PERGAMON INTERNATIONAL LIBRARY
of Science, Technology, Engineering and Social Studies

The 1000-volume original paperback library in aid of education,
industrial training and the enjoyment of leisure

Publisher: Robert Maxwell, M.C.

MEN'S STUDIES MODIFIED

The Impact of Feminism on the Academic Disciplines

THE ATHENE SERIES
An International Collection of Feminist Books
General Editor: DALE SPENDER

The ATHENE SERIES assumes that all those who are concerned with formulating explanations of the way the world works need to know and appreciate the significance of basic feminist principles.

The growth of feminist research has challenged almost all aspects of social organization in our culture. The ATHENE SERIES is committed to the principle of changing the power configurations of society and eliminating all structures of dominance and oppression and will provide an integrated and international collection of books and occasional conference papers.

In preparation

BREAKING OUT
Feminist Research and Feminist Consciousness *by Liz Stanley and Sue Wise*

UNPUBLISHED HERITAGE
The Politics of Selection *by Lou Buchan*

DOCUMENTS OF THE MODERN WOMEN'S MOVEMENT *edited by Bari Watkins and Cindy Patterson*

NOTICE TO READERS
May we suggest that your library places a standing/continuation order to receive all future volumes in this new series immediately on publication? Your order can be cancelled at any time without notice.

Also of interest
WOMEN AND MEDIA, *edited by Helen Baehr*
(A special issue of the journal Women's Studies International Quarterly, Vol. 3, No. 1)

THE VOICES AND WORDS OF WOMEN AND MEN, *edited by Cheris Kramarae*
(A special issue of the journal Women's Studies International Quarterly, Vol. 3, No 2/3)

WOMEN'S STUDIES INTERNATIONAL QUARTERLY*
A Multidisciplinary Journal for the Rapid Publication of Research Communications & Review Articles in Women's Studies
Editor: Dale Spender

Reduced subscription rates to bona fide Women's groups, certain professional associations and for individuals whose institutional Library subscribes to the Journal

*Free Specimen Copy Available on Request

MEN'S STUDIES MODIFIED

The Impact of Feminism on the Academic Disciplines

Editor
Dale Spender

PERGAMON PRESS

OXFORD · NEW YORK · TORONTO · SYDNEY · PARIS · FRANKFURT

U.K.	Pergamon Press Ltd., Headington Hill Hall, Oxford OX3 0BW, England
U.S.A.	Pergamon Press Inc., Maxwell House, Fairview Park, Elmsford, New York 10523, U.S.A.
CANADA	Pergamon Press Canada Ltd., Suite 104, 150 Consumers Road, Willowdale, Ontario M2J 1P9, Canada
AUSTRALIA	Pergamon Press (Aust.) Pty. Ltd., P.O. Box 544, Potts Point, N.S.W. 2011, Australia
FRANCE	Pergamon Press SARL, 24 rue des Ecoles, 75240 Paris, Cedex 05, France
FEDERAL REPUBLIC OF GERMANY	Pergamon Press GmbH, 6242 Kronberg-Taunus, Hammerweg 6, Federal Republic of Germany

First edition 1981

British Library Cataloguing in Publication Data
Men's studies modified — (The Athene series; 1).
1. Higher education of women
I. Spender, Dale   II. Series
376'.65   LC1567   80-41818

ISBN 0-08-026770-X—Hardcover
ISBN 0-08-026117-5—Flexicover

Printed in Great Britain by A. Wheaton & Co. Ltd., Exeter

Men may cook or weave or dress dolls or hunt humming birds but if such activities are appropriate occupations of men, then the whole society, men and women alike, votes them as important. When the same activities are performed by women, they are regarded as less important.

Margaret Mead
1950

Acknowledgements

I would like to thank Glynis Butcher for typing much of this manuscript, sometimes under considerable difficulties, and also to thank Jan Walbe for all her help, and her invaluable assistance in editing the editor.

Contents

x   Contents

Biographical Notes on Contributors

Helen Baehr
Is a senior lecturer in Media Studies and Women's Studies at the Polytechnic of Central London. Member of Advisory Board of Women's Studies International Quarterly and guest editor of a special issue on Women and Media. She is a member of the Women's Research and Resources Centre Collective, Co-founder of Women's Broadcasting and Film Lobby and Co-founder of the Women and Television group. She has produced a video on Women and TV which was transmitted on London Weekend Television in March 1980.

Mary Ann Elston
Has been an active member in the Women's Health Movement for some years and is a member of the Politics of Health Group. Her main research interests are in the sexual division of labour in health care and the medical profession. She teaches Medical Sociology at North-East London Polytechnic.

Marianne A. Ferber
Professor of Economics at the University of Illinois at Urbana-Champaign. She has degrees from McMaster University and the University of Chicago. Many of her publications are concerned with the position of women.

Ruth Hubbard
Professor of Biology at Harvard University where she teaches courses on the interaction between science and society. In recent years she has been thinking, writing and lecturing about the assumptions scientists make, how the society in which they live influences their assumptions and how the assumptions influence their work. She is interested in issues of gender, and also in health care — particularly as it relates to women. She has written articles and reviews on these subjects.

Mercilee M. Jenkins
Has been involved in developing and teaching feminist courses in San Francisco State University, Oregon State University and Santa Rosa Junior College. She is currently conducting research on gender and communication while completing her doctoral program. Her dissertation research is an ethnographic analysis of story telling in a women's rap group.

Annette Kolodny
Her feminist study of the American Pastoral, *The Lay of the Land; Metaphor as Experience and History in American Life and Letters* appeared in 1975 from the University of North Carolina Press. Since then she has continued to publish actively in the areas of American Studies and American Literature, feminist literary criticism, and the status of women in higher education in the United States. She has taught at Yale University, the University of British Columbia (in Canada) and the University of New Hampshire. She is currently completing 'Westering Women', a study of pioneer women's responses to the New World Frontiers, under grants from the Rockefeller and Guggenheim Foundations.

Cheris Kramarae
Teaches a language and gender course in the Speech Communication Department at the University of Illinois at Urbana-Champaign. She helped plan the 'Feminist Scholarship '78' Conference. Her book, *Women and Men Speaking: Frameworks for Analysis* was published by Newbury House in 1981.

Jane Lewis
Has degrees from Reading University (UK) and the University of Western Ontario (Canada); she has taught in Canada and in Britain at the London School of Economics. She is involved in the Feminist History Group and her book *Politics of Motherhood: Maternal and Child Welfare in England 1900–1939* was published by Croom Helm in 1980.

Joni Lovenduski
Born in Providence, Rhode Island, she now lives and works in Britain. A closet feminist since 1964, she came out in 1970. She is an executive of the Political Studies Association of the United Kingdom, a member of the advisory board of Women's Studies International Quarterly, founding member and sometime convenor of the PSA Women's Group and editor of the PSA Newsletter. She is currently engaged on a survey of women in Political Science teaching. She is co-editor of a forthcoming book, 'Feminine Political Participation', to be published by Routledge and Kegan Paul.

Carol MacCormack
Born in the USA she is now a British resident. She has an M.A. from Cambridge University and a Ph.D. from Bryn Mawr. Under the name of Carol Hoffer she contributed to *Women, Culture and Society* (Edited M. Z. Rosaldo and L. Lamphere); she has also contributed to *Signs: Journal of Women in Culture and Society*. She taught in the Women and Society course at Cambridge and is currently a lecturer in Social Sciences, Ross Institute, London School of Hygiene and Tropical Medicine, University of London. Her book, *Nature, Culture and Gender* (Cambridge University Press) which she has edited with M. Strathern has been recently published and her current interest is in rural primary health care, especially women's fertility and childbirth.

Katherine O'Donovan
Was born and educated in Dublin. Has taught law at universities in Belfast, Addis Ababa, Kuala Lumpur and Kent, where she is currently involved in teaching Women's

Studies. She has published papers on family law with an emphasis on feminist theory and is at present working on a book on sex and gender in the law.

Kathy Overfield
Has been through long years of the academic mill, found little of interest, and is now eagerly awaiting the demise of the oil-based competitive economy. She, with friends, is building an alternative to patriarchal oppression — as much as this is possible. She lives in rural Wales on a smallholding (farm) and is helping to bring up children.

Helen Roberts
Is a feminist and a sociologist and editor of books on women's health and on feminist research (Routledge and Kegan Paul). She works as a senior researcher at Ilkley College and is active in the British Sociological Association.

Sheila Ruth
Born in New York City she has degrees in Political Science from Hunter College in N.Y.C. and in Philosophy from SUNY-Buffalo. After a very traditional childhood, marriage, divorce and single parenthood, she turned her thinking, both personal and professional to the analysis of women's experience. She is Associate Professor of Philosophy at Southern Illinois University at Edwardsville and Director of Women's Studies and all her research is in feminist theory. Her book, *Issues in Feminism: A First Course in Women's Studies* has been published by Houghton Mifflin. She is happiest when working with and for women.

Dale Spender
Is an Australian who lives in London. An active feminist she has taught Women's Studies courses on the politics of knowledge and the intellectual aspects of sexism. She has written feminist books on language, and eductaion, and her book, 'Women of Ideas' is forthcoming from Routledge and Kegan Paul.

Michelle L. Teiman
Is currently completing a degree in agricultural economics at the University of Illinois. She is also involved in Women's Studies and serves on The Committee for Women's Concerns under the Vice-Chancellor for Student Affairs at the University.

Beverly Walker
Lectures in Psychology at the University of Wollongong, Australia. She has degrees from the University of Sydney and has interests, particularly at the theoretical level, in the areas of individual differences, personality and life span development. She teaches in an interdisciplinary Women's Studies course and has been involved in the establishment of a women's referral centre in Wollongong.

Introduction

The broad parameters of this book are those of the politics of knowledge. It is not customary to bracket together politics and knowledge: on the contrary, keeping them apart has usually been perceived as a necessary condition for scholarly activity. The essays in this volume, however, are not just concerned with bringing politics and knowledge together, but with demonstrating that their separation has often been both artificial and false, and that those who have assumed or asserted that politics can be kept out of knowledge have frequently been devious or deluded.

There have been many overt and covert reasons given for the separation of politics and knowledge; some of them are more defensible than others. But from the point of view of those who have held the power to decree what scholarship should and should not be, who have had the power to formulate the paradigms of the various disciplines, little could be more convenient than their injunction that politics should be eliminated from the academic enterprise on the grounds that it is a source of contamination in the construction of knowledge. The myth of 'apolitical objective knowledge' (Fitzgerald, 1978) has served the establishment well; those with resources have often been able to use them to protect their existing resources, and to gain more, without their activities being too closely scrutinised.

Research which is addressed to the problems of the production of knowledge in systematic fashion, is a relatively recent phenomenon. Analysing the power base and power relations which are inherent in the codification of knowledge is still — understandably — not always viewed as a laudable or legitimate activity. But in recent years there has been a shift towards the recognition that knowledge is socially constructed, that it is invented by human beings with limited access to explanations and limited claims to infallibility. While all human beings may generate 'explanations' of the world, may devise schemata for organising the objects and events of the world, not all of them become the legitimated and acceptable explanations; there is a selection process at work and it has a power dimension. It can also be a self perpetuating power dimension, for those who have the power to validate their own models of the world can validate their own power in the process.

Although there are numerous bases for the division between those who have power and those who do not, the focus of this book is the division based on *gender*. Most of the knowledge produced in our society has been produced by men; they have usually generated the explanations and the schemata and have then checked with each other and vouched for the accuracy and adequacy of their view of the world. They have created *men's studies* (the academic curriculum), for, by not acknowledging that they are presenting only the explanations of *men*, they have 'passed off' this knowledge as human knowledge. Women have been excluded as the producers of knowledge and as the subjects of knowledge, for men have often made their own knowledge and their own sex, representative of humanity; they have, in Mary Daly's terms, presented false knowledge by insisting that their *partial* view be accepted as the whole (Daly, 1973; 8).

Fundamental to feminism is the premise that women have been 'left out' of codified knowledge; where men have formulated explanations in relation to themselves, they have generally either rendered women invisible or classified them as deviant. This is not necessarily malicious intent on the part of men, but a product of organisation; while men have checked only with men it has been almost inevitable that women should be encoded as an absence or a deficiency.

The description and analysis of the omission of women as autonomous human beings has been one of the most significant contributions made by feminism. Although initial 'discoveries' (in the contemporary women's movement) were sometimes in terms of individual disciplines, the boundary lines were soon broken when feminists began to establish that this omission was not a peculiar development within a particular discipline but a problem common to many disciplines. It was the problem of male dominance in the construction of knowledge and it manifested itself across disciplines.

By asking questions in terms of *women* (and not in terms of a particular framework such as psychology or history, for example) feminists moved beyond some of the limitations which are imposed by 'compartmentalisation'; they reconceptualised the existence of women and began to encode knowledge in a radically new way. They did not have much choice. As Joan Roberts (1976) has said:

> After beginning the search for relevant facts and concepts, some of us came to realize that neither facts nor concepts about females existed in critical scholarly areas. In still other areas, ideas presumed to pertain to both sexes, were in actuality based on the study of males and extended to females. When females were studied, the paucity of fact and the prevalence of opinion were painfully apparent. Thus, *the challenging and arduous task before us was to rethink the concepts inherited from men* — about them, about us, and, therefore, about humanity (Roberts, 1976: 5; my emphasis).

Men's knowledge about women would no longer suffice. What was required was women's knowledge about women. But even stating the problem in this way was to enter the political arena because men had not only often validated the knowledge which women were challenging, they had also usually validated their own authority to construct such knowledge. Men's position in society could not be separated from the knowledge which they had created. It is one thing to challenge the validity of studies on maternal deprivation, but quite another to challenge the power of men to make such knowledge.

Feminists have come to appreciate that the invisibility of women is not a problem of individual male historians or philosophers conducting a personal campaign to keep women out of their respective disciplines (although such individuals can still be found) but a *structural problem* which has been built into the production of knowledge. Because it has been primarily men who have determined the parameters, who have decided what would be problematic, significant, logical and reasonable, not only have women been excluded from the process *but the process itself can reinforce the 'authority' of men and the 'deficiency' of women*.

Dorothy Smith (1978) has outlined the way in which this process works. Men, she says, attend to and treat as significant only what men say with the result that women have been 'largely excluded from the work of producing the forms of thought, and the images and symbols in which thought is expressed and ordered'. There is a circle effect as men check with each other, validating each other's explanations of the world. 'The circle of men whose writing and talk was significant to each other extends backwards in time as far as our records reach. What men were doing was relevant to men, was written by men about men for men. Men listened to and listen to what one another said' (Smith, 1978; 281.)

To Smith, this is how a tradition is formed as a way of thinking develops through the written and spoken word. A 'style' evolves with its own questions, solutions, and standards as the circle of those present builds on the work of the past. And women have not been present in those circles with the result that they have been deprived of the means to participate in the construction of forms of thought which are relevant or adequate to express their own experience. They have never controlled the material or social means, says Smith, to the making of a tradition among themselves for the symbolic modes which are the general currency of thought have been produced or controlled by men:

> Insofar as women's work and experience has entered into it, it has been on terms decided by men and because it has been approved by men. This is why women have had no written history until very recently, no share in making religious thoughts, no political philosophy, no representation of society from their view, no poetic tradition, no tradition in art (Smith, 1978; 281–282).

In referring to this same problem, Shirley Ardener (1975) has classified women and men as muted and dominant groups. She suggests that while both sexes have generated representations of the world, any difference between the two is usually resolved in favour of men. And because men's views come to be legitimated as *the* view for the whole society, the dominance of men and the muteness of women is continually 'reproduced'.

If men have had the power to encode meaning it should not be surprising to find that they have encoded meanings which enhance their own image. 'Once a group is defined as inferior' says Jean Baker Miller (1976) 'the superiors tend to label it as defective or substandard in various ways' (p 6) so that there is a positive and negative polarisation. The 'superior' group, with power, is in a position to provide positive meanings about itself and thereby to reinforce and perpetuate that power. 'Out of the total range of human possibilities' adds Miller, 'the activities most highly valued in any particular culture will tend to be enclosed within the domain of the dominant group: less valued functions are relegated to the subordinates' (p. 7). This is politics.

While the task confronting women of reconceptualising female experience from a female perspective may appear to be a simple one it can lead to confrontation with those who are responsible for the existing representations of females as a 'deficient' or 'deviant' group. As Basil Bernstein (1975) has pointed out, the way a society selects, classifies, distributes, transmits, and evaluates knowledge it considers to be public 'reflects both the distribution of power and the principles of social control' (p. 47) and it is no mere coincidence that women have remained outside the production of knowledge. This is one of the reasons for their position as a subordinate group. In attempting to change their relationship to the construction and dissemination of knowledge they are proposing to change a fundamental power base and, therefore, it should not be surprising that they should encounter resistance.

Because of their dominant position men have often given substance to the maxim that 'might is right' and have been able to appropriate *authority* — among other things — for themselves. As the established philosophers, politicians, legislators etc., they have been in a position to justify and insist on the 'rightness' of their explanations, and the fact that males are granted authority can lead to the situation in which their explanations are granted authority, and such a value judgement can be made without an examination of the inherent strengths and weaknesses of their explanation. Conversely, because women are *not* accorded authority, their explanations may not carry authority and can be discounted without reference to their merits. This conceptualisation of the politics of knowledge, whereby it is women who are wrong — by definition — is at the base of much new knowledge which has been constructed by women.

That women are 'wrong' not because of their arguments or explanations, but because of their gender — is a point which was made by Simone de Beauvoir in 1949 when she said:

> In the midst of an abstract discussion it is vexing to hear a man say: 'You think thus and so because you are a woman'; but I know that my only defence is to reply: 'I think thus and so because it is true', thereby removing my subjective self from the argument. It would be out of the question to reply: 'And you think the contrary because you are a man', for it is understood that the fact of being a man is no peculiarity. *A man is in the right being a man: it is the woman who is in the wrong* (de Beauvoir, 1972; 15; my emphasis).

It has been suggested that this premise of women being in the wrong is at the root of much of our contemporary knowledge about the world and while it remains it will continue to be influential in the construction of knowledge and could lead to more and more 'proofs' about the authoritative, positive, autonomous and superior nature of men, and the negative, derivative and deficient nature of women. Feminists are seeking to change not only the conceptualisation of women as 'wrong' but the processes which have given rise to it.

There are many means by which women's efforts to encode and validate their own experience can be preempted or frustrated: indeed it could be argued that a patriarchal society is predicated on the silence of women (Cora Kaplan, 1976) and that almost any move that women might make can be counteracted. But again and again in feminist literature — and in this volume — there are two issues which arise which seem to be fundamental in the exclusion of women from knowledge. One is the polarised and discrete categories of objectivity/subjectivity, and the other is a linguistic issue, the use of the term *man*. Although these two issues are so very different they have both become political issues because of the way they have functioned to deny or dismiss women.

That the world can be divided into objective versus subjective is an assumption which has been challenged by women at two inter-related levels. First of all they have challenged the appropriation of objectivity by men. It is unlikely that it is just a fortuitous accident that the prestigious capacity to be objective is a distinguishing feature allocated to the dominant group: it is likely that this could be another example of men taking the positive, authoritative capacities for themselves and allocating the less desirable 'opposites' to women.

However, it is at the second level, at the level of disputing the validity of objectivity that women have made perhaps one of their most significant contributions to the debate on the politics of knowledge.

As a legitimating device, *objectivity* has served the dominant group well. Faced with the *objective* evidence that women are inferior, women have been discouraged from promoting change for the very definition of *objective* is 'exhibiting actual facts uncoloured by exhibitors feelings or opinions' (*Oxford English Dictionary*). If women had been presented with an acknowledgement that the 'facts' of women's inferiority had been constructed by men and verified by other men (Smith, 1978) then the way would have been open to declare the *opinions* of men inaccurate and inadequate. But women were confronted with an ideology which would have it that women's inferiority, for example, belonged *not* to 'the consciousness or the perceiving or thinking SUBJECT, but what is presented to this, external to the mind, real' (*Oxford English Dictionary*). They were led to believe that it was not the opinion of men but the truth presented to men, and this has served to intimidate in many instances, for if it is true, and therefore incontestable that women are inferior, little can be gained by contesting.

I think it fair to say that earlier efforts (in the contemporary feminist movement) did not constitute an overall challenge to the validity of objectivity, but a defense against the undue emphasis placed upon it. There was a tendency to accept the conceptual framework in which subjectivity and objectivity were discrete and polarised categories in terms of both knowledge, and the sexes. Taking on the concept that women were the subjective sex, women defended the personal and argued that it was a necessary 'corrective'.

While objectivity persisted as a valid category however I think it worked to constrain feminist intellectual development for feminists tried to construct new knowledge about women in the old mould and there was considerable contradiction, and strain. As Elaine Reuben (1978) has pointed out, many of the new explanations about women stood 'in defiance of the evidence' constructed by men, and could not be legitimated by male decreed criteria. But this contradiction gave way to new understandings.

Moving from a defence of the subjective (and by implication a defence of women) to a critique of objectivity (and a critique of men) there was a growing appreciation that objectivity had been used to discriminate against women. Joan Roberts said:

> In our search for knowledge of ourselves, we find repeatedly that the 'scientific' methods are essentially reasserting with new terminological 'weightiness' the same biases against women. Strangely, the 'objectivity' of science has sustained a subjective bias that maintains, against the woman's experience of her own life, the myths of female inferiority (Roberts, 1976: 5).

Women came to realise that the knowledge which men constructed about women (from their deviant physiology and psychology to the definition of women as non-workers) was frequently rated as 'objective' while the knowledge women began to construct about women (which has its origins in the role of a participant rather than a spectator) was frequently rated as 'subjective'. When men checked with men, their pronouncements were usually seen as credible, but when women checked with women, their explanations were frequently seen as illogical, irrational, emotional and liable to be dismissed by men. The hypothesis arose that legitimacy might be associated with *gender* rather than with the adequacy of an explanation, and this has led Adrienne Rich (1979) to comment that in a patriarchal society, objectivity is the name we give to male subjectivity. (Anna Bexall, 1980, has also suggested that males have a great emotional investment in objectivity.)

With this fundamental challenge to the objectivity of objectivity there has been a shift in feminist development. With it has come the acknowledgement that *subjectivity* plays a crucial role in the construction of knowledge and that rather than construct knowledge about women which 'out-objectives' the knowledge constructed by men, new criteria for credibility are called for (see Thelma McCormack, 1981: in press).

If all that had occurred was simply a reversal — whereby women are decreeing the new orthodoxy in which subjectivity is valued, and then appropriated by women — then there would perhaps be some cause for concern. But there is a significant difference between the way men have checked with men and often presented their explanations as the complete and only truth, and the way women are checking with women and offering their explanations as partial and temporary 'truths'. These partial and temporary truths about women, which have their origin in women's experience of the world, are being fed back into the various disciplines and are changing those disciplines.

It is not just knowledge about women which fills the gaps left by men. It is knowledge which men have not often had access to. Until recently, says Jean Baker Miller (1976) men's understandings have been the only ones generally available to us. 'As other perceptions arise — precisely those perceptions that men, because of their dominant position, could *not* perceive — the total vision of human possibilities enlarges and is transformed. The old is severely challenged' (p. 1).

'Women know a lot about the world and about men, that men do not know' says Liz Stanley (1980) and if what women know becomes part of our culture's general knowledge we will inhabit a very different world. This is partly because women's subordination has relied in large measure on women's explanations being denied or dismissed: once women can hold up their own experience as legitimate and valid — to men as well as women — one of the means of structuring that subordination no longer exists. When women name themselves and the world (this is Mary Daly's phrase) they can no longer be classified as *muted* and *subordinate*.

This is why the essays in this volume are not just an 'academic argument'. They constitute a significant challenge to male authority. They show not just what men left out in the codification of knowledge but indicate why it has been necessary for men — as the ostensibly superior sex — to exclude women. And by putting women into codified knowledge, feminists have transformed not just the knowledge itself but the processes whereby knowledge is produced. This is the politics of knowledge.

The means by which women have been excluded are too numerous to summarise here: indeed, they are the substance of this book. But besides objectivity there is perhaps one other device that deserves mention because it too makes its presence felt in almost every chapter. It is the use of the word *man*.

In virtually every chapter reference is made to the way in which the use of the term *man* to 'embrace woman' has disposed us to devise explanations of the world in terms of men, and not women. The use of *man* is often cited as a key factor in constructing the invisibility of women (see Wendy Martyna 1978 and Elaine Morgan 1972). I endorse this claim. What I do not endorse, however, is the belief that this usage arose mysteriously. In the choice of the term *man* to encompass woman there is a classic example of the way in which men generated this meaning and checked with each other to establish its 'logic' and validity.

Although there is a widespread belief that the term *man* has always been used to refer to women, this is not the case. It was a rule introduced into (male) scholarly circles in the sixteenth century. In 1553, Thomas Wilson suggested that *man* should precede *woman* because it was more natural. No women were consulted about the 'naturalness' of this argument and Wilson's male colleagues apparently agreed on the justice of his case. In

1646, Joshua Poole added his pearls of wisdom and decreed that the male gender was the worthier gender and therefore deserved priority and again it seems that the men he consulted were convinced of the credibility of his case. John Kirkby in 1746 helped to set the seal on the case when he insisted that the male gender was the more comprehensive and an all male parliament found it feasible to pass the 1850 Act which decreed that he/man should stand for woman (Bodine, 1975).

This indicates the way in which women were kept out of the discussion and the production of knowledge, but it also indicates the way in which their absence or invisibility is reinforced and reproduced. There were no women philosophers of language, no rhetoricians, grammarians or parliamentarians in the circles where this rule was ordained. Had women been present they might have quarrelled with the notion that men were the worthier sex and they might have taken exception to the argument that men were more comprehensive. They might have helped to forestall the development of the belief that the *man* is representative and the woman, the exception. Their absence from those circles in which such knowledge was produced was probably crucial for the construction of such knowledge. Men's arguments would not have sufficed in the presence of women.

The way men have used *objectivity* and *man* to promote male primacy are but two examples of the politics of knowledge. They show the way in which male supremacy is bolstered when only males produce knowledge and they indicate the nature and extent of the changes that are being wrought by women when they challenge male knowledge and male power.

Women are now beginning (again[1]) to evolve their own agencies for the production of knowledge, to develop their own style and their own tradition, and it is different from the one that has been established by men. It is not merely a mirror image of male organisation (although Margrit Eichler, 1980, warns that it is possible to be seduced into such a simple but no less sexist reversal) but an attempt to forge a new way of thinking about the world which is more consistent with women's experience.

Because this new style is still being formed (this book is part of the process) it is not possible to categorically define it. What can be said is that it is personal and political, and this constitutes a significant difference. Rather than separate the personal and political from the production of knowledge, feminists are attempting to bring them together and in this synthesis they are striving to construct more accurate, adequate, and comprehensive explanations (Stanley and Wise, in press) than those which emerged under the reign of objectivity, and male supremacy. Feminists have focused on 'research on research' and have been extremely critical of the way in which knowledge has for so long been presented as a *fait accompli* with little or no acknowledgement of the part played by the personal in the process of producing such knowledge. Instead of trying to be 'detached', feminists are blatantly 'involved' in the knowledge which they are producing and unlike the traditional model in which the researcher is presumed to be 'outside' the subject matter being researched, feminist contributions frequently testify to the way in which women are changed by the research process.[2] This is a concrete example of the way women are trying to bring politics and knowledge together.

[1] The more archivist activity that is undertaken, the more it seems that women have been engaged in comparable processes in the past but their efforts are excised with the passing of time.

[2] Liz Stanley and Sue Wise (1979) have documented this and there are many examples to be found in Helen Roberts (Ed.) *Doing Feminist Resesearch,* Routledge and Kegan Paul (in press).

Few, however, would suggest that the task has been accomplished. While this volume documents the gains that feminism has made, both in terms of changing the knowledge which is constructed and distributed, and the social organisation which has permitted such practices, these are still early days. There is still an ongoing debate within feminism about the criteria of credibility and there are signs of some discomfort at being required to accept the current position. While Joan Roberts (1976) and Mary Daly (1979) have made a considerable contribution towards the development of tolerance of ambiguity and contradiction, by suggesting that the world is not monodimensional (as men would have it) but multidimensional, it is perhaps an indication that we are products of our own culture (in which we have been raised to seek the *one* truth and the *one* right answer) when we become uneasy with our 'multiple' explanations.

But we do not have to interpret our lack of certainty as a weakness: it can be reconceptualised as a strength. After all, it is partly because we were 'conned' by the one truth, the one correct and objective evaluation of women as inferior in men's studies, that we have proceeded to construct women's studies with a specific aim of not repeating the same mistakes. If men could be so 'sure' — and so 'wrong' — there is perhaps something suspect in their method.

We have begun to construct knowledge about women and such a task leads us directly into the area of the politics of knowledge. We are changing the 'rules', not just those which apply to content, but those which apply to production. We are changing society by establishing alternative processes and alternative knowledge. In this volume we have documented the extent to which we have been taken into account in various disciplines, and therefore, the extent to which we have begun to alter the power configurations in the construction of knowledge and in society. That there is today a conceptualisation of traditional knowledge as men's studies, and that such men's studies are being modified, suggests that the first decade of the modern women's movement has been productive.

References

ARDENER, Shirley (Ed.) (1975) *Perceiving Women,* Malaby, London.

BERNSTEIN, Basil (1975) 'On the classification and framing of educational knowledge' in Michael F. D. Young (Ed.) *Knowledge and Control,* Collier Macmillan, London, pp. 47–69.

BEXALL, Anna (1980) Private communication.

BODINE, Ann (1975) 'Androcentrism in prescriptive grammar: singular *they* sex indefinite *he* and *he* or *she*' in *Language in Society*, Vol. IV, No. 2, pp. 129–156.

DALY, Mary (1973) *Beyond God the Father,* Beacon Press, Boston.

DALY, Mary (1979) *Gynecology: The metaethics of radical feminism,* Beacon Press, Boston/The Women's Press, London.

de BEAUVOIR, Simone (1972) *The Second Sex,* Penguin, Middlesex.

EICHLER, Margrit (1980) *The Double Standard: A feminist critique of feminist social science,* Croom Helm, London.

FITZGERALD, Anne (1978) 'Teaching interdisciplinary women's studies', Great Lakes College Association, *Faculty Newsletter,* March 27th.

KAPLAN, Cora (1976) 'Language and gender' in *Papers in Patriarchy,* Women's Publishing Collective. London, pp. 21–37.

McCORMACK, Thelma (1981) (in press) 'Good Theory or Just Theory?' in *Women's Studies International Quarterly,* Vol. IV, No. 1.

MARTYNA, Wendy (1978) 'Beyond the he/man approach: The case for language change', Unpublished paper.

MILLER, Jean Baker (1976) *Toward a New Psychology of Women,* Penguin, Middlesex.

MORGAN, Elaine (1972) *The Descent of Woman,* Stein and Day, N.Y.

REUBEN, Elaine (1978) 'In defiance of the evidence: Notes on feminist scholarship' in *Women's Studies International Quarterly,* Vol. I, No. 3, pp. 215–218.

RICH, Adrienne (1979) *On Lies, Secrets and Silences,* Norton, N.Y./Virago, London.
ROBERTS, Joan (Ed.) (1976) *Beyond Intellectual Sexism: A new woman a new reality,* David McKay, N.Y.
STANLEY, Liz (1980) Discussion, Women's Research and Resources Centre Conference, *The Women's Liberation Movement and Men,* London, March 23.
STANLEY, Liz and WISE, Sue (1979) 'Feminist research, feminist consciousness and experiences of sexism' in *Women's Studies International Quarterly,* Vol. II, No. 3, pp. 359–374.
STANLEY, Liz and WISE, Sue (in press) 'Breaking out: Feminist Research and Feminist Consciousness', Pergamon Press, Oxford.
SMITH, Dorothy (1978) 'A peculiar eclipsing: women's exclusion from man's culture' in *Women's Studies International Quarterly,* Vol. I, No. 4, pp. 281–296.

1

A Thief In The House:
Women and Language*

MERCILEE M. JENKINS
CHERIS KRAMARAE

Feminists' reevaluation of women's place in society has included studying our place in language and in speech exchanges. We are studying the ways we have been 'protected' from obscenity, yet made the object of much of it. We are conscious of the ways we have been prevented, through occupational segregation, from hearing speech in some public places and prevented from expressing ourselves in still more. We find that women's sphere includes the interpersonal but seldom the rhetorical. Women have had the responsibility for maintaining relationships but have not had the control. Feminists are challenging and documenting the sexism in language structure and language use, while pointing out the omissions of past communication research which has been restricted by the limitations of a white middle class male perspective.

Feminist language studies have shown the failures of traditional research designs. Women have not been accepted, and do not fit comfortably as participants, in the present research regime. Nor do the present research conventions satisfactorily answer *our* questions. The feminists' work argues strongly the need for a different value system in the research designs. As backdrop to our discussion of the desirability of a language studies approach which includes women as theoreticians and speakers, we briefly review some of the topics and approaches of feminist language studies of the past ten years, and list some contemporary concerns. We cannot in one chapter do justice to the whole topic of language and gender and its impact on academic disciplines. Therefore, we will focus on social interaction, an area which encompasses a substantial amount of the communication and gender research of the past ten years.

Previous Research

According to traditional history books, women have experienced social changes primarily as shadow mates of men. Women are seldom presented as having affected social changes or as having said or written much of lasting value. Second wave feminists finding records of earlier feminists' work, including work on language, experience surprise and joy — as well as resentment toward the voices, votes, and visions of men which have suppressed those of women. We have had to slowly find, through archive and attic searches, our history. In the late 1960's and early 1970's we thought that we

*We thank Lona Jean Turner, Barrie Thorne, and Joanne Finkelstein for their critiques of an earlier draft and Jane McIntosh for typing.

11

were the first women to show concern with sexism in language use and language structure. The terminology was new, but we have since discovered that others had written at length of the phenomenon. For example, Elsie Clews Parson (1913) discusses what she hears as different actual, stereotypical, and socially respectable speech for women and for men. Similarly, Lillian O'Connor (1954) writes of her search for the texts and evidence of the reception of the speeches of pioneer women orators. Our work began, unfortunately, without their help. Yet during the past ten years we have learned much about officially recognized knowledge about language, and about the extent of ignorant arrogance regarding women's speech and women's views on language.

Here we briefly summarize some of the concerns of researchers in this area, before discussing some possible research positions for the future. The summary is based on our reading of much of the recent communication work, but we realize that in such a summary we are glossing over many important details and furthermore, that we are involved in a cooperative, continuing evaluation of language study which has been and will be enriched by many perspectives.[1] What should be made clear at the onset is that topics related to gender and communication cross many disciplinary boundaries, such as linguistics, sociology, speech communication, English, and psychology, as well as being widely dealt with outside academe.[2] Our review of this literature will focus on the issues which we perceive as being most germane to an understanding of women's and men's relationship to language and communication.

Early and contemporary studies explore the extent of sexism in language structure and content by documenting the ways in which language defines, deprecates and ignores women (Miller and Swift, 1977). These studies have included discussion of the language of legislatures and courts, marriage, dictionaries, advertisements, children's books, and teaching materials (e.g. Nilsen, Bosmajian, Gershuny, and Stanley, 1977). 'Women are often defined by their relation to men ('Miss/Mrs.', or 'Harold's widow'), while men have more autonomous and varied linguistic status' (Kramer, Thorne and Henley, 1978; p. 643). Men have the power to name, order and classify while also defining the rules of speaking which help keep women in their place. For example, femininity is not a symbol of women's making in the way that masculinity is a symbol of men's making (Spender, 1980). The exploration has recently been expanded to study the impact of the use of the 'generic' *man* and *he* on women's and men's thought processes (e.g. Martyna, 1980, and MacKay, 1980), the problems with the patriarchal reconstructions of language origin and change (Wolfe and Stanley, 1980) and the ridicule and hostility toward feminists who research these topics (Blaubergs, 1980).

Research on structural features of language has lead to the conclusion that the language we use does not adequately encompass the experiences of women, who are a subordinate 'muted' group in the society (Ardener, 1975). Mary Daly (1978a) writes that 'deceptive perceptions were/are implanted through language — the all-pervasive language of myth, conveyed overtly and subliminally through religion, great art, literature, the dogmas of professionalism, the media, grammar' (p. 3). She believes our liberation from patriarchy will come in part through our studies of male control over language and through our 'wrenching back some word power' (p. 9). Until women take

[1]Because several review essays are available, in this short summary we have included very few references. At the same time we want to stress that the lines of research we mention have been developed by many researchers.

[2]Review essays of this literature include those by Thorne and Henley (1975), Haas (1979), Frank (1978), and Kramer, Thorne and Henley (1978).

some control of naming, Adrienne Rich (1978) writes, much of our experience will remain invisible; self-naming is a revolt against 'namelessness, denial, secrets, taboo subjects, erasure, false-naming, non-naming, encoding, omission, veiling, fragmentation and lying' (p. 18). Judith McDaniel (1978) states, 'If feminism is the final cause — and I believe it is — then language is the first necessity' (p. 17). These women believe that language is profoundly political and that men's control of women is intimately tied to control of naming and restriction on what women can say, when and where.

Historically, language structure has been studied as distinct from language usage (langue and parole). Early studies in gender and communication tended to preserve these distinctions. Work on language usage in the early 70's focused on discrete variables of speaking style, such as phonetic variants, pitch, vocabulary and syntax. Actual differences along these dimensions were not found to be as great as perceived differences. That is, women and men seem to perceive a greater difference between the sexes in patterns of speaking than actually exists. Researchers then began to explore the sterotypes of women's and men's speech in terms of the social functions they may serve in interaction. As Pamela Fishman (1978) demonstrates, women do the interactional work, while men retain the control of topics and turns of talk. Thus, the control men retain over language structure is reinforced in language usage. More recent research has reflected this connection between language structure and language use in the social context. For example, some recent work in discourse analysis considers not only the number of interruptions and the number of reinforcing/encouraging 'uh-huh's' from women and men in same sex and mixed sex groups, but also the way the interruptions (more from men) and the reinforcements (more from women) reflect and conserve the existing social structure (Zimmerman and West, 1975). Further, continuing work by Patricia Nichols (1978) and Giles, Bourhis, and Taylor (1977) has demonstrated the necessity of considering the *interaction* of sex, heritage, expectations, motivations, opportunities, and goals of women and men speakers.

The impact of feminism on the study of communication will perhaps be most strongly felt in the areas of interpersonal and small group research. Since early reports from consciousness-raising groups, feminists have focused on the social interaction of women in small groups as offering a different model of human communication (Jenkins and Kramer, 1978). Out of this work a paradigm is emerging which emphasizes co-operation rather than competition, a dialogue of complementary alternatives rather than a dialectic of opposing forces. Copper, Ethelchild, and Whyte (1974) outline the elements of this new paradigm. Their methodology is as innovative as their theory. They studied themselves studying the process of group interaction, juxtaposing traditional models with the way women work together. They identified differences in the following elements as distinguishing feminist interactions from traditional models: sequence of discourse, ways of interrupting or interjecting comments into the conversation, ways of giving others support, and acceptance of the emotional as a legitimate part of an intellectual discussion. Other researchers have begun work in these areas which will be discussed more fully when we consider new directions for future research.

Theoretical Perspectives

It should be clear by now that the research on gender and communication has not evolved from a unitary theoretical foundation. While originally researchers were concerned with 'sex' differences, we generally agree now that the biological fact of sex is not as significant as the complex of sociological, cultural and psychological associations which form our concepts of gender. Theoretical differences revolve around how gender should be defined and how it operates in everyday life. Divergent perspectives range from the more psychologically oriented to progressively more sociologically and culturally grounded approaches.

Some researchers have focused on the idea of gender identity in terms of psychological sex, that is, the degree to which a person identifies with characteristics associated with masculinity or feminity (Bem, 1974; Eman and Meyers, 1978). A person who possesses a large portion of both types of characteristics is considered androgynous. Theoretically, the androgynous person is more flexible in any communication situation because she/he has a wider range of behaviors from which to choose. Androgyny seems to be the ideal or preferred gender identity and in a sense the solution to the sex dichotomy. These researchers feel that to study sex differences is to perpetuate or reinforce stereotypes and enhance polarization between women and men. They believe that how much a person identifies with her/his gender is a more accurate measure of how gender effects communicative behavior than a person's sex *per se.*

Critics of this approach point out that in regarding gender as primarily a psychological rather than a social phenomenon, they overlook the fact that both masculinity and feminity are man-made creations. As Joanna Russ (1979) points out, femininity is 'a man-made mess' — a paradox (madonna-whore) which has a high cost of living. The concept of androgyny, then, is nothing new, but is rather a combination of two man-made stereotypes.

Further, if gender is considered primarily a psychological rather than sociological phenomenon, then individuals are thought free to choose to change their behavior to best suit themselves. Following from this position, remedies such as assertiveness training have emerged. This training seems to imply that women ought to be more like men, rather than vice versa. For example, assertiveness training for women — teaching women to express their opinions honestly and clearly and thus to stand up for their needs, desires and rights — has sprung up all over the United States. Similar training to help men become more emotionally expressive or less aggressive has not emerged on the same scale. While many women have found assertiveness training helpful in relieving anxiety, helplessness and frustration, other women point out the important limitations of the techniques. Although the goal is to help women control their lives by making their thoughts and feelings known, they are to accomplish this by changing and attacking their own speech and behavior rather than attacking the social and economic conditions which produce what is called their nonassertiveness. Nancy Henley (1979) argues that while assertiveness training is sometimes a valuable program (one available primarily to middle-class women) it is not a prescription for the cure of *social* problems. To regard gender as primarily a set of dispositional traits which the individual can modify, does not give enough consideration to the social and cultural practices which make a 'separate peace' with sexism impossible.

Barrie Thorne and Nancy Henley (1975) offer an alternative conception of gender as a system of relationships. From this perspective, gender is seen not as a collection of psychological traits but as a basic element of social structure, especially of a sexual division of labor which is tied to gender division and male dominance. The division between female and male is socially created, and is deeply woven into the organization of institutions and of everyday life. It is not just a division, but an asymmetry, with men having more power and status. The fact of being male or female carries connotations of different power and status, although other situational and relational factors may mitigate these connotations. Thus, gender does not have a uniform impact across situations. We make subtle shifts in gender related behavior depending on whom we are with and what we are doing. Thus, we need to know more about the situational factors which influence the impact of gender on interaction.

We take the position that experimental studies will not be as valuable as naturalistic observation for developing a theoretical foundation for gender and communication research at this time. For example, we do not see measures such as the Bem questionnaire (1974) as helpful in determining how people actually negotiate their gender identity. If gender is not static, then a one time reporting of degree of identification with stereotypic traits regardless of situation should not be very informative. Here also we might expect a large gap between what people report they do, perhaps in accordance with what is perceived as socially acceptable, and what they actually do.

An Ethnographic Approach

How then do we deal with the fact that gender is always with us but is not always the same? Although researchers generally agree that gender is not static, we disagree as to how it varies and how this variation can be measured. We do not know exactly what gender is or how it operates in terms of communication and, therefore, how to gauge its effects.[3] Many basic questions remain to be asked before we can begin to construct a coherent theory and method for the study of gender and communication. We need to know much more about how communicative behaviors provide a basis for gender definitions in context. Context refers not only to time and place but to the structure and function of a communicative event and the relationships between its members. This leads us directly to an ethnographic approach. We need to know much more about how people actually use speaking as a cultural resource in order to have a firm foundation for communication theory in general.

Philipsen (1975) outlines this cultural approach to the study of communication in context based on the work of Hymes (1972) and other ethnographers of communication. He describes speaking as 'the true nexus of language and social life, a means in and through which language is used and social life conducted' (p. 2). 'People,' he writes,

---

[3]Philip M. Smith *et al.* (1980) pose two important questions which are particularly applicable to the study of gender and communication: Why are speech variables used for assessing others? Why are speech patterns modified from situation to situation? In answer to the first question: Speech cues have informational value because we associate them with social concepts; speech cues reduce uncertainty by indicating a person's group memberships (such as class, race, gender, region). How values become attached to linguistic variations, however, is more difficult to discern. A substantial amount of evidence indicates that men's speech in most cultures is valued more highly than women's. Is this due to the way women speak or the fact that anything women do is valued less highly than what men do? Available evidence supports the latter contention (Chodorow, 1972). In regard to the second question, we can talk in terms of the presentation of self as influenced by norms or rules of speaking and our relationships with others in context. Much research (Jenkins, 1980) has indicated that there are differential norms of communicative behavior for women and men, but we don't know how they may vary from situation to situation.

'define, interpret and judge speaking as a resource which can be exploited to serve human purposes' (p. 2). Different social groups have differing attitudes, beliefs, values and assumptions about speaking. That is, the range of possibilities for speaking in any situation and the standards of evaluation of speech provide a kind of sociocultural regularity to our interactions. Creative innovation and change are always possible but occur within a context of social expectations and practices. To study speaking as a cultural resource, then, involves studying how various social groups use speaking and the value they attach to it in a variety of contexts.

Keeping in mind that we are all members of more than one social group, we can use this approach to see the range of ways language and other means of communication are used and what the criteria are for evaluating these uses in context. Observation of naturally occurring social groups provides the basis for describing regularities in communicative behavior which reflect the implicit or tacit rules of speaking. Once we have documented these communicative patterns, comparative analyses are possible, which can then serve as a basis for generalizations leading to communication theory. Encompassing a broader range of communicative experience than current research typically does, this naturalistic approach has some important implications for communication research in general, and provides a much needed context for the study of gender and communication.

Previous research on interpersonal and small group communication has typically studied interaction in simulated or laboratory situations involving a specific task and using a discrete variable research design. Both the theory and methodology are based on the implicit assumption that the communicative experience of white middle class males is prototypical. The experiences of women and other ethnic groups and classes are treated as deviations from this model of normative behavior. Gender, ethnicity and class are seen as 'demographic variables' which can be controlled and accounted for, often by using *ad hoc* explanations based on cultural stereotypes. If we were to conceive of society as a basically homogeneous group, this might be an appropriate method of study, but to take one group as a standard for all others is not only profoundly biasing but very limiting.

This can be strikingly demonstrated if we consider what we might learn about communication by studying the ways in which women communicate with each other. Based on cross-cultural data which Jenkins is currently compiling, there is evidence to suggest that in many societies, communication networks among women serve as the foundation for social interaction with kinship and social groups.[4] Carol Stack's (1974) study of kinship groups among poor urban American blacks supports this contention, but her observations were seen as peculiar to the black family as matriarchal or female dominated. However, women's work may also be the foundation of white middle class American society — where women are often considered to be the most alienated from

[4]The absurd notion has long been floating around, thanks to Lionel Tiger (1969), that men bond and women don't and that this state of affairs dates back to our prehistorical ancestors. The story goes that men bonded because they had to in order to hunt large animals. Of course, we know that women and children gathered food in groups, food which provided a primary source of sustenance (Slocum, 1975). Thus, early societies may have been similarly based on communication among women. Families and societies have changed much over time but close bonds between women still exist to the extent that if they break down, the social fabric of society is threatened. Thus, what is seen by many as the current malaise of the American family may well be a result of the isolation of women from each other in suburban nuclear family dwellings.

each other. As Elizabeth Bott (1971) indicates in her survey of the literature on family and social network, female friendship has not been adequately studied. If we consider who typically writes the letters to friends and relatives, signed 'love, Joe and Martha', who keeps track of social engagements, makes the phone calls to arrange who's going to bring what to the party, remembers the birthdays and anniversaries for both sides of the family, researches the family tree and keeps in touch with the grown children, spends the most time talking to the kids at home, makes and preserves the family artifacts, we see that it is usually women who do all this work.[5] Surely these are the means by which families and social groups are created and maintained through communication and care.

Women's talk, however, has been trivialized. These exchanges of information, during which social ties are formed and identities emerge, have been called gossip and chit chat. Very little research has been done on communication among women because it has not been considered important. Male researchers have studied communication as they experienced it in institutionalized task groups. These groups in the military and business are the groups they see as powerful. The only type of relational communication which has been studied is male–female lovers or marriage partners. Male–female bonding is considered to be the foundation for the family. However, we might consider whether the female–female bond is not also essential for the maintenance of family life.[6]

The few studies which have been done of interaction in women's groups indicate there are important differences between female, male and mixed sex groups (Aries, 1976; Kalcik, 1975; Copper, Ethelchild and Whyte, 1974; Aebischer, 1978). Currently folklorists are turning their attention to women's verbal art which is often not expressed in public but among women only (see special issue, *Frontiers,* Vol. 3 (3), 1978 on Women as Verbal Artists; Green, 1977; Johnson, 1973; Jones, 1980; and Farrer, 1975). To study woman to woman communication is to open up language and communication research to the full range of communicative experiences of which people are capable. It has now become clear that we need to study communication between and across groups in order to understand the relationship of power and communication. We will then be able to address the question of the relationship of language change to social change.

We do have some guides to the study of naturally occurring interaction, approaches which respect the perspectives of the speakers. For example, Philipsen (1975) in 'Speaking 'Like a Man' in Teamsterville' explains how he, through months of interaction with and listening to the boys and adult males of a U.S. blue-collar neighborhood, learned a great deal about how speech functions in that community. He learned, he felt, the way talk is defined, valued, interpreted and judged by members of the community. His interaction and interest was primarily with males; he said little about women's speech in 'Teamsterville'. Yet seemingly he or another researcher could use the same 'open' methods to derive an understanding of women's speech in a particular neighborhood or group.

---

[5]In discussing women's work which affects the family's relationship with other people, Hanna Papanek (1979) writes, 'Understanding women's work and its worth is difficult — it is less visible, less clearly rewarded in concrete terms, than the work of men, and it is more likely to be seen simply as a source of private comfort and welfare. (p. 781).

[6]For a historical perspective on female friendship see Smith-Rosenberg (1975) and Sahli (1979). Daly (1978b) offers a contemporary feminist vision of female bonding.

A Feminist Perspective

However, we find that our interests and concerns about the future ethnography of women's communication are different in several respects from those of most ethnographers of speaking.

(1) We want to be very cautious as we evaluate the basic assumptions males have often made about speech. Philipsen writes in general terms of speaking as a resource which people hoard, and spend strategically, to purchase things. The use of a monetary/economic metaphor for explaining social interaction is, of course, common to studies labelled small group research, and creates many problems in that work also. It is a disfunctional metaphor for much of women's communication where the emphasis is often *not* on competition, 'public' interaction, power, and rugged individualism. This is not to say that women do not have individual goals or that women are never competitive. We do suggest, however, that the metaphor comes from men's activity in, and control of, capitalism, and not from women's interaction.

(2) We will consider the integration of what are commonly considered dichotomous macro/micro elements of interaction. Discourse analysts are usually considered micro researchers (as opposed to researchers interested in social institutions such as family, church, and school). Sometimes they state that they are uninterested in intention or motivation, working instead to find specific rules of speech (frequently occurring patterns of speaking) which serve as the common base for verbal interaction. However, without knowing the speakers' interpretations of speech construction we know very little about sociological aspects of speaking. The macro/micro dichotomy is perhaps unnecessary if we consider societal institutions as primarily products of people's interaction and interpretation. Discourse should not be considered in isolated instances but as socially and historically situated and inclusive of the dynamics of attitudes, intentions and identities. The use of the macro (institutional structure) and micro (recurring everyday speech patterns) also assumes that social and political issues are separable from the study of everyday interaction. This can only be believed by people who think the present relationship of individuals and groups is equitable or at least irrevocable. Rather than assuming that all speakers make such assumptions, we will want to learn speakers' understanding of the social organization of their everyday interaction.

(3) We will study the attitudes, intentions and identities of speakers by learning about speakers' relationships to groups — those they choose and those which are imposed upon them. While men have worked to maintain the group *women,* by belittling or ignoring our speech and perceptions of reality and by labelling our actions as problems (our problems), they are seldom ready to explicitly categorize themselves as a group with special interests, and particular behavior. Through an ethnography of speaking we can obtain a better understanding of people's relationship to groups.

We do not expect all women to have the same relationship to their gender group. Henri Tajfel (1974), Jennifer Williams and Howard Giles (1978) point out that some members of subordinate groups consider their subordination legitimate and blame themselves or their group for their low status. Some perceive alternate social structures and work for social change, either individually or collectively. Our group identities are not single, or stable over time or across situation. We know very little about what conditions determine whether, or what, group identity is important. We want to know much more.

(4) Our approach recognizes that our studies are interpretations, not reconstructions of reality. We realize that inevitably we will delete and expand aspects of the social interaction we study. However, we will not ignore the one-half of the population which has been largely ignored in past communication research.

(5) Therefore, we would add to studies of social interaction a new goal — to determine the meaning of gender for speakers. We will consider the accumulating evidence that many women in mixed-sex verbal interaction believe that they are only allowed to have a say in interpretation if they conceptualize and categorize reality in terms acceptable to males (cf. Ardener, 1975), and evidence that women establish and maintain not only close same gender friendship networks, but also do much of the bonding work for men.

We do not assume that all women have the same beliefs and values and that all women are conscious of all their intentions and motivations, and will or can talk about them and about their own relationship to the entire social structure. What we do suggest is that we enlarge the study framework to include these relationships by studying the interaction among women as well as among men and between women and men, attending as much as possible to the words, ideas, and culture of women.

Scholarship by women about women's communication is considered by many males as radical scholarship — which indicates to us the extent of the deficiency of most of the previous communication research. Women have never been as apt as men to explain life through the lab, and recently we have been learning and speaking a new respect for our own constructions of reality and using them as a base for our inquiries and investigations. Only by listening to and respecting women's communication can we understand the various knowledge women have of group identity, of cultural expectations of women and their speech and of the perceived impact of male judgement on our speech.

By studying how talk is evaluated and what is expected from talk we can avoid a separation of academic and movement concerns about language. By studying gender and speech as relationships within sociocultural contexts we can derive a theory of communication which clearly includes female voices.

As it is now, in the words of French critic, Claudine Herriman, a woman must be '*valeuse de langue*' — a thief of language (Ostriker, 1979). She must steal the words back, redefine them to include her experience. She is building her own house of words *now* where she will finally be at home.

Impact of Feminist Scholarship

When we examine the impact that gender and communication research has had on the field as a whole, a paradox is evident. The number of recent publications, convention programs, special conferences and course offerings in this area attest to the substantial amount of research being done. Recognition and support for this research on the part of those not involved with it, however, have not always seemed as abundant. Many of our colleagues seem much more worried about the possible biases which might result from the investigation of gender and communication, than about possible biases which are brought about by overlooking these concerns.

Most male academicians seem to be conscious only of the existence of claims of male dominance and sexism in language usage. The use of 'he/she' instead of 'he' for the indefinite third person singular pronoun has been adopted by some academic journals and presses, but such usage is not yet standard or uniform. While such changes in usage have occurred, they have not usually been accompanied by an understanding of the substance of these feminist claims or the corresponding theoretical positions and analyses. Many women see a new consciousness of complex patterns of social arrangements not as a separate area of study but as an integral part of any studies of language structure and speech behavior.

In reviewing the research on sex differences in language and communication, however, it is important to distinguish between research whose primary focus is the investigation of these differences, and research that merely reports such findings as fall-out from statistical analyses of the data. In the latter, hypothetical reasons for these differences based on common gender stereotypes are often put forth with no attempt at validating such conclusions. In the former, a variety of explanations have been offered, as we have seen. It is obviously not enough simply to include gender as another variable in a research design which fails to take into account differences between the experiences of women and men from the outset.

But while most academic men have either dismissed immediately or have not been interested in or willing to read and discuss feminist questions about existing myths, assumptions and values, many women in the disciplines have been benefited from the feminist work in ways we are already beginning to take for granted.

Feminism has made a difference in what we study, how we study it, with whom we study, and who reads what we write. Even though our work may not be greeted with approval and support from many of our male colleagues, at least this work is now being done. But more than that, it is being discussed by large numbers of women. While the major disciplinary journals are still very male dominated, women's studies journals and other feminist journals now serve as vehicles for our work. Women in universities are thereby sharing ideas and research with many women in other occupations who are not reached by traditional academic journals. Women can now sustain the publication of books and articles that deal with our own experiences.

Data on university faculty indicate that the number of women in tenure positions has not increased dramatically in recent years, but there are now feminist faculty in language study disciplines who are working with students and colleagues from a feminist perspective. While the numbers may not have changed significantly, the quality of the relationships among faculty members and among faculty and students has changed. Women scholars no longer have to be isolated from each other. They are cooperating and sharing their work in a network that stretches around the world. (This network has resulted, for example, in international programs on communication and gender at conferences at Uppsala, Sweden; Osnabrück, Germany; and Bristol, England; and in many other national and regional seminars on this topic.) Many of us are attempting to employ feminist values in the work we do and the way we treat each other which counter the one-upmanship so common in the academic struggle to get ahead. Feminist scholarship necessarily implies an interdisciplinary approach: women's relationship to language, for example, cannot be studied apart from women's economic and social position in society. Recognizing this, we have broadened the scope of our scholarship rather than narrowed it as antifeminist critics might suppose. This is ultimately enriching to our research and to the disciplines to which we contribute.

Thus, the impact of feminism must be evaluated qualitatively as well as quantitatively. While every woman scholar does not choose to focus on this area of study, the opportunity for such work is there. The fact that feminist curricula have continued to grow in the face of economic cutbacks at most universities is evidence of a sustained movement for change in academic inquiry. It is a movement toward incorporating the experiences of women as understood by women into what has been until very recently men's studies, otherwise known as mainstream research.

References

AEBISCHER, Verena (1975) Chit-chat: Women in interaction, Paper given at the Ninth world Congress of Sociology, Uppsala, Sweden, August.

ARDENER, Shirley (1975) *Perceiving women,* Malaby Press, London.

ARIES, Elizabeth (1976) Interaction patterns and themes of male, female, and mixed groups, *Small Group Behavior. 7* (1), 7–18.

BEM, Sandra L. (1974) The measurement of psychological androgyny, *Journal of Consulting and Clinical Psychology,* 42 (ii), 155–162.

BLAUBERGS, Maija (1980) An analysis of classic arguments against changing sexist language, *Women's Studies International Quarterly, 3* (2/3).

BOTT, Elizabeth (1971) *Family and Social Network,* Tavistock, London.

CHODOROW, Nancy (1972) Being and doing: A cross cultural exmination of the socialization of males and females. In Vivian Gornick and Barbara K. Moran (Eds.) *Women in a Sexist Society,* Signet, New York.

COPPER, Babette, Maxine ETHELCHILD and Lucy WHYTE (1974) Feminist Process: Developing a non-competitive process within work groups, Manuscript, c/o Maxine Spencer, 1628 Grove Street, Berkeley, CA 94709, $1.50.

DALY, Mary (1978a) *Gyn/Ecology: The metaethics of radical feminism,* Beacon Press, Boston.

DALY, Mary (1978b) Sparking: The fire of female friendship, *Chrysalis,* No. 6, 27–35.

EMAN, Virginia A. and Renee MEYERS (1978) A symbolic interaction perspective of sexual identity and its relation to language use, Paper given at the Central State Speech Communication Association.

FARRER, Claire R. (1975) *Women and folklore,* University of Texas Press, Austin.

FISHMAN, Pamela M. (1978) Interaction: The work women do, *Social Problems, 26,* 397–406.

FRANK, Francine Wattman (1978) Women's language in America: Myth and reality. In Douglas Butturff and Edmund L. Epstein (Eds.) *Women's language and style.* Published with the assistance of the Department of English, University of Akron.

GILES, Howard, Richard Y. BOURHIS and Donald M. TAYLOR (1977) Towards a theory of language in ethnic group relations. In Howard Giles (Ed.) *Language, ethnicity and intergroup relations.* European monographs in social psychology 13, Academic Press, London.

GREEN, Rayna (1977) Magnolias grow in dirt: The bawdy lore of southern women, *Radical Teacher,* 6, 26–31.

HAAS, Adelaide (1979) Male and female spoken language differences: Stereotypes and evidence, *Psychological Bulletin,* 86, (3), 616–626.

HENLEY, Nancy M. (1979) Assertiveness training: Making the political personal. Paper written for the annual meetings of the Society for the Study of Social Problems, Boston.

HYMES, Dell (1972) Models of the interaction of language and social life. In John J. Gumperz and Dell Hymes (Eds.) *Directions in sociolinguistics: The ethnography of communication,* Holt, Rinehart and Winston, New York.

JENKINS, Lee, and Cheris KRAMER (1978) Small group process: Learning from women, *Women's Studies International Quarterly,* 1 (1), 67–84.

JENKINS, Mercilee M. (1980) Toward a model of human leadership. In Virgina Eman and Cynthia L. Berryman (Eds.) *Communication, language and sex,* Newbury house, Rowley, Mass.

JOHNSON, Robbie Davis (1973) Folklore and women: A social interactional analysis of the folklore of a Texas madam. *Journal of American Folklore,* 86 211–224.

JONES, Deborah (1980) Gossip: Notes on women's oral culture, *Women's Studies International Quarterly, 3* (2/3).

KALCIK, Susan (1975) ". . . like Ann's gynecologist or the time I was almost raped." In Claire R. Farrer (Ed.) *Women and Folklore,* University of Texas Press, Austin.

KRAMER, Cheris, Barrie THORNE and Nancy HENLEY (1978) Review essay: Perspectives on language and communication, *Signs: Journal of Women in Culture and Society, 3* (3) 638–651.

MacKAY, Donald. Prescriptive grammar and the pronoun problem. In Nancy Henley, Barrie Thorne and Cheris Kramarae (Eds.) *Language and Sex II* (Working Title) Newbury House, Rowley, Mass., in preparation.

McDANIEL, Judith (1978) Paper given as part of a panel at the 1977 Annual Modern Language Association Convention. The panel papers were published with the title, The transformation of silence into language and action, *Sinister Wisdom, 6* (Summer).

MARTYNA, Wendy (1980). Beyond the 'he/man' approach: The case for nonsexist language, *Signs: Journal of Women in Culture and Society.*

MILLER, Casey and Kate SWIFT (1977) *Words and women: New language in new times,* Anchor Press/Doubleday, New York.

NICHOLS, Patricia (1978) Dynamic variation theory as a model for the study of language and sex. Paper given at the Ninth World Congress of Sociology, Uppsala, Sweden, August.

NILSEN, Allen Pace, Haig BOSMAJIAN, H. Lee GERSHUNY and Julia P. STANLEY (1977) *Sexism and language,* National Council of Teachers of English, Urbana, IL.

O'CONNOR, Lillian (1954) *Pioneer women orators: Rhetoric in the ante-bellum reform movement,* Columbia University Press, New York.

OSTRIKER, Alicia (1979) Her cargo: Adrienne Rich and the common language, *The American Poetry Review, 8* (4), 6–10.

PAPANEK, Hanna (1979) Family status production: The 'work' and 'non-work' of women, *Signs: Journal of Women in Culture, 4* (4) 775–781.

PARSONS, Elsie Clews (1913) *The old-fashioned woman: Primitive fancies about the sex,* G. P. Putnam's Sons, New York.

PHILIPSEN, Gerry (1975) Speaking 'like a man' in Teamsterville: Cultural patterning of role enactment in an urban neighborhood, *Quarterly Journal of Speech 61,* 13–23.

PHILIPSEN, Gerry. (1975). Speaking as a cultural resource. Paper presented at the Speech Communication Association, Houston, Texas.

RICH, Adrienne (1978) Paper given as part of panel discussion of the 1977 Annual Modern Language Association Convention. The panel papers were published with the title, The transformation of silence into language and action, *Sinister Wisdom, 6* (Summer).

RUSS, Joanna (1979) Review of Mary Daly's Gyn/Ecology: The metaethics of radical feminism, *Frontiers: A Journal of Women Studies, 4* (1), 68–70.

SAHLI, Nancy (1979) Smashing: Women's relationships before the fall, *Chyrsalis,* No. 8, 17–28.

SLOCUM, Sally (1975) Woman the gatherer; Male bias in anthropology. In Rayna R. Reiter (Ed.) *Toward an anthropology of women,* Monthly Review Press, New York.

SMITH, Philip M., Howard GILES and Miles HEWSTONE (1980) Sociolinguistics: A social psychological perspective. In Robert St. Clair and Howard Giles (Eds.) *Social and Psychological Perspectives of Language,* Erlbaum: Hillsdale, N.J.

SMITH-ROSENBERG, Carroll (1975) The female world of love and ritual: Relations between women in nineteenth-century America, *Signs: Journal of Women in Culture, 1* (1), 1–29.

SPENDER, Dale (1980) *Man Made Language,* Routledge and Kegan Paul, London.

STACK, Carol B. (1974) *All our kin: Strategies for survival in a black community,* Harper & Row, New York.

STOLTJE, Beverly (1973) Bow-legged bastard: A manner of speaking: Speech behavior of a black woman, *Folklore Annual, 4* and *5,* 152–178.

TAJFEL, Henri (1974) Social identity and intergroup behavior, *Social Science Information,* 13 (2), 65–93.

THORNE, Barrie and Nancy HENLEY (1975) Difference and dominance: An overview of language, gender, and society. In Barrie Thorne and Nancy Henley (Eds.) *Language and sex: Difference and dominance,* Newbury House, Rowley, Mass.

THORNE, Barrie and Nancy HENLEY (Eds.) (1975) *Language and sex: Difference and dominance,* Newbury House, Rowley, Mass.

TIGER, Lionel (1969) Why men need a boy's night out. In Betty Roszak and Theodore Roszak (Eds.) *Masculine/feminine: Readings in sexual mythology and the liberation of women,* Harper Colophon Books, New York.

WEST, Candace and Don H. ZIMMERMAN. Small insults: A study of interruptions in cross-sex conversations between unacquainted persons. In Nancy Henley, Barrie Thorne and Cheris Kramarae (Eds.) *Language and Sex II* (Working Title) Newbury House, Rowley, Mass., in preparation.

WILLIAMS, Jennifer A. and Howard GILES (1978) The changing status of women in society: An intergroup perspective. In Henri Tajfel (Ed.) *Differentiation between social groups; Studies in the social psychology of intergroup relations,* European Monograph in Social Psychology, 14, Academic Press, London.

WOLFE, Susan and Julia Penelope STANLEY (1980) Linguistic problems with patriarchal reconstructions of Indo-European culture: A little more than kin, a little less than kind, *Women's Studies International Quarterly, 3* (2/3).

ZIMMERMAN, Don H. and Candace WEST (1975) Sex roles, interruptions and silences in conversation. In Barrie Thorne and Nancy Henley (Eds.) *Language and sex: Difference and dominance,* Newbury House, Rowley, Mass.

2

Dancing Through the Mine-Field: Some Observations on the Theory, Practice, and Politics of a Feminist Literary Criticism*

ANNETTE KOLODNY

During the years that I was in college, from 1958 to 1962, no one thought to ask why so few women poets and novelists appeared on required reading lists or, even less, why women's names were only rarely mentioned when we discussed the 'important' or 'influential' critics of the day. Where women writers were taught, as in the courses on the history of the English novel, a supposedly exceptional work might be remarked for its 'large scope' or 'masculine thrust'; but, more often than not, women's novels were applauded for a certain elegance of style, an attention to detail or nuance, and then they were curtly dismissed for their inevitably 'feminine' lack of humor, weighty truths, or universal significance. If possible, things were even more dismal in the American literature courses, where Anne Bradstreet was treated as a Puritan anomaly, and Emily Dickinson was presented as a case study who had offered biographer after biographer the occasion to identify the peculiar pathology which *must* explain (or explain away) her otherwise apparently incomprehensible prolific poetic output. These were the years, after all, when no one blinked at Norman Mailer's 'terrible confession' that he could not read 'any of the talented women who write today' (1959: 434–435), and most nodded in agreement when Theodore Roethke listed among the frequent charges made against women's poetry, its 'lack of range — in subject matter, in emotional tone — and a lack of a sense of humor'.[1] Elizabeth Janeway (1979) has noted that women writers of that period quite properly attempted to reject the label 'women's literature', reacting against the 'automatic disparagement of their work' which it implied (p. 342). For readers as for writers then, as Adrienne Rich recalled, 'it seemed to be a given fact that men wrote poems and women frequently inhabited them' (Rich, 1972: 93).

But just beneath the many surface complacencies of the 1950's an anger was brewing. With the radical critiques of American society that emerged in the 1960's there emerged also, though perhaps more slowly, a gradual recognition by women that it was not just the blacks or the other minority groups who were being deprived of their basic civil

---

[1]See Theodore Roethke's 'The Poetry of Louise Bogan' in *Selected Prose of Theodore Roethke,* Ralph J. Mills, Jr. (Ed.) (Seattle: University of Washington Press, 1965), pp. 133–134. For an illuminating analysis of the contradictions in Roethke's remarks, see Sandra M. Gilbert and Susan Gubar, *The Madwoman in the Attic: The Woman Writer and the Nineteenth-Century Literary Imagination* (New Haven: Yale University Press, 1979), pp. 541–542.

rights; that women, too, regardless of their class or education, were also, in a real sense, second-class citizens. As this perception was shared, especially in the consciousness-raising groups that marked the beginning of the 'new feminism' at the end of the 1960's and the beginning of the 1970's, 'the sleepwalkers', as Adrienne Rich called us, began 'coming awake'; and, even more important, 'for the first time this awakening' took on 'a collective reality' (1972: 90). By the time I was completing my Ph.D. thesis at the University of California at Berkeley, in 1969, that new collective consciousness had permeated campus study groups and social gatherings sufficiently to make it at least uncomfortable for anyone to merely laugh at or accept as witty Norman Mailer's dismissal of women writers on the grounds 'that a good novelist can do without everything but the remnant of his balls' (1959: 435). And few of the *women* graduate students, at any rate, were willing to accept without further investigation Roethke's pronouncement that women writers had always contented themselves with 'the embroidering of trivial themes' or shown only 'a concern with the mere surfaces of life — that special province of the female talent in prose — hiding from the real agonies of the spirit' (Roethke, 1965: 134). That further investigation which began so tentatively at the end of the 1960's became, of course, what we now call 'feminist literary criticism'.

Had anyone the prescience back then to pose the question of defining a 'feminst' literary criticism, she might have been told, after the appearance of Mary Ellmann's *Thinking About Women,* in 1968, that it involved exposing the sexual stereotyping of women in both our literature and our literary criticism and, as well, demonstrating the inadequacy of established critical schools and methods to deal fairly or sensitively with works written by women. And, for the most part, such a prediction would have stood well the test of time. What could not have been anticipated as the 1960's drew to a close, however, was the long-term catalyzing effect of an ideology that, for many of us, had helped to bridge the gap between the world as we found it and the world as we wanted it to be. For those of us who studied literature, a previously unspoken sense of exclusion from authorship, and a painfully personal distress at discovering whores, bitches, muses, and heroines dead in childbirth where we had once hoped to discover ourselves, could now, for the first time, begin to be understood as more than 'a set of disconnected, unrealized private emotions' (Geertz, 1973: 232). With a renewed courage to make public our otherwise private discontents, what had once been 'felt individually as personal insecurity' came at last to be 'viewed collectively as structural inconsistency' (Geertz, 1973: 204) within the very disciplines we studied. Following unflinchingly the full implications of Ellmann's percipient early observations, and emboldened to do so by the liberating energy of feminist ideology — in all its various forms and guises — feminist criticism very quickly moved beyond merely 'expos[ing] sexism in one work of literature after another' (Robinson, 1972: 51), and promised, instead, that we might at last 'begin to record new choices in a new literary history' (Showalter, 1977: 36). So powerful was that impulse that we experienced it, along with Adrienne Rich, as much 'more than a chapter in cultural history:' it became, rather, 'an act of survival' (1972: 90). What was at stake was not so much literature or criticism *per se* but the historical, social, and ethical consequences of women's participation in, or exclusion from either enterprise.

The pace of inquiry these last ten years has been fast and furious — especially after Kate Millett's 1970 analysis of the sexual politics of literature added a note of urgency to what had earlier been Ellmann's sardonic anger — while the diversity of that inquiry easily outstripped all efforts to define feminist literary criticism as either a coherent system or a unified set of methodologies. Under its wide umbrella everything has been thrown into question: our established canons, our aesthetic criteria, our interpretive strategies, our reading habits, and, most of all, ourselves as critics and as teachers. To delineate its full scope would require nothing less than a book — a book that would be outdated even as it was being composed. For the sake of brevity, therefore, let me attempt only a summary outline.

Perhaps the most obvious success of this new scholarship has been the return to circulation of previously lost or otherwise ignored works by women writers. Following fast upon the initial success of the Feminist Press in reissuing gems like Rebecca Harding Davis' 1861 novella, *Life in the Iron Mills,* and Charlotte Perkins Gilman's 1892 *The Yellow Wallpaper,* published in 1972 and 1973 respectively,[2] numbers of commercial trade and reprint houses vied with one another in the reprinting of anthologies of lost texts and, in some cases, in the reprinting of whole series. For those of us in American literature especially, the phenomenon promised a radical reshaping of our concepts of literary history and, at the very least, a new chapter in understanding the development of women's literary traditions. So commercially successful were these reprintings, and so attuned were the reprint houses to the political attitudes of the audiences for which they were offered, that many of us found ourselves being wooed to compose critical introductions which would find in the pages of nineteenth-century domestic and sentimental fictions some signs of either muted rebellions or overt radicalism, in anticipation of the current wave of 'new feminism'. In rereading with our students these previously lost works, we inevitably raised perplexing questions as to the reasons for their disappearance from the canons of 'major works', and worried over the aesthetic and critical criteria by which they had been accorded diminished status.

This increased availability of works by women writers led, of course, to an increased interest in what elements, if any, might comprise some sort of unity or connection among them. The possiblity that women had developed either a unique, or at least a related tradition of their own, especially intrigued those of us who specialized in one national literature or another, or in historical periods. Nina Baym's (1978) *Women's Fiction: A Guide to Novels by and about Women in America, 1820–1870* demonstrates the Americanists' penchant for examining what were once the 'best sellers' of their day, the ranks of the popular fiction writers, among which women took a dominant place throughout the nineteenth century, while the feminist studies of British literature emphasized instead the wealth of women writers who have been regarded as worthy of canonization. Not so much building upon one another's work as clarifying, successivly, the perameters of the questions to be posed, Sydney Janet Kaplan, Ellen Moers, Patricia Meyer Spacks, and Elaine Showalter, among many others, concentrated their energies on delineating an internally consistent 'body of work' by women which might stand as a female counter-tradition. For Kaplan, in 1975, this entailed examining women writers' various attempts to portray feminine consciousness and self-consciousness not as a

[2]Rebecca Harding Davis, *Life in the Iron Mills,* orig. publ. in *The Atlantic Monthly,* April 1861; rpt. with 'A Biographical Interpretation' by Tillie Olsen (New York: Feminist Press, 1972). Charlotte Perkins Gilman, *The Yellow Wallpaper,* orig. publ. in *The New England Magazine,* May 1892; rpt. with an Afterword by Elaine R. Hedges (New York: Feminist Press, 1973).

psychological category, but as a stylistic or rhetorical device;[3] that same year, arguing essentially that literature publicizes the private, Spacks placed her consideration of a 'female imagination' within social and historical frames, to conclude that, 'for readily discernible historical reasons women have characteristically concerned themselves with matters more or less peripheral to male concerns', and attributed to this fact an inevitable difference in the literary emphases and subject matters of female and male writers (Spacks, 1975: 6). The next year, Moers's *Literary Women* (1976) focussed on the pathways of literary influence that linked the English novel in the hands of women. And, finally, in 1977, Showalter took up the matter of a 'female literary tradition in the English novel from the generation of the Brontës to the present day' by arguing that, since women in general constitute a kind of 'subculture within the framework of a larger society', the work of women writers, in particular, would thereby demonstrate a unity of 'values, conventions, experiences, and behaviors impinging on each individual' as she found her sources of 'self-expression relative to a dominant [and, by implication, male] society' (p. 11).

At the same time that women writers were being reconsidered and reread, male writers were similarly subjected to a new feminist scrutiny. The continuing result, to put ten years of difficult analysis into a single sentence, has been nothing less than an acute attentiveness to the ways in which certain power relations — usually those in which males wield various forms of influence over females — are inscribed in the texts (both literary and critical) that we have inherited, not merely as subject matter, but as the unquestioned, often unacknowledged *given* of the culture. Even more important than the new interpretations of individual texts which such attentiveness has rendered is its probings into the consequences (for women) of the conventions which inform those texts. In surveying selected nineteenth- and early twentieth-century British novels which employ what she calls 'the two suitors convention', for example, Jean Kennard (1978) sought to understand why and how the structural demands of the convention, even in the hands of women writers, inevitably work to imply 'the inferiority and necessary subordination of women' (p. 164). Her 1978 study, *Victims of Convention,* points out that the symbolic nature of the marriage which conventionally concludes such novels 'indicates the adjustment of the protagonist to society's values, a condition which is equated with her maturity' (p. 18). Kennard's concern, however, is with the fact that the structural demands of the form too often sacrifice precisely those 'virtues of independence and individuality', or, in other words, the very 'qualities we have been invited to admire in' the heroines (p. 14). If Kennard appropriately cautions us against drawing from her work any simplistically reductive thesis about the mimetic relations between art and life, her approach does nonetheless suggest that what is important about a fiction is not whether it ends in a death or a marriage, but what the symbolic demands of that particular conventional ending imply about the values and beliefs of the world that engendered it.

Her work thus participates in a growing emphasis in feminist literary study on the fact of literature as a social institution, embedded not only within its own literary traditions

[3]In her *Feminine Consciousness in the Modern British Novel* (Urbana: Univ. of Illinois Press, 1975) Sydney Janet Kaplan explains, p. 3, that she is using the term 'feminine consciousness' 'not simply as some general attitude of women toward their own femininity, and not as something synonymous with a particular sensibility among female writers. I am concerned with it as a literary device: a method of characterization of females in fiction.'

but within the particular physical and mental artifacts of the society from which it comes. Adumbrating Millett's 1970 decision to anchor her 'literary reflections' to a preceding analysis of the historical, social, and economic contexts of sexual politics,[4] more recent work — most notably Lillian Robinson's — begins with the premise that the process of artistic creation 'consists not of ghostly happenings in the head but of a matching of the states and processes of symbolic models against the states and processes of the wider world' (Geertz, 1973: 214). The power relations inscribed in the form of conventions within our literary inheritance, these critics argue, reify the encodings of those same power relations in the culture at large. And the critical examination of rhetorical codes becomes, in their hands, the pursuit of ideological codes, since both embody either value systems or the dialectic of competition between value systems. More often than not, these critics also insist upon examining not only the mirroring of life in art but, as well, the normative impact of art on life. Addressing herself to the popular arts available to working women, for example, Lillian Robinson is interested in understanding not only 'the forms it uses', but, more importantly 'the myths it creates, the influence it exerts'. 'The way art helps people to order, interpret, mythologize, or dispose of their own experience', she declares, may be 'complex and often ambiguous, but it is not impossible to define'.[5]

Whether its focus be upon the material or the imaginative contexts of literary invention; single texts or entire canons; the relations between authors, genres, or historical circumstances; lost authors or well-known names, the variety and diversity of all feminist literary criticism finally coheres in its stance of almost defensive re-reading. What Adrienne Rich (1972) had earlier called 're-vision', that is, 'the act of looking back, of seeing with fresh eyes, of entering an old text from a new critical direction' (p. 90), took on a more actively self-protective coloration in 1978, when Judith Fetterley called upon the woman reader to learn to 'resist' the sexist designs a text might make upon her — asking her to identify against herself, so to speak, by manipulating her sympathies on behalf of male heroes, but against female shrew or bitch characters. Underpinning a great deal of this critical re-reading has been the not-unexpected alliance between feminist literary study and those feminist studies in linguistics and language acquisition examined in the chapter by Mercilee Jenkins and Cheris Kramarae. Tillie Olsen's (1978) commonsense observation of the danger of 'perpetuating — by continued usage — entrenched, centuries-old oppressive power realities, early-on incorporated into language' (p. 239–240), has been given substantive analysis in the writings of feminists who study 'language as a symbolic system closely tied to a patriarchal social structure'. Taken together, their work demonstrates 'the importance of language in establishing, reflecting, and maintaining an asymmetrical relationship between women and men' (see Kramer et al., 1978: 646).

To consider what this implies for the fate of women who essay the craft of language is to ascertain, perhaps for the first time, the real dilemma of the poet who finds her most cherished private experience 'hedged by taboos, mined with false-namings'[6] and, as well,

---

[4]See Millett, Part III, 'The Literary Reflection', pp. 235–261.

[5]Robinson, 'Criticism — and Self Criticism', *College English* 36 (1974) and 'Criticism: Who Needs It?' in *The Uses of Criticism* A. P. Foulkes (Ed.) (Bern and Frankfurt: Lang, 1976); both rpt. in *Sex, Class, and Culture*, p. 67; p. 80.

[6]See Adrienne Rich's discussion of the difficulty in finding authentic language for her experience as a mother in her *Of Woman Born* (New York: W. W. Norton and Co., 1976), p. 15.

the dilemma of the male reader who, in opening the pages of a woman's book, finds himself entering a strange and unfamiliar world of symbolic significance. For if, as Nelly Furman (1978) insists, neither language use nor language acquisition are 'gender-neutral', but, instead, are both 'imbued with our sex-inflected cultural values' (p. 184); and if, additionally, reading is a process of 'sorting out the structures of signification' (Geertz, 1973: 9) in any text, then male readers who find themselves outside of and unfamiliar with the symbolic systems that constitute female experience in women's writings, will necessarily dismiss those systems as undecipherable, meaningless, or trivial. And male professors will find no reason to include such works in the canons of 'major authors'. At the same time, women writers, coming into a tradition of literary language and conventional forms already appropriated, for centuries, to the purposes of male expression, will be forced virtually to 'wrestle' with that language in an effort 'to remake it as a language adequate to our conceptual processes' (Stanley and Robbins, 1977: 63). To all of this, feminists concerned with the politics of language and style have been acutely attentive. 'Language conceals an invincible adversary', observes French critic Helene Cixous (1976), 'because it's the language of men and their grammar' (p. 87). But equally insistent, as in the work of Sandra M. Gilbert and Susan Gubar, has been the understanding of the need for *all* readers — male and female alike — to learn to penetrate the otherwsie unfamiliar universes of symbolic action that comprise women's writings, past and present.[7]

*   *   *   *

To have attempted so many difficult questions and to have accomplished so much — even acknowledging the inevitable false starts, overlapping, and repetition — in so short a time, should certainly, one would imagine, have secured feminist literary criticism full partnership in that academic pursuit which we term, loosely enough, 'critical analysis'. But, in fact, as the 1979 *Harvard Guide to Contemporary American Writing* makes all too clear, our situation is, at best, ambiguous; at worst, precarious. Boasting that it 'undertakes a critical survey of the most significant writing in the United States between the end of World War II and the end of the 1970's', the *Guide's* Preface promises 'first, ... a survey of intellectual commitments and attitudes during the period' and then 'an examination of the theories and practices of literary criticism which have accompanied and to some extent even influenced the writing of these decades'. The opening chapter by Alan Trachtenberg on the 'Intellectual Background', however, while it pays respectful and often probing attention to the social critics and the 'revolutionary criticism' which marked the 1960's and early 1970's, never mentions what remains as perhaps the most enduring legacy of that critique: the women's liberation movement. Similarly, in his overview of 'American literary criticism since 1945', A. Walton Litz notes a 'general trend ... from consensus to diversity', but he fails to note feminist literary criticism as any contributor to that growing critical diversity. To be sure, the *Guide* includes two chapters by women — Elizabeth Janeway's study of 'Women's

---

[7]Gilbert and Gubar suggest, for example, that women's writings are in some sense 'palimpsestic' in that their 'surface designs conceal or obscure deeper, less accessible (and less socially acceptable) levels of meaning' (p. 73). It is, in their view, an art designed 'both to express and to camouflage' (p. 81).

Literature' and Josephine Hendin's survey of 'Experimental Fiction'.[8] And both, in different ways, point to the importance of women writers and the new feminism for current developments in American Literature. That only the women contributors marked this fact, though, suggests the continuing ghettoization of women's interests and demonstrates again how fragile has been the impact of feminist criticism on our non-feminist colleagues and on the academic mainstream in general.

Indeed, for all our efforts, instead of being welcomed into that mainstream, we've been forced to negotiate a mine-field. The very energy and diversity of our enterprise has rendered us vulnerable to attack on the grounds that we lack both definition and coherence; while our particular attentiveness to the ways in which literature encodes and disseminates cultural value systems calls down upon us imprecations which echo those heaped upon the Marxist critics of an earlier generation. If we are scholars dedicated to rediscovering a lost body of writings by women, then our finds are questioned on aesthetic grounds. And if we are critics, determined to practice revisionist readings, it is claimed that our focus is too narrow, and our results only distortions or, worse still, polemical misreadings.

The very vehemence of the outcry, coupled with the fact of our total dismissal in some quarters,[9] suggests not our deficiencies, however, but the potential magnitude of our challenge. For what we are asking be scrutinized are nothing less than shared cultural assumptions so deeply rooted and so long ingrained that, for the most part, our critical colleagues have ceased to recognize them as such. In other words, what is really being bewailed in the claims that we distort texts or threaten the disappearance of the great western literary tradition itself[10] is not so much the disappearance of either text or tradition but, instead, the eclipse of that particular *form* of the text, and that particular *shape* of the canon, which previously reified male readers' sense of power and significance in the world. Analogously, by asking whether, as readers, we ought to be 'really satisfied by the marriage of Dorothea Brooke to Will Ladislaw? of Shirley Keeldar to Louis Moore?' or whether, as Jean Kennard (1978) suggests, we must reckon with the ways in which 'the qualities we have been invited to admire in these heroines [have] been sacrificed to structural neatness' (p. 14), is to raise difficult and profoundly perplexing questions about the ethical implications of our otherwise unquestioned aesthetic pleasures. It is, after all, an imposition of high order to ask the viewer to attend to Ophelia's sufferings in a scene where, before, he'd always so comfortably kept his eye fixed firmly on Hamlet. To understand all this, then, as the real nature of the challenge

[8]See Daniel Hoffman's 'Preface'; Alan Trachtenberg's 'Intellectual Backgrounds', p. 34; A. Walton Litz's 'Literary Criticism', p. 51; Elizabeth Janeway's 'Women's Literature', pp. 342–395; and Josephine Hendin's 'Experimental Fiction', pp. 240–246, in *Harvard Guide.*

[9]Consider, for example, Paul Boyers' reductive and inaccurate generalization that 'what distinguishes ordinary books and articles about women from feminist writing is the feminist insistence on asking the same questions of every work and demanding ideologically satisfactory answers to those questions as a means of evaluating it', in his 'A Case Against Feminist Criticism' in *Partisan Review* XLIII, no. 4 (1976): 602; and, partly as a result of such misconceptions, the paucity of feminist critics granted a place in English Departments which otherwise pride themselves on the variety of their critical orientations.

[10]Ambivalent though he is about the literary continuity which begins with Homer, Harold Bloom nonetheless somewhat ominously prophesies 'that the first true break ... will be brought about in generations to come, if the burgeoning religion of Liberated Women spreads from its clusters of enthusiasts to dominate the West', in his *A Map of Misreading* (New York: Oxford Univ. Press, 1975), p. 33; on p. 36, he acknowleges that while something 'as violent [as] a quarrel would ensue if I expressed by judgment' on Robert Lowell and Norman Mailer, 'it would lead to something more intense than quarrels if I expressed my judgment upon ... the "literature of Women's Liberation".'

we have offered and, in consequence, as the motivation for the often overt hostility we've aroused, should help us learn to negotiate the mine-field, if not with grace, then with at least a clearer comprehension of its underlying patterns.

The ways in which objections to our work are usually posed, of course, serve to obscure their deeper motivations. But this may, in part, be due to our own reticence at taking full responsibility for the truly radicalizing premises that lie at the theoretical core of all we have so far accomplished. It may be time, therefore, to redirect discussion, forcing our adversaries to deal with the substantive issues and pushing ourselves into a clearer articulation of what, in fact, we are about. Up until now, I fear, we have only piece-meal dealt with the difficulties inherent in challenging the authority of established canons and then justifying the excellence of women's traditions, sometimes in accord with standards to which they have no intrinsic relation.

At the very point at which we must perforce enter the discourse — that is, claiming excellence or importance for our 'finds' — all discussion has already, we discover, long ago been closed. 'If Kate Chopin were *really* worth reading', an Oxford-trained colleague once assured me, 'she'd have lasted — like Shakespeare'; and he then proceeded to vote against the English Department's crediting a Women's Studies seminar I was offering in American women writers. The canon, for him, conferred excellence; Chopin's exclusion demonstrated only her lesser worth. As far as he was concerned, I could no more justify giving English Department credit for the study of Chopin than I could dare publicly to question Shakespeare's genius. Through hindsight, I've now come to view that discussion as not only having posed fruitless oppositions but as having entirely evaded the much more profound problem lurking just beneath the surface of our disagreement: and that is, that the fact of canonization puts any work beyond questions of establishing its merit and, instead, invites students to offer only increasingly more ingenious readings and interpretations, the purpose of which is to validate the greatness already imputed by canonization.

Had I only understood it for what it was then, into this circular and self-serving set of assumptions I might have interjected some statement of my right to question why *any* text is revered and my need to know what it tells us about 'how we live, how we have been living, how we have been led to imagine ourselves, [and] how our language has trapped as well as liberated us' (Rich, 1972: 90). The very fact of our critical training within the strictures imposed by an established canon of major works and authors, however, repeatedly deflects us from such questions; instead, we find ourselves endlessly responding to the *riposte* that the overwhelmingly male presence among canonical authors was only an accident of history — and never intentionally sexist — coupled with claims to the 'obvious' aesthetic merit of those canonized texts. It is, as I say, a fruitless exchange, serving more to obscure than to expose the territory being protected and dragging us, again and again, through the mine-field.

It is my contention that current hostilities might be transformed into a true dialogue with our critics if we at last made explicit what appear, to this observer, to constitute the three crucial propositions to which our special interests inevitably give rise. They are, moreover, propositions which, if handled with care and intelligence, could breathe new life into now moribund areas of our profession:

1. Literary history (and, with that, the historicity of literature) is a fiction;
2. insofar as we are taught how to read, what we engage are not texts but paradigms; and, finally,

3. that since the grounds upon which we assign aesthetic value to texts are never infallible, unchangeable, or universal, we must re-examine not only our aesthetics but, as well, the inherent biases and assumptions informing the critical methods which (in part) shape our aesthetic responses.

For the sake of brevity, I won't attempt to offer the full arguments for each but, rather, only sufficient elaboration to demonstrate what I see as their intrinsic relation to the potential scope of and present challenge implied by feminist literary study:

1. *Literary history (and, with that, the historicity of literature) is a fiction.* To begin with, an established canon functions as a model by which to chart the continuities and discontinuities, as well as the influences upon and the interconnections between works, genres, and authors. That model we tend to forget, however, is of our own making. It will take a very different shape, and explain its inclusions and exclusions in very different ways, if the reigning critical ideology believes that new literary forms result from some kind of ongoing internal dialectic within pre-existing styles and traditions or if, by contrast, the ideology declares that literary change is dependent upon societal development and thereby determined by upheavals in the social and economic organization of the culture at large.[11] Indeed, whenever in the previous century of English and American literary scholarship one alternative replaced the other, we saw dramatic alterations in canonical 'wisdom'.

This suggests, then, that our sense of a 'literary history' and, by extension, our confidence in a so-called 'historical' canon, is rooted not so much in any definitive understanding of the past, as in our need to call up and utilize the past on behalf of a better understarding of the present. Thus, to paraphrase David Couzens Hoy (1978), it becomes 'necessary to point out that the understanding of art and literature is such an essential aspect of the present's self-understanding that this self-understanding conditions what even gets taken' as comprising that artistic and literary past. To quote Hoy fully, 'this continual reinterpretation of the past goes hand in hand with the continual reinterpretation by the present of itself' (p. 166–167). In our own time, uncertain as to which, if any, model truly accounts for our canonical choices or accurately explains literary history, and pressured further by the feminists' call for some justification of the criteria by which women's writings were largely excluded from both that canon and history, we suffer what Harold Bloom (1975) has called 'a remarkable dimming' of 'our mutual sense of canonical standards' (p. 36).

Into this apparent impasse feminist literary theorists implicitly introduce the observation that our choices and evaluations of current literature have the effect either of solidifying or of reshaping our sense of the past. The authority of any established canon, after all, is reified by our perception that current work seems to grow, almost inevitably, out of it (even in opposition or rebellion), and is called into question when what we read appears to have little or no relation to what we recognize as coming before. So, were the larger critical community to begin to seriously attend to the recent outpouring of fine literature by women, this would surely be accompanied by a concomitant re-searching of the past, by literary historians, in order to account for the present phenomenon. In that process, literary history would itself be altered: works by

---

[11]The first is a proposition currently expressed by some structuralists and formalist critics; the best statement of the second probably appears in Georg Lukacs, *Writer and Critic* (New York: Grosset and Dunlap, 1970), p. 119.

seventeenth, eighteenth, or nineteenth century women writers, to which we had not previously attended, for example, might be given new importance as 'precursors' or as prior influences upon present-day authors; while selected male writers might also be granted new prominence as figures whom the women today, or even yesterday, needed to reject. I am arguing, in other words, that the choices we make in the present inevitably alter our sense of the past that led to them.

Related to this is the feminist challange to that patently mendacious critical fallacy that we read the 'classics' in order to reconstruct the past 'the way it really was', and that we read Shakespeare and Milton in order to apprehend the meanings that they intended. Short of time machines or miraculous resurrections, there is simply no way to know, precisely or surely, what 'really was', what Homer intended when he sang, or Milton when he dictated. Critics more acute than I have already pointed up the impossibility of grounding a reading in the imputation of authorial intention, since the further removed the author is from us, so too must be his or her systems of knowledge and belief, points of view, and structures of vision (artistic and otherwise).[12] (I omit here the difficulty of finally either proving or disproving the imputation of intentionality since, inescapably, the only appropriate authority is unavailable: deceased.) What we have really come to mean when we speak of competence in reading historical texts, therefore, is the ability to recognize literary conventions which have survived through time — so as to remain operational in the mind of the reader — and, where these are lacking, the ability to translate (or perhaps transform?) the text's ciphers into more current and recognizable shapes. But we never really reconstruct the past in its own terms. What we gain when we read the 'classics', then, is neither Homer's Greece nor George Eliot's England *as they knew it* but, rather, an approximation of an already fictively imputed past made available, through our interpretive strategies, for present concerns. Only by understanding this can we put to rest that recurrent delusion that the so-called 'continuing relevance' of the classics serves as 'testimony to perennial features of human experience' (Altieri, 1978: 90). The only 'perennial feature' to which our ability to read and reread texts written in previous centuries testifies is our inventiveness — in the sense that all of literary history is a fiction which we daily recreate as we reread it. What distinguishes feminists in this regard is their desire to alter and extend what we take as historically relevant from out of that vast storehouse of our literary inheritance and, further, their recognition of the storehouse for what it really is: a resource for remodelling our literary history, past, present, and future.

2. *Insofar as we are taught how to read, what we engage are not texts but paradigms.* To pursue the logical consequences of the first proposition leads, however uncomfortably to the conclusion that we appropriate meaning from a text according to what we need (or desire), or, in other words, according to the critical assumptions or predispositions (conscious or not) that we bring to it. And we appropriate different meanings, or report different gleanings, at different times — even from the same text — according to our

---

[12]John Dewey offered precisely this argument in 1934 when he insisted that a work of art 'is recreated every time it is esthetically experienced. ... It is absurd to ask what an artist "really" meant by his product: he himself would find different meanings in it at different days and hours and in different stages of his own development.' Further, he explained, 'It is simply an impossibility that any one today should experience the Parthenon as the devout Athenian contemporary citizen experienced it, any more than the religious statuary of the twelfth century can mean, esthetically, even to a good Catholic today just what it meant to the worshipers of the old period', in *Art as Experience* (rpt. New York: Capricorn Books/G. P. Putnam's Sons, 1958), pp. 108–109.

changed assumptions, circumstances, and requirements. This, in essence, constitutes the heart of the second proposition. For insofar as literature is itself a social institution, so too, reading is a highly socialized — or learned — activity. What makes it so exciting, of course, is that it can be constantly relearned, so as to provide either an individual or an entire reading community, over time, infinite variations of the same text. It *can* provide that; but, I must add, too often it does not. Frequently our reading habits become fixed so that each successive reading experience functions, in effect, normatively, with one particular kind of novel stylizing our expectations of those to follow, the stylistic devices of any favorite author (or group of authors) alerting us to the presence or absence of those devices in the works of others, and so on. 'Once one has read his first poem', Murray Krieger (1976) has observed, 'he turns to his second and to the others that will follow thereafter with an increasing series of preconceptions about the sort of activity in which he is indulging. In matters of literary experience, as in other experiences', Krieger concludes, 'one is a virgin but once' (p. 6).

For most readers, this is a fairly unconscious process, and not unnaturally, what we are taught to read well and with pleasure, when we are young, predisposes us to certain specific kinds of adult reading tastes. For the professional literary critic, the process may be no different, but it is at least more conscious. Graduate schools, at their best, are training grounds for competing interpretive paradigms or reading techniques: affective stylistics, structuralism, and semiotic analysis, to name only a few of the more recent entries. The delight we learn to take in the mastery of these interpretive strategies is then often mistakenly construed as our delight in reading specific texts, especially in the case of works that would otherwise be unavailable or even offensive to us. In my own graduate career, for example, with superb teachers to guide me, I learned to take great pleasure in *Paradise Lost,* even though as both a Jew and a feminist, I can subscribe neither to its theology nor to its hierarchy of sexual valuation. If, within its own terms (as I have been taught to understand them), the text manipulates my sensibilities and moves me to pleasure — as I will affirm it does — then, at least in part, that must be because, in spite of my real-world alienation from many of its basic tenets, I have been able to enter that text through interpretive strategies which allow me to displace less comfortable observations with others to which I have been taught pleasurably to attend. Though some of my teachers may have called this process 'learning to read the *text* properly', I have now come to see it as learning to effectively manipulate the critical strategies which they taught me so well. Knowing, for example, the poem's debt to epic conventions, I am able to discover in it echoes and reworkings of both lines and situations from Virgil and Homer; placing it within the ongoing Christian debate between Good and Evil, I comprehend both the philosophic and the stylistic significance of Satan's ornate rhetoric as compared to God's majestic simplicity in Book III. But, in each case, an interpretive model, already assumed, had guided my discovery of the evidence for it (see Fish, 1978: 627–628).

When we consider the implications of these observations for the processes of canon-formation and for the assignment of aesthetic value, we find ourselves locked in a chicken-and-egg dilemma, unable easily to distinguish as primary the importance of *what* we read as opposed to *how* we have learned to read it. For, simply put, we read well, and with pleasure, what we already know how to read; and what we know how to read is to a large extent dependent upon what we have already read (works from which we've developed our expectations and learned our interpretive strategies). What we then choose to read — and, by extension, teach and thereby 'canonize' — usually follows upon our previous reading. Radical breaks are tiring, demanding, uncomfortable, and sometimes wholly beyond our comprehension.

Though the argument is not usually couched in precisely these terms, a considerable segment of the most recent feminist rereadings of women writers allows the conclusion that, where those authors have dropped out of sight, the reason may be due not to any lack of merit in the work but, instead, to an incapacity of predominantly male readers to properly interpret and appreciate women's texts — due, in large part, to a lack of prior acquaintance. The fictions which women compose about the worlds they inhabit may owe a debt to prior, influential works by other women or, simply enough, to the daily experience of the writer herself or, more usually, to some combination of the two. The reader coming upon such fiction, with knowledge of neither its informing literary traditions nor its real-world contexts, will thereby find himself hard-pressed, though he recognize the words on the page, to competently decipher its intended meanings. And this is what makes the recent studies by Spacks, Moers, Showalter, Gilbert and Gubar, and others so crucial: for, by attempting to delineate the connections and inter-relations that make for a female literary tradition, they provide us with invaluable aids for recognizing and understanding the unique literary traditions and sex-related contexts out of which women write.

The (usually male) reader who, both by experience and by reading, has never made acquaintance with those contexts — historically, the lying-in room, the parlor, the nursery, the kitchen, the laundry, and so on — will necessarily lack the capacity to fully interpret the dialogue or action embedded therein; for, as every good novelist knows, the meaning of any character's action or statement is inescapably a function of the specific situation in which it is embedded (again, see Fish, 1978: 643). Virginia Woolf therefore quite properly anticipated the male reader's disposition to write off what he could not understand, abandoning women's writings as offering 'not merely a difference of view, but a view that is weak, or trivial, or sentimental because it differs from his own'. Grappling most obviously with the ways in which male writers and male subject matter had already preempted the language of literature, in her essay on 'Women and Fiction', Woolf was also tacitly commenting on the problem of (male) audience and conventional reading expectations when she speculated that the woman writer might well 'find that she is perpetually wishing to alter the established values [in literature] — to make serious what appears insignificant to a man, and trivial what is to him important'.[13] 'The "competence" necessary for understanding [a] literary message ... depends upon a great number of codices', after all; as Cesare Segre has pointed out, to be competent, a reader must either share or at least be familiar with, 'in addition to the code language ... the codes of custom, of society, and of conceptions of the world' (Segre, 1976: 272–273) (what Woolf meant by 'values'). Males ignorant of women's 'values' or conceptions of the world will necessarily, thereby, be poor readers of works that in any sense recapitulate their codes.

The problem is further exacerbated when the language of the literary text is largely dependent upon figuration. For it can be argued, as Ted Cohen (1978) has shown, that while 'in general, and with some obvious qualifications ... all literal use of language is accessible to all whose language it is ... figurative use can be inaccessible to all but those

[13]Virginia Woolf, 'Women and Fiction' in *The Forum,* March 29, 1929. Reprinted, Leonard Woolf (Ed.) 1972, *Collected Essays, Virginia Woolf,* Vol II, Chatto and Windus, London, p. 146.

who share information about one another's knowledge, beliefs, intentions, and attitudes' (p. 9). There was nothing fortuitous, for example, in Charlotte Perkins Gilman's decision to situate the progressive mental breakdown and increasing incapacity of the protagonist of *The Yellow Wallpaper* in an upstairs room that had once served as a nursery (with barred windows, no less). But the reader unacquainted with the ways in which women traditionally inhabited a household might not have taken the initial description of the setting as semantically relevant; and the progressive infantilization of the adult protagonist would thereby lose some of its symbolic implications. Analogously, the contemporary poet who declares, along with Adrienne Rich, the need for 'a whole new poetry beginning here' is acknowledging the fact that the materials available for symbolization and figuration from women's contexts will necessarily differ from those that men have traditionally utilized:

> Vision begins to happen in such a life
> as if a woman quietly walked away
> from the argument and jargon in a room
> and sitting down in the kitchen, began turning in her lap
> bits of yarn, calico and velvet scraps,
>
>   *   *   *
>
> pulling the tenets of a life together
> with no mere will to mastery,
> only care for the many-lived, unending
> forms in which she finds herself.[14]

What, then, the fate of the woman writer whose competent reading community is composed only of members of her own sex? And what, then, the response of the male critic who, on first looking into Virginia Woolf or Doris Lessing, finds all of the interpretive strategies at his command inadequate to a full and pleasurable deciphering of their pages? Historically, the result has been the diminished status of women's products and their consequent absence from major canons. Nowadays, however, by pointing out that the act of 'interpreting language is no more sexually neutral than language use or the language system itself', feminist students of language, like Nelly Furman (1978), help us better understand the crucial linkage between our gender and our interpretive, or reading, strategies. Insisting upon 'the contribution of the . . . reader [in] the active attribution of significance to formal signifers' (p. 184), Furman and others promise to shake us all — male and female alike — out of our canonized and conventional aesthetic assumptions.

3. *Since the grounds upon which we assign aesthetic value to texts are never infallible, unchangeable, or universal, we must re-examine not only our aesthetics but, as well, the inherent biases and assumptions informing the critical methods which (in part) shape our aesthetic responses.* I am, on the one hand, arguing that men will be better readers, or appreciators, of women's books when they have read more of them (as women have always been taught to become astute readers of men's texts); on the other hand, it will be noted, the impact of my remarks shifts the act of critical judgment from assigning aesthetic valuations to texts and directs it, instead, to ascertaining the adequacy of any interpretive paradigm to a full reading of both male and female writing. My third proposition — and, I admit, perhaps the most controversial — thus calls into question

---

[14]From Adrienne Rich's 'Transcendental Etude' in her *The Dream of a Common Language: Poems 1974–1977* (New York: W. W. Norton and Co., 1978), pp. 76–77.

that recurrent rendency in criticism to establish norms for the evaluation of literary works when we might better serve the cause of literature by developing standards for evaluating the adequacy of our critical methods.[15] This does not mean that I wish to discard aesthetic valuation. The choice, as I see it, is not between retaining or discarding aesthetic values; rather, the choice is between having some awareness of what constitutes (at least in part) the bases of our aesthetic responses and going without such an awareness. For it is my view that insofar as aesthetic responsiveness continues to be an integral aspect of our human response system — in part spontaneous, in part learned and educated — we will inevitably develop theories to help explain, formalize, or even initiate those responses. Indeed, in a sense, this is what criticism is all about.

In challenging the adequacy of received critical opinion or the imputed excellence of established canons, therefore, feminist literary critics are essentially seeking to discover how aesthetic value is assigned in the first place, where it resides (in the text or in the reader), and, most importantly, what validity may really be claimed by our so-called aesthetic 'judgments'. What ends do those judgments serve, the feminist asks; and what conceptions of the world or ideological stances do they (even if unwittingly) help to perpetuate? She confronts, for example, the reader who simply cannot entertain the possibility that women's worlds are symbolically rich, the reader who, like the male characters in Susan Glaspell's 1917 short story, 'A Jury of Her Peers', has already assumed the innate 'insignificance of kitchen things'.[16] Such a reader, she knows, will prove himself unable to assign significance to fictions which attend to 'kitchen things' and will, instead, judge such fictions as trivial and as aesthetically wanting. For her to take useful issue with such a reader, she must make clear that what appears to be a dispute about aesthetic merit is, in reality, a dispute about the *contexts of judgment*; and what is at issue, then, is the adequacy of the prior assumptions and reading habits brought to bear on the text. To put it bluntly: we have had enough pronouncements of aesthetic valuation for a time; it is now our task to evaluate the imputed norms and normative reading patterns that, in part, led to those pronouncements.

By and large, I think I've made my point. Only to clarify it do I add this coda: when feminists turn their attention to the works of male authors which have traditionally been accorded high aesthetic value and, where warranted, follow Tillie Olsen's advice that we assert our 'right to say: this is surface, this falsifies reality, this degrades' (1978: 45), such statements do not necessarily mean that we will end up with a diminished canon. To question the source of the aesthetic pleasures we've gained from reading Spenser, Shakespeare, Milton, *et al,* does not imply that we must deny those pleasures. It means only that aesthetic response is once more invested with epistemological, ethical, and moral concerns. It means, in other words, that readings of *Paradise Lost* which analyze its complex hierarchal structures but fail to note the implications of gender within that hierarchy; or which insist upon the inherent (or even inspired) perfection of Milton's figurative language but fail to note the consequences, for Eve, of her specifically gender-marked weakness, which, like the flowers to which she attends, requires 'propping up';

[15]'A recurrent tendency in criticism is the establishment of false norms for the evaluation of literary works' notes Robert Scholes in his *Structuralism in Literature: An Introduction* (New Haven: Yale University Press, 1974, 1976), p. 131.

[16]For a full discussion of the Glaspell short story which takes this problem into account, please see my 'A Map for Re-Reading: Or, Gender and the Interpretation of Literary Texts' in *New Literary History* (XI, no. 3 (Spring 1980): 451–467.

or which concentrate on the poem's thematic reworking of classical notions of martial
and epic prowess into Christian (moral) heroism but fail to note that Eve is stylistically
edited out of that process — all such readings, however useful, will no longer be deemed
wholly adequate. The pleasures we had earlier learned to take in the poem will not be
diminished thereby; but they will become part of an altered reading attentiveness.

*   *   *

These three propositions I believe to be at the theoretical core of all current feminist
literary criticism, whether acknowledged as such or not. If I am correct in this, then that
criticism represents more than a profoundly skeptical stance towards all other pre-
existing and contemporaneous schools and methods, and more than an impassioned
demand that the variety and variability of women's literary expression be taken into full
account, rather than written off as caprice and exception, the irregularity in an
otherwise regular design; it represents that locus in literary study where, in unceasing
effort, female self-consciousness turns in upon itself, attempting to grasp the deepest
conditions of its own unique and multiplicitous realities, in the hope, eventually, of
altering the very forms through which the culture perceives, expresses, and knows itself.
For, if what the larger women's movement looks for in the future is a transformation of
the structures of primarily male power which now order our society, then the feminist
literary critic demands that we understand the ways in which those structures have been
— and continue to be — reified by our literature and by our literary criticism. Thus,
along with other so-called 'radical' critics and critical schools, though our focus remains
the power of the word to both structure and mirror human experience, our overriding
commitment is to a radical alteration — an improvement, we hope — in the nature of
that experience.

What distinguishes our work from those similarly oriented 'social consciousness'
critiques, it is said, is its lack of systematic coherence. Pitted against, for example,
psychoanalytic or Marxist readings, which owe a decisive share of their persuasiveness
to their apparent internal consistency as a system, the aggregate of feminist literary
criticism appears woefully deficient in system, and painfully lacking in program. It is, in
fact, from all quarters, the most telling defect alleged against us, the most explosive
threat in the mine-field. And my own earlier observation that, as of 1976, feminist
literary criticism appeared 'more like a set of interchangeable strategies than any
coherent school or shared goal orientation', has been taken by some as an indictment,
by others as a statement of impatience. Neither was intended. I felt then, as I do now,
that this would 'prove both its strength *and* its weakness' (Kolodny, 1976: 420), in the
sense that the apparent disarray would leave us vulnerable to the kind of objection I've
just alluded to, while the fact of our diversity would finally place us securely where, all
along, we should have been: camped out, on the far side of the mine-field, with the other
pluralists and pluralisms.

In our heart of hearts, of course, most critics are really structuralists (whether or not
they accept the label), since what we are seeking are patterns (or structures) that can
order and explain the otherwise inchoate; thus, we invent, or believe we discover,
relational patternings in the texts we read which promise transcendence from difficulty
and perplexity to clarity and coherence. But, as I've tried to argue in these pages, to the
imputed 'truth' or 'accuracy' of these findings, the feminist must oppose the painfully

obvious truism that what is attended to in a literary work, and hence what is reported about it, is often determined not so much by the work itself as by the critical technique or aesthetic criteria through which it is filtered or, rather, read and decoded. All the feminist is asserting, then, is her own equivalent right to liberate new (and perhaps different) significances from these same texts; and, at the same time, her right to choose which features of a text she takes as relevant since she is, after all, asking new and different questions of it. In the process, she claims neither definitiveness nor structural completeness for her different readings and reading systems, but only their usefulness in recognizing the particular achievements of woman-as-author and their applicability in conscientiously decoding woman-as-sign.

That these alternate foci of critical attentiveness will render alternate readings or interpretations of the same text — even among feminists — should be no cause for alarm. Such developments illustrate only the pluralist contention that, 'in approaching a text of any complexity . . . the reader must choose to emphasize certain aspects which seem to him crucial' and that 'in fact, the variety of readings which we have for many works is a function of the selection of crucial aspects made by the variety of readers'. Robert Scholes, from whom I've been quoting, goes so far as to assert that 'there is no single "right" reading for any complex literary work', and, following the Russian formalist school, he observes that 'we do not speak of readings that are simply true or false, but of readings that are more or less rich, strategies that are more or less appropriate'.[17] The fact that those who share the term 'feminist' nonetheless practice a diversity of critical strategies, leading, in some cases, to quite different readings, requires us to acknowledge among ourselves that sister critics, 'having chosen to tell a different story, may in their interpretation identify different aspects of the meanings conveyed by the same passage'.[18] In other words, just because we will no longer tolerate the specifically sexist omissions and ignorances of earlier critical schools and methods does not mean that, in their stead, we must establish our own 'party lines'.

In my view, our purpose is not and should not be the formulation of any single reading method or potentially procrustean set of critical procedures nor, even less, the generation of prescriptive categories for some dreamed-of non-sexist literary canon.[19] Instead, as I see it, our task is to initiate nothing less than a playful pluralism, responsive to the possibilities of multiple critical schools and methods, but captive of none, recognizing that the many tools needed for our work of analysis will necessarily be largely inherited and only partly of our own making. Only by employing a plurality of methods will we protect ourselves from the temptation to so oversimplify any text — and especially those particularly offensive to us — that we render ourselves unresponsive to what Robert Scholes (1974) has called 'its various systems of meaning and their interaction' (p. 151–152). Any text we deem worthy of our critical attention is usually, after all, a locus of many and varied kinds of (personal, thematic, stylistic, structural, rhetorical, etc.) relationships. So, whether we tend to treat a text as a *mimesis,* in which words are taken to be recreating or representing viable worlds; or

[17]Scholes, p. 144; pp. 144–45. These comments appear within his explication of Tzvetan Todorov's theory of reading.

[18]I borrow this concise phrasing of pluralistic modesty from M. H. Abrams' 'The Deconstructive Angel' in *Critical Inquiry* 3, no. 3 (Spring 1977): 427.

[19]I have earlier elaborated my objection to prescriptive categories for literature in my 'The Feminist as Literary Critic', Critical Response in *Critical Inquiry* 2, no. 4 (Summer 1976): 827–28.

whether we prefer to treat a text as a kind of equation of communication, in which decipherable messages are passed from writers to readers; and whether we locate meaning as inherent in the text, the act of reading, or in some collaboration between reader and text — whatever our predilection, let us generate from it not some strait jacket which limits the scope of possible analysis but, rather, an ongoing dialogue of competing potential possibilities — among feminists and, as well, between feminist and non-feminist critics.

The difficulty of what I describe does not escape me. The very idea of pluralism seems to threaten a kind of chaos for the future of literary inquiry while, at the same time, it seems to deny the hope of establishing some basic conceptual model which can organize all data — the hope which always begins any analytical exercise. My effort here, however, has been to demonstrate the essential delusions which inform such objections: If literary inquiry has historically escaped chaos by establishing canons, then it has only substituted one mode of arbitrary action for another — and, in this case, at the expense of half the population. And if feminists openly acknowledge ourselves as pluralists, then we do not give up the search for patterns of opposition and connection — probably the basis of thinking itself; what we give up is simply the arrogance of claiming that our work is either exhaustive or definitive. (It is, after all, the identical arrogance we are asking our non-feminist colleagues to abandon.) If this kind of pluralism appears to threaten both the present coherence of and the inherited aesthetic criteria for a canon of 'greats', then, as I have earlier argued, it is precisely that threat which, alone, can free us from the prejudices, the strictures, and the blind-spots of the past. In feminist hands, I would add, it is less a threat than a promise.

What unites and repeatedly reinvigorates feminist literary criticism, then, is neither dogma nor method but, as I have indicated earlier, an acute and impassioned *attentiveness* to the ways in which primarily male structures of power are inscribed (or encoded) within our literary inheritance; the consequences of that encoding for women — as characters, as readers, and as writers; and, with that, a shared analytic *concern* for the implications of that encoding not only for a better understanding of the past, but on behalf of an improved reordering of the present and future as well. If that *concern* identifies feminist literary criticism as one of the many academic arms of the larger women's movement, then that *attentiveness,* within the halls of academe, poses no less a challenge for change, generating, as it does, the three propositions explored here. The critical pluralism which inevitably follows upon those three propositions, however, bears little resemblance to what Lillian Robinson has called 'the greatest bourgeois theme of all, the myth of pluralism, with its consequent rejection of ideological commitment as "too simple" to embrace the (necessarily complex) truth' (Robinson; 1971: 11). Only ideological commitment could have gotten us to enter the mine-field, putting in jeopardy our careers and our livelihood. Only the power of ideology to transform our conceptual worlds, and the inspiration of that ideology to liberate long-suppressed energies and emotions, can account for our willingness to take on critical tasks that, in an earlier decade, would have been 'abandoned in despair or apathy'.[20] The fact of differences among us proves only that, despite our shared commitments, we

---

[20]'Ideology bridges the emotional gap between things as they are and as one would have them be, thus insuring the performance of roles that might otherwise be abandoned in despair or apathy', comments Geertz in 'Ideology as a Cultural System', p. 205.

have nonetheless refused to shy away from complexity, preferring rather to openly disagree than to give up either intellectual honesty or hard-won insights.

Finally, I would argue, pluralism informs feminist literary inquiry not simply as a description of what already exists but, more importantly, as the only critical stance consistent with the current status of the larger women's movement. Segmented and variously focussed, the different women's organizations, in the United States at least, neither espouse any single system of analysis nor, as a result, express any wholly shared, consistently articulated ideology. The ensuing loss in effective organization and political clout is a serious one, but it has not been paralyzing; in spite of our differences, we have united to *act* in areas of clear mutual concern (the push for the Equal Rights Amendment, [ERA], is probably the most obvious example). The trade-off, as I see it, has made possible an ongoing and educative dialectic of analysis and preferred solutions, protecting us thereby from the inviting traps of reductionism and dogma. And so long as this dialogue remains active, both our politics and our criticism will be free of dogma — but never, I hope, of feminist ideology, in all its variety. For, 'whatever else ideologies may be — projections of unacknowledged fears, disguises for ulterior motives, phatic expressions of group solidarity' (and the women's movement, to date, has certainly been all of these, and more) — whatever ideologies express, they are, as Clifford Geertz astutely observes, 'most distinctively, maps of problematic social reality and matrices for the creation of collective conscience'. And despite the fact that 'ideological advocates . . . tend as much to obscure as to clarify the true nature of the problems involved', as Geertz notes, 'they at least call attention to their existence and, by polarizing issues, make continued neglect more difficult. Without Marxist attack, there would have been no labor reform; without Black Nationalists, no deliberate speed' (Geertz, 1973 p. 220: 205); without Seneca Falls, I would add, no enfranchisement of women, and without 'consciousness raising', no feminist literary criticism nor, even less, Women's Studies.

Ideology, however, only truly manifests its power by ordering the *sum* of our actions.[21] If feminist criticism calls anything into question, it must be that dog-eared myth of intellectual neutrality.[22] For, what I take to be the underlying spirit, or message, of any consciously ideologically-premised criticism — that is, that ideas are important *because* they determine the ways we live, or want to live, in the world — is vitiated by confining those ideas to the study, the classroom, or the pages of our books. To write chapters decrying the sexual stereotyping of women in our literature while closing our eyes to the sexual harrassment of our women students and colleagues; to display Katherine Hepburn and Rosalind Russell in our courses on 'The Image of the Independent Career Woman in Film', while managing not to notice the paucity of female administrators on our own campus; to study the women who helped make universal enfranchisement a political reality while keeping silent about our activist colleagues who are denied promotion or tenure; to include segments on 'Women in the Labor Movement' in our American Studies or Women's Studies courses while

[21]I here follow Frederic Jameson's view in *The Prison-House of Language: A Critical Account of Structuralism and Russian Formalism* (Princeton: Princeton Univ. Press, 1972; rpt. 1974), p. 107, that 'Ideology would seem to be that grillwork of form, convention, and belief which orders our actions'.

[22]On this point, I take issue with Spacks's view, p. 4, that 'criticism need not be political in order to be aware'. In my opinion, it is only our politics that initiates our awareness of the need for critical stances in the first place.

remaining wilfully ignorant of the department secretary fired for her efforts to organize a clerical workers' union; to glory in the delusions of 'merit', 'privilege', and 'status' which accompany campus life in order to insulate ourselves from the millions of women who labor in poverty — all this is not merely hypocritical; it destroys both the spirit and the meaning of what we are about. It puts us, however unwittingly, in the service of those who laid the mine-field in the first place. In my view, it is a fine thing for many of us, individually, to have traversed the mine-field; but that happy circumstance will only prove of lasting importance if, together, we expose it for what it is (the male fear of sharing power and significance with women) and deactivate its components, so that others, after us, may literally dance through the mine-field.

References

ALTIERI, Charles (1978) 'The Hermeneutics of Literary Indeterminacy: A Dissent from the New Orthodoxy' in *New Literary History,* x, no. 1.

BAYM, Nina (1978) *Women's Fiction: A Guide to Novels by and about Women in America, 1820–1870,* Cornell University Press, Ithaca.

BLOOM, Harold (1975) *A Map of Misreading,* Oxford University Press, N.Y.

CIXOUS, Helene (1976) 'The Laugh of the Medusa', transl. Keith Cohen and Paula Cohen, in *Signs,* 1, no. 4.

COHEN, Ted (1978) 'Metaphor and the Cultivation of Intimacy' in *Critical Inquiry,* 5, no. 1.

ELLMAN, Mary (1968) *Thinking About Women,* Harcourt, Brace, Jovanovich, N.Y.

FETTERLEY, Judith (1978) *The Resisting Reader: A Feminist Approach to American Fiction,* Indiana University Press, Bloomington.

FISH, Stanley E. (1978) 'Normal Circumstances, Literal Language, Direct Speech Acts, the Ordinary, the Everyday, the Obvious, What Goes Without Saying, and Other Special Cases' in *Critical Inquiry,* 4, 4.

FURMAN, Nelly (1978) 'The Study of Women and Language: Comment on Vol. 3, No. 3' in *Signs* 4, no. 1.

GEERTZ, Clifford (1973) 'Thick Description: Toward an Interpretive Theory of Culture' and 'Ideology as a cultural system' in his *The Interpretation of Cultures: Selected Essays,* Basic Books, N.Y.

HOY, David Couzens (1978) 'Hermeneutic Circularity, Indeterminancy, and Incommensurability, in *New Literary History* x, 1.

JANEWAY, Elizabeth (1979) 'Women's Literature' in Daniel Hoffman (Ed.) *Harvard Guide to Contemporary American Writing,* Belknap Press/Harvard University Press, Cambridge, Mass.

KENNARD, Jean E. (1975) *Victims of Convention,* Archon Books, Hamden Ct.

KOLODNY, Annette (1976) 'Literary Criticism' Review Essay,in *Signs* 2, no. 2.

KRAMER, Cheris, Barrie THORNE and Nancy HENLEY (1978) 'Perspectives on Language and Communication' Review Essay, in *Signs,* 3, no. 3.

KRIEGER, Murray (1976) *Theory of Criticism: A Tradition and its System,* The John Hopkins University Press, Baltimore.

MAILER, Norman (1959) 'Evaluations — Quick and Expensive Comments on the Talent in the Room' in *Advertisements for Myself,* Berkley, Medallion Book/G.P. Putnam's Sons, New York.

MILLETT, Kate (1970) *Sexual Politics,* Doubleday, Garden City, N.Y.

MOERS, Ellen (1976) *Literary Women: The Great Writers*, Doubleday, Garden City, N.Y. and The Women's Press, London.

OLSEN, Tillie (1978) *Silences,* Delacorte Press/Seymour Lawrence, N.Y.

RICH, Adrienne (1972) 'When We Dead Awaken: Writing as Re-Vision' in *College English* 34, 1: reprinted in Barbara Charlesworth Gelpi and Albert Gelpi (Eds.) 1975 *Adrienne Rich's Poetry,* Norton, N.Y.

ROBINSON, Lillian S. (1971) 'Dwelling in Decencies: Radical Criticism and the Feminist Perspective' in *College English* 32, no. 8: reprinted in her 1978 *Sex, Class, and Culture,* Indiana University Press, Bloomington.

ROBINSON, Lillian S. (1972) 'Cultural Criticism and the *Horror Vacui*' in *College English* 33: reprinted as 'The Critical Task' in her 1978 *Sex, Class, and Culture,* Indiana University Press, Bloomington.

ROETHKE, Theodore (1965) 'The Poetry of Louise Bogan, in Ralph J. Mills Jr. (Ed.) *Selected Prose of Theodore Roethke,* University of Washington Press, Seattle.

SEGRE, Cesare (1976) 'Narrative Structures and Literary History' in *Critical Inquiry,* 3: 2.

SCHOLES, Robert (1974) (1976) *Structuralism in Literature: An Introduction,* Yale University Press, New Haven.

SHOWALTER, Elaine (1977) *A Literature of their own: British Women Novelists from Brontë to Lessing,* Princeton University Press, N.J. and Virago, London.

SPACKS, Patricia Meyer (1975) *The Female Imagination,* Knopf, N.Y.

STANLEY, Julia Penelope and Susan W. ROBBINS (1977) 'Toward a Feminist Aesthetic, in *Chrysalis,* 6.

WOOLF, Virginia (1929) 'Women and Fiction' in The *Forum,* March 29: reprinted Leonard Woolf (Ed.) 1972, *Collected Essays, Virginia Woolf,* Chatto and Windus, London, pp. 141–148.

3

Methodocracy, Misogyny and Bad Faith: The Response of Philosophy*

SHEILA RUTH

> We have been foreigners not only to the fortresses of political power but also to those citadels in which thought processes have been spun out ... women are beginning to recognize that the value system that has been thrust upon us by the various cultural institutions of patriarchy has amounted to a kind of gang rape of minds as well as of bodies (Mary Daly, 1973; pp. 6, 9).

> When I refuse to commit myself to genuine argument involving persuasion, I in effect make a refusal of philosophy itself; I will not risk myself and I will not risk my world. ... In Sartrean language, this is one of the modalities of 'Bad Faith' ... (Maurice Natanson, 1975; 16).

I am a philosopher and a feminist. I have never doubted the compatibility of the two world-views, either in my life-style or in my profession. On the contrary, I have been convinced that they overlap: as a philosopher I might address myself to an analysis of women's experience and to the beliefs and institutions which surround it; as a feminist I might bring new insights and perspectives to the intellectual quest. The Women's Movement has had its philosophical component from its inception, and it seemed obvious to me that philosophy, as the attempt to 'know one's way around ... the intellectual landscape as a whole' (Sellars, 1964; 2) could not legitimately omit 51% of that landscape. I had no doubt that a feminist analysis of philosophical issues would be welcomed into the profession as a felicitous addition to our tools.

I was wrong. Feminism is not happily received. While overt misogyny is out of vogue in most mixed intellectual gatherings, the rejection of uppity womanizing is accomplished more delicately through the intervention of a variety of considerations which are very persuasive to most philosophers.

Originally I had embarked upon a career in Philosophy seeking answers to 'ultimate' questions: What is the meaning of life? Why did I exist? How shall I behave? What is good? What is excellence in humanity? I wanted to be excellent.

I remember the quest: Plato through Marcuse — the ultimate questions pursued by the Greats. So what if my student's mind had to squeeze my woman's experience into perspectives not quite alien, not quite my own: Socrates asks the women to leave his death chamber because they cry. No matter; I would not have been like that. Aristotle says that human excellence consists of courage, temperance, intelligence, justice, wisdom .... The excellence of women (and her ever-present addenda, children) is of another variety:

*An earlier version of the essay appeared in *Metaphilosophy* and grateful acknowledgement is made of their permission to reprint this revised version.

A similar question may be raised about women and children, whether they too have virtues: ought a woman to be temperate and brave and just? . . . all things rule and are ruled according to nature. But the kind of rule differs; — the freeman rules over the slave in other ways from that in which the male rules over the female . . . For the slave has no deliberate faculty at all; the woman has, but it is without authority . . . the temperance . . . courage . . . and justice of a man and a woman are not . . . the same . . . the courage of a man is shown in commanding, of a woman in obeying . . . as the poet says of women, 'Silence is a woman's glory' (Aristotle, *Politics,* Book I, Ch. 13: 1259b–1260a).

I certainly did not care for this excellence as well as the first. But I had my choice — the first was *human* excellence, and I was certainly more human than female. Some confusion in that? No matter; I could make the necessary mental involutions. (Haven't you heard of generic man?) William Ebenstein tells us that Rousseau was a philosopher of the 'people', extolling *natural man* at the expense of *civilized man* (generic, of course). 'Nature destined man to live a healthy, simple life and to satisfy his essential needs ('food, a female, and sleep')' (Ebenstein, 1969; 440–441). Substitutions, involutions, and more substitutions! No matter, just an oversight. After all, these were men of their times, and modern women know how to seek their models.

Modern thinkers, we are told, are more understanding of the situation. Joel Feinberg, for example, liberal, (author, even, of a book on abortion) speculates upon the meaning of respect:

> In olden days, when power and authority went hand in hand . . . the scale of respect was one with the scales of power and status. This was the background against which the earliest moralists could begin demanding that respect be shown to various classes of the *deserving weak,* too. Hence our rude and unimpressed ancestors were urged to 'show respect' for women, for the aged, for the clergy . . . . Christianity gave dignity even to the *meek and humble.* Respect could then be extended to the aged, to women, to the clergy (Feinberg, 1973 pp. 1–3; my emphasis).

I don't think I like this grouping (women, the aged, and the clergy) any better than 'women and children'. I wonder if I perceive myself as the 'deserving weak', or the 'meek and humble'. Feinberg continues:

> To see a woman as having dignity now is to see her as in a moral position to make claims against *our* conduct, even though she may lack physical or political power over *us.* Certain minimal forms of consideration are her due, something she has coming, and can rightfully claim, even when she is in no position to make demands in the gunman sense. Insofar as *we* think of her that way we have respect for her . . . and insofar as she shares this image of herself she has self-respect (Feinberg, 1973, pp. 1–3).

Indeed! And would any *man* in such a position — weak, meek, humble and without power — perceive himself with self-respect? Who is this author to speak for me? And who is this *us, we, our* Feinberg speaks of? A club he belongs to? He is a philosopher addressing philosophers. But he could not mean that only philosophers grant respect in this fashion. (Besides, I am a philosopher.) No, Feinberg is analyzing the concept of respect as it is used, given, and granted in society, among people. Which people? Society surely must include women. Do women grant respect that way? Am I part of that *we, us*? I certainly don't perceive women and their worthiness that way. Generic *we*? Rather not. This is a substitution, a mental involution, impossible for me to make without plunging myself into marked self-alienation.

Feinberg's essay and his use of the term *we* (*us, our*) in juxtaposition to the term *women* is only one example among many of a world-view that constitutes humanity as male and relegates woman to the status of out-group, of 'other'.[1] Comfortable and confident that 'we boys' are 'we everyone', Feinberg exhibits the masculist usurpation of universality. The usurpation, conceptual in nature, with wide conceptual implications, is conveniently masked by the linguistic device of 'generic man', and is so generally accepted that it has become invisible to the naked (i.e. masculist, i.e. non-feminist) eye. A recent film entitled *Why Man Creates* (Bosustow, 1968) ostensibly an inquiry into the nature and motivation of *human* creativity, is composed of sequences in which scientists, artists, inventors and symbols are all male, and women appear only as wives, foils, or subjects of art. *The Uncommitted: Alienated Youth in Modern Society,* (Keniston, 1960) a sociopsychological study based upon profiles of alienated young people, contains not *one* female profile, yet purports to be a study of alienated *youth*. A modern textbook for logic asks the (supposedly general) reader, 'She won't give you a date?' (Moore, 1967). The Constitution of the United States declared 'We the people', although women were totally disfranchised. The conceptual confusing of 'human' and 'male' historically and in the present in all disciplines is so pervasive as to be the rule rather than the exception.

It is not difficult to understand how such confusion came about. The various disciplines were historically owned and operated by and for men. Women were simply not an issue nor a force. The construction of a universe where man (male) and human were coextensive was not problematic in a belief system that deemed women not quite human if it deemed them at all. Women simply did not function for the male conceptually, because they did not function politically, economically or, for that matter, intellectually. Women's perspectives are absent because they were permitted no entry into the club. When 'woman' does appear in the 'sacred writings', she does not talk herself, but rather is talked about, usually in a subsidiary chapter that grudgingly gives some attention to the troublesome but persistent presence of the subsidiary of the human race. Aquinas, for example, inquires whether, 'in the first state, women would have been born?' (Aquinas, Pegis, [Ed] 1945; 936–937)[2].

Women have had stolen from us 'the power of naming', the power to put 'words' (i.e. interpretations and meanings) to the experiences we have and the images we see. We have been denied the right and the opportunity to view the world and our own lives from *our* own stance and within our own perspectives. Instead, men have put their 'words', their definitions, their analyses, their values, to *our* experiences, and from thence into *our* mouths. Denied education, self-assertion, contact with one another, the tools of analysis, we have been long in realizing that the 'names' we have been uttering are not our own.

> We have not been free to use our own power to name ourselves, the world, or God. The old naming was not the product of dialogue — a fact inadvertently admitted in the Genesis story of Adam's naming the animals and the woman. Women are now realizing that the universal imposing of names by men has been false because partial. Inadequate words have been taken as adequate (Daly, 1973; 8).

As women have lost the power of naming, the intellectual landscape has lost the power of women. There is a skewing to official judgments of values, priorities, and actions.

[1]For a discussion of woman as 'other' see Simone de Beauvoir, 1961, *The Second Sex*, (translated H. M. Parshly) Bantam, New York.

[2]'Summa Theologica' in *Basic Writings of Saint Thomas Aquinas,* Anton C. Pegis (Ed.), 1945, Part I, Question 99, Vol. I, Random House, New York, pp. 936–937. The peculiarity of such treatment becomes clearer if we consider how we would respond to a general work on political theory that contained a special chapter on 'males'.

Male voices, perspectives, interests, ideas, and modes dominate all thinking. For all intents and purposes, 'official' intellection and male intellection have become coextensive. In the realm of thought the male is universalized. As a result the categories of relevance have been appropriated by the male frame of reference: If male = human, universal primacy, then: That which is of importance is [what the male perceives as important]; that which is holy is [what the male perceives as holy]; that which can persuade is [what the male perceives as persuasive]; the way one reaches conclusions is [the way men reach conclusions], and so on. Not only have women had no part in defining the content of philosophical speculation, but they have had even less influence over the categories of concern and the modes of articulation.

Some time ago, a feminist friend and I, discussing the nature and strength of ethical obligation, differed on the matter of justifying certain behavior. I said that I had always believed that to be good, one must carefully consider every act that involves another being, must live by rationally justified general principles, must always require of oneself the virtue one might wish for in others . . . etc. Smiling, she said, 'But, Sheila, that was when you thought that God was male'.

God the father; Father, the god: deification of the father, culmination and manifestation of deification of the male. It is a truism, almost a cliche, that Western culture has divided humanness into separate and seemingly incompatible halves, the one, maleness, represented (significantly) by the symbol of Mars ($\male$), God of War, and the other by that of Venus ($\female$), Goddess of Love. It is a truism that the prevailing definition of masculinity is pervaded by the Martial qualities: competitiveness, aggression, power, dominance, courage and the like. The contemporary imperatives of femininity are those of love and sexuality.[3]

What is not a truism and is often overlooked (although it is just as obvious) is that the mandates of masculinity and femininity are not adequately satisfied simply by the expression of the required qualities in the respective sex. Western culture has appended a further requirement of the individual: that he or she also display an absence of the qualities and characteristics ascribed to the opposite sex. That is, to be fully male, one must not only incarnate the Martial qualities; one must also display, in whatever way possible, that he does not contain anything of the feminine. He is courageous *and* he feels no fear. He is dominant *and* he is not submissive. The ideal woman is not only tender, receptive, and emotional; she is also not-aggressive, not-courageous, not-intelligent.

Given that the culture, controlled *by* men, functions *for* men, it is not surprising that the male composite (masculine/not-feminine) should be valued and have precedence over the female composite.[4] One would expect the policy-maker to favor his own interests. Further, since male *is* power, and men *have* power, and maleness includes rejection of the female, one could expect a disparagement and a crushing of all that is ascribed female, including both the female within and the woman without. Men, if they would maintain their status, must ever wage war against the female within; the 'flight

---

[3]I must underscore here that in the following discussion, maleness and femaleness, masculinity and femininity, are taken in their *cultural* definitions. There is no evidence that tenderness, receptivity and the like are more inherent in the female than in the male, nor courage, power etc., inherently in the male and not in the female.

[4]Since culture governs the internalization of values, and our culture is masculist, it is not surprising that both women and men value men and maleness over women and femaleness.

from woman' (Stern, 1965) as Karl Stern calls it, includes a profound rejection of all of her ascriptions.

It is the vilification of femaleness in conjunction with the deification of maleness, the tension between the two, that creates the dynamic of sexist consciousness. Man is Mars, woman Venus. Man is Apollo, woman Dionysius. Mars/Apollo is power, strength, intellect, linearity, control, discipline, cognition, abstraction, order; Venus/Dionysius is love, spontaneity, pleasure, impulse, feeling. Mars/Apollo is odd, light, trustworthy, desirable. Venus/Dionysius is even, dark, capricious, to be controlled and avoided. Flee! Flight from woman is flight from feeling, from experiencing, from the affective; it is flight into distance. It is mind/body split, priority of cognition over feeling, fear of ambiguity (loss of control), preference for deduction over induction, faith in systems rather than responses, preoccupation with logic to the detriment of aesthetics, and so on.

Men and women express their consciousness not only in *what* they think, but *how* they think. Men think, perceive, select, argue, justify malely. *What* they have thought, *how* they have thought, world-views and Lebenswelten imbedded necessarily in a male consciousness, become manifest in their intellectual constructions, their philosophies. That is perhaps as it should be. What should not be is the raising of these male constructs to the status of universals — the identification of male constructs with all allowable constructs so that women cannot 'legitimately' think, perceive, select, argue, etc. from their unique stance. Ultimately, of course, it is impossible to detect what in our perceptions is genuinely universal, and what is male or female.

Professional philosophy is essentially male. Even the few women in it have been there by virtue of their identification with, their acceptance of, their competencies in the established (male) norms — 'she thinks like a man'. She is trained in male schools by male instructors teaching male philosophers. She resides in the philosophic establishment.

In the philosophic establishment, mind supersedes feeling; that which you can deduce from general principles supersedes that which is derived from experience; abstraction is more impressive than the concrete; we are supposed to avoid discussions and analyses in the first person singular; we extol the rational, split it from the feelings, flee from ambiguity — A is A, A is not — A, etc.; men in war, a worthy topic, men in love, not so worthy; austerity, sobriety, sternness — proper signs of respect; laughter, whimsy — disrespectful; dry, didactic, linear, abstruse — scholarly; light, humorous, easy — substandard. What is abstract and abstruse is impressive; metaethics is more impressive than ethics, metaphysics even better, and epistemology, the best (i.e. the most impressive), while aesthetics is a kind of step-sister to the family. What is most completely separable from the agent is most respectable, most trustworthy.

Women, lodged between the female and the human, have experienced this skewing, are becoming more aware of it, and are expressing it more often and more expertly. After sitting for years in classrooms and colloquia dominated by men and male perspectives, aware somewhere in ourselves that something was not quite right, afraid to voice that dissonance, we are beginning to put 'names' to those insights and experiences. At a recent conference[5] on feminist scholarship, a philosopher from an important

---

[5]*The Feminist and the Scholar*, 1974, Barnard College, New York City, May 20th.

university was asked how her work had changed since adopting a feminist perspective. She answered that it had changed in many ways including focus and method. Particularly, she said, she no longer felt it necessary to participate in the 'hunt'. There was a rustle of laughter in the room, shared recognition, assent. She had put women's 'names' to her experience of the situation. Female consciousnesses heard and knew. Someone reads a paper; he is quarry. The others, hunters, listen, waiting for a weak point, sniffing for blood. They attack; the quarry defends. Combat. So male. Is this the way to do philosophy? Is this the way to do any investigation?

These very questions are the basis of a feminist critique of philosophy; they are a challenge and a threat to the elders, and, predictably, the way in which women are naming philosophy is not welcomed. The feminist challenge is met with all the anger and resistance one would expect from a company of threatened warriors trying to preserve their own territory. That they have had to have recourse to their arsenal of weapons however is an indication of their response to feminism. Once feminists began to examine philosophy, to expose and confront its sexism, the battle lines were drawn. Those (males) who were in control could so readily camouflage their position and by calling on the 'rules' — which they themselves had decreed — attempted to counter the charges by ruling them out of order. The way in which feminism could be dismissed by appealing to the paradigm of philosophy itself, was convenient — and for some, convincing — and feminists were required, in Elaine Reuben's (1978) terms, to defy the evidence. For, in 'traditional' terms:

> Feminism is a 'specialized' pursuit, not part of the mainstream' of philosophy.
>
> Philosophy is universal in scope, dealing with all mankind (sic), but feminism only applies to a segment of the population.
>
> Feminist issues are trivial compared to the ultimate questions philosophers ought to address.
>
> Feminist concerns are transient, bound to a particular time and place; philosophy transcends particular time and place.
>
> Feminism is sociological, political, or anthropological; it asks no genuinely *philosophic* questions.
>
> Feminists haven't yet learned to argue properly; they have not learned to give proper evidence for their claims, no general principles, just vignettes and metaphors.
>
> Philosophy is neutral in its analysis; feminism is a bias.

All in all, such statements mean to say, either overtly or in veiled terms, that feminist philosophy is not 'real' Philosophy; feminist thought, its presuppositions, methodology and even its content, is somehow illegitimate in the enterprise.

There are many definitions of philosophy, many senses of the word. One thing is clear, philosophy ranges where it will across the intellectual landscape: it is the philosophers (male) who build these particular fences.

But if this in insufficient to intimidate, there are more weapons available.

Weapon 1: *Methodolatry*

In the socio-political realm, God the Father dictates and legitimizes the ascendancy of male over female.

The symbol of the Father God, spawned in the human imagination and sustained as plausible by patriarchy has in turn rendered service to this type of society by making its mechanisms for the oppression of women appear right and fitting. If God in 'his' heaven is a father ruling 'his' people, then it is in the 'nature' of things and according to divine plan and the order of the universe that society be male dominated.

Within this context a mystification of roles takes place — the husband dominating his wife represents God 'himself'. The images and values of a given society have been projected into the realm of dogmas and 'Articles of Faith', and these in turn justify the social structure (Daly, 1973; 13).

In philosophy, too, there is a legitimating god — method — and its functions in the same way:

The tyranny of methodolatry hinders new discoveries. It prevents us from raising questions never asked before and from being illumined by ideas that do not fit into pre-established boxes and forms. The worshippers of Method have an effective way of handling data that doesn't fit into the Respectable Categories of Questions and Answers. They simply classify it as nondata, thereby rendering it invisible (Daly, 1973; 11).

According to Herbert Marcuse, contemporary philosophy, when it is suffused with the values of neo-Positivism and the ideology of linguistic analysis, subverts its proper function, which is therapy for the human condition through the full grasping of reality and its possibilities. Committed to clarity, it beclouds by disallowing the historical (i.e. political-contextual) analysis of terms and events; committed to empiricism, it violates empiricism by rejecting all experience but that expressible and verifiable within the limited, 'mutilated' discourse of the system.

In barring access to the realm [of knowledge beyond common sense and formal logic] positivist philosophy sets up a self-sufficient world of its own, closed and well-protected against the ingression of disturbing external factors. In this respect, it makes little difference whether the validating context is that of mathematics, of logical propositions, or of custom and usage. In one way or another, all possible meaningful predicates are prejudged. The prejudging judgment might be as broad as the spoken English language, or the dictionary, or some other code or convention. Once accepted, it constitutes an empirical *a priori* which cannot be transcended (Marcuse, 1964; 182).

Invalidation by reduction to non-data through the limiting of legitimate modes of discourse, language, and argumentation, i.e. 'Respectable Categories of Questions and Answers', is a superb defense against feminist criticism, because, as women, we have been so wholly outside of the arena that defines and determines the legitimate modes of discourse, both in our persons and our perspectives.

The Politics of Experience is a method of generating creatively new political insights from an analysis of personal experience. It is the heart and process of consciousness-raising, a group effort to 'speak the unspoken', bring to conscious awareness what is far from consciousness (Mitchell, 1973). It is a powerful tool for cracking the rigidity of a closed universe. Yet despite its power (or because of it) its theoretical products are rejected not only in substance ('I don't think you women have it as bad as you say' but in its mode of validation. 'What do you mean you perceive philosophic discussion as a hunt. I don't see any hunt', i.e. You're wrong; your experience doesn't coincide with mine, and you can't *prove* your experience. That is, you can't (or did not) fit it into a verifiable proposition deducible from general principles, and that's what you must do according to the rules of the game (which *we* males created). Besides, it's our game; we say there is no hunt, only the pursuit of truth in a most rigorous manner, and if we can't *prove* our experience either, that's okay because we own the 'names' to this situation, and possession is nine tenths of the law. Besides, that is not what we talk about when we discuss the processes of philosophical investigation. And if you disagree with me you set yourself in conflict with the entire philosophic establishment, which I represent.

Weapon 2: *Assimilation*

Borrowing again from Marcuse, one way to devitalize the unpalatable is to co-opt it, to rob it of its revolutionary power by giving it small acceptance and recognition in a non-dangerous sphere. Give a few women visible, well-salaried positions in the administration with ostensible status but no real power, and they have nothing to 'bitch' about. In the intellectual realm, accept feminist theory as a marginally important enterprise, necessary for women, part sociology, part political science, acceptable as Women's Studies, one of those anomalous specialities sometimes found in universities, and you do not have to give it full status as philosophic investigation with universal significance. A place on the program at APA (all the women's papers together) is less threatening than one paper in Ethics, one in Metaphysics, etc. To allow women their arguments so long as they are made within the limits of traditional issues, categories and methods is to assimilate the developing woman-consciousness into the existent male context.

Weapon 3: *Ridicule*

Ridicule is a familiar device for silencing any opponent, and most familiar to women. Only its concrete expression in philosophical circles is new, because in those circles she is new. 'Well, of course, you women aren't getting your fair share, but is this stuff really worthy of serious scholarly effort?' 'Juliet Mitchell, who's she?' (No philosopher willingly admits to not knowing 'important' philosophers.)

Weapon 4: *A succession of tomfooleries that would not be tolerated in any other sphere*

'Yes, but my wife stays home, and she doesn't feel oppressed'. 'How can a feminist fairly teach a course in feminist philosophies?' No philosopher would reject Sartrean insights on the ground that his/her cousin the clerk felt no bad faith, nor would (s)he question the metaphysician's right to teach metaphysics on the ground that (s)he would be biased toward metaphysics.

In the language of some contemporary psychologies, these are games philosophers play. By definition, games are crooked ways of filling crooked needs. They are destructive to the game-player and to the opponents he or she hooks. They subvert appropriate ends, in this case, the ends of philosophy, and of those who wish genuinely to pursue it.

Should the feminist philosopher endeavor to acquaint her non-feminist colleagues with her perspectives, she runs the risk of finding herself in a peculiar interchange, another game, where words are traded, arguments are constructed, 'general principles' pleaded, but where there is no sense of what one expects in a philosophic enterprise: what Maurice Natanson calls 'genuine argument', where 'the self is risked' (Natanson, 1965; 12).

> ... what is 'genuine' is nothing more than the commitment of the self to the full implications of a philosophical dialectic, a saying, in effect, 'if you argue you choose to open yourself to the risk of discovering the argument has a fundamental structure that has, in turn, profound implications for your own being' (Natanson, 1965; 15).

Genuine argument takes place on the level of our most 'primordial' and concrete experience, otherwise we are engaged merely in an exercise which seeks to 'convince' (i.e. gain power) rather than 'persuade' (change the self or selves involved). To retreat into the games philosophers play, to refuse genuine engagement, is to refuse philosophy itself:

> When I refuse to commit myself to genuine argument involving persuasion, I in effect make a refusal of philosophy itself; I will not risk myself and I will not risk my world . . . . In Sartrean language, this is one of the modalities of 'Bad Faith' (Natanson, 1965; 16).

As women need the therapeutic function of philosophy — salvation through clarification of reality and its possibilities, philosophy, in its therapeutic function, needs women.

> The real emancipation of man [sic] can take place only in a different society after a fundamental change in values . . . a new rationality and sensibility . . . at least some human beings with new values and new aspirations must exist and do their work prior to the massive change that will make general liberation possible . . . [What is required is] enough distance and dissociation from the society to be anguished rather than absorbed by it (Marcuse et al; 1971; 40).

On 'the boundary of patriarchal space' (Daly, 1973; 132) the feminist scholar, against weapons economic, political, and psychological, must trust her woman's consciousness and insights, must insist upon status in the 'mainstream', must resist the quest for the male seal of approval, and assert her right to philosophize as philosophy, not the philosophic establishment, means her to.

We all know that the history of philosophy has been sexist. That philosophers brought to their work the conventional misogyny and ignorance of their times has been chronicled by many. We know that the consequences of their prejudice have been horribly damaging: 'verification' of misogynist beliefs in the 'learned' writings legitimated sexist ideas and practices in religion, medicine, and social institutions, and reinforced the worst kinds of oppression, from witch-burning to clitoridectomy.[6] Moreover, we know that as the 'Mother of the Sciences', philosophy has transmitted her aberrations to all her children — psychology, law, political theory, and the others. Some of us are acutely aware that socio-ethical, biological, and even metaphysical misconceptions about women still appear in current philosophical literature, although they tend now to take a less acerbic form,[7] and we know that they are still doing harm in all the familiar ways. Feminism is a response to this misogyny, an attempt to 'right the balance', to serve as a 'corrective' as Forence Howe (1977) terms it. A philosophy that responds positively to feminist critiques will be a more complete philosophy.

There is an old Jewish saying that if you dig a grave for someone else, you may fall in yourself. The entire intellectual/academic enterprise, including philosophy, has spent centuries digging a grave for women. I contend that it has, indeed, fallen in. Because philosophers have been sexist, because the philosophic establishment (those who control the profession through journals, boards, chairs, etc.) has been sexist, because

---

[6]See: Henricus Institoris, 1970, *Malleus Malificorum* (translated Montague Summers) B. Blom, New York. See: Ben Barker-Benfield, 'The spermatic economy: a nineteenth-century view of sexuality' *Feminist Studies*, Vol I, No. 1, pp. 45–74.

[7]See: Maryellen MacGuigan, 1973 'Is woman a question?' *International Philosophical Quarterly*, Vol. XIII, No. 4 (Dec.) pp. 485–505. See: Mary Daly, 1973, *Beyond God the Father*, Beacon Press, Boston, pp. 3–4.

women — their perspectives, values, and attitudes — have been barred from the enterprise, because a kind of *gynophobia* has not been uncommon among practitioners in the field, because of these and yet other reasons, sexism in philosophy has become philosophical sexism, meta-sexism, if you will, and has become self-destructive to the profession. The rejection of 'womaning' has produced a distortion so complete and so pervasive that it has embedded itself almost invisibly in the very heart of the pursuit: meta-sexism is epistemological, permeating philosophy to its roots — the structure of its method and the logic of its criticism. Feminist analysis is *not* the bias: rather it is the prophylactic against the distorted, exquisitely subtle bias of masculism.

Aggressive response to the threat posed by feminism however, is not the only result that feminism has procured. Inroads have been made: the very articulation of philosophy as masculist is an insight which once realized, will not fade. But in attempting to assess what, if any, positive accommodations philosophy is making to feminist insights, we must make at least two important distinctions: first, we must separate those responses made by philosophy itself from those made by male philosophers (who represent, after all, only one segment of the enterprise); second, we must distinguish what is happening now from what might or should happen in the future.

As it was pointed out, most men in the field do not take feminist philosophy seriously. They barely read work written by women at all unless it is presented in the most rigidly traditional style or mode, and unless it is sufficiently familiar not to cause stress. By and large very few take the trouble to read the longer, more systematic statements of theoretical feminists such as Mary Daly, Susan Griffin, Kate Millett or the like (some of them not even 'philosophers'!). Therefore, one could hardly expect these men to be integrating these tremendously creative and philosophically radical perspectives into their own work. For the present, the establishment is safe from feminist change in the conceptual arena — in epistemology, metaphysics, even aesthetics.

No one in academe, however, can be fully insulated from feminist activism. Nearly everyone, like it or not, has been touched by affirmative action, by publishing house guidelines for non-sexist language, or by strong women (students or teachers) in the classroom. Male philosophers, then, like the rest, have been sensitized to the most blatant expressions of sexism, and at least on the surface, may try to be careful. A growing minority sincerely seek change: for example some have added feminist issues to course curricula; they avoid overtly sexist texts, offer realistic encouragement to female graduate students, hire women. In other words, in their behavior as academicians, if not in their research as philosophers, many male members of the establishment are changing. These changes have set the groundwork for the other more substantive changes.

Increasingly, women are being attracted into the field of philosophy, so long a masculine preserve. Philosophy, after all, is really a natural place to explore the essential issues of feminism. Where else, if not in ethics or political philosophy, would one consider the principles involved in abortion, ERA, male/female/human relationships, subordination, freedom, etc? Where else if not in epistemology or language philosophy would one explore sexist rhetorical devices, words and naming, male/female or masculist/feminist consciousness? Where if not in metaphysics would one explore matriarchal religion, the implications of female/male divinities, and so on?

While in the past women acquired reputability in philosophy by going low profile (as women), today many of us are far more assertive about taking whatever stance seems most constructive, most true to us, including feminism. More and more women are thinking, writing, publishing, and even teaching as freed people. There is a Society For Women in Philosophy and an active women's caucus in the American Philosophical Society. As women become integrated into the philosophical establishment, our work, our insights, will become integrated into the philosophical enterprise. Philosophy itself, the doing of it, will change.

References

ARISTOTLE, *Poliics*, Book I, Ch. 13.

BARKER-BENFIELD, Ben (1972) 'The spermatic economy: A nineteenth-century view of sexuality' in *Feminist Studies*, Vol. I, No. 1, pp. 45–74.

de BEAUVOIR, Simone (1961) *The Second Sex* (translated by H. M. Parshly) Bantam, New York.

BOSUSTOW, Steven (1968) *Why Man Creates*, Prod. Saul Bass and Associates, for Kaiser Aluminium and Chem. Corp. Distributed Pyramid Film Prod., Santa Monica, California.

DALY, Mary (1973) *Beyond God the Father*, Beacon Press, Boston.

EBENSTEIN, William (1969) *Great Political Thinkers*, 4th edition, Holt, Rinehart & Winston, New York.

FEINBERG, Joel (1973) 'Some conjectures about the concept of respect' in *Journal of Social Philosophy*, Vol. III, No. 2, pp. 1–3.

HOWE, Florence (1977) *Seven years later: women's studies programs in 1976*. Report of the National Advisory Council on Women's Educational Programs, USA.

INSTITORIS, Henricus (1970) *Malleus Malificorum* (translated by Montague Summers), B. Blom, New York.

KENISTON, Kenneth (1960) *The Uncommitted: Alienated Youth in American Society*, Dell, New York.

MacGUIGAN, Maryellen (1973) 'Is woman a question?' in *International Philosophical Quarterly*, Vol. XIII, No. 4, Dec. pp. 485–505.

MARCUSE, Herbert (1964) *One-Dimensional Man*, Beacon Press, Boston.

MARCUSE, H in S. KEEN and J. RASER (1971) 'Conversations with Herbet Marcuse' in *Psychology Today*, February, pp. 35–40, 60, 62, 64 & 66.

MITCHELL, Juliet (1973) *Women's Estate*, Vintage, New York.

MOORE, Edgar (1967) *Creative and Critical Thinking*, Houghton Mifflin, New York.

NATANSON, Maurice (1965) 'The claims of immediacy' in M. Natanson and H. Johnstone, jr. (Eds.) *Philosophy, Rhetoric, and Argumentation*, Pennsylvania University Press, University Park, pp. 10–19.

PEGIS, Anton C. (Ed.) (1945) *Basic Writings of Saint Thomas Aquinas*, Random House, New York.

REUBEN, Elaine (1978) 'In defiance of the evidence: notes on feminist scholarship' in *Women's Studies International Quarterly*, Vol. I, No. 3, p. 215–218.

SELLARS, Wilfred (1964) 'Philosophy and the scientific image of man' in *Science, Perception and Reality*, Routledge & Kegan Paul, London, pp. 1–40.

STERN, Karl (1965) *Flight from Woman*, Farrar, Strauss and Giroux, New York.

4

Women, Lost and Found: The Impact of Feminism on History

JANE LEWIS

When the women's movement turned its attention to sexism in the schools, one measure used was the way women were portrayed in text books. In the case of history, it was concluded that women were remarkable chiefly by their absence. More or less the same was true of scholarly writing. The fact that women's contribution to society had been ignored in the past made it easier to deny women's contribution in the present; it also helped to perpetuate woman's poor self-image. Keenly aware of this, writers of the new women's history were fired with the dual purpose of 'restoring women to history and history to women' (Kelly-Gadol, 1976: 809). *Hidden from History* and *Becoming Visible* are two of the titles that reflect this preoccupation with discovering women's past (Rowbotham, 1973; Bridenthal and Koonz, 1977).

One of the first women to insist that all women made an active contribution to history was Mary Beard (Beard, 1946). While her book on the role of American women in the past was on the whole well received, the comments of one critic, J. H. Hexter, give some indication as to why women nevertheless failed to become subjects of historical study during the following two decades. Hexter argued that historians were concerned with the process of change and that since women did not play a decisive role in such processes, they were not the legitimate subject of history: 'We know who is mainly behind those trends and developments and movements . . . . For better or for worse it was men' (Degler, 1974a : 73; Berenice Carroll, 1976). As long as Hexter's view of history as the record of the powerful and articulate prevailed, it was inevitable that the past of the great majority of women and of men would be ignored. Only the deeds of the occasional woman of note would find a place in the history books.

It was the rapid development of the new social history during the 1960's which made it increasingly difficult for Hexter's view of history to be sustained. The new social history claimed that the experience of the powerless and inarticulate, which had been neglected by political, constitutional, economic, diplomatic and intellectual history was important. With this development, we might also have expected a fuller treatment of women's history. But, disappointingly, the work of social historians continued to ignore women. Women often took a back seat during times of crisis (in strikes or revolts) and played little part in the labour movements that were studied. Their most common form of work in the nineteenth and early twentieth centuries, domestic service, was passed over by historians eager to explain the transition to factory production. To social historians, the working class was defined implicitly as male. For example, examination of working class leisure patterns meant an analysis of the pub, the working man's club,

55

the football match and the music hall. As Gareth Stedman Jones (1977:162) recently remarked: 'it is a fair generalization to say that the relation between one-half of the working class and leisure remains to be explored'.

Similarly, gender does not figure at all in one of the most important debates among labour historians on the emergence of a 'labour aristocracy' during the late nineteenth century. Women were low wage earners and were therefore not members of the labour aristocracy themselves, but the gender component should nevertheless be considered. Labour historians have sought explanations for the emergence of the labour aristocracy at the workplace in wage data and in the relationships between groups of workers and employers (e.g., Hobsbawm, 1964; Foster, 1974). The labour aristocrat's 'culture of respectability' has been largely ignored (an exception is Gray, 1976). Yet it is this aspect that has most impressed the women's historians who have begun to document the meticulous housework routines of the wives of labour aristocrats, performed in the name of respectability (e.g., Roberts, 1977). Did these values come from within or were they imposed from without? And, within the family, was the husband or the wife the more concerned to aspire to and preserve respectability?

It is likely that the gender component helped determine the male labour aristocrat's attitude towards the wage. For example, the extent to which the demand for a family wage was an expression of masculinity merits consideration. We know from women's autobiographies that most men kept back a portion of their wage, no matter how small, for the sake of 'self respect', even though no such sum was either expected or given women (Scannell, 1974). Masculinity has never been studied and yet it is probable that the desire for badges of respectability, such as pocket money, or at another level, a wage that would enable wives to stay at home, should be examined in relation to this concept.

Even when historians turned to look at the family — as crucial to women's past as to their present — they did not discuss gender. Pioneering work with aggregate family data revealed family composition, fertility fluctuations, illegitimacy patterns and sex ratios,[1] all of vital importance, but the family was treated very much as an undifferentiated unit and relations between husband and wife and patterns of dependence and decision making within it were not considered. It has been argued that Aries's (1962) influential history of childhood paid insufficient attention to different patterns of socialization for the sexes, with the result that his conclusions about the emerging concept of childhood refer more accurately to boyhood (Smith, 1976). Similarly, Smelser's (1959) early effort to link changes in the cotton industry to changes in the structure of family life allowed no room for discussion of the significance of sex roles, despite obvious changes in the nature of male and female occupations during the period he studied.

Family history and women's history cover very similar ground, indeed, in one popular English history text book an index entry for women turns out to be a section on the family (Webb, 1974). Historians of the family work with topics of crucial concern to women, for example, fertility and childrearing practices, which standard survey histories confine to a few pages, but this does not guarantee sympathetic consideration of the woman's point of view. Some recent writings in family history have assumed that the family is a natural, biological rather than socially constructed phenomenon (e.g., Lasch, 1977). As a result, the analysis deals inadequately with social forces and institutions exterior to the family, such as the state, availability of work and kin and neighbourhood

[1]See for example the *Journal of Interdisciplinary History* 2 (Autumn, 1971) for articles by Joseph Lett, Robert Wells, Peter Laslett and Kenneth Keniston.

networks, all of which affect family members and which are therefore important to our understanding of the institution of the family (Rapp, Ross and Bridenthal, 1979).

Edward Shorter (1975) explains the 'making of the modern family' in terms of a revolution of sentiment. He believes that capitalism produced a transition to modern values: free individual choice rather than a preference for authority, spontaneous creativity rather than a preference for custom, and sexual liberation. By implication, this is better than anything we have had before. He also assumes that capitalism had a liberating effect on single women, although he produces no evidence to prove it and the picture other works give of low wages being turned over to the family coffers is hardly that of a 'liberated' nineteenth century flapper. While a study like this does not ignore women, it is essentially unsympathetic to their experiences. Moreover, its portrayal of change as a series of spontaneous and functional responses masks the power relations within the family and society that are so important to a real understanding of women's past (Breines, Cecillo and Stacey, 1978).

During the late 1960's, it became clear to a number of historians who were also involved in the women's movement that it was necessary to include women as a new category of historical analysis. Extrapolating from their own position, these women hypothesized that women's experience in the past had been significantly different from that of men. But there was little information available as to what women did in the past: how many worked and whether they were married or single, how much they earned, how they coped with their children, their own bodies, in widowhood. And, where a general picture of one group of women had emerged, for example, the 'perfect', idle middle class Victorian 'lady', the texts provided no explanations of their behaviour.

Thus women began the empirical research necessary to reconstruct (and in so doing to reinterpret) women's role in the past and to establish turning points of particular significance to women: for example in the management of childbirth and attitudes towards sexuality. Class and racial differences had also to be considered; not all women were powerless or white. Of necessity, consideration of gender roles complicates rather than simplifies historical analysis, sex cuts across all the existing variables used including class, the most common in social history. Peter Stearns (1976) has recently suggested that social history is not another sub-discipline like intellectual history, but rather 'an approach to the entirety of the past'. Such a perspective is necessarily incomplete if women are ignored.

The new women's history, like the new social history, took many forms. In what follows, I shall examine some examples of two main approaches: the one adds to our information about women's behaviour in the past, while relying on already established approaches and methodologies, and the other attempts to re-examine history from a 'woman-centred' point of view, which involves asking new questions of new topics. While the latter approach is both more exciting and more valuable because it has resulted in substantial clarification and reinterpretation of the ideas we had about women's position in the past, methodological problems arise. Perhaps because they have always been conscious both of their close relationship to social historians and yet of their separate status, women's historians have constantly reviewed the methodology they employ (Gordon, 1975; Lerner, 1969; Smith Rosenberg, 1975; Zemon-Davis, 1976).

The most successful woman-centred studies combine an understanding of theoretical concepts (often drawn from other disciplines) with careful research. Very early efforts, (such as that by Ivy Pinchbeck, 1930), to describe the nature of women's work between

1750 and 1850, provided a wealth of empirical detail but no theoretical framework. Many women's historians have continued in this vein, although few have done as thorough work as Pinchbeck. The development of feminist theory since the late 1960's and its application to history is crucial to the development of women's history. The record of women's experience in the past can all too easily become a backwater — literally 'other' in terms of historical studies — but a strong theoretical framework which relates women's experience to that of men has the potential to make the consideration of gender as automatic as consideration of class.

I shall go on to sketch one research design which I think provides concrete illustration of how some of these concepts may be worked out in practice and then discuss some of the influential explanatory models that have been used as feminist theory has developed. The development of women's history since the late 60's has been uneven. First, it is important to recognize that not all historical writing about women can be called either women's or feminist history. Some work, such as Shorter's is riddled with implicit assumptions that make it essentially anti-feminist. For the rest, studies using traditional approaches continue to parallel attempts to radically rethink women's past. It is important to be aware of these different types of women's history if we are to determine which is the most useful and to press for its integration into the mainstream of social history.

Much early women's history began with what Natalie Zemon Davis (1976) has called the study of 'women worthies': the chronicling of famous or exceptional women. Doris Mary Stenton's *The English Woman in History* (1957) relies heavily on this approach. Because it arose from women's desire for a better self-image and a greater sense of self-worth, it is not surprising that a substantial amount of the recent work in women's history has continued in this vein. Not only have women's historians (who were influenced by the women's movement) been particularly anxious to seek the origins of feminism and to describe the activities of earlier feminist movements, but also many male historians interested in women's past have been able to relate easily to this aspect, because it concentrates on public figures and on the whole uses traditional source materials. The historiography of the suffrage movement in particular is still growing (Liddington and Norris, 1978; Mackenzie, 1975; Morgan, 1975; Raeburn, 1974).

It *is* important to analyze the personal circumstances and external pressures which led women such as the suffragettes to take the public stage; to explain how they dealt with the conflicts between their prescribed role and their behaviour; and to give their views on matters other than the suffrage. Andrew Rosen has made a start by asking who the suffragettes were and by identifying a majority of them as single women. This indicates, perhaps, that we should look more carefully at both the opportunities and restrictions experienced by single women in Edwardian society. Apart from this Rosen's analysis is traditional. He examines the interactions between the movement's leaders and politicians and seeks to re-define the nature of militancy as a political strategy. This tends to be descriptive rather than explanatory. It does not bring us nearer to understanding the suffragette's world view. For example, I have yet to see a satisfactory analysis of Christabel Pankhurst's demand for 'Purity for Men and Votes for Women' in a history of suffrage. Christabel's attitude might well be related to the recent suggestion that middle class Victorian women feared to divorce sexuality from reproduction because their vested interest in home and family was so great. It is interesting that this suggestion was made in a book on birth control (Gordon, 1976), which sets out to ask new questions about women's experience, rather than in analyses of suffrage, which tend to ask questions designed to analyse male rather than female power. It should be remembered that as suffrage became universal so the power vested in it declined and in the final event women's suffrage had little direct influence on politics or women. Thus a suffrage historian must be prepared to look beyond the immediate details of the struggle itself if he or she is to make a significant contribution to the study of women's past.

Some writers have continued in the Pinchbeck tradition and have provided us with valuable additional information on ordinary women which may find its way into other works on the period in question. However, these tend not to add to our understanding of why the women being written about experienced life as they did. Kitteringham's piece (1975) on farm girls in the late nineteenth century falls into this category. We get a very convincing reconstruction of the rhythms and routines of the work they did, but are given no context for it, nor any idea of the reasons for and the effects of the changes that take place. For example, child labour is discussed without reference to any of the work done on the concept of childhood, or to the contribution made by the child to the family economy, and while we are told that indoor service declined we are not told how this affected women. A more extreme example still is that of Lee Holcombe's *Victorian Ladies at Work* (1973). Holcombe's theme is that economic, demographic and organizational factors had more to do with the expansion of women's employment than the women's movement. But while she describes the kind of work women did in detail, she does not relate it to the factors she promised and the opening of the professions is explained chiefly in terms of greater educational opportunities for women.

Yet another group of works in women's history have taken movements or events already established as important and have examined the role women played in them: what Gerda Lerner has called 'women's contribution' history (Lerner, 1976). Dorothy Thompson (1971) made an early attempt to include documents written by women in her collection of Chartist materials. More recent examples are Jane Abray's attempt (1975) to describe the part played by feminists in the French Revolution and a collection of essays describing women's contribution to the labour movement (Middleton, 1977). Undoubtedly there is merit in redressing the balance in this way. (Major histories of the Labour Party, for example, make no mention of women.) However, this approach accepts what has been defined as important to men's past as its subject matter and requires no new conceptualization of history. Lerner (1976) has argued that such studies miss the opportunity of studying women 'on their own terms', that is to say, their contribution is judged by its effect on the movement or event and by standards appropriate to men. *Women in the Labour Movement*, edited by Lucy Middleton, is a case in point. The authors are anxious to portray labour women supporting the ideals of male leaders and actually ignore the well-documented controversy that develops during the 1920's, when the labour women's sections support free access to birth control information. Here, the determination to chronicle the activities of united women in a united movement at the expense of an analysis of the context in which labour women lived and worked adds little to our understanding of women's experience. The force of Lerner's point becomes clearer if an example of an alternative approach is considered. Hufton's study (1971) of the way in which all classes of women experienced the French Revolution takes women out of the 'also ran' category and forces a re-evaluation of this pivotal historical event from their point of view.

'Women's contribution' history tends to concentrate on the experiences of relatively few women. Women's role is analysed only when they make a contribution to 'male' history, which means that the writer is implicitly defining women as marginal to history (Smith Rosenberg, 1975). If we want to know more about the lives of the majority of women, we must discover what was central to those lives. Woman-centred history demands that we rethink what is 'important' in the past and how we analyse it. From our position today, we may suppose that family size and the relationship between reproduction (including the socialization of children) and production are likely to have been central. In an effort to write woman-centred history, many women's historians have consciously adopted and developed Juliet Mitchell's categories of analysis: production, reproduction, socialization and sexuality. Richard T. Vann (1974) has abstracted one of Mitchell's categories and gone so far as to suggest that a new periodization for women's history should be worked out based on women's emancipation from the reproductive process. Certainly, major demographic changes or major changes in sexual practice may be of far greater importance to women than the existing divisions usually made on the basis of major political events and intellectual or economic trends. But it is difficult to locate a new periodization appropriate to all women. For example, family size alone ignores the important effect of industrialization on women and the family. Joan Kelly-Gadol (1976) recommends keeping history's traditional periodization and asking how women reacted and were affected differently. Naturally this would involve greater consideration of women-centred variables, such as fertility. Hufton's article on women in the French Revolution, for example, considered the effect of the Revolution on the family economy of the poor, on women's health, on the death rate of their infants and on women's work and wages.

Obviously, historical events affected women as well as men and it is important to decide whether working class women were affected in the same way as middle class women and single women in the same way as married women; whether women's roles became more or less circumscribed; and whether their status rose or fell compared to that of men in their social class. As Sheila Ryan Johansson (1976) has pointed out, measurement of status alone is enormously complicated. Determinants of her 'status pattern' include: age, marital status, class, motherhood, legal rights, political and military factors, religion, cultural and intellectual variables, health and women's perceptions of their own status. Naming a few of the effects of World War I on women shows the difficulties of such a process of balancing and assessment. Women's wages rose dramatically during the war and married women in the home also achieved a measure of economic independence through separation allowances. Child and maternal welfare services improved and the infant mortality rate fell. However, the greater economic independence of women was shortlived and the renewed strength of the ideology of motherhood which resulted from the concern about both the huge loss of life and a falling birth rate worked to restrict rather than to enlarge the opportunities of all classes of married women.

The attempt to record female experiences in the past from a woman-centred point of view has already resulted in substantial reinterpretations of women's role. For example, the popular sterotype of the middle and upper class Victorian woman as 'the completely ornamental, completely helpless and dependent . . . wife or daughter with no function besides inspiring inspiration and bearing children' (Perkin, 1969: 159) has been challenged. Patricia Branca (1975) has argued that for the majority of middle class women budgets were tight and servants few. Thus, these women took the initiative in adapting to technological changes (she feels that the sewing machine played a more important part in their lives than the piano, for example) and in seeking to improve their personal comfort and well-being by using birth control to limit their families and by demanding relief from pain in childbirth. However, Branca's work has many methodological problems, one of the most serious being that her main source, domestic manuals, were probably not used by the middle class group she describes. More subtle, perhaps, is Leonore Davidoff's (1973) treatment of nineteenth-century society. Rather than seeking new meaning in Society women's lives, Davidoff chooses to explore the real significance of the rituals they performed. Why was so much time spent in observance of the etiquette surrounding introductions, calls and dining? She concludes that these should not be dismissed as idle ways of passing time but recognized as elaborate access rituals, vitally important in a rapidly expanding society, where 'new wealth' had to be differentiated from old.

The image of working class women has also been revised. Most early accounts of the effect of industrialization stressed the destructive impact of married women's work on home life. Ivy Pinchbeck (1930) made it clear that she felt it to be an improvement when men's wages reached a sufficiently high level for women to stay at home and look after their children. In her study, *Wives and Mothers in Victorian Industry* (1958), Margaret Hewitt agreed with nineteenth and early twentieth century opinion which blamed married women's work for the high infant mortality rate, arguing that the infants of working mothers were consigned to the vicissitudes of both the feeding bottle and the child minder. However, a recent study by Carol Dyhouse (1978) has tested the hypothesis that the larger the proportion of married working women in the population the higher the associated infant mortality rate and has arrived at results which do not suggest a positive relationship between the two variables. Moreover, Anderson's work on family structure in nineteenth century Lancashire has indicated that less than 2% of children would have been left with professional minders (Anderson, 1971:74). In the vast majority of cases relations and neighbours helped out. More recently Edward Shorter (1975) has again asserted that working class women only became good mothers when they left the workforce and devoted themselves to their children. Shorter (1975) and Demause (1974) go one step further to assert that women in the recent past did not love their children if they chose to work outside the home. But love is not a definable or measurable variable over long periods of time. What can be assessed is the degree to which parents strove to protect and nurture their children within the bounds of the possibilities open to them. In the case of my own research on maternal and child welfare, one of my respondents referred to her second baby who died of bronchitis in 1909 as a 'November baby', a phrase that evinces a degree of fatalism. But she also recalled nursing him night and day and doing her best to follow the instructions of a doctor, who was called in at great expense.

Perhaps the most important factor affecting middle and working class married women during the late nineteenth and early twentieth centuries was the rapid fall in family size due to the increased practise of birth control. Between 1860 and 1925 the proportion of couples who were childless doubled, the proportion with one child increased five fold and with two, four fold. The middle class birth rate declined more rapidly than that of the working class and it has been assumed that knowledge of newer methods of contraception (especially the cap and the condom) diffused downwards from the middle to the working class. In fact, as Angus McLaren (1978) has shown, the working class were using traditional birth control methods of withdrawal and abortion long before the birth rate began its steady decline in the 1870's. Thus the diffusion of birth control practice should be seen more as a process of adaptation than innovation. The working class birth rate began to decline rapidly in the 1930's due to changing goals in regard to family size rather than because of the availability of any new method of contraception.

Gender is crucial to a consideration of the motives behind the practice of birth control. In his classic study of the nineteenth century decline in the middle class birth rate, Joe Banks (1954) concluded that economic reasons were responsible for the increased use of contraceptives among the middle class. This implied that as breadwinners, men played the more important role in decision making. But both Branca's book (1975) and an article by Daniel Scott Smith (1974) argue for the existence of a 'domestic feminism', which they define as the middle class British and American woman's search for greater personal autonomy within the home, including her desire to control her own fertility. In the case of working class women, McLaren (1977a, 1977b) has pointed out that one of the main traditional methods of birth control was abortion, an exclusively female practice and Diana Gittens (1977) showed from her study of oral evidence that the decline in working class fertility during the inter-war period was closely related to such variables as women's desire for more leisure time and the opportunity available to them for learning about more effective methods of contraception.

This woman-centred history is not without problems. Reinterpretations such as those of Branca and Scott Smith place a premium on women as actors rather than victims. This tension between an 'active' and 'passive' interpretation of women's behaviour is fundamental to any study in women's history. Does the historian portray women as an oppressed group and 'acted upon', or does he/she concentrate on the positive way women have acted and responded in the past? Timely warnings have been issued about interpreting the prescriptive literature which is often a major source for women's history. Women did not always behave as they were expected to. Using an 1890's survey of women's attitudes towards sexuality, Carl Degler (1974b) has concluded that American women did not follow the prescriptions laid down by the marriage and advice manuals which assumed women to be sexually passive and Jay Mechling (1975) has identified four main problems that arise when historians use childrearing literature to predict behaviour: manuals can either reflect established practice or be advocating something new; manual writers usually address a particular (class-based) audience; parents learn parenting from sources other than manuals (mothers are often more likely to do what *their* mothers did than what the manuals say); and finally manuals are likely to tell us more about the childrearing values of their authors than of the wider society. These writers are of course correct in their insistence that people will often resist prescribed behaviour. But, in a patriarchal and capitalist society, resistance should not be confused with free choice. It is important to be aware of the realities of power and to establish the bounds within which women could and did resist. These will of course vary for women of different classes, races, ages and marital status. In her enthusiasm to overthrow the stereotype of passivity, Branca neglects to make clear the very real constraints upon the behaviour of the nineteenth century middle class woman. On the other hand, Leonore Davidoff's essay, 'Mastered for Life: Servant and Wife in Victorian and Edwardian England' (1974), has been criticised on the grounds that she articulates the structure of oppression common to servant and wife but does not devote enough attention to the reactions and emotions of the servants and wives themselves.

Awareness of the actor-victim problem of interpretation can result in some finely drawn analyses. Carroll Smith Rosenberg's (1972) recognition of hysteria as an alternative role option for middle class women faced with conflicting expectations as to their behaviour is one such piece of work. The middle class Victorian woman was expected both to conform to the ideal of the 'perfect lady' and at the same time to manage the house efficiently and undergo frequent and often painful childbirth. One of the few lines of resistance open to her was that of the hysteric's sick role; while sick nothing could be expected of her.

Full understanding of the nature of women's options and choices can only come from greater familiarity with women's universe in the past. There are as yet few works of synthesis in women's history and so we are often forced to assess one aspect of women's experiences — family, or work outside the home, or sexuality — with incomplete knowledge of the value and belief systems of the women under discussion. Oral testimony and some of the recently published women's autobiographies can help the historian struggling to analyse and explain by providing an all encompassing portrait, albeit of only one individual. For example, Francie Nichol's tale of her life in South Shields provides a complete picture of courtship, childbirth, husband/wife relations and work, as a lodging housekeeper and small business woman (Robinson, 1975). Her attitudes could well be interpreted as fatalistic: painful childbirth and a drunken husband are to be endured and hard times expected. The limitations imposed on Francie Nichol by class, poverty and poor education are all too clear to an observer, but she never refers to them directly or complains about them, they are the accepted bounds within which she behaves with unlimited energy and vitality. She is neither victim nor free agent.

The most striking feature of her story is the central place occupied by her family. All her efforts are directed towards its defence and preservation. It is for the sake of her children that she opens a fish and chip shop and when her husband drinks away the profits it is for their sake that she tries again. Obviously, it is impossible to compartmentalize her life neatly into categories of home and work. As Tilly and Scott (1975) have so perceptively shown in their work, nineteenth century working class women's familial orientation underlies a whole range of behaviour and is a key factor explaining their physical sacrifice within the family as well as their work patterns outside it. Married working class women worked to supplement the family income. Thus, until the late nineteenth century, a majority of them would be most likely to go out to work when their children were young and expenses were greatest, dropping out of the labour force when their children began to earn. As Tamara K. Hareven (1974) has pointed out, it is extremely important for the historian to consider the family life cycles of family members rather than to adopt the 'census snapshot' approach of most historians of the family. Hareven has been extremely successful in using a woman-centred perspective to revise the methodology of family history. The close relationship between what she calls 'family time' (marked by marriage, childbirth, maturation) and 'social time' (occupation, migration, and changing government policy and legislation) in women's lives must be explored if we are to make sense of the strategies and attitudes they adopted.

Women's history makes its strongest impact upon social history when it not only describes and interprets women's position in the past but also attempts to explain and account for the changes that have occurred. Attempts at explanation are built on careful empirical inquiry, an awareness of the problems that might be encountered in interpreting the material (such as the 'woman as victim' approach) and a sense of the way in which the patterns of association among the central factors in women's lives differ from those of men and differ between women of various classes and races. To develop a woman-centred historical perspective and at the same time to add gender to the already established categories of analysis makes it difficult to grasp the full dimensions of a particular topic. For valid analysis and soundly based explanation, historical inquiry must therefore proceed systematically, using theoretical constructs to guide research and testing these against the empirical evidence.

Many women's historians employ this kind of analysis to a greater or lesser extent in their work, testing evidence against theory, but because their preparatory work is always buried in their analyses, an example of some of the initial steps I went through in my own work might help to illustrate some of the problems involved in formulating the right questions to ask about women's experience in the past.[2]

The history of childbirth practices is of vital importance in terms of the history of women's experiences and bears directly on the concern of many women today to take control of the childbirth process and give birth at home rather than in hospital. The first crucial step is to decide which aspect of childbirth to study and what exactly it is that we are trying to explain. For example, one alternative title to 'childbirth practices' might be 'the management of childbirth'. Consideration of the difference between these two serves to clarify the issue under investigation. Management of childbirth is the phrase commonly used in medical texts since the inter-war years and implies a measure of control being exerted over the childbearing process. Childbirth practice is a more neutral term and does not lead the reader to expect a particular style of delivery, on the contrary it implies a certain diversity. Looking at the recent history of childbirth in one or more western countries, this difference in description suggests the centrality of the changing relationship between woman and attendant. In most cultures women have been and are attended by another person in childbirth and basic changes in the nature of that relationship must be explained. Was it caring and supporting or cold and alienating? Was there dependency involved? First the context in which childbirth takes place must be established. How does a particular society view pregnancy? What are the rituals and symbols involved and do these give any indication as to whether childbirth is regarded as a sickness or a natural physiological functions, whether it is regarded as polluting or held in awe? For example, the practice of 'churching' women after childbirth, which was common in our own society until very recent times, shows that childbirth and possibly also women themselves were regarded as unclean. Identification of the meanings of important rituals or sexual symbols has led some authors to make unwarranted leaps in terms of causation. For example, Oakley (1976) pointed out that midwifery practice was commonly shunned by male practitioners in the nineteenth century because it was regarded as dirty. The connection between women and pollution

---

[2]The subject I shall discuss ended up occupying a subsidiary place in my research. Thus what follows represents a genuine attempt to discuss a preliminary approach to the topic. Several books have appeared in this area (Donnison, 1977; Litoff, 1978; Wertz and Wertz, 1977), but none attempts the kind of enquiry described here.

is imaginatively developed in Oakley's explanation of the changing relationship between attendant and parturient woman, but other possible factors, including the actions and reactions of women themselves are not considered.

The basic changes in childbirth practice must be established within the context of the central relationship between woman and attendant. First, considering the woman's side in the relationship: obviously the place of birth has changed. Home births were once the rule and now they are, to say the least, exceptional. The preparations women made for childbirth have changed as a result of this and of changes in medical practice, such as the introduction of pre-natal care. There have been changes in women's attitudes towards childbirth (for example in their classification of it as a state of sickness or health) and a change in their expectations as to the nature of the experience with regard to pain control and technique. When childbirth took place in the home, women were responsible for the preparations and in the final event for labour itself. They booked an attendant if they could afford it and were usually responsible for providing whatever equipment was needed. The degree and extent of these changes may have varied between regions, classes and ethnic groups and a number of other variables such as educational levels may also be found to be significant. The aim of the study must be to explain the changes. For example, what prompted women to choose a midwife rather than a doctor in twentieth century England: economic factors, a belief that parturition was a normal function, the social class of the midwife as opposed to the doctor, or the influence of neighbours, kin or childbirth literature? It is possible that the evidence will not answer many of the numerous questions the researchers have in mind before they begin, but it is often as important to know what contemporaries did not record as what they did. Because it is impossible for us to put ourselves into the past and predict all the likely causes of change, it is also probable that questions will have to be added.

In the case of the attendant: it is clear that the sex and status of the attendant has changed from that of untrained female midwife to male midwife to doctor to obstetrician. In some countries female midwives remain and in some they do not. Where they still practise they are now professionals. Attendance in childbirth has become increasingly medicalized. Here again we must look at the attitudes towards pregnancy as sickness that accompanied this; the influences of changes in medical education and in medical technology; the place of midwifery in medical practice as a whole, in the practice of the general practitioner and in the range of jobs open to women; and the influence of intra-professional conflicts and rivalries.

Finally we must be aware of the interactions between attendant and woman. For example, did women want to go into hospital for childbirth? If so, was this desire spontaneous, or a reflection of what the medical profession told them was best? The issue of anaesthaesia illustrates this sort of problem neatly. During the late nineteenth century pain relief in childbirth was often denied by the medical profession on religious grounds and because it was feared that somehow women might be stimulated sexually by the experience. By World War I government health officials were giving every encouragement to the development of anaesthaesia and analgaesia because it was recognized that fear of childbirth could be one of the factors accounting for the decline in the birth rate. Pain relief was more commonly available in hospital and there is evidence that middle class women especially desired hospitalization for that reason. However, there are scattered references to indicate that as late as the inter-war years, working class women resisted pain relief because they regarded it as unnatural. The issue was complicated at another level by the intra-professional rivalry between doctors and midwives which led to the British Medical Association's opposition to midwives giving gas and air in domiciliary practice.

Such a preliminary set of questions has the makings of a model which may be extended and modified as research proceeds. The idea is not to force the evidence into a framework as Smelser did in his effort to build a model to explain the rise of the cotton industry, but rather to take account of the acknowledged complexity of historical inquiry and to have some means of keeping all the issues that arise in perspective. The dynamics of one relatively small issue such as anaesthaesia can be related to the central relationship being studied and conclusions drawn from this one case can readily inform the whole. It is also apparent that such systematic inquiry involves a tremendous amount of work. Most studies have abstracted one element of the relationship I have described, for example, the change from female midwife to male attendant and have sought to explain this alone. While this is perfectly valid, the conclusions drawn will be more soundly based if the author keeps in mind the wider perspective. For example, in her study of nineteenth century midwives, Jean Donnison (1977) explained the shift to male midwife in terms of the intra-professional rivalry between midwives and doctors without giving adequate consideration to the place of midwifery in medicine, the attitudes of midwife and doctor towards pregnancy and the possible preferences of the clients. While her empirical investigation of the questions she raised was impeccable, the conceptual framework of the study was narrow. Of course, the questions asked depend on the initial definition of the particular issue in the history of childbirth that is to be explained, but the same elements or variables will merit consideration, even though they will be weighted differently in each inquiry. Donnison missed some of the main elements, probably because she allowed her research to shape her questions.

Other works in the history of medicine and women have looked more generally at the relationship between patient and physician and have shown how the new approach of women's historians can break completely new ground. The treatment of 'female complaints' by male doctors during the Victorian period has attracted much attention. Two accounts, seeing only the sexual violence implicit in such practices as ovariotomy and the invasion of the uterus (made common by doctors who were convinced that the creation of women had involved taking a uterus and building a woman around it), have characterized the relationship as one of sexual hostility between doctor and patient or 'victim' (Barker Benfield, 1976; Wood, 1974). This component is important but is at best a partial explanation (Morantz, 1974; Verbrugge, 1976). Carroll Smith Rosenberg's (1972, 1973a, 1973b) contributions on this issue have been more finely drawn. She has concentrated on the relationship between social structure and the role options of women and in particular on how medical ideas about women's biology and sexuality affected women's role. She avoids the 'woman as victim' trap, being always conscious that prescription is not behaviour and that prescriptive literature and unpublished personal documents are both essential for a valid assessment of women's experience in the past. Her explanation of the interaction between doctors' ideas and women's roles tries to work at the level of the individual and thus relies heavily on psychological theory to the exclusion of economic and political forces. Nevertheless, these historians have, by their approach to the subject, by the kinds of questions they have asked, and in the case of Smith Rosenberg, by an ability to use a range of theoretical constructs drawn from other disciplines, put themselves in the forefront of the social history of medicine.

Other women's historians' efforts to develop models of change to explain women's experiences in the past have been equally fruitful. As more research is done and as feminist theory develops, these are constantly being criticized and modified. These theories of change have provided us with a woman-centred perspective of social change, while also making clear the theoretical importance of the consideration of gender in social history. First, women's historians have stressed the relationship between family and work, between a woman's reproductive and productive life. As Alice Rossi (1973) recently pointed out, this is something that male historians have tended to ignore even in biographies especially if the subject happened to be male. In the case of working class married women, familial values seem to have been the main impetus prompting them to work for wages or to take in lodgers. What is needed now is more study of the emergence of a 'family wage' which was paid to the male breadwinner and which permitted women to choose to stay at home and men to encourage them to do so. As long ago as 1924, Eleanor Rathbone (1924), a feminist, complained that the 'family economy' had been neglected by investigators; it seems that women's historians in the 1980's are beginning to address themselves to this crucial area. Women's closeness to familial values can also explain certain aspects of working class, single women's work experience. It is well-known that women are more poorly organized than men at the workplace. Lewenhak's recent book (1977) has given us details of women's trade union membership although she does not attempt to explain it. Joanna Bornat's (1977) findings, though, show how indirect women's association with their union was likely to be. Their jobs were often found by male relatives and they were usually signed up as union members by another member of the family, subscriptions being paid by the mother or grandmother out of the family kitty into which the vast majority and sometimes the whole of the young woman's wage had been paid. (Young men seem to have kept a larger proportion of their wage.)

As Kelly-Gadol (1976) has pointed out, analyses using the production/reproduction dichotomy are subject to confusion because of the debate over whether housework is productive work. She therefore prefers to use the structural model which was developed by the anthropologist, Rosaldo (1974) to account for what the latter perceived as universal sexual asymmetry. This focuses on another dichotomy: the public/domestic Historians early recognized that the removal of the workplace from the home and the more rigid separation of spheres into public and private which followed played an important part in determining the withdrawal of middle class women from the labour force and in sharpening the distinction between the productive and reproductive roles of working class women (Clark, 1919; Pinchbeck, 1930). In Rosaldo's hands domestic and public cease to be merely categories for analysis and assume a predictive power: the more definitely separated the two spheres the lower women's status and sense of self-worth. This model has difficulties as Natalie Zemon Davis (1976) has shown. While most feminists would agree with Rosald's contention that women's present strategy should be to bring men into the domestic sphere if the public is ever to belong to more than an elite of women, the categories domestic and public have to be very carefully defined over time, especially for the more distant past. Davis points out that during the Medieval period the concept of 'public might apply to religious as well as to political activity at one point and be much eroded at another'.

Nineteeth century studies have also found the model wanting. During the nineteenth century the separation of the public from the domestic sphere was extrmely rigid, yet it has been argued that such a separation provided real opportunities for women. Branca and Scott Smith have insisted on the existence of what they call a 'domestic feminism' whereby women took certain initiatives to make their lives more comfortable. But they did so within the bounds of the domestic sphere, something Rosaldo's model makes allowance for. A more satisfying challenge comes from Ellen DuBois (1975, 1978), whose analysis of the suffrage movement shows that suffragists used the ideology of domesticity to demand a role for women in the public sphere. A similar case can be made for the temperance movements in the United States and Canada. Here, the ideology of domesticity and the importance of home and family was accepted, but in seeking to make the family a more secure sanctuary by abolishing the demon drink, women took their protest into one of the most forbidden public places, the saloon. Rosaldo's model seeks to clearly differentiate the female experience from that of the male and in doing so it does not make provision for such contradiction between ideology and behaviour amongst women.

The compartmentalization inherent in these forms of dichotomous thinking led Nancy Osterud (1978) to comment on the value of sexual divisions theory,[3] which cuts across the divisions created by production and reproduction and public and domestic. As Kelly (1979: 221) has noted, this is important because feminists are becoming increasingly aware of the way in which 'the social relations arising from each sphere [the family and social production] structure experience in the other'. Sexual divisions arise in both the family and in the workplace. This focus also orients research towards an explanation of the process by which sex roles become differentiated at a particular time and place. In particular women's historians have sought to explain how the sexual division of labour was extended to the wage labour market. A new appreciation of the structure of women's oppression has emerged from this, especially in regard to the important role played by patriarchy. Patriarchal relations within the family played a large part in determining the division of labour when production took place in the home and Osterud has shown that in hosiery production in Leicester this division of tasks was carried over to the factory. Within the cotton industry, Lazonick (1976) has argued that the division of labour between male spinners and women power loom weavers was dictated not so much by economic considerations as by the capitalist's need for a spinner who could direct the work of others, particularly children; in other words for an authority figure. Hartman (1976) has pointed out that male workers as well as male capitalists played a major role in maintaining job segregation through their unions and she has emphasized that women's historians must consider patriarchy as seriously as capitalism. The state's role in reinforcing patriarchal structures and attitudes is also crucial. Several writers have arrived at the conclusion that the state promulgates and enforces either implicitly or explicitly a family policy (Land and Parker, 1978; McIntosh, 1978; Rapp *et al.*, 1979). The concept of patriarchy is subject to changing definitions over time. These have yet to be explored and a means of successfully integrating them into feminist theory and analysis has yet to be found. These two tasks are amongst the most pressing facing feminist scholars.

The value of the work done by committed women's historians who employ careful methods of enquiry and develop strong models to explain social change stands out clearly against the more doubtful contribution made by studies which either choose not

[3]This term was first used by Diana Leonard Barker and Sheila Allen (1976).

to go beyond painstaking description or provide inadequate explanations. Many proponents of modernization theory, for example, tend to miss some of the relationships that are crucial to an analysis of gender. It is Branca's (1975) preoccupation with modernization that leads her to insist so strongly that middle class women began to take positive control over their own lives during the later nineteenth century. She leaves the impression that all women had to do was to be a little more active in order to be completely liberated. Theresa McBride (1976) used the theory better in her analysis of domestic servants. Service provided the major setting for female urban labour, recruited from rural areas during the transitional stages of industrialization. Thus traditional work patterns were combined with a new form of behaviour for women: migration over long distances. McBride thus maintains that the rise and decline of domestic service constituted a distinct phase in the modernization of western society. But it is important, as Tilly and Scott have shown, that the traditional values and mores the servants brought with them to the towns not be overlooked. Indeed, it seems likely that women 'modernized' more slowly than men.

It is important to distinguish carefully between the various approaches to women's history and uses of theory, feminist and otherwise, because so many different strands are to be found in current writings in women's history. During the last few years many examples of women's contribution to history have been published (these tend also to be heavily empirical) and there have been several examples of family history treating issues of great importance to women and discussing women's past directly while ignoring or rejecting a feminist perspective. There is no doubt that consideration of gender has made a substantial impact on social history, but the status of women's history is far from clear. While it is too early for women as a category to have entered history texts (let alone the rapid re-interpretations of women's past that are in progress), women are now a respectable topic of enquiry and some establishment journals regularly publish pieces on women's history and review books in the field.[4] But this does not necessarily mean that feminist theory goes unquestioned. A feminist perspective is still regarded by many as biased history and graduate students must often fight to include the word feminist in their research titles. It is significant too that most theoretical pieces appear in feminist rather than establishment journals. Yet if feminist theory is ignored, two things may happen: either research on women is absorbed by works that ignore or are antithetical to feminism or women's history becomes an antiquarian backwater. We must be wary of the book of essays in which only one contribution is devoted to women, while the majority of the remainder are careful to make their comments class specific (regardless of their subject matter) and yet ignore gender.

The development of women's history courses exhibits similar strengths and weaknesses. Such courses are well-established in American but not in British universities. Their lack need not necessarily impede acceptance of the importance of the study of gender, but the dimensions of women's experience must be known if they are to be discussed and if students are to choose research topics wisely. (There is still a marked tendency for students to tread the well-known, safe paths of institutional and labour history rather than choosing more innovative lines of enquiry.) In England, at the University of Essex, where the study of sexual divisions in the past as well as in the

---

[4]The *Journal of Social History, Social History, History Workshop Journal, Victorian Studies* and the *Journal of Family History* are some of the most important.

present is well established in the Sociology Department, the archives of oral source material include a wealth of information on women's past which in turn has been largely responsible for an extensive treatment of women in two general texts on the Edwardian period (Thompson, 1975; Meacham, 1977). However, the existence of separate women's history courses also makes it easier for the subject to become a backwater. A degree of separation between women's history and social history would nonetheless seem to be productive and healthy. Like labour history, women's history needs its specialists if it is to develop. In addition, many women's historians are active feminists and have no desire to neglect the political implications of their work.

The women's history most feminists want to see combines thorough research of what is still in many respects uncharted territory with interpretation and explanation soundly based in feminist theory. If we want this sort of work to be fully integrated into the mainstream of social history, the study of gender must be proved to be of too great importance to be ignored. It has often been remarked that women have had to prove themselves better than men in any chosen field before gaining acceptance. It is unfortunate for women's historians that history is probably no exception.

References

ABRAY, Jane (1975) 'Feminism in the French Revolution', *American Historical Review* 80 (February), pp. 43–62.

ANDERSON, Michael (1971) *Family Structure in Nineteenth Century Lancashire*, Cambridge University Press, Cambridge, U.K.

ARIES, Philippe (1962) *Centuries of Childhood*, Vintage Bks., New York:

BANKS, Joseph A. (1954) *Prosperity and Parenthood*, Routledge & Kegan Paul, London.

BARKER, Diana Leonard and Sheila, ALLAN (eds.), (1976) 'Sexual Divisions in Society', (Edited by Diana Leonard Barker and Sheila Allen), In *Sexual Divisions and Society*, Tavistock, London.

BEARD, Mary (1946) *Woman as Force History*, MacMillan, New York.

BENFIELD, G. J. Barker (1976) *The Horrors of the Half-Known Life,* Harper, New York.

BORNAT, Joanna (1977) 'Home and Work: A New Context for Trade Union History', *Oral History* 5 (Autumn), pp. 124–135.

BRANCA, Patricia (1975) *Silent Sisterhood*, Croom Helm, London.

BREINES, Wini, Margaret CECILLO and Judith STACEY (1978) 'Social Biology, Family Studies and the Anti-Feminist Backlash', *Feminist Studies* 4 (February), pp. 43–67.

BRIDENTHAL, Renate and Claudia KOONZ (Eds.) (1977) *Becoming Visible. Women in European History,* Houghton Mifflin, Boston.

CLARK, Alice (1919) *The Working Life of Women in the Seventeenth-Century*, Routledge, London.

DAVIDOFF, Leonore (1973) *The Best Circles*, Croom Helm, London.

DAVIDOFF, Leonore (1974) 'Mastered for Life: Servant and Wife in Victorian and Edwardian England', *Journal of Social History* 7 (Summer), pp. 446–459.

DEGLER, Carl (1974(a)) 'Woman as Force in History by Mary Beard', *Daedelus* 103 (Winter), pp. 67–74.

DEGLER, Carl (1974(b)) 'What Ought to Be and What Was: Women's Sexuality in the Nineteenth-Century', *American Historical Review* 79 (December), pp. 1467–1490.

DEMAUSE, Lloyd (1974) 'The Evolution of Childhood', Edited by Lloyd Demause In *The History of Childhood,* Psycho-history Press, New York.

DONNISON, Jean (1979) *Midwives and Medical Men,* Heinemann, N.Y. and London.

DuBOIS, Ellen (1975) 'The Radicalism of the Woman Suffrage Movement: Notes Towards the Reconstruction of Nineteenth-Century Feminism', *Feminist Studies* 3 (Fall), pp. 63–71.

DuBOIS, Ellen (1978) *Feminism and Suffrage: The Emergence of an Independent Women's Movement in America, 1848–1869*, Cornell U.P., Ithaca.

DYHOUSE, Carol (1978) 'Working Class Mothers and Infant Mortality in England, 1895–1914', *Journal of Social History* 12 (Winter), pp. 248–267.

FOSTER, John (1974) *Class Struggle and the Industrial Revolution,* Methuen, London.

GILLIS, John R. (1979) 'Servants, Sexual Relations and the Risk of Illegitimacy in London, 1801–1900', *Feminist Studies* 5 (Spring), pp. 142–173.

GITTENS, Diana (1977) 'Women's Work and Family Size Between the Wars', *Oral History* 5 (Autumn), pp. 84–100.

GORDON, Linda (1975) 'A Socialist View of Women's Studies: A Reply to the Editorial, Vol. I, #1', *Signs* 1 (Winter), pp. 559–566.

GORDON, Linda (1977) *Woman's Body Woman's Right*, Penguin, Middlesex.

GRAY, Robert Q. (1976) *The Labour Aristocracy in Victorian Edinburgh*, Clarendon Press, Oxford.

HAREVEN, Tamara K. (1974) 'The Family as Process: The Historical Study of the Family Cycle', *Journal of Social History* 7 (Spring), pp. 322–329.

HARTMAN, Heidi (1976) 'Capitalism, Patriarchy and Job Segregation by Sex', *Signs* 1 (Spring), pp. 137–169.

HEWITT, Margaret (1958) *Wives and Mothers in Victorian Industry*, Rockcliffe, London.

HOBSBAWN, Eric (1964) *Labouring Men*, Weidenfeld and Nicholson, London.

HOLCOMBE, Lee (1973) *Victorian Ladies at Work*, David and Charles, Newton Abbott: London.

HUFTON, Olwen (1971) 'Women in Revolution, 1789–1796', *Past and Present* #53 (November), pp. 90–108.

JOHANNSON, Sheila Ryan (1976) 'Herstory as History: A New Field or Another Fad?' (Edited by Berenice Carroll), In *Liberating Women's History*, University of Illinois Press, Urbana.

JOHANSSON, Sheila Ryan (1978) 'Sex and Death in Victorian England', (Edited by Martha Vicinus), In *A Widening Sphere*, Indiana University Press, Bloomington, Indiana.

JONES, Gareth Stedman (1977) 'Class Expression versus Social Control?' *History Workshop Journal* (Autumn), pp. 162–170.

KELLY-GADOL, Joan (1976) 'The Social Relations of the Sexes: Methodological Implications of Women's History'. *Signs* (Summer), pp. 809–824.

KELLY, Joan (1979) 'The Doubled Vision of Feminist Theory: A Postscript to the 'Women and Power' Conference', *Feminist Studies* 5 (Spring), pp. 216–227.

KITTERINGHAM, Jennie (1975) 'Country Work Girls in Nineteenth Century England', (Edited by Raphael Samuel), In *Village Life and Labour*, Routledge & Kegan Paul, London.

KNIGHT, Patricia (1977) 'Women and Abortion in Victorian and Edwardian England', *History Workshop Journal* (Autumn), pp. 57–69.

LAND, H. and R. PARKER (1978) 'Family Policies in Brittain: The Hidden Dimension', (Edited by J. Kahn and S. B. Kammerman), In *Family Policy*, Columbia University Press, New York.

LASCH, Christopher (1977) *Haven in a Heartless World*, Basic Bks., New York.

LAZONICK, William H. (1976) 'Historical Origins of the Sex-Based Division of Labour under Capitalism: A Study of the British Textile Industry during the Industrial Revolution', Discussion Paper #479, Harvard Institute of Economic Research, Boston.

LERNER, Gerda (1960) 'New Approaches to the Study of Women in American History', *Journal of Social History* 3 (Fall), pp. 5–14.

LERNER, Gerda (1976) 'Placing Women in History', (Edited by Berenice Carroll), In *Liberating Women's History*, University of Illinois Press, Urbana.

LEWENHAK, Sheila (1977) *Women and Trade Unions: An Outline History of Women in the British Union Movement*, E. Benn, London.

LITOFF, Barbara (1978) *The American Midwives 1860 to the Present*, Greenwood Press, Westport, Conn.

McBRIDE, Theresa (1976) *The Domestic Revolution, 1820–1920*, Croom Helm, London.

McINTOSH, Mary, (1978) 'The State and the Oppression of Women', (Edited by Annette Kuhn and Ann Marie Wolp), In *Feminism and Materialism*, Routledge and Kegan Paul, London.

MacKENZIE, Midge (Ed.) (1975) *Shoulder to Shoulder: A Documentary*, Allen Lane, London.

McLAREN, Angus (1977(a)) 'Abortion in England, 1890–1914', *Victorian Studies* XX (Summer), pp. 379–400.

McLAREN, Angus (1977(b)) 'Women's Work and the Regulation of Family Size', *History Workshop Journal* (Autumn), pp. 70–81.

McLAREN, Angus (1978) *Birth Control in Nineteenth-Century England*, Croom Helm, London.

MEACHAM, Standish (1977) *A Life Apart: The English Working Class, 1890–1914*, Thames and Hudson, London.

MECHLING, Jay (1975) Advice to Historians on Advice to Mothers', *Journal of Social History* 9 (Fall) pp. 44–63.

MIDDLETON, Lucy (Ed.) (1977) *Women in the Labour Movement*, Croom Helm, London.

MITCHELL, Juliet (1971) *Women's Estate*, Penguin, Middlesex.

MORANTZ, Regina (1974) 'The Lady and Her Physician', (Edited by Lois Banner and Mary Hartman), In *Clio's Consciousness Raised*, Harper, New York.

MORGAN, David (1975) *Suffragists and Liberals: The Politics of Woman Suffrage in England*, Rowman and Littlefield, New Jersey.

OAKLEY, Ann and Juliet MITCHELL (Eds.) (1976) *Rights and Wrongs of Women*, Penguin, Middlesex.

OREN, Linda (1974) 'The Welfare of Women in Labouring Families: England, 1860–1950'. (Edited by Lois Banner and Mart Hartman)In *Clio's Consciousness Raised*, Harper, New York.

OSTERUD, Nancy Grey (1978) 'Women's Work in Nineteenth Century Leicester: A Case Study in the Sexual

Division of Labour', Paper given at the 4th Berkshire Conference, Mount Holyoke, South Hadley, Mass (August).

PERKIN, Harold (1969) *The Origins of Modern English Society, 1780–1880,* Routledge and Kegan Paul, London.

PINCHBECK, Ivy (1930) *Women Workers and the Industrial Revolution,* Cass, London.

RAEBURN, Antonia (1976) *The Suffragette View,* St. Martin's Press, New York.

RATHBONE, Eleanor (1924) *The Disinherited Family,* Arnold, London.

RAPP, Rayna, Ellen ROSS and Renate BRIDENTHAL (1979) 'Examining Family History', *Feminist Studies* 5 (Spring), pp. 174–200.

ROBERTS, Elizabeth (1977) 'Working Class Women in the North West', *Oral History* 5 (Autumn) pp. 7–30.

ROBINSON, Joe (1975) *The Life and Times of Francie Nichol of South Shields,* Allen and Unwin, London.

ROSALDO, Michelle Zimbalist (1974) 'Woman Culture and Society: A theoretical Overview', (Edited by Michelle Zimbalist Rosaldo and Louise Lamphere), In *Women Culture and Society,* Stanford U.P., Stanford.

ROSEN, Andrew (1974) *Rise Up Women! The Militant Campaign of the Women's Social and Political Union, 1903–1914,* Routledge and Kegan Paul, London.

ROSSI, Alice S. (1973) 'Feminist History in Perspective: Sociological Contributions to Biographic Analysis', (Edited by Dorothy Gies McGuigan), In *A Sampler of Women's Studies,* Michigan: University of Michigan Press, Ann Arbor.

ROWBOTHAM, Sheila (1973) *Hidden from History,* Pluto, London.

SCANNELL, Dorothy (1974) *An East End Childhood,* MacMillan, London.

SHORTER, Edward (1975) *The Making of the Modern Family,* Basic Books, New York.

SMELSER, Neil (1959) *Social Change in the Industrial Revolution,* Chicago: Routledge and Kegan Paul, London.

SMITH, Daniel Scott (1974) 'Family Limitation, Sexual Control and Domestic Feminism in Victorian America', In *Clio's Consciousness Raised,* (Edited by Lois Banner and Mary Hartman), Harper, New York.

SMITH, Hilda (1976) 'Feminism and the Methodology of Women's History', (Edited by Berenice A. Carroll), In *Liberating Women's History,* University of Illinois Press, Urbana.

SMITH ROSENBERG, Carroll (1972) 'The Hysterical Woman: Sex Roles and Conflict in Nineteenth-Century America', *Social Research* 39, pp. 652–678.

SMITH ROSENBERG, Carroll and Charles ROSENBERG (1973(a)) 'The Female Animal: Medical and Biological Views of Woman and Her Role in Nineteenth Century America', *Journal of American History* 60 (September), pp. 332–356.

SMITH ROSENBERG, Carroll (1973(b)) 'Puberty to Menopause: The Cycle of Feminity in Nineteenth-Century America', *Feminist Studies* 1 (Winter-Spring), pp. 58–72.

SMITH ROSENBERG, Carroll (1975) 'The New Woman and the New History', *Feminist Studies* 3 (Fall), pp. 185–198.

STEARNS, Peter (1976) 'Coming of Age', *Journal of Social History* 10 (Winter), pp. 246–255.

STEARNS, Peter N. (1974) 'Working Class Women in Britain, 1890–1914', (Edited by Martha Vicinus), In *Suffer and Be Still,* Indiana U.P., Bloomington.

STENTON, Doris Mary (1957) *The English Woman in History,* George Allen and Unwin, London.

THOMPSON, Dorothy (1971) *The Early Chartists,* MacMillan, London.

THOMPSON, Paul (1975) *The Edwardians,* Indiana U.P., Bloomington, Indiana.

TILLY, Louis and Joan SCOTT (1975) 'Women's Work and the Family in Nineteenth Century Europe', *Comparative Studies in Society and History* 17 (January) pp. 36–64.

VANN, Richard T. (1974) 'Towards a Periodization of Women's History', Paper given at the 2nd Berkshire Conference, Radcliffe.

VERBRUGGE, Martha (1976) 'Women and Medicine in Nineteenth-Century America', *Signs* 1 (Summer) pp. 957–972.

WEBB, R. K. (1974) *Modern England,* Dodd, Mead and Co., New York.

WERTZ, D. C. and R. W. WERTZ (1977) *Lying-In: A History of Childbirth in America,* Free Press, New York.

WOOD, Ann Douglas (1974) 'The Fashionable Diseases: Women's Complaints and their Treatment in Nineteenth-Century America', (Edited by Lois Banner and Mary Hartman), In *Clio's Consciousness Raised,* Harper, New York.

ZEMON-DAVIS, Natalie (1976) 'Women's History in Transition: The European Case', *Feminist Studies* 3 (Spring-Summer), pp. 83–103.

5

Some of the Boys Won't Play Any More: The Impact of Feminism on Sociology

HELEN ROBERTS

While contributors asked to assess the impact of feminism on such disciplines as medicine, physics or theology might find themselves writing rather a short chapter, there can be no doubt that although the impact of feminism on sociology has not been as significant so far as some might hope, it has been all too significant for others.

The last ten years have seen considerable change both within the organisation of the discipline and within the structure of the profession and to a very large extent, these changes have been a direct or indirect result of an increased level of awareness brought about through the women's movement.

Given the subject matter of sociology and its concern with social structure and social change, given a significant interest in the discipline in the sociology of social movements, and given that a majority (and in some universities and colleges a substantial majority) of sociology undergraduates are women, the resurgence of the women's movement in the late sixties could not be ignored by sociologists, or as Professor Sheila Allen pointed out on reading a first draft of this chapter, could not be ignored for ever. Of course, it might well have been ignored for a little longer had there not been, despite the normal barriers, a certain number of practising women sociologists in the late sixties in positions of relative power who were willing to use their influence on behalf of other women.

In this chapter, I will be describing some of the historical antecedents of the more recent impact of feminism on sociology, developments within the subject matter of the discipline, and changes in social relations within the profession. It is undoubtedly the case that to a very large extent the increased awareness of the importance of sexual divisions in sociology owes an enormous debt to ideas stemming from the women's movement, but one would be doing a serious injustice to certain women scholars if one were to date all significant developments in this area as being post second wave feminism (i.e., late 1960's onwards). While sexism as such might yet have been unnamed, there were those who realised that the raw conflicts between home and work were not a purely personal concern, but had enormous social structural ramifications. At a time when Bowlby's views on maternal deprivation were at their height, women sociologists were writing on women's two roles (Myrdal and Klein, 1954). At a time when studies of the working class meant studies of working class men, Margaret Hewitt (1958) was writing on wives and mothers in Victorian industry. Even earlier, Jephcott (1949) had written on *Girls Growing Up* and Margery Spring Rice's *Working Class Wives* (1939) remains a classic. The differentiated pay of women was well documented before the second world war, and there were also women doing early important work in social administration, which was not at the time clearly differentiated from sociology in terms of university departments.

We might, of course, wish to take issue with some of the earlier approaches, and Veronica Beechey (1978) has done so, on the grounds, among others, of the optimism of studies such as those of Myrdal and Klein. But whatever their shortcomings (and those of us judging the work now have an enormous historical advantage) they played a very significant part in providing a basis for work that was to come later. And however isolated feminist sociologists may feel within the discipline now, those working before the rise of the current women's movement must have been isolated to a much greater extent.

Apart from a very few studies, then, women were notable in British sociology up until the last few years mainly by their absence, except in one important respect. Just as even medicine cannot exclude a consideration of women from the study of obstetrics and gynaecology, there was one area of social institutions from which women could not be excluded, and this was the area where virtually all sociological studies of women were focussed — the sociology of the family. Of course, there were exceptions or partial exceptions.

In the field of community studies, Frankenberg (1957, 1966), Littlejohn (1963) and Stacey (1960) all discussed the status of women, and while it was largely in relation to the family, they also looked at the implications the family role had on the social interaction of women in the wider society.[1] But on the whole, the family was all-subsuming. When men and work were being discussed, it would be within the context of industrial sociology. On the rare occasions when studies were made of women's work outside the home, it would invariably be within the context of the effect of their work on the family. As Oakley (1974) has pointed out, the sociology of ithe family is one of the few areas where the visibility of women is extraordinarily high; and one might add that that of men is extraordinarily low. This is not, of course, unrelated to the 'real' world. The British Sociological Association's working party on the status of women in the profession (BSA 1975) in a survey of male and female sociologists found that 26 of the 148 women, but none of the 179 male respondents to their questionnaire commented on professional difficulties arising from having children. For some women, their status as mothers had presented problems in getting in to study sociology: 'At 28, I had an insulting interview to get into x to read sociology. I was told that 'having spent five years at the kitchen sink with two children' I would find it hard to study. The suggestion was made at that interview that I do a course in flower arrangement. I was also told that 'You won't be able to use your children as an excuse for not keeping up'.' In other cases, job interviews when the candidate was female elicited concern about child-care from the interviewers: 'At every interview, I am asked what provision *I* shall make for *my* children. This is never asked of my husband' (BSA 1975). Perhaps it should be of some comfort to us that only a few years later, such comments are a good deal rarer. Whether this is due to lobbying and pressure within the profession, the effects of the Sex Discrimination Act, or due to an increased level of cunning among the interviewers rendering such a crude approach unnecessary is a matter for speculation. The above merely serve as examples of the very acute relationship between social relations within

[1]Frankenberg discusses the lack of a perspective on sexual divisions in his own and others' work on community studies in his article 'In the Production of their lives, men (?) . . . : Sex and gender in British Community Studies' (Barker and Allen, 1976a).

the profession and the structure of knowledge within the discipline. Others have pointed to a similar problem in medicine. Until recently, the sociology and psychology taught to medical undergraduates was pitifully inadequate, but even so, few young doctors emerged without some knowledge of Bowlby's views on maternal deprivation, a view which cannot have been insignificant in the subsequent home and career plans of the female medical graduate.

The problems which feminists face in sociology however, are not ones which deal only with the visibility or invisibility of women. As David Morgan (1981) has pointed out: '... sexism is as much to do with the ways in which taken-for-granted notions of 'men' and 'masculinity' are handled in sociological enquiry, notions which are most frequently manifested in absences and silences, as it is with the way women are ignored or stereotyped in such work'.

If, however, we were to look at the problem only within the context of the visibility or otherwise of women (or men) in sociology, then the content of sociology could very probably be put right, and one could adjust the balance in terms of gender by a certain amount of resourcefulness, hard work and historical raking over. To a very large extent, this has been and is being done, and in this context, one cannot underestimate the contributions made by postgraduate students choosing to write their theses in the area of gender differentiation and social structure, thus rendering women's history and participation in social institutions more visible.

There are probably students and academics producing work influenced by the impact of feminism in all the mainstream areas of sociology. In the sociology of education for instance, Jenny Shaw is working on sex segregated education and girls and absenteeism. Kathy Clarricoates on sexism in the primary school and Ann Marie Wolpe on education and the sexual division of labour (see for instance, Shaw, 1976; Clarricoates, 1980; Wolpe, 1978)

In the sociology of health and illness, Ann Oakley (1979, 1980) and Hilary Graham (1977) have produced important work on childbirth and Lesley Doyal and Imogen Pennell (1979) have carefully analysed the particular situation of women in their *Political Economy of Health.* Carol Smart (1976, 1978) is producing work on deviance, Sheila Allen on work and race (1977; 1980) and Margaret Stacey and Marion Price (1979) on power. But as Ann Oakley (1974) has pointed out: 'Male orientation may so colour the organisation of sociology as a discipline, that the invisibility of women is a structural weakness, rather than simply a superficial flaw'. Women can be 'put back' into sociology, and to a certain extent, our view of what constitutes valid sociological knowledge can be reconstituted to take account of new work on gender differentiation and social structure, but how far will this affect the mainstream theoretical and methodological basis of the subject? The core of the discipline, and the high status areas of study have been theoretical and methodological issues, largely based around analyses of power, class, conflict, and the problem of order. There is nothing about the concepts as such, of course, which excludes either women or a feminist analysis. Indeed, one could well see the issue of gender differentiation as being crucial to these areas, but traditionally, studies of sexual divisions have been accorded somewhat low status and certainly seen as peripheral to the central concerns of the subject. Part of the problem, as Oakley (1974) has pointed out, lies in the foundations of the discipline. For good historical reasons (by which, of course, one means bad historical reasons), the founding fathers of sociology *are* founding fathers and not founding mothers. The ideas of Marx,

Weber, Spencer and Durkheim provided the bedrock of the discipline, and these continue to have an important influence, a factor which provides us with some basis for understanding the fact that in a subject purporting to be concerned with social structure and social relations, an enormous amount of emphasis has been given to those areas from which women have normally been excluded.

Particularly significant is the lack of serious analysis of women in terms of social class within the sociological framework. Certainly within the British tradition, studies of social class have a central place in sociological theory, and many a long hour has been spent by sociologists in devising increasingly sophisticated indices for social class allocation. Not only are class analyses central to British sociology, but a good deal of work in social policy is also related to class. I have described elsewhere (Roberts, 1979) the breathtaking sexism of the instructions given to interviewers working for the Office of Population Censuses and Surveys where interviewers are advised: 'So long as the husband is resident he takes precedence over the wife in being HOH (head of household). This means that if you have a married couple living together, even if the wife owns the property, or has her name on the rent book, you count her husband as the HOH' (Atkinson, 1971).

Sociologists however, can hardly be expected to take the blame for the worst excesses of categories used by the OPCS, and indeed, sociologists inside and outside OPCS are pressing for change. What sociologists do have to look at carefully are the categories used in their own analyses.

Some sociologists refuse to recognise that there is a problem, arguing that the family is the primary unit of stratification, and that the position of the woman is subsumed within this. Such an argument poses problems for those with even the most rudimentary sociological training. Even at a very basic level, this creates problems in looking at those women who do not live in families, problems which some sociologists have overcome by looking at the occupations of the fathers of unmarried women, the ex-husbands of divorced or separated women and the deceased husbands of widows. At the level of family income and standard of living, the inadequacy of looking at class through the occupation of the male 'head of household' when there is more than one income is clear.

In spite of this, and in spite of the fact that in those studies where the class position of women has been looked at, such as work on the educational achievement of children (Douglas, 1964) it has been shown to be crucial, the social class position of women has consistently been ignored in the very important studies on class and mobility which have been undertaken by British sociologists. The recent and massively funded Nuffield mobility study is an appalling example of the willingness of funding agencies to continue to fund research where a lack of analysis in terms of gender is seen as unproblematic. In a review of one of the books arising from this study (Halsey *et al.*, 1980) Blackstone (1980) highlights the significance of the fact that the survey (of 10,000) was confined to men. ' ... it means that the next major mobility survey in 10 or 15 years time, which will surely include women, will not be able to make any comparisons with the findings of this study as far as half the population is concerned. Since one of the most important social changes of the last decade has concerned the educational and occupational advance of women ... this is a great pity' (Blackstone is clearly a mistress of understatement). Of course, there are enormous methodological problems in looking at women and class in terms of women's own occupations, but as Gouldner (1971) has pointed out, 'the use of particular methods of study implies the existence of particular assumptions about man' (sic) 'and society'. The work of competent sociologists is surely to examine and analyse these assumptions rather than reinforce them, and such an analysis was in fact, attempted by two of the women workers on the Nuffield mobility study (Llewellyn and Graham, 1981).

With problems of sexism in both the theory and methods of the subject, it is hardly surprising that much of the basic literature leaves something to be desired. It is not without significance that an introductory booklet for the social sciences produced by the BBC in 1969 was entitled *Man in Society*, that many sociology courses in the late sixties and early seventies had similar titles, and that courses on the sociology of work meant men's work, and preferably the work of working class men in the factory. If we turn to a popular undergraduate textbook, *The Sociology of Modern Britain* (Butterworth and Weir, 1976), we may have some indication of what is happening at the basic level of sociology teaching. The book is split into seven sections, each dealing with an issue of major concern within sociology. The sections deal with the family, the community, socialisation, work, class, power and values. Women and gender relations are well-represented in the section on the family, and indeed, part of this section is devoted to an extract from Ann Oakley's work on sex roles in western society. The section on community has only one reference to women, in an extract from Margaret Stacey's work. Gender differentiation is fairly well-represented in the section on socialisation, and indeed, one article in this section looks at unequal access in education in terms of sex and class. Interestingly, women do not get a mention in the sections on work and class, and one can detect a rather 'macho' emphasis in the work section, which deals with issues dear to the heart of the radical male sociologist. 'Dock work', 'On the shop floor', 'Social relations in the mining industry' and 'A night at the dogs' all provide a good read with valuable insights into work and leisure habits, but they are quite extraordinarily partial in the section of the community they chose to examine.

In the section on power, women are referred to only in the most superficial way (for instance in terms of the number of women MP's), although in an article on class and party divisions, Richard Rose has a little more to say. Rose delineates thirteen hypotheses to explain party preference, one of which is 'working class men are more likely to vote labour than working class women'. Although he goes on to say that when one controls for age 'sex is of limited theoretical interest' this does not prevent him from throwing in the odd red herring that: 'In support of this hypothesis, one could advance a 'depth psychology' argument that Labour was a more 'masculine' party, or a simple sociological assertion that first hand experience of the work situation is more likely to increase class oriented voting than is the situation of a housewife' (Butterworth and Weir, 1976, p. 383). Clearly, what Rose means by a 'work situation' is a 'paid employment outside the home situation'. The gratuitous reference to the 'depth psychology' argument (sic) that Labour is a more 'masculine' party reflects certain taken-for-granted assumptions about the nature of gender, which one might expect a social scientist to be questioning rather than describing.

The final section is on values, and includes an excerpt from Juliet Mitchell's work on the position of women, but disappointingly, other chapters on inequality in this section tend to see inequality only in class terms.

In a very real sense, the content of the book bears out an observation made by one of the contributors, Ann Oakley. 'Even when there is change', she writes, 'people often hold to traditional ways of thinking and behaving' (Butterworth and Weir, 1976, p. 73). What we see from this textbook is that although women and gender differentiation can no longer be ignored in studies of social structure, there is frequently a lack of imagination about the contexts within which such studies may be seen as appropriate.

But in focussing on the areas which still leave something to be desired as far as a feminist analysis or even the inclusion of women is concerned, one would not want to paint too pessimistic a picture. There is a large and growing feminist literature in sociology, some of it very much within the mainstream of theoretical and methodological debate. The two volumes arising from the British Sociological Association's 1974 conference on Sexual Divisions in Society (Barker and Allen, 1976(a), 1976(b)) were influential and provided much of the reading matter in early women's studies courses in sociology departments. Many of the insights in these articles have since been re-worked or taken further.

The domestic labour debate, in which the main protagonists have been sociologists, has been influential in a rather different way. In pinpointing a serious omission in materialist analyses (i.e., that of unpaid labour by women within the home) crucial questions about the material basis of women's oppression have had to be asked (if not yet answered). Such impact as feminism has had on sociology has been very closely related to the individual and group efforts of women working in the profession and refusing to accept a perspective which they know is partial and unsociological. Arlene Daniels (1975) in advocating a feminist perspective refers to Dorothy Smith (1974) who, she says, 'underscores the basic limitations of a sociological discipline where women's place is subordinate, ignored, invisible. Women appear only as they are relevant to a world governed by male principles and interests. To the extent that women sociologists accept that perspective, they are alienated from their own personal experience. They speak a language, use theories, and select methods in which they are excluded or ignored'.

One of the ways in which advances have been made is through the organisation of women within the profession. In 1975 when the Working Party of the Status of Women in the Profession reported to the British Sociological Association, out of the 14 members who sat on the BSA executive committee, there had never been more than three women at any one time. And in March 1975, there had only been two women officers since the foundation of the BSA. Barbara Wootton was president from 1959–1964 and Margaret Stacey was Honorary General Secretary from 1968–1970. Since 1975, we have had another woman President, Sheila Allen, and Margaret Stacey has served a term as chairperson. In 1980, of an executive committee of 15 members, 7 are women. There is a standing committee on Sex Equality in the Profession arising from the working parties on sex gender and the status of women in the profession, and a study group on Sexual Divisions in Society. Representations have been made by the Association to the Social Science Research Council concerning the low representation of women on the Sociology and Social Administration Committee of that Council, and while Margaret Stacey was chairperson, a document was issued to all BSA members responsible for running BSA activities reminding them that 'It is the policy of the British Sociological Association actively to promote the equality of the sexes. To this end all members who are involved in appointing committees or personnel to run, teach or talk at seminars, conferences, summer schools and the like, are asked to ensure as far as they are able that women and men are equally represented on all such bodies and in all capacities.' On a more informal level, a women's caucus, set up at the 1974 BSA annual conference, which was on Sexual Divisions in Society, operates as a pressure group within the profession.[2] If such issues appear to the outsider as 'mere' professionalism, and rather remote from the concerns of the feminist in the street, it is perhaps significant to point out that the idea for the Women's Research and Resources Centre was first mooted at a BSA Sexual Divisions in Society study group meeting, and sociologists were among those active in its inception and subsequent development.

The past ten years then, have seen significant developments, both within the way in which knowledge is organised within sociology, and in the organisation of social relations within the profession. Many sociology departments run a Women in Society or Sexual Divisions course as part of their degrees, but whether this leads to the ghettoisation of work concerning women in these areas and a sigh of relief all round from male colleagues who do not feel the pressure to look at gender differentiation within their own areas, is open to question. The rampant and crude sexism one might have found ten years ago would not now escape comment in most departments. Books dealing with gender differentiation and social structure are much more readily available, and professional as well as women's studies journals appear more willing to accept articles written from a feminist perspective. There are areas, however, where one remains pessimistic. The *British Journal of Sociology* for winter 1979 ran a special issue on stratification which ignored the whole issue of gender and stratification, for instance, and the distribution of research funds by the Equal Opportunities Commission and the Social Science Research Council on 'Women and Under-Achievement' (surely an unfortunate choice of title) does not give one enormous cause for optimism. By far the largest contract awarded in the year ending April 1979, went to A. McIntosh and Miss J. Lovell of Industrial Facts and Forecasting Ltd., with £51,550 over 8 months to look at women and underachievement in employment: a sample survey of employers. Much smaller sums went on the application of maternity provision (£8072 over 2 years at Nene College, Northampton) and the situation of women who return to work (£6964 over 1 year 3 months at Sunderland Polytechnic) (SSRC newsletter, November 1979). Clearly, in the sense of obtaining large sums of grant money, women are indeed 'under-achievers'.

Notwithstanding this, there is a very real sense in which the impact of feminism on sociology has led to important insights in our understanding of the importance of sexual divisions in society and it is now unlikely that any sociology student will graduate without having at least some understanding of sexual divisions. The Chairman of the British Sociological Association is now a chairperson, and the iron grip of the old boy network in the profession has slackened somewhat (although one cannot help wondering whether the drop in membership of the senior male professoriat in the BSA is a sign of some of the old boys taking their bats home in protest). Whilst it can be argued that some of these changes are superficial, that they do not touch the core of the discipline, that women sociologists are merely being accommodated or even co-opted, the weight of the evidence supports a cautious optimism. The changes which have taken place, relatively rapidly by standards of social change within an academic discipline, have been real ones. A good deal more careful theoretical work needs to be

[2]This article is based on the experience of sociology in Great Britain. In the United States, *Sociologists for Women in Society* is an important and influential pressure group, performing much the same roles as a combination of the Sociology Women's Caucus and the Sexual Divisions Study Group in this country.

done, and since theory does not drop from the skies, in the sense that some seem to imagine, a good deal more empirical work too. Perhaps one of the strengths of developments of feminist analyses within sociology has been the active participation of many feminist sociologists within the women's movement.

In other words, the current of ideas has not been one way and does have a firm social base. In that sense, it is unlikely that feminism will be a transitory phenomenon in the discipline and indeed one has some reason to hope that the influence of feminist analyses will come to be taken more seriously and feminist ideas within sociology seen as a valid area for important theoretical work.

I am grateful to Sheila Allen, Rodney Barker, Dale Spender, Margaret Stacey and Diana Woodward for comments on a first draft of this chapter.

References

ATKINSON, Jean (1971) *A Handbook for Interviewers* (Produced for OPCS Survey Division) London.

ALLEN, Sheila (1980) 'Perhaps a Seventh Person', In *Women's Studies International Quarterly* Vol. III, No. 4.

BARKER, D. L. and S. ALLEN, (Eds.) (1976(a)) *Sexual Divisions and Society: Process and Change,* Tavistock, London.

BARKER, D. L. and S. ALLEN (Eds.) (1976(b)) *Dependence and Exploitation in Work and Marriage,* Longman, London.

BEECHEY, Veronica (1978) 'Women and Production: A Critical Analysis of Some Sociological Theories of Women's Work', (Annette Kuhn and Ann Marie Wolpe (Eds.)) In *Feminism and Materialism* Routledge and Kegan Paul, London.

BLACKSTONE, T. (1980) 'Falling short of Meritocracy', *Times Higher Educational Supplement,* January 18.

BRITISH SOCIOLOGICAL ASSOCIATION (1975) Unpublished Report on the Status of Women in the Profession.

BUTTERWORTH E. and D. WEIR (Eds.) (1970) (Revised 1976) *The Sociology of Modern Britain,* Fontana, London.

CLARRICOATES, Kathy (1980) Contribution in Rosemary Deem (Ed.) *Schooling for Women's Work* Routledge and Kegan Paul, London, and 'All in a day's work' In Dale Spender & Elizabeth Sarah (Eds.) *Learning to Lose: Sexism and Education,* The Women's Press, London.

DANIELS, Arlene (1975) 'Feminist Perspectives in Sociological Research', In Marcia Millman and Rosabeth Moss Kanter (Eds.) *Another Voice,* Anchor, New York.

DOUGLAS, J.W.B. (1964) *The Home and the School,* Penguin, London.

DOYAL, L. with Imogen PENNELL (1979) *The Political Economy of Health,* Pluto, London.

FRANKENBERG, R. (1957) *Village on the Border,* Cohen and West. London.

FRANKENBERG, R. (1966) *Communities in Britain,* Penguin, London.

GOULDNER, Alvin (1971) *The Coming Crisis of Western Sociology,* Heineman Educational Books, London.

GRAHAM, Hilary (1977) 'Women's Attitudes to Conception and Pregnancy', In R. Chester and J. Peel (Eds.) *Equalities and Inequalities in Family Life,* Academic Press, London and New York.

HALSEY, A. H., A. F. HEATH, and J. M. RIDGE (198) *Origins and Destinations: Family class and education in modern Britain,* Oxford University Press.

HEWITT, M. (1958) *Wives and Mothers in Victorian Industry,* Rockliff, London.

HIMMELWEIT, H. and D. SIMMONS (1969) *Man in Society,* B.B.C. publications, London.

JEPHCOTT, Pearl (1949) *Girls Growing Up,* Faber & Faber, London.

LITTLEJOHN, J. (1963) *Westrigg: The Sociology of a Cheviot Parish.* Routledge and Kegan Paul, London.

LLEWELLYN, C. and S. GRAHAM (1981) 'Women in the Occupational Structure: A Case Study of Banking', In H. Roberts (Ed.) *Doing Feminist Research,* Routledge and Kegan Paul, London.

MORGAN, David (in press) 'Men, Masculinity and the Process of Sociological Enquiry', In H. Roberts (Ed.) *ibid.*

MYRDAL, A. and V. KLEIN, (1956) *Women's Two Roles,* Routledge and Kegan Paul, London.

OAKLEY, Ann (1974) *The Sociology of Housework,* Martin Robertson, London.

OAKLEY, Ann (1979) *Becoming a Mother,* Martin Robertson, London.

OAKLEY, Ann (1980) *Women Confined: Towards a Sociology of Childbirth,* Martin Robertson, London.

ROBERTS, Helen (1979) 'Women, Social Class and I.U.D. Use', *Women's Studies International Quarterly* Vol. 1, 1979, pp. 492–56.

ROBERTS, Helen (Ed.) (in press) *Doing Feminist Research,* Routledge and Kegan Paul.

SHAW, Jenny (1976) 'Sex segregated education', In Barker and Allen, 1976a.

SMART, Carol (1976) *Women, Crime and Criminology,* Routledge and Kegan Paul, London.

SMART, C. and B. SMART (Eds.) (1978) *Women Sexuality and Social Control,* Routledge and Kegan Paul, London.

SMITH, Dorothy (1974) 'Women's Perspective as a Radical Critique of Sociology', In *Sociological Enquiry* 44 (1) pp. 7–13.

SPRING RICE, Margery (1939) *Working Class Wives,* Penguin, London.

STACEY, M. (1960) *Tradition and Change: A Study of Banbury,* Oxford University Press.

STACEY, Margaret and Marion PRICE, (1979) 'The law is not enough: The continued oppression of women', Paper presented at the British Sociological Association Conference, University of Warwick.

WOLPE, A. (1978) 'Education and the sexual division of labour', In A. Kuhn and A. M. Wolpe (Eds.), *Feminism and Materialism,* Routledge and Kegan Paul, London.

6

Toward the Emasculation of Political Science: The Impact of Feminism

JONI LOVENDUSKI

The arguments which follow are centred on two related contentions. These are: firstly, that mainstream Political Science itself is not what it ought to be or what it could be or even what it used to be; and secondly, that so long as feminist political science continues to situate itself within this mainstream it will fail to realise its potential.

No-one would deny that the long-standing dissociation of political scientists from the female half of the population has distorted the discipline. But this failure is, I would argue, best regarded as one of many symptoms of a fundamental failure by the vast majority of Political Scientists to come to terms with our object of study. It need not have been this way. Political Science has a thoroughly honourable history. It has been multi-disciplinary in construction, modest in its assumptions, wide-ranging in its pre-occupations and radical in its outlook. These origins should have led to a relatively untroubled union between a developed and confident Political Science on the one hand, and a radical, innovative Feminist Scholarship on the other. Instead, in what is one of the minor tragedies of contemporary scholarship, an absorption of a rather constrained branch of women's studies by a one-dimensional academic discipline has taken place.

Determining the causes of such an unnecessary and unfortunate development is far from simple and it is probably impossible to supply a complete explanation. It is possible, however, to identify a number of key elements in the process. Post World War Two developments in the study of politics have combined to produce a dominant form of Political Science which has lost touch with the resources inherent in its manifold origins. Whilst techniques are still regularly borrowed from cognate disciplines, related theoretical developments are not scrutinised. Additionally, there has been a growing American dominance of the discipline of Political Science. In contrast to a greater European concern with moral philosophy, the American study of politics has stressed

> '... instruments and practices of popular government. It (is) an applied discipline, an exercise in pragmatism ...' (Apter, 1977: 16).

Indeed, the American Political Science Association was founded in 1904 largely as a way to collect facts. It was Americans

> 'more than any other, ... (who) ... made Political Science into a practical discipline and the preferred style was always empirical' (Apter, 1977: 29).

And today Americans dominate the discipline in terms of numbers: 70% (McKenzie, 1970), 28,000 of 30,000 (Apter, 1977), in terms of output, and in terms of access to funding (McKenzie, 1967). The impact of this quantitative dominance becomes a qualitative one when it is remembered that the study of politics is not simply an intellectual pre-occupation, it is also a profession with a coherent hierarchical structure within which dominance by a particular kind of scholarship is likely to lead to increasing dominance by that kind of scholarship. Finally, these developments have been combined with a general erosion of the traditional integration of applied politics specialists and the more explicitly normative political philosophers and theorists.

It is these three developments which have, in my view, been crucial in both impeding the development of a Feminist Political Science and in limiting the effect of feminist scholarship, or indeed, of any theoretically demanding and radical scholarship, on the manner in which politics is normally studied. These assertions are central to the arguments of this chapter and they determine the structure of the essay which follows. Thus the first section of this essay will cover a brief and admittedly somewhat simplified examination of how an originally fruitful internal tension[1] amongst professional students of politics has resulted in the ossification of the discipline. This will be followed by an outline of the sexist biases in Political Science practice and such modifications as have ensued in response to feminist criticism. Finally, attention will be given to the potential feminist challenge to the manner in which Political Science has constructed its object and some concluding comments on the likely impact of this challenge will be offered.

The Construction of the Study of Politics:
The Emergence of a Positivist[2] Discipline

Political Science is said to have properly begun with Aristotle's investigation of some 158 Constitutions in a search for the 'best' method of government (Aristotle, 1962). In his study of *The Politics*, the moral philosopher's pursuit of the good society was combined with the applied researcher's investigation of extant and recorded political arrangements. Origins such as these involve both normative preoccupations and a commitment to objective description, a dualism which has continued to be a feature of the study of politics. Until recently this dualism had never taken the form of a simple bi-polarity, rather there existed an uneasy synthesis in which vulnerability to criticism was balanced by an ability to absorb the content of the critique. The argument here is a straightforward one: the object of study, politics, has an active element, and is in fact epiphenomenal — it cannot exist independently of social and economic forces. Thus, so long as society and economy continue to alter, politics will alter. It follows therefore that the Political Science of each generation will develop in response to events in the political arena, and the location of the political arena itself will vary with changing definitions of what is political. Until recently this has been largely a process of expansion. The concerns of Political Science have tended to increase exponentially and theoretical reflection at each stage has been unable to encompass all of what has gone before. Hence, divided as we are, Political Scientists have long experienced difficulty in

[1]A particularly lucid discussion of this tension is to be found in J. Blondel (1976), *Thinking Politically*, Penguin.
[2]'Positivist' and 'Positivism' are used throughout this essay as terms referring to the so-called 'scientific' strands of empiricism.

producing a comprehensive definition of our subject. Efforts by the most eminent practitioners to produce such a definition (Apter, 1977; Blondel, 1976; McKenzie, 1970; Easton, 1965a, 1965b, 1968) have had to take into account not only the changes in the object of study, but also the duality of the subject and have thus had some difficulty in locating Political Science squarely in the social sciences. It has been argued that a case might be made for its status as a bridge between the humanities and the social sciences, (McKenzie, 1970) the reasoning being that the study of politics is as much an art based on scholars' intuitions and abilities as it is a science based on the skills of established methods of enquiry. The existence of these two characteristics has been responsible for friction within the discipline which has caused divisions between both the different schools and the different generations of specialists. This has been exacerbated by two important post-war developments: the growth and eventual dominance of the applied side of the subject and increasing specialisation which has cut Political Science off from the humanities and the other social sciences. The connectedness of the two parts of Political Science has inevitably been eroded at the same time as routes via which possible reconnecting theoretical innovations could enter have been blocked. Nevertheless, the traditional duality continues to be present, albeit in a less fruitful form and Political Science remains without a generally agreed definition, which is acceptable to all of the profession. The boundaries of the range of proper objects of study are more or less permanently in dispute and scholars have found it impossible to outline a single distinctive, unifying epistemological basis.

Critics of contemporary Political Science (usually sociologists) suggest that it is at best a form of enlightened journalism which fails to achieve its very modest aims. Such critics would also hold that a strong normative element has meshed with a pseudo-scientific attempt at objectivity which has tended to make the academic study of politics status quo orientated and uncritically reflective of prevailing belief systems. Whilst these sallies may sometimes be richly deserved, they fail to take account of the vast range of the subject. Although the 'Science' in the appellation may be limiting, the 'Political' is a clear invitation to expansion. Failure on the part of many students of politics to take up this invitation has been of crucial significance to feminist scholarship as this academic and intellectual self-limitation has, as much as conscious and subconscious sexism, impeded the emergence of a Feminist Political Science.

The absence of a commonly agreed definition of Political Science obviously poses certain problems for a critique of this nature. After all, one needs to be able to recognise the object of criticism. There is, however, clear evidence that identification difficulties are surmountable. There are, in most nations, institutions which employ persons (normally men) as Political Scientists. Indeed, outside of the U.S.A. there are very few ways in which it is possible to be a Political Scientist if one is not a member of a research or educational institution of some kind. These Political Scientists have managed to arrange themselves into the normally accepted educational hierarchies, to form national and international associations, to publish academic journals, to write scholarly articles, books and papers, to transmit a common body of agreed knowledge to undergraduates and graduate students, to generate proposals and receive funding for research. They may be observed meeting regularly at national and international conferences, conventions and seminars to discuss their work. Even if this entire edifice were the result of a monumental confidence trick, it would still be necessary for co-conspirators to know how to identify each other and to select recruits to continue the conspiracy into future generations. The crucial point here is that Political Science has become a profession with a recognised set of professional interests. The relative health and elaborate nature of the structure of this profession is an indication that the lack of a definition has not been particularly debilitating problem. Indeed, it might be argued that such a deficiency has been a positive advantage.

Clearly, Political Science is not without an agreed object and the lack of a definition as such may well arise from the polymorphous nature of politics itself. To the extent that there is an intellectual unity amongst political scientists it is to be found in an inchoate commonality of preoccupation with the component elements of political life. The locus of the commonality varies nationally and the process of defining the area of what is political has itself been a constituent preoccupation. Within the postulated commonality there has been a clear bi-furcation of approach which became subject to particular imbalance in the 1950's and early 1960's, the time of the subject's greatest growth.[3]

The argument which follows would normally be a complex one, developed via a painstaking exposition of the major works of influential proponents of the two main types of approaches which have been present in the development of Political Science. Space constraints do not allow this here and documentation is in any case available elsewhere.[4] Hence, the exposition which follows is limited to the arguments of two widely cited and talented representative scholars of the period whose work illustrates the two sides of the bi-furcation.

Making a case which underlines the interdisciplinary spirit and philosophical origins of the subject's development, Sheldon Wolin has argued that the process of defining the object of political study has been little different from that which has taken place in other fields of enquiry.

> 'No-one', he writes,
> ' ... would seriously contend ... that the fields of physics or chemistry have always existed in a self-evident determinate form waiting only to be discovered by a Galileo or Lavoisier ... ' (Wolin, 1961; 4).

Similarly, Political Science has been a product of the interplay of its practitioners rather than a set of truths or laws discovered by them. The field is, and always has been,

> ... ' a created one. The designation of certain activities and arrangements as political, the characteristic way that we think about them and the concepts we employ to communicate our observations and reactions — *none of these are written into the nature of things* but are ... (an accruing) ... legacy ... ' (Wolin, 1961: 5 my emphasis).

In other words, Political Science is a construct of Political Scientists. It is a convention.[5]

The other side of the bi-furcation is illustrated by David Easton who makes extremely strong claims for the potential of Political Science as objective, discoverable truth. Stressing its empirical preoccupations, Easton recognised the social construction of Political Science and the first section of his essay on the subject for the 1968 edition of

---

[3]This raises the interesting question of why such developments took place in that period of history. Discussion of this is beyond the scope of this essay but the author plans to take it up in a future article of the development of the Political Science profession.

[4]See works by McKenzie (1967, 1970), Apter (1977), Wolin (1961), Blondel (1976).

[5]I am grateful to Jean Hardy of the Department of Government, Brunel University for pointing out the relevance of this insight.

the *International Encyclopaedia of the Social Sciences*[6] is an account of the development of this construction. In Easton's very influential view.

> 'Two widely differing sets of criteria have emerged in the last hundred years or so, for differentiating political life from all other aspects of society and thereby for isolating the subject-matter of Political Science' (Easton, 1968: 283).

These two sets of criteria have been (1) institutional, which Easton caustically suggests has 'not very profoundly' defined government institutions or the state as proper objects of study; and (2) functional, which has concentrated on the study of power or decision-making, emphasising the active or behavioural dimension of politics. Easton's sympathies are clearly with proponents of the second set of criteria which he sees as having developed largely out of dissatisfaction with the first.[7]

However, political power and political decisions must still be distinguished from all other types of power and decisions, a problem which Easton reckons should be solved by applying the criteria generated by the use of the Eastonian model of the political system. Widespread acceptance of this model has been (he modestly asserts) the breakthrough which, combined with major advances in techniques of data collection and analysis, finally released Political Science 'from its *synthetic* past' (my emphasis) and thrust it forward into its more appropriate concern of discovering a theoretical consensus (Easton, 1968: 297). In effect, truth only awaited the diligence of Eastonian researchers for its discovery.

On the face of it, Easton and Wolin are often saying similar things. The divergence to be found in their perspectives is at root, an epistemological one. Whilst both recognise the social construction of Political Science, Wolin confronts and accepts this as a characteristic of any information which has the status of knowledge. Easton, on the other hand, regards this social construction as a passing phase, as the *synthetic* false start of a discipline which with the assistance of his insights, has finally been offered a route to truth.

As with division at other levels of understanding, epistemological duality is a perennial characteristic of Political Science. Unfortunately, critical appreciation of the implications of this is not characteristic. Whilst Wolin's philosophical study of the nature of political enquiry shows an acute sensitivity to the implications of his own epistemological predilictions, Easton appears to be unaware that he has any. Throughout a long period of positivist ascendency this rather important difference went largely unexamined within the discipline. Such an oversight becomes particularly striking when it is considered that neighbouring disciplines of Philosophy, Sociology, and Linguistics have regularly subjected their methodologies to fundamental criticism. Tragically, this oversight became critical failure for Political Science leading to a virtual termination of its classical marriage between moral philosophy and empirical research.

Easton and Wolin were writing in the ten-year period immediately before second-wave feminism had become politically visible, by which time Easton's views were representative of the mainstream preoccupations of the profession. Political Science,

---

[6]In terms of its claim for the utility of systems analysis and its views of the development of Political Science, the IESS essay is representative of the views expressed by Easton in his major works.

[7]Noteworthy here is Easton's de-facto exclusion of any philosophical components from his conceptualisation of Political Science.

particularly American Political Science, became more and more concerned with studying what politicians regarded as political (Apter, 1977: 28) with an increasing number of research efforts being Government commissioned. As Apter argues, the

> 'management of government business led political scientists to emphasise *pragmatic common sense* and search out alternatives that would work ... ' (1977: 29, my emphasis).

What this effectively meant was that

> 'After WWII ... political science professionals embraced the behavioural approach to the discipline ...' (Apter, 1977: 29).

and

> 'The once conventional political science curriculum-political theory, comparative government, public administration, constitutional law, international politics, state and local government — has been drastically altered. New titles: legislative behaviour, political modernization, political socialization, political psychology have moved to center stage' (Apter, 1977: 30).

Political Scientists such as Dahl (1956a, 1956b, 1963, 1971), Almond and Verba (1963), Davies (1964), Deutsch (1963), and Lipset (1960) produced regular studies of the various aspects of the disposal of or relations to public power by various institutions and groups of individuals. Although Easton's political systems model, and the variations on it developed by his contemporaries[8] has yet to deliver its promised theoretical unity, these types of initiatives traced the grid which was to be mapped out by today's generation of Political Scientists. It has been their work and the work of their students which has dominated the literature for a generation. Whilst few of these 'pioneers' were so immodest in their claims as Easton, their influence in defining the object, range and research priorities of Political Science is inescapable. Thus, in a very real sense, it has been the research methods and models of the first full post-war generation of professional Political Scientists with which Feminist Political Science has had to contend (see below). Instead of inheriting the eccentric, self-consciously constructed discipline of Wolin, Feminist Political Science has inherited the de-constructed version proselytised by Easton and other American positivists. That this was the case has a considerable effect on the directions taken in the new studies of women and politics and it is appropriate that our attention should now be turned to the emergence of these studies.

Sexist Bias in the Study of Politics

The framework acccepted for the study of politics during the late 1950's and early 1960's was clearly inadequate for a feminist, or indeed any other radical perspective. Whilst any radical critic of a socially constructed discipline must contend with the cultural biases such a construction contains; the dominance of Political Science by scholars who had not developed the habit of systematically engaging even rudimentary theories of knowledge compounded the problem enormously. There is, of course, no doubt that Political Science has been sexist. Not only did it exclude women from its

---

[8]For examples of these variations see the *Contemporary Political Theory* series edited by David Easton for Prentice-Hall, and the Little, Brown series in *Comparative Politics* edited by G. Almond, J. Coleman and L. Pye.

concerns, it also excluded them from membership in the profession (Converse and Converse, 1974; Lovenduski and Evans, 1979).

The complication here is that there never was any way that the modern study of politics could fail to be sexist. Its empirical concerns have been almost exclusively those of the exercise of public power, aspects of political elites and aspects of the institutions of government. Such studies are bound to exclude women, largely because women usually do not dispose of public power, belong to political elites or hold influential positions in government institutions. Nor, until fairly recently, have issues of concern to women exercised those who do dispose of public power, belong to political elites, or hold influential positions in government institutions. In an increasingly positivistic discipline, no-one thought to question this. The only enquiries in which political woman was scrutinised were empirical studies of the various components of political participation and, predictably these studies contained numerous examples of sexist bias.

Such examples have been well documented. Bourque and Grossholtz (1974) examined several widely used and cited texts[9] for the way in which data on the participation of women was handled and checked later material to see if Political Scientists had come to see the error of their ways. (They had not). They found four by no means mutually exclusive categories of distortion in common use.

The first, FUDGING THE FOOTNOTES, comprised

> 'those statements of female political characteristics, attitudes or behaviour which are not substantiated in the manual cited or in the source' (Bourque and Grossholtz, 1974: 229).

Such misuse of the data was normally a matter of removing the 'qualifications and careful language of the original study'. The second category, THE ASSUMPTION OF MALE DOMINANCE, comprised 'pervasive expectations about sex differences in politics', resulting in failure to question male preponderance in political office and leading to the assumption of male dominance in the family for evidence from which to draw conclusions about actual sex differences in politics. Bourque and Grossholtz's third category, the acceptance of MASCULINITY AS IDEAL POLITICAL BEHAVIOUR, exposes the use of

> 'unexplained and unexamined assumptions that those stereotyped characteristics held up as the masculine ideal (e.g. aggressiveness, competitiveness, pragmatism, etc.) are the norms of political behaviour as well' (1974: 229).

This distortion is most frequently found in discussions of explicit political behaviour (e.g. candidate preference, issue preference and saliency, etc.). The final category, COMMITMENT TO THE ETERNAL FEMININE, explains feminine political behaviour as a direct product of women's domestic role. Based on society's reliance upon the services of women in the social realm, the distortion involves

> 'an assumption that women's present weak political position is necessary and functional ...' (1974: 229).

[9]Including: Greenstein, *Children and Politics*, Yale 1965; Hess and Torney, *The Development of Political Attitudes of Children*, Aldine 1967; Dawson and Prewitt, *Political Socialisation*, Little, Brown and Co. 1969; Merriam and Gasnell, *Non-Voting: Causes and Methods of Control*, University of Chicago 1969; Campbell *et al.*, *The American Voter*, Wiley 1960; Almond and Verba, *The Civil Culture*, Princeton 1963; Robert Lane, *Political Life*, The Free Press 1959; Floyd Hunter, *Community Power Structure*, University of North Carolina 11953; R. Dahl, *Who Governs*, Yale 1961; R. Presthus, *Men at the Top*, 1964.

This results in the implication that the limited participation of women is to be tolerated in order to ensure that 'we have wives and mothers to preserve the race' (1974: 229).

Besides explicit sexist bias, the most striking feature of pre-feminist political science research on women has been how little of it there was. Although gender was normally a background variable in research involving social surveys and data on women was regularly collected, it was rare for a study to concern itself seriously with the political behaviour of women. The outstanding exception to this was the IPSA[10]/UNESCO study undertaken under the direction of Maurice Duverger in 1952 and 1953 and published in 1955 as *The Political Role of Women.* Working in somewhat debilitating conditions of time and money constraints, Duverger's team undertook a comparative investigation of the political behaviour of women in France, West Germany, Norway and Yugoslavia. The investigators aimed to cover the part played by women in elections and in political leadership. Initially, they experienced considerable difficulty in acquiring the necessary data, which Duverger attributed to a degree of disinterest due to the fact that

> 'The political scientists and most of the organisations invited to supply information often tended to regard its purpose as a secondary one, of no intrinsic importance. This ... was accompanied by ... the reserve shown, at the outset, by certain women's associations of importance ... ' (Duverger, 1955: 8).

These obstacles, combined with the above mentioned time and money constraints, meant that the data on which the report was based were often inadequate, a fact acknowledged by Duverger. Nevertheless, the study was an important one, not the least because it investigated feminine political behaviour during a period now regarded as a patriarchal apogee. Additionally, the research plan and report pretty well anticipated the range of questions which were to be raised by future research on women. Finally, many of Duverger's conclusions came, albeit indirectly, to constitute the assumptions about women and politics which are today being challenged by feminists.[11]

The report's analysis of election data indicated that there were more women than men non-voters, but that this difference was small and varied considerably by type of election, size of community, age group, occupational category and marital status. Duverger held that the variations indicated that such slight overall sex differences as could be detected were likely to be diminishing ones. The study indicated that actual voting differences between men and women were also small and revealed a strong tendency for husbands and wives to vote in the same way. The most important sex difference was seen to be a greater tendency on the part of women to vote for parties of the centre-right when that option was available. This difference was held to be important because conservative victories in elections immediately prior to the study had been gained at the margins and and therefore could not have been obtained without the 'extra' women's vote (Duverger, 1955: 72). More speculative was a comment suggesting that women voters might have been more likely to be swayed by candidate personalities than issues. On this point Duverger is to be credited with pointing out that German women had been less likely than German men to vote for the National Socialists during the 1930's (Duverger, 1955: 71).

[10]International Political Science Association.

[11]Ironically, Duverger may well have been a victim of a certain amount of 'footnote fudging'. His conclusions are very carefully worded and their speculative character acknowledged. A careful reading of his report reveals considerable sensitivity to the dangers of sexist interpretation of the data.

In contrast to the electoral surveys, data on political leadership indicated an enormous discrepancy in the representation of women. Few women held electoral office anywhere and these numbers decreased dramatically as the hierarchy of office was ascended. Duverger held that this phenomenon was not solely due to the hostility of the electorate toward women, but was 'primarily due to the fact that few women stand as candidates' (Duverger, 1955: 77). This was duly investigated and causes included both feminine 'self-selection' and discrimination against women candidates by men. Even if women did manage the hurdles of qualification, candidacy and election, their impact in assemblies was minimal, characterised by three essential features: (1) Women seldom appeared in the role of political leaders; (2) spoke less than men in debates; (3) concerned themselves largely with issue areas such as health, family policy, children, and women's rights (Duverger, 1955: 95); that is, they were seldom to be found in the political 'mainsteam'. Similar patterns were present in public administration posts, and women's participation in the political parties was characterised by an analogous fall-off.

Women's membership in the political parties was small and their role in party executives even smaller. Investigation of national variations showed the highest feminine party participation to be in the 'Christian Parties', followed by the Communist and Socialist parties. Liberal and Radical parties contained the smallest numbers of women participants.

All of these tendencies are by now common knowledge (some would argue cultural myth), but Duverger was the first to attempt such a systematic investigation. Interestingly, Duverger's research was extremely sensitive to possibilities of sexism and sex discrimination as causal factors, and his explanation for the relative absence of women from political life is a lucid one. He points out that there has 'always been extremely keen competition for political leadership' and that in circumstances of intense rivalry

> 'To give a post to a woman is to deprive a man of it, and in these circumstances, the posts given to women are cut down to the minimum required for propaganda purposes ... The mechanism at work here is ... the same as that which makes it difficult for younger men to get into politics and to bring new blood into political leadership, *but the unity of the older generation is less solid than that of the male sex or, more exactly, it is not founded on the same psychological and social substructure*' (Duverger, 1955: 125, my emphasis),

Although this point is mitigated a few paragraphs later by the comment that

> 'men's opposition to the participation of women in political life would not have succeeded so well if it had come against vigorous resistance from women. There can be no doubt that women are less interested in politics than men' (Duverger, 1955: 126).

this was still a remarkable statement to make in the early 1950's.

A careful reading of *The Political Role of Women* shows that Duverger had all the necessary clues for an understanding of women's political behaviour as well as the sensitivity and intuition to use many of them. Additionally, he seemed sympathetic to the plight of women political aspirants. However, he was ultimately incapable of taking the necessary extra step which involved questioning the basis of the definition of what is political as an alternative to pointing to women's inadequacies when faced with what was commonly accepted by men as political. That this was the case may well be due to the fact that he was a political scientist as it is to his sex or the time at which the study was done.

Despite its faults, the IPSA/UNESCO study was in many respects a pioneering one and an outstanding piece of preliminary research in its own right. Nevertheless, the response over the next fifteen years was a resounding silence. Indeed, there is little indication that the study was actually read by students of political participation during the late 1950's and 1960's (Milbrath, 1965; McCloskey, 1968; R. Lane, 1959; S. M. Lipset, 1960). Scrutiny of the bibliographies of these myth-originating works confirms a suspicion that the stereotype of a-political woman has more to do with the processes ascribed by Bourque and Grossholtz than it does to a reading of some solid, if sometimes mistaken, research on the subject. The lack of impact of Duverger's study is more than likely to be due to the American dominance of the discipline (see Apter, 1977; McKenzie, 1970) and their well documented ethno-centricity — the report, after all, did not concern itself with American women (see MacIntyre, 1971). Another factor which may be of relevance here is that the Duverger study appeared at about the same time as positivism was beginning to dominate the profession.

To the relatively limited extent that political scientists in the ensuing fifteen years gave attention to the phenomenon of low levels of feminine political participation, their explanations tended to rest upon psychological assumptions. Women were said to be more traditionalist and right-wing, to be temperamentally unsuited to masculine styles of political activity, to unquestioningly adopt their husbands' political allegiances, to be more swayed by candidates than issues, to be more moralistic, more emotional and less politically aware and interested than men. Possibly stemming from the isolation of the housewife role, such attitudes were explained by references to a low feminine sense of political efficacy (Milbrath, 1965; Campbell, 1960; R. Lane, 1959). But these explanations were often inconsistently supported or not supported at all by such data as was available (Goot and Reid, 1975). Standard explanations of low feminine participation relied therefore on women's insufficient socialisation into their civic duty or on 'insufficient masculinisation' (Currell, 1974; Jaquette, 1974). And Evans (1979) has pointed out that whilst women's preferences for the conservative and the traditional

'merely posit a sex difference in political attitudes ...'

the other assertions

'imply that women are less competent than men as citizens'.

Competence is, of course, a normative concept and the problem is not as simple as that. But sexism was endemic in the Political Science of the period under discussion. Goot and Reid (1975) argue that the few Political Scientists who did turn their (passing) attention to feminine political participation apparently viewed the under-representation of women in political life with a certain amount of equanimity, if not outright approval. Dahl (1956a: 74) and Sartori (1956: 230–77) saw no diminution in the claim of democracy made by states which withheld the vote from women altogether. Other researchers limited their more intensive data analyses to male respondents (Abrams, 1966; Lane, 1962). Davies (1964: 137) felt comfortable in asserting that 'Politics is a game, in one simple sense for middle-aged men'. Whilst the limiting tendencies to scientism is the behavioural era combined with an attendant commitment to 'value free' social science could in part account for a failure to explain properly, and sometimes even notice an evident disenfranchisement of half of the world's citizens; these same tendencies often did not prevent sexist attitudes from being substituted for analysis. Admittedly, few went so far as Robert Lane, who wrote

> 'That working girls and career women and women who insistently serve the community, and women with extra-curricula interests of an absorbing kind are often borrowing their time and attention and capacity for relaxed play and love from their children to whom it rightfully belongs. As Kardiner points out, the rise in juvenile delinquency (and, he says homosexuality) is partly to be attributed to the feminist movement and what it did to the American mother' (1959: 355).

To be fair to Political Science, Lane's comments are unusually blatant and sex roles were never more than a passing concern for these scholars.

Towards a Feminist Political Science?

In most of the relevant disciplines it was only with the development of a feminist consciousness amongst academic women that the study of women was seriously engaged. In Political Science this response was late in coming and tended to correspond with political developments within professional associations. In the United States, articles and papers on women and politics only began to be a regular feature of academic journals and conferences after protests by the Women's Caucus of the American Political Science Association;[12] and it was only after 1970 that full length books on women and politics began to appear.

Until very recently, most of the new research on women and politics was situated squarely within mainstream political science; this despite a tendency to interdisciplinarity in feminist scholarship generally. The narrow base of the early studies of women and politics may well have been due to the peculiar isolation of Political Science from the other disciplines; and this was probably aggravated by the structure of academic careers. A continuing dominance of traditional single-discipline based departments may have meant that there is a perceived career penalty attached to multi-disciplinary scholarship. This consideration, combined with the fact that full-time women's studies posts are still relatively scarce, could well have been an inhibiting factor in the development of a feminist study of politics.

Whatever the causes, the main contribution of feminism to political studies has been limited to the areas of reinforcement of existing method and the exposure of sexist myths. A major initial concern was with identifying and publicising sexist bias in the standard literature on political participation, political socialisation and voting behaviour (Goot and Reid, 1975; Morgan, 1974; Bourque and Grossholtz, 1974). This was a necessary task, but not one likely to involve a fundamental challenge to the discipline. Similarly, studies involving the collection of new research material (Kirkpatrick, 1974; Currell, 1974), whilst innovative in terms of devising methods to acquire a non-sexist data base, remained well within the acceptable limits of positivist Political Science. The point here is not that the above-mentioned studies were not worthy and necessary, this patently is not the case. Rather, the question is one of why these studies were not accompanied or succeeded by a number of works of critical theory which challenge the manner in which Political Studies has constructed its object of study.

[12] Women's Caucus for Political Science.

It seems likely that this is an area in which the influence of the positivists of the 1950's and 1960's has been extremely important. The models and methods constructed in that era are the ones in which most of us were trained and remain important elements of undergraduate and graduate courses. Moving from combatting the sexist application of these approaches to a position of challenging their foundations will be a crucial step for feminist political scholarship. Unfortunately it is not an obvious one. The continuing dominance of American scholarship over the applied side of the discipline has its effect here. This dominance should be seen not only in conjunction with the strong positivistic tendencies discussed in the first section of this essay, but also in conjunction with a strong national reluctance to engage materialist philosophy, socialist thought or radical theory. When all of these elements are taken into account it becomes fair to suggest that certain important tensions conducive to the construction of a radical critique are not present amongst most of the Political Science profession. Hence the kind of critical feminist scholarship which has informed debates within Sociology and Social Psychology does not appear to have obtained access to Political Science. Additionally, the lack of a tradition of searching self-criticism within the profession has impeded the internal development of habits of thought conducive to a feminist challenge.

Thus one is forced ultimately to face the question of whether there is a Feminist Political Science to assess. Following Reuben (1978) one may state that there does exist a growing body of 'research by and/or about women', but this is, as Reuben points out, not necessarily synonymous with feminist scholarship. However, this research is undoubtedly generated by feminist goals. It is ideological in the sense that it has been motivated by a clear commitment to combat sexist bias in the way the discipline views feminine political behaviour. Lately too, studies of political issues thrown up by the women's movement have become more common; but this may be explained by the fact that the political success of 'second wave' feminism has now been sufficient for such issues to loom large enough to be on the policy agenda, forcing a pragmatic profession to take notice.

All in all, the feminist initiative in the study of politics has been a cautious and not entirely successful one, largely corresponding to the early stages of feminist scholarship outlined by Sherif (1978). Women are today more studied, but mainly by women and few of these women hold prestigious chairs or other important positions in the hierarchy of the profession. Whilst most major new political behaviour research includes sex differences as a major concern (Verba, Nie and Kim, 1979), such efforts as there have been to combat sexist perspectives in undergraduate politics literature appear so far to have been unsuccessful (WCPS Quarterly, 1979: 6). The work completed so far has been confined to a very narrow area of study and a great deal of effort has been expended towards the explosion of sexist myths which have arisen from observations of often minute political differences between men and women. In areas where political differences between the sexes are large, research has tended to be concentrated on what insights might be gleaned from the study of the few women who are there (Kirkpatrick, 1974; Tolchin and Tolchin, 1974). The somewhat larger questions relating to the many women who are not there are only beginning to receive attention.

In the U.S.A., the CAWP[13] has undertaken a major project involving using educational institutions in a programme of training women for public office. Research

[13]Center for the American Women and Politics, Eagleton Institute, Rutgers University, New Brunswick, New Jersey.

proposals have recently been submitted in the U.K. for a study of dropout rates amongst women candidates for electoral office. There have also been a number of studies produced which have as their avowed aim the object of comparing the political behaviour of women with women rather than the more usual comparisons of women with men (Kirkpatrick, 1979; Iglitzin & Ross, 1976; Wulff, 1979). Whilst at a very early stage, developments such as these might be the first indications of a turn from an 'exposé of biases in the discipline' to 'defining new areas for study that will explicate the biases and lead to new scholarship' (Sherif, 1978: 220), that, is, they may represent a turn toward the development of a genuinely feminist Political Science.

The way in which Political Science reacts to such a turn will depend upon four factors: (1) openness and responsiveness; (2) developments in the object; (3) on internal professional political developments; and to a certain extent on (4) the quality of the new scholarship itself. Taking each of these in their turn — firstly, there is theoretically no reason why Political Science should not be open to what will inevitably be interdisciplinary research iniatives. The study of politics is, as has been argued above, a convention . . . an evolved and agreed construct and that construct is an interdisciplinary one (see Blondel, 1976). Indeed, in many ways, the early development of the academic study of politics bears marked similarities to the perspectives Sherif[14] has suggested for feminist scholarship. Secondly, the impact of developments in the object will depend largely upon the performance of women politicians. There are indications of cause for optimism in this regard, and evidence from recent European elections suggests that at least the Duverger 'Minimum representation of women necessary for propaganda purposes' has been raised. Thirdly, there is also cause for optimism about internal professional political developments. Organisation by women to promote both women and feminist scholarship is at the time of writing taking place in many of the national associations and the Sex Roles and Politics Group of the International Political Science Association appears to be well subscribed.

The fourth factor, the quality of the scholarship, is a more difficult element to assess as said scholarship is in its infancy. Certainly there are likely to be problems in that for a feminist Political Science to come into being, current definitions of political and public must be expanded and attention must be given to factors traditionally regarded as belonging to the private sphere. Tools for such analysis are being forged within other areas of feminist scholarship, however, and may be found particularly in the literature generated by the Capitalism-Patriarchy debate (see especially Kuhn and Wolpe, 1979). So far this debate has not been engaged by Political Scientists, however, and there are reasons for being concerned that it won't be. Certainly the theoretical propensities of the profession have been such that this and similar debates could pass unnoticed by all but a peripheral few. Indeed, if a route into Political Science for discussions of a radical feminist nature is found, it is likely to be through the success the women's movement itself has in politicising new issues, the study of which will require the development of new analytical frameworks.

Statements about possible future developments must therefore be hedged with uncertainty. Too many of the important variables are outside of our control. Whilst new

---

[14]Sherif's view is that the development of an interdisciplinary feminist scholarship will involve the refining of 'the art of judicious borrowing of both information and techniques from the various disciplines concerned with a problem, then to coordinate them, recognising their differing levels and units of analysis . . . ' (1978: 223).

research techniques and theoretical perspectives are necessary, this necessity does not automatically mean they will be developed. It is also a fact that a situation of contracting finance for scholarly pursuits is likely to worsen, causing increasing competition in which less well-established feminist scholars may be pushed out. Whilst much in the way of socio-political research may be undertaken on little or no funding, sooner or later, expensive data collection is going to be necessary and the prospects for the required funding look bleak.

At the time of writing, feminists seeking to establish the study of women as a legitimate concern for Political Science have gained a toehold. Our concerns have, not surprisingly, been shaped by our training and this training has been predominantly in the scientism of Easton and Almond rather than in the theoretical and normative tradition of Aristotle. Hence our concentration has been on the adjustment of spurious analysis within an existing construct. We have concentrated on removing culturally determined, often implicit sexist assumptions from existing models. In other words, our efforts have been directed at generating a revised standard version of the political science of women, instead of at the development of a radical, altogether innovative feminist Political Science. We have done this because it was the obvious thing to do and only now that the task is nearing completion has it become apparent that for our work to mean anything at all, it must be seen as preliminary to a confrontation with and a challenge to the way in which knowledge has come to be constructed in the Political Science profession. The success of such an endeavour is not assured. The alacrity with which those employed in the study of politics have abandoned or ghettoised an honourable and traditional strand of critical theory has been outlined above and closely argued elsewhere.[15] Nevertheless, that strand has been responsible for much of what has been attractive and compelling about Political Science, and the imperatives of both feminist scholarship and the study of politics demand its restoration.

References

ABRAMS, M. (1966) 'Social Tends and Electoral Behaviour' in Rose, *Studies in British Politics*, MacMillan; London.

ALMOND, G. A. and S. VERBA (1963) *The Civic Culture*, Little, Brown and Company: Boston.

APTER, D. E. (1977) *Introduction to Political Analysis* Winthrop: Cambridge, Mass.

ARISTOTLE (1962) *The Politics*, Penguin (T. A. Sinclair Trans.): Middlesex.

BLONDEL, J. (1976) *Thinking Politically*, Penguin: Middlesex.

BOURQUE, S. C. and J. GROSSHOLTZ (1974) 'Politics an Unnatural Practice: Political Science Looks at Female Participation', *Politics and Society*, Winter, pp. 225–266.

CAMPBELL, A., P. E. CONVERSE, W. E. MILLER and D. E. STOKES (1960) *The American Voter*, John Wiley: New York.

CONVERSE, P. E and J. M. CONVERSE (1971) 'The Status of Women as Students and Professionals in Political Science', *PS* 4, Summer, pp. 328–48.

CURRELL, M. E. (1974) *Political Woman*, Croom Helm: London.

DAHL, R. A. (1956a) *A Preface to Democratic Theory*, Chicago Univesity Press: Chicago.

DAHL, R. A. (1956b) *Who Governs*, Yale University Press: New Haven.

DAVIES, A. F. (1964) *Australian Democracy*, 2nd edition, Longmans, Green: Melbourne.

DEUTSCH, K. W. (1963) *The Nerves of Government: Models of Political Communication and Control*, Free Press: New York.

DUVERGER, M. (1955) *The Political Role of Women*, UNESCO.

EASTON, D. (1953) *The Political System: An Inquiry into the State of Political Science*, Knopf: New York.

[15]See especially Carol Pateman (1970), *Participation and Democratic Theory*, Cambridge University Press, Cambridge.

EASTON, D. (1965a) *A Framework for Political Analysis*, Englewood Cliffs, Prentice-Hall: New Jersey.

EASTON, D. (1965b) *A Systems Analysis of Political Life*, Wiley: New York.

EASTON, D. (1968) 'Political Science', *International Encyclopaedia of the Social Sciences*, Vol. 12, pp. 282–298.

EVANS, J. (in press) 'Attitudes to Women in American Political Science', *Government and Opposition*, forthcoming.

GOOT, M. and E. REID (1975) *Women and Voting Studies: Mindless Matrons or Sexist Scientism?* Sage Professional Papers in Comparative Political Sociology.

IGLITZIN & ROSS, (1976) *Women in the World: A Comparative Study*, Clio Press: Santa Barbara.

JAQUETTE, J. (Ed.) (1974) *Women in Politics*, John Wiley and Sons: New York.

KIRKPATRICK, J. (1974) *Political Woman*, Basic Books: New York.

KUHN, A. and A. M. WOLPE (1978) *Feminism and Materialism*, Routledge and Kegan Paul: London.

LANE, R. E. (1959) *Political Life*, Free Press: Glencoe.

LANE, R. E. (1962) *Political Ideology*, Free Press: Glencoe.

LANE, R. E. and D. O. SEARS (1964) *Public Opinion*, Prentice-Hall: Englewood Cliffs.

LIPSET, S. M. (1960) *Political Man: The Social Bases of Politics*, Heinemann: London.

LOVENDUSKI, J. and J. EVANS (1979) 'Women as Academic Staff and As Students in Political Studies', Paper presented to 1979 Political Studies Conference, Sheffield, April.

MacINTYRE, A. (1971) 'Is a Science of Comparative Politics Possible?' in *Against the Self Images of the Age*, Duckworth: London.

McKENZIE, W. J. M. (1967) *Politics and The Social Sciences*, Penguin: Middlesex.

McKENZIE, W. J. M. (1970) *The Study of Political Science Today*, MacMillan: London.

McCLOSKEY, H. (1968) 'Political Participation', In D. L. Sills (Ed.) *International Encyclopedia of the Social Sciences*, MacMillan: New York.

MILBRATH, L. (1965) *Political Participation*, Rand McNally: Chicago.

REUBEN, E. (1978) 'In Defiance of the Evidence: Notes on Feminist Scholarship', *Women's Studies, International Quarterly*, Vol. I, No. 3, pp. 215–218.

SARTORI, G. (1956) *Democratic Theory*, Praeger: New York.

SHERIF, C. W. (1978) 'Climbing Disciplinary Walls and Learning How to Borrow', *Women's Studies, International Quarterly*, Vol. I, No. 3, pp. 219–224.

TOLCHIN, S. and M. TOLCHIN (1974) *Clout: Woman, Power and Politics,* Coward, McCann and Geoghegan: New York.

VERBA, S., N. NIE and KIM (1979) *Participation and Political Equality,* Cambridge University Press: Cambridge.

WOLIN, S. (1961) *Politics and Vision,* George Allen and Unwin: London.

WCPS (Women's Caucus for Political Science Quarterly) (1979) 'Scholarly Treatment of Women in Political Science Texts Subjects of Study', May, 6.

WULFF, C. (1979) 'Women Activists in the British Constituency Labour Parties', European Consortium for Political Research, April.

7

Anthropology: A Discipline with a Legacy

CAROL P. MacCORMACK

Relativity and Comparison

Anthropology, as an academic discipline, began with systematic enquiry into the nature of *Homo sapiens* as a species. How did we come to be what we are, and how do we differ from other animals? Compared with other animals, our brain has evolved to be quite large in relation to body weight. It is also qualitatively different from other animals, having a thick cortex of associating neurons which allow memory and perception to link in variable patterns of meaning. Much of the behaviour of lower animals is pre-programmed but little of human behaviour is truly instinctive, allowing for greater variability in thought and resultant behaviour. The question of how much human behaviour, including gender specific behaviour, is biologically ordained is fiercely debated, but all agree that we are the only self-conscious and self-domesticated animal (see Tanner and Zihlman, 1976; Leibowitz, 1978). We are therefore curious to know how we evolved the capacity for language which allows us to communicate plans for a better tool or a better society. Language, and the normative patterns it encodes, help to make behaviour predictable, and cooperative human society possible. But normative patterns are a kaleidoscope which undergo transformations through historical time in a single society, and also vary between societies. Some broad norms, such as constraint on wanton murder, or the obligation of elders to nurture and teach the young, are common to all thriving societies. But there are many possible roles and methods for successfully nurturing and teaching the young. Morally correct behaviour in one society may be considered incorrect in another, thus we speak of the relativity of culture. The question then becomes one of the *range* of variability in socially approved thought and behaviour, charted through cross-cultural comparative studies. For example, in 1949 Margaret Mead cast her eye over a sample of human societies, and although she took the debatable position that women are to be defined with reference to maternity, she concluded that little else in gender roles was biologically innate. Much behaviour considered masculine in one society would be considered feminine in another.

Most cross-cultural studies of social organization have been explicitly or implicitly influenced by functionalist theory. Societies consist of structures of statutes and roles. The anthropologist's job is to describe the structure of a society and analyze the relationship between elements of the structure. An assumption of functionalism is that the elements are articulated in an orderly fashion to make an integrated whole society which persists over time. On an intellectual level, anthropologists agree that an integrated whole society includes children, adults, elders, and even shades of the dead, as well as males and females. In practice, children and women, if they lacked political power, were seldom written about in historical accounts, nor interviewed in cross-cultural field studies. It is a sad irony that most of the elegant functionalist case studies of the 1940s and 1950s, written with the aim of explaining the structure of integrated whole societies, revolved around the thoughts and acts of politically elite males only. There are notable exceptions, however. Rather than ignore or attempt to explain away the politically and economically prominent women he encountered in coastal West Africa, Kenneth Little incorporated them into his account of *The Mende of Sierra Leone* in 1951. Working as a husband and wife team, E. J. Krige and J. D. Krige wrote of *The Realm of the Rain Queen: A Study of the Patterns of Lovedu Society* in 1943. Earlier, in America, writers like Robert Lowie included women's activities in his analysis of *The Crow Indians* (1935). He wrote a chapter on women in *Primitive Society* (1920) which continues to instruct us today.

Formative Years

Anthropology is perhaps different from other social sciences in having been relatively welcoming to women researchers from its beginning as a discipline. This difference arises in part from anthropology's focus on every-day life in integrated whole societies that unquestionably include women and children. For example, in the 1870s, Matilda Cox Stevenson did field work with her husband in the Zuñi area of the American southwest. After her husband's death, she returned to do extensive research under the sponsorship of the Bureau of American Ethnology, producing publications ranging from the first serious anthropological observations of children to a study of Zuñi origin myths published in 1905. (Mead and Bunzel, 1960: 205). Alice Cunningham Fletcher, perhaps best known for her work with the Omaha tribe, published in 1911, collaborated with Francis La Flesche, an Omaha Indian 20 years her junior. Regarding each other as adopted mother and son, they worked together for over a quarter of a century. She was the first ethnologist to join the staff of the Peabody Museum, Harvard University, in 1882, and helped to set the course of anthropology as a discipline by emphasizing indigenous interpretations and meanings in her work (Eggan, 1968: 126; Mead and Bunzel, 1960: 227-8).

A photograph of Elsie Clews Parsons (de Laguna, 1960: 925) confirms that she was indeed a beautiful woman, of a wealthy and socially prominent New York family. But she side-stepped conventional expectations, attended Barnard College, and took a Ph.D in sociology in 1899. During the next 15 years she wrote a number of books dealing with the pressure of society upon the individual. She then discovered that the comparative framework anthropology offers might give her added insight into social process, and did distinguished field work in societies which demanded even greater social conformity than did her own (Mead and Bunzel, 1960: 546).

One cannot designate these anthropologists as feminist scholars, but they helped to shed light on the larger philosophical context in which feminist issues are embedded. Ruth Benedict, for example, born in 1887, was not interested in the movement for women's suffrage, and considered women's education a battle which was won in her mother's day (Mead, 1966: 5). But in common with Elsie Clews Parson, she shared an intellectual interest in the relationship between individual freedom and cultural integration, culminating in *Patterns of Culture* in 1934. She was in sympathy with functionalism, focussed on integrated wholes, but differed with the British functionalist

Bronislaw Malinowski. He began his analysis with the individual, deriving patterns from human need satisfaction. Benedict began with 'cultural configurations' and viewed individual behaviour as largely conforming to cultural imperatives. Margaret Mead carried on in this tradition, observing how individuals develop in relation to their culture.

The influence of these anthropologists was not only felt through their publications, but also as teachers: Fletcher at Harvard, Parsons, Benedict and Mead at Columbia. They also exerted their influence in professional organizations. The society precursing the American Anthropological Association was founded in Washington D.C. in 1879. Its membership was limited to men, but women such as Stevenson and Fletcher, already experienced researchers, organized the Women's Anthropological Society of America in 1885. In 1899 the two societies merged, then became the present American Anthropological Association in 1902 (de Laguna, 1960: 93—101). Several presidents of that association have been women.

In Britain, Victorian women such as Mary Kingsley made excellent ethnographic observations before anthropology was organized as an academic discipline. An interesting parallel might be drawn between American and British anthropology in that the towering figures, largely responsible for formulating a literature and methodology for the new discipline, were immigrants who welcomed women students into their departments. Franz Boas at Columbia, a German immigrant, and Bronislaw Malinowski, at the London School of Economics, a Polish immigrant, are renowned for their extensive, painstaking field work in non-Western societies. They attracted brilliant men and women students, and expected the women to endure the rigors of solitary field work as a matter of course. Audrey Richards, for example, the only woman president of the Royal Anthropological Institute, was born at the end of the 19th century, lived in India as a child, read natural sciences at Newnham College, did field work in Africa, completing her Ph.D. under Malinowski's supervision in 1931 (La Fontaine, 1972: x-xi). Similar to their American contemporaries, early British women anthropologists displayed some sensitivity to gender roles in human societies. The subjects Richards has taken up in a long and distinguished career are quite varied and could not be described as women's topics. However, she has ranged over social roles in a matrilineal society and written perceptively about a girl's initiation ceremony. Lucy Mair wrote on marriage, and Phyllis Kayberry studied women's rituals and economic activities. Phyllis Kayberry studied women's rituals and economic activities.

Malinowski's early work was slightly colored by romantic escapism; the search for the 'untouched primitive' on a south seas island. But perhaps under the stimulation of work done by the first generation of students, British anthropology began to directly acknowledge the impact that colonialism was having on small scale societies. Lucy Mair has been a powerful figure influencing policies of colonial rule so that the impact of those policies has been less damaging than it might otherwise have been (Mair, 1936, 1950). Monica Wilson, in collaboration with her husband Godfery, co-authored the first anthropological monograph addressing itself directly to processes of social change (1945).

Early women anthropologists on both sides of the Atlantic sometimes worked under government sponsorship, occasionally were asked to look specifically at women's activities, and throughout their professional lives ranged widely over a variety of theoretical problems. For example, in the early 1940s the Cameroons Development

Corporation informed the Colonial Office that the Bamenda area, although rich in resources, was underpopulated and underdeveloped economically. Feeling that a very high infant mortality rate, the status of women, and other social factors might be correlated, the assistance of a social anthropologist was requested. Phyllis Kayberry's study, *Women of the Grassfields*, alerted researchers to the discrepancy between normative statements about how a society ought to be organized and how it actually functioned. In Bamenda, men in the role of chief or head of kin group officially controlled land, but women exercised real control over land by virtue of their right to produce crops (Forde in Kayberry, 1952: vi). A quarter of a century later, anthropologists doing research on the topic of women and development are rediscovering that truth. Similarly, Audrey Richards' *Chisungu* was not merely a description of girl's puberty rite. She distinguished between different types of interpretations of symbols that are obtained from (1) ordinary participants, (2) ritual specialists, and (3) the anthropologist as observer. Many anthropologists have been stimulated by her work, for example Victor Turner has further developed the concept of 'level of exegetical analysis' as well as Richards' concept of the polyvalence of symbols (La Fontaine, 1972: xv-xvi).

We might conclude that in the formative years of British and American anthropology most anthropologists were men, and heads of influential departments of anthropology were men. This inevitably resulted in a degree of male bias in the literature (Ardener, 1972: Milton, 1979). However, anthropology, perhaps to a greater degree than other social sciences, has welcomed women, who have exerted a wide-ranging intellectual influence, and served as inspiring role models for other women coming into the discipline.

The 1960s and After: Search for Models that Transcend Relativism

Questions raised by the women's movement in the West have stimulated anthropologists in two ways. They are collecting new data on gender roles in field studies, and they are reassessing the models that have been used to generate hypotheses and analyse data. The two activities, of course, have a feed-back effect on each other. Goodale (1971) asked how the complicated Australian aborigines' marriage system was viewed by the women who become wives in it, and gave us insights not only into kinship but women's economic and symbolic roles as well. Goodale's work, together with the earlier work by Kayberry (1939); began to give us a much more accurate picture of aboriginal societies. Strathern (1972), working in Papua New Guinea, asked what it was like to be a woman born into one patrilineage, married into another, mediating between two groups within the social structure. Weiner (1976) went to the Trobriand Islands to study artists, was taken to a huge women's ceremonial exchange ceremony on her first day in the field, immediately changed the focus of her study, and filled in the parts of Trobriand social organization and symbolism which Malinowski had left ouf of his otherwise excellent and exhaustive ethnography. Her work not only tells us more about women in this matrilineal society, but for the first time we begin to understand some of the puzzles about the role of men as well.

This kind of field work has stimulated male as well as female anthropologists to become aware of new theoretical perspectives. Milton (1979: 52) is quite correct in her view that these new theoretical perspectives are not the exclusive domain of women researchers; to say so would be to imply that theories in anthropology are biologically determined. She suggests that new theoretical perspectives arise out of particular problem solving experiences. Many men as well as women are seeking to free themselves from the extreme demands of pre-1960s gender roles, and both men and women who struggle with the same problem are likely to adopt similar theoretical frameworks when analyzing the social organization of non-Western societies. Although we are disciplined to discover the folk models of non-Western people, and to understand them on their own terms, we cannot be entirely free from the preoccupations of our own society. If nothing else, they shape the kinds of questions one sets out to investigate.

For some anthropologists the roles of analyst and activist merged in the 1960s and 1970s (Rosaldo and Lamphere, 1974: 2; Friedl, 1975: 6; Reiter, 1975: 11). As they attempted to achieve greater autonomy and influence for women in their own society, they also turned to the question of male dominance in pan-human social organization. Some have insisted that men are dominant in all societies (e.g. Rosaldo, 1974), while others have attempted to explain the nature of real power women exert (e.g. MacCormack, 1972, 1974, 1977; Van Allen, 1972). Part of the problem in the debate about universal male dominance is a lack of agreement on exactly how dominance is to be defined, and which sociopolitical powers are to be recognized, given that women's influence is often less overt than men's. The other problem is male bias in the anthropological literature itself. If we use comparative ethnographic literature to prove that women are universally devalued, the very ethnographies are products of male bias, and the evidence itself is biased and not valid for the conclusion reached (Milton, 1979: 44).

Even in case studies where there may be little bias, for example Robert Lowie's work on the Crow Indians, where he was careful to note the kinds of influence women had, we do feel intuitively that it was a rather 'male dominated' society. But to label Crow society as male dominated with a concluding finality, as though that was all there is to say about it (Ortner, 1974: 70), is to reach closure before examination of more subtle social processes at a deeper level of analysis can be taken up. To say that men and women have separate but interdependent spheres of power is not necessarily to say that men's and women's spheres are 'complementary but equal', a phrase Lamphere (1977: 616) has used perhaps too hastily. We must carefully report women's real prerogatives and powers, no matter how subtle they are, for it is the dynamic interplay between genders, whatever their relative power, that should be a focus of studies in social organization.

Marxist Materialist Analysis

In America, anthropological gender studies had been initially inspired by Engels' *Origin of the Family, Private Property and the State* (1884), which in turn had been based on partially incorrect 19th century ethnography, organized in an evolutionary paradigm by Lewis Henry Morgan (1877). In Britain and France the inspiration has come more from Althusserian interpretations of Marx, with work concentrating on the nature of pre-capitalist modes of production (Hindess and Hirst, 1975; Meillassoux, 1975).

The American writers began by postulating preclass hunting and gathering societies where the relations between genders are egalitarian. Whatever male dominance now exists in pre-industrial societies is the consequence of colonialism with its intrusion of private property and wage labour. Empirical enquiry has especially focussed on the

Kung Bushmen of the Kalahari Desert, some North American Indian groups, and Australian aborigines. The arguments are again dogged by the lack of a suitable definition of what constitutes male dominance, or what kinds of female prerogatives might be counted as political power.

Looking at the aborigines, for example, we know from the work of Kayberry (1939) and Goodale (1971) that women gather, hunt, and distribute food to others. Land is not owned, nor are crops planted, stored or controlled. Production is for immediate *use* by the domestic group or clan, not for *exchange*. There is no corporate control of productive resources neither as private property nor as corporate property. Decision making is diffuse, and women's decisions are as important to group survival as are men's. In this kind of society one cannot speak of a female domestic sphere and a male public political sphere.

In settled agricultural societies the asymmetrical power relationship between genders arises when the reproduction of labourers becomes a critical element. Men gain control over the reproductive potential of women through rules of marriage exchange. Once men control women as reproducers of the labour force, and as substantial producers in the farming economy, they accumulate surpluses over immediate subsistence needs (Aaby, 1977: 38). With a shift from clans and extended family structure to the isolated nuclear family, women's labour is privatized in the domestic sphere and the product of women's labour is easily appropriated by men who use it in political exchanges. Exchanges made by men in the public domain help them to build their political networks, where women confined to the domestic sphere cannot do the same. Friedl (1975) has developed this theme of dominance based upon men's control and extra-domestic distribution of valuable objects in a sample of societies with different modes of production.

Anthropologists working with Engels' evolutionary paradigm relate the low status of women to the rise of class formation (Leacock, 1972; Sacks, 1974; Bujra, 1978). Empirical validation of this hypothesis takes two forms: (1) historical-archaeological studies and (2) cross-cultural studies of contemporary pre-industrial and industrial societies. Rapp (1979) discusses a sample of such case studies, her own work (1977) representing the historical approach, while Shapiro's work represents the cross-cultural approach (1976). The weight of evidence from these studies indicates that an Engel's type progression is oversimplified. Changes caused by colonialism and neo-colonialism, introducing capitalistic relations of production, do not always lead to further powerlessness and oppression for women. Such changes are clearly beneficial for some women, for example Peruvian hacienda women who are able to transcend a servile status (Deere, 1977). In other cases, colonialism and production for cash profits has put women in an economically and politically dependent situation where they once had relatively more autonomy (Boserup, 1970; Babb, 1980; Etienne, 1977).

A social organization of nuclear families often divides and isolates women, weakening gender solidarity. Furthermore, within complex societies caste and class solidarity preempts gender solidarity. Women in high socioeconomic groups in urban India, for example, are active in enhancing their husbands' careers, and distance themselves from less fortunate women by giving charity to them (Caplan, 1978). In some pre-capitalist societies women's extra-domestic sodalities, such as the Sande society in Sierra Leone, enhance the organized political power of women. But these groups are internally stratified, with older women appropriating the labour of younger ones (MacCormack,

1979). Such age-graded societies, however, are not class systems since every exploited young woman eventually becomes an exploiting elder woman.

These women's organizations mitigate male control over women as producers and reproducers. But even without the advantage of solidarity groups, field studies describe how some women manage to work their own strategies to accumulate wealth, power and autonomy. In the Kpelle area of Libera, for example, formal jural rules regarding gender rights and duties indicate that married women are indeed jural minors, without rights. But when Bledsoe (1980) looked at their actual strategies and achievements, many seemed quite adept at appropriating the product of men's labour, using it for their own purposes. In an urban industrial setting, Stack (1974) has described how poor black women at the bottom of class structure build social networks for mutual assistance. Relationships with men, who may father their children, are fragile. When the relationship with the man ends, the relationship with his mother, sisters, and other kin does not end. With each subsequent union the woman builds a network of 'affinal' kin who come to her assistance with money, food, child care and a range of other support in time of need.

Many recent studies call into question Rosaldo's insistence in *Woman, Culture and Society* (1974) on a strict dichotomy between the private domestic domain and the public political domain, with women universally inside the former. MacCormack (Hoffer) questioned the universality and utility of that dichotomy in the same volume (1974: 173), and Rapp (1979: 508-11) summarizes a number of subsequent studies which demonstrate that political activity is not as distinct from domestic activity as Rosaldo suggested. Furthermore, the domestic domain of an African farming or trading woman is quite different from that of an American housewife, and so also are the social transformations needed to enhance their political power.

Symbolism

Initiation ritual, rich with gender symbolism, has been another focus of enquiry. Using a sample of societies for comparative study, Brown (1963) concluded that female puberty rites tend to occur in situations where a young woman continues to have a close relationship with her parents' domestic group following marriage, and where her economic contribution is significant. Brown has given a useful overview, drawing out statistical correlations, which in a sense highlight the exceptions. Strathern (1981: 174–222), describes the Mt. Hagen area of Papua New Guinea where women work very hard at productive tasks, but men successfully appropriate the product of their labour, categorizing women and their activities as 'rubbish'. There are no puberty rites for girls. Indeed, there is no concern with formally socializing a child to 'make' it into a responsible adult, as there is in some parts of West Africa (MacCormack, 1981: 95–118).

Throughout much of Papua New Guinea adult males and females are residentially separate for considerable parts of their adult life. Men are afraid of contact with women, feeling it will lead to weight loss, illness, and other signs of illness and death (Goodale, 1981: 119–142). In actual fact, there is a painful awareness on the part of men of their interdependence on women, especially on women's essential role in releasing men's persona at death, and in the regeneration of social groups. (Weiner, 1976; Gillison, 1981: 143–173). On a more empirical level, women in the highlands work very hard at farming, are not well nourished for this arduous physical labour, and are made even thinner by pregnancy and lactation. Menopause comes early compared with other parts of the world, and women die earlier than men in the highlands of Papua New Guinea. For these reasons, Gray (in press) suggests that men see very clearly the debilitating aspects of female fertility and do not wish to be 'contaminated' by it.

Paradoxically, men often display ritually their preoccupation with powers of fertility. Much has been written to 'explain' women's inferior status by the fact that they bleed and pollute. But in Papua New Guinea male semen also pollutes. Faithorn's work (1975) suggests that blood of menstruation and birth, and semen, are not so much polluting as powerful substances which create children. Men may express disgust at menstruation and birth, but in their ritual they symbolically appropriate both female processes in areas of Papua New Guinea (Meigs, 1976).

In an African context, bleeding takes on different symbolic meaning. La Fontaine (1972) has suggested that defloration is an important symbolic act for men because by rupturing the hymen they can, at least once, produce blood connoting the fertility of menstruation and birth on demand. MacCormack (1979), looking at another kind of ritual bleeding 'on demand', suggests that clitoridectomy in West Africa, performed on young women by elder more politically powerful women, is a metaphor for childbirth itself. In clitoridectomy the ceremonial official, who is also local midwife, controls the time, duration and pain of bleeding, just as she will later in childbirth through her skill as midwife. Indeed, there has been new interest in the whole question of the cultural meaning of fertility and birth (Jordan, 1978; MacCormack, in press).

In Yemen, menstruation, far from polluting, is defined as purifying. The blood itself is regarded as unclean, but the process of menstruation is purifying. If a woman does not bleed enough she is 'locked up', the uterus is 'closed' and she is infertile. When women do not menstruate their bodies become 'dense' in a way that male bodies cannot, and women suffer resultant aches and pains. They therefore take traditional medicines to encourage menstrual flow, and avoid contraceptives which inhibit it (Myntti, 1981).

The weight of the above observations suggests that women's fertility and childbirth is very much a matter of cultural meanings, modified and shaped at all stages by ritual acts and chemical and mechanical therapies. It is not a thing of 'nature', explaining women's universal devaluation, as Ortner (1974) has suggested. Indeed, the cultural 'belief' that nature is to culture as female is to male is a Western meaning which we must understand within our own intellectual history (Mathieu, 1973; Bloch and Bloch, 1980; Jordanova, 1981), and must not be imposed upon the whole world as a universal structuralist explanation of gender roles (MacCormack and Strathern, 1981).

Structuralist studies concerned with gender symbolism do not necessarily constitute an exclusive category, and some promising recent work combines Marxist and structuralist analysis into a single theoretical framework.

Conclusion

I have only touched upon a sample of the literature on the meaning of gender which has welled up in anthropology since the 1960s. The discipline is relatively open to the questions raised by the women's movement. That is not to say that all is entirely lovely in the garden. Women are not represented in academic posts, especially in the higher ranks, in numbers which reflect their contribution to the discipline. But the American

Anthropological Association at least, has taken this as a 'social fact' to be analysed and be acted upon, and has talked of censuring some of the most powerful universities in America (Sanjek, 1978; American Anthropological Association, 1979).

This openness to questions of gender, and respect for women in the profession of anthropology arises directly from the formative period in British and American anthropology when women were among the giants who walked the land. They were tireless field workers and tough-minded, rigorous, creative thinkers. We treasure the legacy they have left.

References

AABY, P. (1977) 'Engels and Women', *Critique of Anthropology* 3:25-54.
    American Anthropological Association (1981) 'Censure of Departments Proposed', *Newsletter* 22(1):1ff.
ARDENER, Edwin (1972) 'Belief and the Problem of Women' in *The Interpretation of Ritual* Edited. by J. S. La Fontane, London: Tavistock.
BABB, Forence, E. (1980 *Women and Men in Vicos, Peru: A Case of Unequal Development*, Ann Arbor: Michigan Occasional Papers No. 11, University of Michigan.
BENEDICT, Ruth, (1934) *Patterns of Culture,* Boston: Houghton Mifflin.
BLEDSOE, Caroline (1980) *Women and Marrriage in Kpelle Society,* Stanford: Stanford University Press.
BLOCH, Maurice and Jean BLOCK (1981 'Women and the Dialectics of Nature in Eighteenth-Century French Thought' in *Nature, Culture and Gender* Edited by C. P. MacCormack and M. Strathern, Cambridge: Cambridge University Press.
BOSERUP, Esther, (1970) *Women's Role in Economic Development*, London: Allen and Unwin.
BRIGGS, J. L. (1974) 'Eskimo Women: Makers of Men' in *Many Sisters*, Edited by C. J. Mathiasson, New York: Free Press.
BROWN, Judith K. (1963) 'A Cross-Cultural Study of Initiation Rites', *American Anthropologist* 65:837-53.
BUJRA, Janet M. (1978) 'Introductory: Female Solidarity and the Sexual Division of Labour' in *Women United, Women Divided,* Edited by P. Caplan and J. M. Bujra, London: Tavistock.
CAPLAN, Patricia (1978) 'Women's Organizations in Madras City, India' in *Women United, Women Divided,* Edited by P. Caplan and J. M. Bujra, London: Tavistock.
DEERE, Carmen D. (1977) 'Changing Social Relations of Production and Peruvian Peasant Women's Work', *Latin American Perspectives* 4: 38-47.
de LAGUNA, Frederica (1960) 'The Development of Anthropology' in *Selected Papers from the American Anthropologist 1888-1920,* Edited by F. de Laguna, Evanston, Ill.: Row, Peterson.
EGGAN, Fred (1968) 'One Hundred Years of Ethnology and Social Anthropology' in *One Hundred Years of Anthropology,* Edited by J. O. Brew, Cambridge, Mass.: Harvard University Press.
ENGELS, Frederick (1972) [1884] *The Origin of the Family, Private Property and the State: In the Light of the Researches of Lewis H. Morgan,* New York: International Publications.
ETIENNE, Mona (1977) 'Women and Men, Cloth and Colonization: The Transformation of Production-Distribution Relations Among the Baule', *Cahiers d'etudes africaines* 65:41-64.
FAITHORN, E. (1975) 'The Concept of Pollution Among the Kafe of the Papua New Guinea Highlands' in *Toward an Anthropology of Women*, Edited by R. R. Reiter, New York: Monthly Review Press.
FRIEDL, Ernestine (1975) *Women and Men*, New York: Holt, Rinehart and Winston.
GILLISON, Gillian (1980) 'Images of Nature Culture and Gender in Gimi Thought' in *Nature Culture and Gender*, Edited by C. P. MacCormack and M. Strathern, Cambridge: Cambridge University Press.
GOODALE, Jane (1971) *Tiwi Wives*, Seattle: University of Washington Press.
GOODALE, Jane (1981) 'Gender, Sexuality and Marriage: A Kaulong Model of Nature and Culture' in *Nature Culture and Gender,* Edited by C. P. MacCormack and M. Strathern, Cambridge: Cambridge University Press.
GRAY, Brenda (in press) 'Enga Birth, Maturation and Survival: Physiological Characteristics of the Life Cycle in the New Guinea Highlands' in *Ethnography of Fertility and Birth*, Edited by C. P. MacCormack, London: Academic Press.
HINDESS, B. and P. Q. HIRST (1975) *Pre-Capitalist Modes of Production,* London: Routledge and Kegan Paul.
JORDAN, Brigiette (1978) *Birth in Four Cultures*, Montreal: Eden Press.
JORDANOVA, L. J. (1981) 'Natural Facts: A Historical Perspective on Science and Sexuality' in *Nature, Culture and Gender*, Edited by C. P. MacCormack and M. Strathern, Cambridge: Cambridge University Press.
KAYBERRY, Phyllis (1939) *Aboriginal Woman: Sacred and Profane*, London: Routledge and Kegan Paul.

KAYBERRY, Phyllis (1952) *Women of the Grassfields: A Study of the Economic Position of Women in Bamenda, British Cameroons,* London: Her Majesty's Stationery Office, 'Preface' by Daryll Forde.

KRIGE, E. J. and J. D. KRIGE (1943) *The Realm of the Rain Queen: A Study of the Pattern of Lovedu Society,* Oxford: Oxford University Press.

LA FONTAINE, Jean S. (1972) 'Introduction' and 'Ritualization of Women's Life-Crisis in Bugisu' in *The Interpretation of Ritual: Essays in Honour of A. I. Richards,* London: Tavistock.

LAMPHERE, Louis (1977) 'Anthropology', *Signs* 2:612-627.

LEACOCK, Eleanor B. (1972) 'Introduction to Frederick Engels' in *The Origin of the Family, Private Property and the State,* New York: International Publications.

LEIBOWITZ, Lila (1978) *Females, Males and Families: A Biological Approach,* North Scituate, Mass.: Duxbury Press.

LITTLE, Kenneth (1951) *The Mende of Sierra Leone,* London: Routledge and Kegan Paul.

LOWIE, Robert H. (1920) *Primitive Society,* New York: Horace Liveright.

LOWIE, Robert, H. (1956) 1935 *The Crow Indians,* New York: Holt, Rinehart and Winston.

MacCORMACK (Hoffer), Carol P. (1972) 'Mende and Sherbo Women in High Office', *Canadian Journal of African Studies,* 6:151-64.

MacCORMACK (Hoffer), Carol P. (1974) 'Madam Yoko: Ruler of the Kpa Mende Confederacy' in *Woman Culture and Society,* Edited by M. Z. Rosaldo and L. Lamphere, Stanford: Stanford University Press.

MacCORMACK, Carol P. (1977) 'Biological Events and Cultural Control' in *Women and Development: The Complexities of Change,* Edited by Wellesley Editorial Committee, Chicago: University of Chicago Press.

MacCORMACK, Carol P. (1979) 'Sande: the Public Face of a Secret Society' in *The New Religions of Africa,* Edited by Bennetta Jules-Rosette, Norwood, N. J.: Ablex Press.

MacCORMACK, Carol P. (1981) 'Nature Culture and Gender: A Critique' and 'Proto-social to Adult: A Sherbro Transformation' in *Nature Culture and Gender,* Edited by C. P. MacCormack and M. Strathern, Cambridge: Cambridge University Press.

MacCORMACK, Carol P. (Ed.) (in press) *Ethnography of Fertility and Birth,* London: Academic Press.

MacCORMACK, Carol P. and Marilyn STRATHERN (Eds.) (1981) *Nature Culture and Gender,* Cambridge: Cambridge University Press.

MAIR, Lucy P. (1936) *Native Policies in Africa,* London: HMSO.

MAIR, Lucy P. (1950) 'The Role of the Anthropologist in Non-Autonomous Territories' in *Principles and Methods of Colonial Administration,* London: HMSO.

MATHIEU, Nicole-Claude (1973) 'Homme-culture et femme-nature?', *L'Homme* 13:101-41, reprinted 'Man-culture and woman-nature' (translated Diana Leonard) in *Women's Studies International Quarterly,* 1978, Vol. I, No. 1, pp. 55—66.

MEAD, Margaret (1949) *Male and Female,* New York: Dell.

MEAD, Margaret (1966) *An Anthropologist at Work: Writings of Ruth Benedict,* New York: Atherton Press.

MEAD, Margaret and Ruth L. BUNZEL (Eds.) (1960) *The Golden Age of American Anthropology,* New York: George Braziller.

MEIGS, Anna S. (1976) 'Male Pregnancy and the Reproduction of Sexual Opposition in a New Guinea Highlands Society', *Ethnology* 15:393-407.

MEILLASSOUX, C. (1975) *Femme, grenier et capitaux,* Paris: Maspero.

MILTON, Kay (1979) 'Male Bias in Anthropology?', *Man* 14:40-54.

MORGAN, Lewis Henry (1963) [1877] *Ancient Society, or Researchers in the Lines of Human Progress from Savagery through Barbarism to Civilization,* New York: World.

MYNTTI, Cynthia (1980) *Traditional Medicine in Rural North Yemen,* Ph.D. thesis, Department of Social Anthropology, London School of Economics, University of London.

ORTNER, Sherry (1974) 'Is Female to Male as Nature is to Culture?' in *Woman Culture and Society,* Edited by M. Z. Rosaldo and L. Lamphere, Stanford: Stanford University Press.

RAPP, Rayna (1977) 'Gender and Class: An Archaeology of Knowledge Concerning the Origin of the State', *Dialectical Anthropology* 2:309-16.

RAPP, Rayna (1979) 'Anthropology', *Signs* 4:497-513.

REITER, R. R. (Ed.) (1975) *Toward an Anthropology of Women,* New York: Monthly Review Press.

ROSALDO, Michelle Z. (1974) 'Woman Culture and Society: A Theoretical Overview' in *Woman Culture and Society,* (Edited by M. Z. Rosaldo and L. Lamphere, Stanford: Stanford University Press.

ROSALDO, Michelle Z. and Louise LAMPHERE (1974) 'Introduction', *Woman Culture and Society,* Edited by M. Z. Rosaldo and L. Lamphere, Stanford: Stanford University Press.

SACKS, Karen (1974) 'Engels Revisited: Women, the Organisation of Production, and Private Property' in *Woman Culture and Society,* Edited by M. Z. Rosaldo and L. Lamphere, Stanford: Stanford University Press.

SANDAY, Peggy R. (1973) 'Toward a Theory of the Status of Women'. *American Anthropologist* 75:682-700.

SANJEK, Roger (1978) 'The Position of Women in the Major Department of Anthropology 1967-76', *American Anthropologist* 80:894-904.

SHAPIRO, Judith (1976) 'Sexual Hierarchy among the Yanomama' in *Sex and Class in Latin America*, Edited by June Nash and Helen I. Safa, New York: Praeger.

STACK, C. B. (1974) *All our Kin*: *Strategies for Survival in a Black Community*, New York: Harper and Row.

STRATHERN, Marilyn (1972) *Women in Between*: *Female Roles in a Male World*: *Mount Hagen, New Guinea*, London: Seminar Press.

STRATHERN, Marilyn (1981) 'No Nature, No Culture: The Hagen Case' in *Nature Culture and Gender*, Edited by C. P. MacCormack and M. Strathern, Cambridge: Cambridge University Press.

TANNER, Nancy and Adrienne ZIHLMAN (1976) 'Women in Evolution: Innovation and Selection in Human Origins', *Signs* 1:585-608.

VAN ALLEN, Judith (1972) 'Sitting on a Man: Colonialism and the Lost Political Institutions of Igbo Women', *Canadian Journal of African Studies* 6:165-182.

WINER, Annette B. (1976) *Women of Value and Men of Renown*: *New Perspectives in Trobriand Exchange*, Austin: University of Texas Press.

WILSON, G. and Monica WILSON (1945) *The Analysis of Social Change Based on Observations in Central Africa*, Cambridge: Cambridge University Press.

8

Psychology and Feminism — If you Can't Beat Them, Join Them[1]

BEVERLY M. WALKER

Before writing this paper I asked many of my academic colleagues: 'What effect do you think the women's movement has had on psychology?' Most replied: 'a great deal'. When pressed for details they spoke of their increasing concern to avoid sexist terminology, their greater awareness of possible sex differences when constructing and analyzing their experiments, the more frequent papers given by women in areas of psychology previously dominated by men and the increasing rate of research on sex roles and fear of success.

I tried to push my colleagues further. 'Surely', I suggested, 'these are fairly superficial changes. I'm more interested in the kinds of theory and types of methodology used.' However, it was rare to find anyone who could offer suggestions in this area. This corroborated my own perception of the situation. The changes in the fundamental nature of psychology have not yet been great — in many cases they are merely token. Feminism has provided psychology with a few extra problems to look at, and some additional ways to analyze data. In short, to a large extent the feminst critique has been coopted by mainstream psychology without any widescale corresponding change in psychology's nature, theory or practice.

The initial attack on psychology came from outside the discipline with the assault of major feminist writers such as De Beauvoir (1953), Millett (1971), Greer (1971), Firestone (1971), and others on psychoanalysis. The publication of Weisstein's (1971) article, in particular, was crucial because it broadened the consideration of feminism's attack to more general issues rather than those pertaining to a particular theory.

The feminist critique was facilitated by meetings of psychologists held in many countries to dicuss the issues involved. In Australia, a Log of Claims evolved out of a 'Hearing' on Women and Psychology in 1974 (Dalgleish, 1975) and subsequently, a symposium on Women and Psychology was held. Una Gault edited an edition of the Australian Psychologist on *Women and Psychology* (1975, 10 (3)). In Britain a symposium was held, the proceedings of which were subsequently published (Chetwynd, 1975). A task force on the status of women in Canadian Psychology was set up and its report published in the *Canadian Psycholgical Review* (1977, 28 (1)). Crucial also was the setting up in the United States of the American Psychological Association's (APA) Committee on Women in Psychology and the establishment of Division 35 of the APA in the area of Psychology of Women.

[1] I am indebted to Dr. Una Gault, Senior Lecturer, Department of Behavioural Science, Macquarie University, Sydney, for the title of this paper.

The log of claims proposed by these meetings and organizations are far-reaching. In this paper I will only be able to select certain areas to explore. I have chosen to consider the effect of feminism on academic theory and research because I regard this as crucial to change in applied areas such as psycho-therapeutic practice. For convenience I have also restricted my review to literature written in English.

I have chosen many of the major underlying criticisms made by feminists of psychology, and the research and theory proposed to vitiate them. Since the feminist critique is an ongoing one, this paper must be considered as an interim report. The pessimism expressed in the title of this paper is a consequence of my concern that many of the important issues have been avoided because they challenge the basic assumptions held, and methodology adopted by psychology.

Psychology and the Feminist Critique

(a) An objective or a value-laden discipline?

Central to the feminist critique is the argument that psychology is not objective, and that it and its practitioners have contributed to the oppression of women by theory and practice. This view is antithetical to the way most psychologists had seen and taught about their discipline.

Psychology in recent times has been dominated by positivism. The model of psychology adopted, particularly in the United States, was that of the supposedly 'objective' natural and physical sciences, so that the methodology adopted was the traditional scientific method applied to psychological problems.

Although the so-called objectivity of the physical sciences has been questioned (e.g. Barnes, 1974; Easlea, 1973) only recently has this become an issue in psychology. Marxist and other 'radical' psychologists have pointed to the value-laden nature of psychological theory and practice (e.g. Armistead, 1972, 1974; Brown, 1973). The Jensen (1969) controversy provoked a re-consideration of the values involved in concepts of intelligence and IQ testing. The issues have been broadened by other writings such as Bart (1972) on psychotherapy, Riegel (1972) in developmental psychology, Israel and Tajfel (1973) and Rawson (1976) in social psychology and Kvale's (1976) courageous assault on the bastion of assumed objectivity, learning theory. A broader framework for the consideration of this issue was provided by Buss's (1975) paper on the sociology of psychological knowledge.

The feminist critique of psychology gained extra impetus and legitimacy within the context of this debate. But, most importantly, it contributed greatly to the issues raised concerning the value-laden nature of psychology, as is acknowledged by many of the writers cited (e.g. Brown, 1973).

Thus the feminist critique of psychology can be seen as something that cannot be remedied by a few patches here and there. It is an attack on the way psychologists have seen and practised their discipline, on the fundamental assumptions and methodologies that they have used.

(b) The male as the prototype/standard

In psychological theory and research the male has been regarded as the prototype of humanity and the female considered largely in relationship to him; males are considered as the norm, the criterion, whereas females are merely considered in comparison to this standard. A few examples illustrate this point:

(i) Psychoanalysis

This point is exemplified in Freudian psychoanalytic theory. Freud saw male development as the prototype — the penis being central to an understanding of the Oedipus complex and all subsequent development. The resolution of the Oedipus complex was seen by Freud to be critical to the development of the moral component of the personality (the superego) and was central to the repression of the all-critical earlier phases of development which, by virtue of their denial to consciousness, recur to haunt us in our subsequent growth throughout life. Thus for both males and females, development is to be understood in relation to the penis — for males its presence, for females its absence. For the female, the recognition that she has no penis (which Freud argues occurs during the Oedipal stage) is the critical experience. Here, Freud claimed, lay the reason for her sense of inferiority, her passivity, her under-developed superego and subsequent dependence on the male.

Traditional Freudian theory was attacked and dismissed by most of the classic feminist writers, as mentioned previously. Not all their criticisms were new however. Female psychoanalysts such as Horney and Thompson had criticised Freud's phallocentric position previously, putting forward alternative theoretical accounts within the broad framework of psychoanalysis (Moulton, 1975). However, their criticisms had been largely ignored, particularly in those influential textbooks of personality theory and in the traditional psychoanalytic literature.

The dismissal of Freudian theory by most feminists was challenged by the publication of Juliet Mitchell's (1974) book *Psychoanalysis and Feminism*, which argued that psychoanalytic theory was valuable as an analysis of the individual within a patriarchal society. Like many of the ignored psychoanalytic women theorists, she has taken the broad framework, concepts and theories of psychoanalysis and used them in a less dogmatic fashion. Largely as a consequence of the controversy surrounding her book, many have turned again to psychoanalytic theory as a flexible rubric to consider issues not developed by Freud himself. Revisions of Freud's account of the psychology of women have followed (Schafer, 1974; Gillespie, 1975; Strouse, 1974) as well as an awakening of interest, in Britain in particular, of the work of French writers such as Lacan, who was discussed by Mitchell (1974). Much of this exploration of Lacan, however, has been outside of the academic psychological journals (Coward, 1978 a & b; Sayers, 1979; Adams, 1978) and as yet has had little or no effect on mainstream theory.

This widescale re-evaluation of psychoanalysis has been a concerted attempt to avoid the Freudian phallocentric assumption that the male is the prototype for the female.

(ii) Male Subjects

In psychology, male subjects have been studied much more frequently in research than have female subjects. In 1960, Carlson and Carlson reported that in their survey of the *Journal of Abnormal and Social Psychology* between 1958 and 1960, males were used far more frequently than females as research subjects. (Of the 298 studies, only 5% used all-female subjects, while 38% used all-male samples.) More recent surveys have indicated that this bias has continued (Peay, 1976) and even applies to the study of rodents (Doty, 1974). The reasons for this imbalance are diverse (Prescott, 1978). Further, Schwabacher (1970) found that when the sex of the subjects was not specified in the abstract of the paper, examination of the original article indicated that the subjects were more likely to have been males than females. She indicates that there is a clear tendency to generalize from all-male samples to humanity in general ('the results indicate dramatically that an individual . . .') while research on women is only generalized to a female population.

In fact there are large bodies of research purporting to be of general psychological significance, which have only been validated on males and have been found not to apply in the same way to females. The convergent-divergent thinking distinction of Hudson (1967) and the need for achievement research of McClelland and Atkinson exemplify this point. Despite this restriction in the range of demonstrated applicability of such research, many of these proponents continue to write and speak about their findings as if they were generally applicable.

(iii) Male is normal — female is abnormal

It had long been established that behaviour and characteristics stereotypically ascribed to men and women are differentially valued —masculine traits are perceived as more socially desirable than feminine traits (Kitay, 1940; McKee and Sherriffs, 1959). However, the implications of this finding had not been carefully considered.

A study by Broverman, Broverman, Clarkson, Rosenkrantz and Vogel (1970), investigated the perception of mental health professionals of a 'healthy, mature, socially competent adult' person (sex unspecified), male and female. They found that mental health professionals were more likely to attribute traits characteristic of the healthy adult to men than to women. Their concepts of the healthy adult and man, did not differ significantly, whereas those of the healthy adult and female did. This particular finding of Broverman *et al.* (1970) has been corroborated elsewhere. In Australia, Anderson and the Feminist Psychology Group (1975) drew similar conclusions based on a sample of clinical psychologists.

This demonstration of the pervasiveness of stereotypes has been interpreted by many as exemplifying a female dilemma — the choice between being a healthy person or a healthy women. This has contributed towards the focus of attention that has been directed towards clinical practice and theory. However, the relationship between Broverman *et al.*'s (1970) study and the behaviour of clinicians in a treatment situation remains to be demonstrated. As Coie, Pennington and Buckley (1974), Maxfield (1976) and Spence, Helmreich and Stapp (1975) suggest, a double standard of mental health may exist only to the extent that when individuals are asked to think of a mentally healthy adult in the abstract, they think of a male; when more details are given about the person to be rated, there is less stereotyping (Maxfield, 1976). The relationship between attitudes and behaviour is not clear-cut.

A re-evaluation of women and mental health has begun. The literature has expanded greatly with among others, Chesler's (1972) *Women and Madness,* Smith and David (eds.) *Women Look at Psychiatry* (1975), Franks and Burtle, *Women in Therapy* (1974), and Rawlings and Carter, *Psychotherapy for Women: Treatment Towards Equality,* (1977). How far-reaching these arguments have been on psychotherapeutic practice is too great an issue to be dealt with here, although my opinion is that, as yet, it has made little impact on the majority of practitioners or training programmes for clinicians. It is to be hoped that the recently published *Guideline for Therapy with Women* (1978), prepared by the task force on sex bias and sex role stereotyping in psychotherapeutic practice, will assist in this regard.

Thus feminists have criticised psychology for its approach regarding the male as the standard or prototype and only considering the female in comparison to this standard. Success at overcoming this problem has been variable. Steps have been taken to revise psychoanalysis in the light of these criticisms, to redress the balance with regard to subject choice and to increase awareness among clinicians of the bind they place women in with their concepts of mental health. However, as yet, these attempts have not been completely successful. The change necessitated is so far-reaching that the process can only be slow.

(c) *The magnification of sex differences — or the emphasis on similarities?*

The nature of research in psychology has focused attention on differences between the sexes and the ignoring of similarities. Many extensive reviews have been published, considering hundreds of studies and concluding that certain sex differences were established (e.g. Burt and Moore, 1912; Anatasi, 1958; Tyler, 1965; Maccoby, 1966; Garai and Scheinfield, 1968; Sherman, 1971; Hutt, 1972; Maccoby and Jacklin, 1974; Fairweather, 1976; Willerman, 1979). However, consideration of the conclusions of these studies can only lead to confusion since they are frequently contradictory. Evidence regarded by one researcher as establishing a particular difference is contradicted by other evidence presented in another review.

For example, Hutt (1972) points to the 'law of greater variability in the male', namely the assertion that males are more extreme than females on whatever dimension is being studied. Thus there are more male geniuses and mental retardates, whereas females are more homogeneous with respect to intelligence. Heim (1970) termed this 'the mediocrity of women'. This view has a long history. It has persisted despite the fact that as early as 1897 Pearson termed it a 'pseudo-scientific superstition', while Anastasi (1958) presented extensive evidence to contradict it. More recently Shields (1975) traced the historical context of the advocacy of this view, suggesting that theories such as this, which have been used to keep women in their place, and which are 'politically and socially useful', have 'an uncanny knack of reappearing, albeit in an altered form'.

The method most frequently used by psychologists is to construct and analyse data so as to falsify a null hypothesis (postulating no differences between groups). Acceptance of a directional alternative hypothesis, postulating differences between groups, is preferred. Thus the accepted methodology in psychology mitigates against finding similarities in favour of the demonstration of significant differences (Furedy, 1978; Greenwald, 1975).

Thus methodology is important for the study of sex differences since publication practice, as well as experimenters' personal preferences for directional significance, has meant that studies showing no differences between the sexes tend not to be published. Experiments are generally constructed with the assumption that 5 times out of 100 the true null hypothesis would be rejected, in favour of the incorrect directional alternative. Since we have no idea, for any one dimension, how many studies confirming the null hypothesis have been carried out but not published, many of the sex differences reported may be spurious.

In this context Maccoby and Jacklin's (1974) book is of major importance. They consider the consistency of published sex differences for 83 dimensions. They conclude that there are only four 'well-established' differences, viz. girls excel in verbal ability, boys in visuo-spatial and mathematical ability, and boys are more aggressive. They assert that there are a number of 'unfounded beliefs' about sex differences viz. girls are more social, more suggestible, lower in self-esteem, and less motivated toward achievement. Further, they reject the views that girls are better at simple repetitive tasks, whereas boys excel at tasks requiring more complex or analytic reasoning. Finally they found no consistent evidence to support the view that girls are more influenced by the environment, boys by heredity or the argument that girls are auditorally oriented while boys are visual. They also specified certain areas where the evidence is equivocal.

Block (1976) has criticised certain features of Maccoby and Jacklin's work. Her arguments suggest that the differences indicated are conservative, and that some of those they class as equivocal could be seen as substantiated sex differences. However, Maccoby and Jacklin's work remains of central importance in indicating the tenuous nature of many of the assumed differences.

Psychologists have always stressed the fact that when they are speaking of differences they are concerned with average differences. Thus if males on the average have higher scores on spatial ability measures than females, many females are still higher than the average male on spatial ability, as the distribution of scores for males and females show substantial overlap.

However, the practical application of the findings on sex differences have frequently overlooked this important point. In the past, vocational guidance testing ignored overlaps. In many cases mechanical reasoning tests were not administered to females, thus avoiding findings that might disconfirm the stereotypes that all women are inadequate in comparison to males on mechanical tests and tasks.

Thus the feminist critique of sex difference research has begun a major re-evaluation of the widespread assumptions about sex differences. Psychologists are less prone to making sweeping generalisations about their nature, irrespective of their interpretation of their origin. Similarities are still not regarded as important as differences but writers can no longer make the extensive sweeping sexist interpretations which were characteristic of some of the earlier reviews in this area.

(d) *The perpetuation of sex-role stereotypes — and the alternatives*

Psychology has contributed in a number of ways to the reinforcement of sex-role stereotypes by its theory and practice. The following are some important examples which illustrate this point.

(i) Masculinity — Femininity

The terms 'masculinity' (M) and 'femininity' (F) were taken from everyday parlance and investigated as traits of personality. The literature on this area has been a confused one (Constantinople, 1973). Different approaches have been used to develop measures of M and F. Terman and Miles (1936), for example, used measures that they considered distinguished between the sexes (viz. word association, ink-blot association, information, interests, introversion, emotional and ethical attitudes, and opinions). This method of choosing items that discriminate between the sexes has in some cases been corroborated by distinctions made between homosexual and heterosexual individuals (e.g. Hathaway and McKinley (1943) in the MF scale of the MMPI, and the Femininity scale included in Gough's (1964) California Personality Inventory).

In view of the suspect nature of many so-called sex differences, this approach calls into question the adequacy of measures of masculinity and femininity. Further, many other issues obscure the interpretation of these measures (Constantinople, 1973). For example Jenkin and Vroegh (1969) criticised the assumption that M – F is a single bipolar continuum, postulating that it could be two separate dimensions. Problems have arisen particularly, however, when the traditional scales have been interpreted as measuring normality, so that males who score low on M and high on F are seen as deviant (probably homosexual), and vice versa for the non-stereotypic females.

The research of Bem (1974, 1975) has gone some way towards clarifying some of these issues. She used as criterion for inclusion of items in the Bem Sex-Role Inventory (BSRI), their being rated as consistent with American society's conception of sex-typed standards. Thus items such as aggressive, ambitious, dominant and self-reliant were rated as socially desirable for men, whereas items such as affectionate, compassionate, loyal and shy were rated as socially desirable for a woman.

Because Bem allowed for two separate dimensions of M and F, subjects responding to the questionnaire could be categorized as high on both M and F or low on both, an outcome which was precluded by most previous investigators of M and F who assumed that these lay at extremes of the one continuum. This then introduced an important new concept to be investigated by psychologists, namely androgyny. Bem (1974) defines androgynous individuals in the following way:

> '. . . they might be both masculine and feminine, both assertive and yielding, both instrumental and expressive — depending on the situational appropriateness of these various behaviours . . .'.

The use of the BSRI and the exploration of androgyny has become an industry. Hundreds of papers have related these dimensions to every conceivable other dimension. Recently however the scale has come under substantial criticism for many reasons (e.g. Locksley and Colten, 1979; Rowland, 1979; Spence and Helmreich, 1978). An important problem with the scale that has not been given sufficient attention centres around the lack of correspondence between Bem's definition of androgyny, which stresses the appropriateness of behaviour in differing situations, and the measure itself, which requires subjects to rate the appropriateness of descriptions of themselves *without reference to situational context*. The ignoring of the situation is a general problem in the study of personality in psychology. The investigation of sex roles has not avoided the glaring inadequacies of traditional psychological research.

However, the BSRI and other such inventories, including the Personal Attributes Questionnaire (Spence and Helmreich, 1978), have served a useful function in that they have effectively questioned the assumption that it is desirable for males to be 'masculine' and females 'feminine'. An alternative view of the healthy individual has been proposed — the androgynous person who can react appropriately to the particular situation.

(ii) Psychological testing

The construction and use of certain psychological tests has contributed toward the perpetuation of sex-role stereotypes (Harmon, 1973; Linden, Linden and Bodine, 1974; Sweet, 1974). Tests have been developed which preclude non-stereotypic responses.

Males are given one form and females another, the nature of the form being determined by the stereotype. Certain tests can only be interpreted adequately if given to one sex, since the norms (which enable comparison of scores between individuals) are provided for a particular sex only.

Many of these tests are used extensively for vocational guidance. Some of the issues can be illustrated by reference to a widely used test of vocational interests, the Strong Vocational Inventory Blank (SVIB), which had separate response forms for each sex, one pink and one blue. (No prizes for guessing which was which.) Males were given a wider option of vocational choice, and the occupations specified entailed more responsibility than those available to women. For example items like astronomer, auto salesman, building contractor and carpenter appeared only on the men's form, and items like dental assistant, artist's model, beauty specialist and book-keeper appeared only on the women's form. The options checked favourably by the client seeking vocational guidance could be used as suggestions for job choice. Thus the effect of this was ordinarily to confine discussion with female clients to traditionally female occupations, and male clients to traditionally male occupations, thus inhibiting exploration of non-sterotypic occupational roles.

This test and others have been revised in view of the critique presented by feminists. A new form of the SVIB has been devised (Campbell, Crichton, Hansen and Webber, 1974) which reduces substantially the difference between the occupations offered to males and females. However, this can only be a partial solution. The test is normed actuarially. In this context this means that in order to decide on the interests of a particular client, responses to the test are compared to groups of people successful in particular jobs. Thus, for example, if the client's responses are similar to a group of the same sex, successful in an occupation, that occupation would be suggested to the client; if their response is dissimilar to a particular occupational group of the same sex, the client is not encouraged to consider this option. Since there are many occupations in which one sex predominates almost exclusively in our culture, the test still precludes occupational suggestions of a non-traditional kind. Thus actuarially-based norms serve to maintain the status quo. Although in many contexts this approach can be extremely effective for prediction, at times of social change in dimensions relevant to the test, it is clearly inappropriate.

(iii) Women and their children

A further area where sex-role stereotypes have been perpetuated is that concerning the role of women as mothers. Psychologists have contributed substantially to the perpetuation of the view that women's prime function is that of mother.

The view popularized by Bowlby and Dr. Spock that it is necessary for the healthy development of the child for women to have as their primary responsibility the continuous care of their children, at least for the early years, has been taken up by psychologists who regard the first few years of life as crucial for subsequent development.

The evidence proposed by the 'maternal deprivation' theorists has been increasingly recognized as inadequate (Morgan, 1975; Cox, 1978). The evidence generally relates to cases where deprivation is much more extensive than lack of a continuous, caring mother. Thus a more sensible interpretation of the data would be that young children need consistent loving care and nurturance, but this implies nothing about the necessity for this to be given solely by their biological parent of the female sex. Further the assertion that the first five years are crucial for subsequent development has also come under attack in the bald form in which it has been asserted (Clarke and Clarke, 1976).

Developmental psychologists have perpetuated the female as mother by studying primarily relationships between children and their mothers. However, one of the important changes resulting from the feminist movement has been the recent studies concerning fathers (Biller, 1974; Lynn, 1974; Heath, 1976; Lamb, 1976; Parke and Sawin, 1976; Russell, 1978).

Previously the study of fathers' relationships with their children had been primarily in terms of their absence. Psychologists studied 'maternal deprivation' but 'father absence', the value-laden notions of these terms and studies only being recently recognized (e.g. Hochschild, 1973). More recently, researchers have studied the contributions that fathers make to child care and the nature of the interactions they have with their children with the clear conclusion that fathers can be as effective caretakers of children as can mothers. This research and viewpoint has been included in most recent developmental texts, redressing, to some extent at least, the inequities present in earlier publications.

(e) *A psychology 'of' women — or a psychology for women*

Initially feminists were concerned that little had been published in psychology specifically concerning women. The major exception to this was the study of women as mothers, as discussed. The female psychoanalysts had published articles and books, attempting to redress the phallocentric perspective of traditional psychoanalysis; examples include Helene Deutsch, *Psychology of Women* vol. 1 (1944) and vol. 2 (1945); Karen Horney's papers and lectures, published between 1922 and 1936 and reprinted in *Feminine Psychology* (1967); and in the 1940's Clara Thompson's papers on women.

To redress this dearth of writing on women a number of books were published including Bardwick's *Psychology of Women: a Study of Biocultural Conflicts* (1971); Sherman's *On the Psychology of Women: a Survey of Empirical studies* (1971); Hyde and Rosenberg, *Half the Human Experience* (1975); Cox, *Female Psychology: The Emerging Self* (1976); Donnelson and Gullahorn, *Women: a Psychological Perspective* (1977); Williams, *Psychology of Women* (1977): Kopp, *Becoming Female: Perspectives on Development* (1979); and Rohrbaugh, *Women: Psychology's Puzzle* (1979).

These books take varying positions. Many would disagree with Bardwick's emphasis on biological factors (Parlee, 1973) or her assumptions about the nature of sex differences (Maccoby, 1972). Nevertheless, she and the other writers have collected together research from disparate sources, thus providing challenges to the 'male — as — prototype' research termed by Henley (1974) 'psychology against women' (section b).

However, as Parlee (1975) points out this new approach, which Henley (1974) calls the 'psychology 'of' women', implies that separate laws and theories are needed to account for the nature, experience and behaviour of females.

This approach would seem to contradict the stress which many feminists would like to place on the similarities between the sexes, rather than the differences (section c). Further, reviewing many of these studies without extensive criticism ignores the problems inherent in these studies. As Parlee (1975) comments:

'Methodological inadequacies of individual studies or inconsistencies among the results of several investigations may be noted, of course, but the underlying conceptual framework, as reflected in the formuluation of problems and operationalization of terms, remains fundamentally unchanged' (Parlee, 1975, p. 121).

Some research, however, avoids these pitfalls by attempting to redefine an area to produce a 'psychology for women'. One example is the study by Matina Horner (1970, 1972) of fear of success. Horner began with a criticism of the research and theory of achievement motivation and its failure to be relevant to women. McClelland (1953) wrote that the attempts to study women and achievement motivation were 'totally puzzling' (cited in Mednick, Tangri and Hoffman, 1975, p. xii). Horner proposed that the traditional approaches should be extended to incorporate her observation that 'most women have a motive to avoid success, that is, a disposition to become anxious about achieving success because they expect negative consequences (such as a social rejection and/or feelings of being unfeminine) as a result of succeeding'.

This proposal met with immediate interest and the methods she devised led to a proliferation of studies. Other studies conducted later did not report the same preponderance of fear of success in women compared to men (Tresemer, 1977). Other writers have argued that the concept is of little interest because it was merely tapping sex role stereotypes rather than a basic underlying stable motive (Feather and Raphelson, 1974; Monahan, Kuhn and Shaver, 1974).

Basically Horner's technique involved giving an incomplete story to her subjects. The most well-known of these projective stories for women was 'After first term finals, Anne finds herself at the top of her medical school class'. The same cue was given for males except that 'John' was substituted for 'Anne'. The assumption of Horner is that the writer of the story will identify with the character and hence write a story about what they would imagine would happen to them if they were in that situation. This response could then be interpreted in terms of to what extent they themselves 'fear success'.

However, the alternative interpretation of this data is that subjects are responding, not by identifying with the character, but in terms of stereotyped expectations about what happens to women or men who succeed — and in the case of the 'Anne' cue, what happens to the women who succeed in a male-dominated, high-status occupation. The issues raised by Horner's research have, as yet, not been satisfactorily resolved.

Theories and publications concerned specifically with women have clearly served a useful function in pointing out the inadequacy of a 'psychology against women'. However, their ultimate value is limited; they serve to divert attention away from the similarities between women and men to emphasise the differences. Redefining methodology, theory and research to develop a 'psychology for women' (and for men, for that matter), would seem desirable, but as yet this has not been attempted on a large scale.

Conclusion

In this paper I have considered the criticisms that feminists have made of psychology and the effects that this critique has had.

The changes have, however, been limited in comparison to the challenge proposed. This has occurred because feminists have continued, in the main, to work within the inherently conservative framework of methodology and theory of their discipline, without substantial revision of its structure. Carlson (1972) made the point when she considered personality theory and reseach that psychology has an 'agentic' orientation, consistent with a 'masculine principle', emphasizing 'mastery, separation and ego-enhancement.' She contrasts this with a 'communion' oriented discipline which she sees as more compatible with femininity and which emphasises 'fusion, expression, acceptance'.

Although Carlson's arguments are not clearly explored, her views seem compatible with the argument presented in this paper. Psychologists cannot develop a non-sexist psychology without a broader revision of their methodology and practice. We continue to act as if our discipline is value-free. We perpetuate a methodology which accentuates differences and mitigates against an emphasis on similarities. We develop tests which serve to maintain the status quo by reinforcing stereotypes. Thus our endeavours to re-orient psychology are limited by the impoverishment of the discipline as traditionally practised. Feminists and non-feminists have churned out research (and to a lesser extent theory) which has had the result of making a psychology of women just another topic (analogous to the psychology of the rat). This co-option, epitimized in the title of this paper, has diverted attention away from the strategy necessary if a feminist or a non-sexist psychology is to be achieved, nameley the re-definition of both theory and practice. This would involve an assault on the nature of the scientific method as used by psychologists, a rejection of psychological practice which preserves the status quo in favour of a more flexible alternative.

References

ADAMS, S. P. (1978) Representation and Sexuality, *M/F, 1,* 65–82.

ANASTASI, A. (1958) *Differential Psychology: MacMillan:* (N.Y.)

ANDERSON, M and Feminist Psychology Group (1975) Sex role stereotypes and clinical psychologists: an Australian study, *Australian Psychologist, 10* (3), 325–331.

ARMISTEAD, N. (1972) Values in psychology, in *Rat, Myth and Magic,* Russell Press: N.Y.

ARMISTEAD, N. (1974) *Reconstructing social psychology.* Penguin: Harmondsworth.

BARDWICK. J. (1971) *Psychology of women: a study of biocultural conflicts,* Harper & Row: (N.Y.).

BARNES, B. (1974) *Scientific Knowledge and Sociological Theory,* Routledge & Kegan Paul: London.

BART, P. B. (1972) The myth of a value-free psychotherapy, In W. Bell & A. Mau (Eds.) *The Sociology of the Future,* Russell Sage: (N.Y.).

BEM, S. L. (1974) The measurement of psychological androgyny, *Journal of Consulting and Clinical Psychology,* 42 (2), 155–162.

BEM, S. L. (1975) Sex-role adaptability: one consequence of psychological androgyny, *Journal of Personality and Social Psychology, 31* (4), 634–643.

BILLER, H. B. (1974) *Paternal deprivation: family, school, sexuality & society,* Heath: (Lexington, Mass).

BLOCK, J. H. (1976) Issues, problems and pitfalls in assessing sex differences: a critical review of *The Psychology of Sex Differences,* Merrill-Palmer Quarterly, *22* (4), 283–308.

BROVERMAN, I. K., D. M. BROVERMAN, F. E. CLARKSON, P. S. ROSENKRANTZ and S. R. VOGEL (1970) Sex role stereotypes and clinical judgements of mental health, *Journal of Consulting and Clinical Psychology 34* (1), 1–7.

BROWN, P. (1973) (Ed.) *Radical Psychology,* Tavistock: London.

BURT, C. and R. C. MOORE (1912) The mental difference between the sexes: IV theories: *Journal of Experimental Pedagogy and Training College Record, 1,* 355–388.

BUSS, A. R. (1975) The emerging field of the sociology of psychological knowledge, *American Psychologist, 30* (10) 988–1000.

CAMPBELL, D. P., L. CRICHTON, J. I. HANSEN and P. WEBBER (1974) A new edition of the SVIB: the Strong-Campbell Interest Inventory, *Measurement and Evaluation in Guidance, 7* (2), 92–95.

CARLSON, R. (1972) Understanding women: implications for personality theory and research, *Journal of Social Issues, 28* (2), 17–32.

CARLSON, E. R. and R. CARLSON (1960) Male and female subjects in personality research, *Journal of Abnormal and Social Psychology, 61,* 482–483.

CHESLER, P. (1972) *Women and Madness,* Avon Books: N.Y.

CHETWYND, J. (Ed.) (1975) The role of psychology in the propagation of female stereotypes, *British Psychological Society Conference* (April).

CLARKE, A. M. and A. D. B. CLARKE (1976) *Early experience: myth and evidence,* Open Books: London.

COIE, J. D., B. F. PENNINGTON and H. H. BUCKLEY (1974) Effects of situational stress and sex roles on the attribution of psychological disorder, *Journal of Consulting and Clinical Psychology, 42,* 559–568.

CONSTANTINOPLE, A. (1973) Masculinity — femininity: an exception to a famous dictum, *Psychological Bulletin, 80* (5), 389–407.

COWARD, R. (1978a) Sexual Liberation and the Family, *M/F 1,* 7–24.

COWARD, R. (1978b) Rereading Freud: the making of the feminine, *Spare Rib, 70* 43–46.

COX, E. (1978) Beware the call of nature, *Women and Labour Conference Papers: The Politics of Sexuality* (May), 51–58.

COX, S. (1978) *Female psychology: the emerging self,* Science Research Associates: Chicago.

DALGLEISH, L. (1975) Women and psychology 'Learning' group report, *Australian Psychologist, 10,* (3), 339–344.

DE BEAUVOIR, S. (1953) *The Second Sex,* Jonathan Capem: London.

DEUTSCH, H. (1944/45) *Psychology of Women,* Grune & Stratton: Vol. 1, Vol. 2, N.Y.

DONNELSON, E. and J. E. GULLAHORN (1977) *Women: a psychological perspective,* John Wiley & Sons: N.Y.

DOTY, R. L. (1974) A cry for the liberation of the female rodent: courtship and copulation in rodentia, *Psychological Bulletin 18,* 181–192.

EASLEA, B. (1973) *Liberation and the aims of science,* Chatto & Windus: London.

FAIRWEATHER, H. (1976) Sex differences in cognition, *Cognition, 4,* 231–280.

FEATHER, N. T. and A. C. RAPHELSON (1974) Fear of success in Australian and American student groups: motive or sex-role stereotype? *Journal of Personality, 42,* 190–201.

FIRESTONE, S. (1971) *The dialectic of sex: the case for feminist revolution,* Cape: London.

FRANKS, V. and V. BURTLE (1974) *Women in therapy: new psychotherapies for a changing society,* Brunner/Mazel: N.Y.

FUREDY, J. J. (1978) *Negative results: abolish the name but honour the same,* In Sutcliffe, J. P. (ed.) Conceptual Analysis and Method in Psychology: essays in honour of W. M. O'Neil. Sydney University Press: Sydney.

GARAI, J. E. and A. SCHEINFIELD (1968) Sex differences in mental and behavioural traits, *Genetic psychology monographs,* (May), *77,* 169–299.

GILLESPIE, W. H. (1975) Woman and her discontents. A reassessment of Freud's views on female sexuality, *International Review of Psychoanalysis, 2,* (1), 1–9.

GOUGH, H. G. (1964) *California Psychological Inventory:* Consulting Psychologists Press: Palo Alto.

GREENWALD, A. C. (1975) Consequences of prejudice against the null hypothesis, *Psychological Bulletin, 82,* 1.20.

GREER, G. (1971) *The female eunuch:* MacGibbon & Kee: London.

HARMON, L. W. (1978) Sexual bias in interest measurement, *Measurement and Evaluation in Guidance, 5* (4), 496–501.

HATHAWAY, S. R. and J. C. McKINLEY (1943) *The Minnesota Multiphasic Personality Inventory* Psychological Corporation: N.Y.

HEATH, D. H. (1976) Competent fathers: their personalities and images, *Human Development, 19,* 26–39.

HEIM, A. W. (1970) *Intelligence and Personality: Their assessment and relationship,* Penguin.

HENLEY, N. (1974) Resources for the study of psychology and women, *RT: Journal of Radical Therapy, 4,* 20–21.

HOCHSCHILD, A. R. (1973) A review of sex role research, In J. Huber (Ed.), *Changing women in a changing society,* University of Chicago Press: Chicago.

HORNER, M. (1970) Femininity and successful achievement: A basic inconsistency, In J. M. Bardwick, E. Douvan, M. S. Horner and D. Gutman, *Feminine Personality and Conflict,* Brooks/Cole: Belmont, California.

HORNER, M. (1972) Toward an understanding of achievement-related conflicts, in women: *Journal of Social Issues, 28* (2).

HORNEY, K. (1967) *Feminine Psychology,* Routledge & Kegan Paul: London.

HUDSON, L. (1967) *Contrary Imaginations,* Penguin: Harmondsworth, Middlesex.

HUTT, C. (1972) *Male and Female,* Penguin: Harmondsworth, Middlesex.

HYDE, J. S. and B. C. ROSENBERG (1975) *Half the human experience: the psychology of women,* D. C. Heath: Lexington Mass.

ISRAEL, J. and H. TAJFEL (Eds.) (1972) *The context of social psychology: A critical assessment,* Academic Press: London.

JENKIN, N. and K. VROEGH (1969) Contemporary concepts of masculinity and femininity, *Psychological Reports, 25,* 679–697.

JENSEN, A. R. (1969) How much can we boost IQ and scholastic achievement, *Harvard Educational Review, 39,* 1–123.

KITAY, P. M. (1940) A comparison of the sexes in their attitudes and beliefs about women, *Sociometry, 34,* 399–407.

KOPP, C. B. (Ed.) (1979) *Becoming female: perspectives on development,* Plenum: N.Y.

KVALE, S. (1976) The psychology of learning as ideology and technology, *Behaviourism, 4,* 97–116.

LAMB, M. E. (1976) *The Role of the Father in Child Development,* Wiley: N.Y.

LINDEN, K. W., J. D. LINDEN and R. L. BODINE (1974) Test bias: fuss'n'facts, *Measurement and Evaluation in Guidance, 7* (3), 163–168.

LOCKSLEY, A. and M. E. COLTEN (1979) Psychological androgyny: A case of mistaken identity? *Journal of Personality and Social Psychology, 37* (6), 1017–1031.

LYNN, D. B. (1976) Fathers and sex-role development, *The Family Co-ordinator,* 403–409.

MACCOBY, E. (Ed.) (1966) *The development of Sex Differences,* Stanford University Press: Stanford, California.

MACCOBY, E. E. (1972) The meaning of being female, *Contemporary Psychology, 17,* (7), 369–372.

MACCOBY, E. E. and C. N. JACKLIN (1974) *The psychology of sex differences,* Stanford University Press: Stanford, California.

McKEE, J. P. and A. C. SHERRIFFS (1959) Men's and women's beliefs, ideals and self-concepts, *American Journal of sociology, 64,* 356–363.

MAXFIELD, R. B. (1976) Sex role stereotypes of psychotherapists, *Dissertation Abstracts International, 37,* 1914 B.

MEDNICK, M. T. S., S. S. TANGRI and L. W. HOFFMAN (Eds.) (1975) *Women and achievement: social and motivational analyses,* Hemisphere: Washington.

MILLETT, K. (1971) *Sexual Politics,* Rupert Hart — Davis: London.

MITCHELL, J. (1974) *Psychoanalysis and feminism,* Allen Lane: London.

MONAHAN, L., D. KUHN and P. SHAVER (1974) Intrapsychic versus cultural explanation of the 'fear of success' motive, *Journal of Personality and Social Psychology, 29,* 60–64.

MORGAN, P. (1975) *Child care: sense and fable,* Temple-Smith: London.

MOULTON, R. (1975) Early papers on women: Horney and Thompson, *American Journal of Psychoanalysis, 35,* 207–223.

PARKE, R. D. and D. B. SAWIN (1976) The father's role in infancy: a re-evaluation, *Family Coordinator,* 365–371.

PARLEE, M. B. (1973) The pre-mentstrual syndrome, *Psychological Bulletin, 80,* (6), 454–465.

PARLEE, M. B. (1975) Psychology, *Signs: Journal of Women in Culture and Society, 1,* (1) 119–138.

PEAY, M. Y. (1976) Use of the sex variable in social psychological research, *Australian Psychologist,* 11 (2) 139–146.

PRESCOTT, S. (1978) Why researchers don't study women: The response of 62 researchers, *Sex Roles, 4* (6) 899–905.

RAWLINGS, E. I. and D. K. CARTER (1977) *Psychotherapy for women: Treatment towards equality,* Charles C. Thomas: Springfield, Ill.

RAWSON, D. (1976) Reconstructing value-issue reconsiderations of social psychology, unpublished paper.

RIEGEL, K. F. (1972) Influence of economic and political ideologies on the development of developmental psychology, *Psychological Bulletin, 78* (2), 129–141.

ROHRBAUGH, J. B. (1979) *Women: Psychology's puzzle,* Basic Books: N.Y.

ROWLAND, R. (1979) Australian attitudes to the traditional cultural sex role stereotypes, Ph.D. Thesis, *University of Wollongong.*

RUSSELL, G. (1978) Father — missing factors in descriptions of development, Paper presented to a Symposium on *Cultural Effects and Environment Factors on Cognitive Development,* Australian Conference on Cognitive Development, Canberra, February.

SAYERS, J. (1979) Anatomy is destiny: variations on a theme, *Women's Studies International Quarterly, 2* (1), 19–32.

SCHAFER, R. (1974) Problems in Freud's psychology of women, *American Psychoanalytic Association Journal* (Nov.), 459–485.

SCHWABACHER, S. (1972) Male versus female representation in psychological research: An examination of the Journal of Personality and Social Psychology, 1970, 1971, in *Catalogue of Selected Documents in Psychology, 2,* 20–21.

SHERMAN, J. A. (1971) *On the psychology of women: A survey of empirical studies,* Charles C. Thomas: Springfield, Ill.

SHIELDS, S. A. (1975) Functionalism, Darwinism and the psychology of women, *American Psychologist, 30* 739–754.

SMITH, D. E. and S. J. DAVID (Eds.) (1975) *Women Look at psychiatry,* Press Gang Publishers: Vancouver.

SPENCE, J. T. and R. L. HELMREICH (1978) *Masculinity and femininity: Their psychological dimensions, correlates and antecedcents,* University of Texas Press: Austin, Texas.

SPENCE, J. T., R. HELMREICH and J. STAPP (1975) Ratings of self and peers on sex role attributes and their relation to self-esteem and conceptions of masculinity and femininity, *Journal of Personality and Social Psychology, 32,* 29–39.

STROUSE, J. (Ed.) (1974) *Women and analysis: Dialogues on psychoanalytic views of femininity,* Grossman: N.Y.

SWEET, R. (1974) *On anti-feminism in the theory and practice of vocational psychology,* Research Report, Division of Vocational Guidance Service, N.S.W. Australia.

SWEET, R. (1978) Task-force on sex bias and sex role stereotyping in psychotherapeutic practice, Guidelines for therapy with women, *American Psychologist,* 1122–1123.

TERMAN, L. and C. C. MILES (1936) *Sex and Personality,* McGraw-Hill: N.Y.

TRESEMER, D. W. (1977) *Fear of success,* Plenum Press: N.Y.

TYLER, L. (1965) *The Psychology of Human Differences,* Appleton Century Crofts: N.Y.

WAND, B. (Ed.) (1977) Special issue: report of the task force on the status of women in Canadian Psychology, *Canadian Psychological Review, 28* (1).

WEISSTEIN, N. (1971) *Kinder, Kuche, Kirche as scientific law,* New England Free Press: Boston, Mass.

WILLERMAN, L. (1979) *The psychology of Individual and Group Differences,* W. H. Freeman: San Francisco.

WILLIAMS, J. H. (1977) *Psychology of women: Behavior in a biosocial context,* Norton: N.Y.

9

The Oldest, the most Established, the most Quantitative of the Social Sciences — and the most Dominated by Men: The Impact of Feminism on Economics

MARIANNE A. FERBER AND MICHELLE L. TEIMAN

I. Introduction

Economics is the oldest of the social sciences, the most established, the most quantitative — and has been the most dominated by men. It is easy to document the extent of this domination in the past, and the slow but nonetheless perceptible diminution in recent years. This is done in the first section of this chapter, which shows data on the percent of economics degrees earned by women, on the participation of women in professional economics associations, their representation on university faculties, on editorial boards of scholarly journals, and in relevant governmental positions.[1]

The second section is devoted to the more substantive question of the extent to which the discipline of economics has reflected the virtual absence of women and women's concerns, and the degree to which this has changed in recent years as the feminist movement increased the visibility of women in society at large, and as the representation of women in the economics profession began to expand somewhat. Several approaches to this question are used. First, we examine the widespread neglect of those segments of the economy where women have been traditionally dominant, and the recent developments that have done much to redress this unbalance. Second, we critically review the extensive literature of recent years in the field of labor, economic development, and to a lesser extent taxation that has addressed specifically women's economic role, and their economic concerns, as distinct from those of men. Last, we shall attempt to gauge the effect of these changes on the discipline as it has been offered to students by examining several editions of the best selling economic text, spanning virtually the whole post World War II period.

---

[1] Because the author lives in the U.S., data will be primarily from this country.

II. **Representation of Women in the Economics Profession**

According to the 1970 Census there were 66,000 people employed as economists in the U.S. Of these 11 percent were women. But of the approximately 12,000 with Ph.D.'s, only 5 percent were women. Even by the end of the decade only 8 percent of Ph.D.'s in economics were being awarded to women.[2] Women's representation on the faculties of the universities awarding these degrees has been even lower, not exceeding 5 percent of full time employees. Furthermore, while most men are in the upper ranks of associate and full professor, women are mainly instructors and assistant professors. Thus over 10 percent of instructors, but only two percent of full professors of economics, are women. Fully 30 percent of economics departments at these large, Ph.D. granting institutions, continue to have all male departments.

Given this situation it is not surprising that the hierarchy of the profession has been male. In the U.S. all 81 presidents of the prestigious American Economic Association, founded in 1886, have been men, as have all the 42 recipients of medals, honorary awards and distinguished fellowships, and all but one of the 36 honorary members from other countries.[3] Nonetheless, at all but the most august levels there are signs of change.[4] Of the 215 annual positions of officer since 1953, twenty two were filled by women, 16 of them since 1969. Of the 375 annual positions on the editorial boards of the two official journals of the association,[5] 33 were held by women, all of them since 1970. In 1979 three of the 28 other associations related to economics had a woman president.[6]

Inspection of a number of associations and journals which are either international or based in other countries indicates that the situation in the U.S. is not atypical.[7] The Royal Economic Society in Great Britain, the Canadian Economic Association, the German Verein fur Sozialpolitik, the International Economic Association, are all headed by men, though the president of the Econometric Society is a woman. The editors of the *British Economica* and the *Italian Giornale Degli Economisti* are all male, but the *Economic Journal*, organ of the Royal Economic Society, has had a woman editor along with two or three men for some years now.

The most influential government organization in the U.S. which has invariably been staffed by economists since its inception in 1946 is the Council of Economic Advisors.

---

[2] One reason for the failure to make greater advances is the very considerable diversion of young women who might have previously considered entering economics into MBA programs. The number of MBA's awarded by the late seventies was in excess of 40,000 a year (compared with about 700 Ph.D.'s in Economics) and the proportion going to women reached about 12 percent. U.S. Department of Health, Education and Welfare National Center for Education Statistics, *Digest of Education Statistics 1977–1978*.

[3] The one woman so honored is Joan Robinson of Cambridge University.

[4] In 1972 the American Economic Association adopted a set of principles disavowing sex discrimination in the profession of economics, and established the Committee on the Status of Women in the Economics Profession. This group has worked ever since to provide more information about women economists, to increase their visibility within the profession and to advance their economic status in general.

[5] *The Journal of Economic Literature* began publication in 1969. Prior to that the *American Economic Review* was the only AEA journal.

[6] It is interesting to note that one of these is the Union of Radical Political Economists, one the association of Black economists.

[7] Two obstacles defeated our efforts to do a thorough study: 1. Many associations and journals give only initials and last names for their officers', 2. The author's inability to distinguish male and female names in many languages.

Only one woman[8] has ever been appointed to this prestigious three member body, and that was in 1973. Women economists have, however, been considerably better represented in the top echelons of the Federal Government by the late seventies than ever before, from the first woman Secretary of Commerce and first Governor of the Federal Reserve System, to such other important posts as Director of the Congressional Budget Office, Commissioner of the Bureau of Labor Statistics, Chief of the Office of Plans and Policy of the Federal Communications Commission, Director of the National Commission for Employment Policy, Embassador for UNESCO, and about another dozen positions rarely before held by women.

As women economists are gradually, if slowly, making progress in universities, professional associations and government, it should gradually become easier for young women to advance in this male-dominated field. Not only do they provide role models, but their success also helps to break down existing prejudices.[9] They are forming at least the beginnings of a network that will do for women what the old-boy network continues to do for men. More important, especially in the long run, they have had some success in providing more open access to such important outlets as professional meetings and scholarly journals.

The American Economics Association has in recent years begun to have sessions where submitted papers are read, rather than having invited papers exclusively, and the Committee on the Status of Women in the Economics Profession[10] has made it a point to have a general call for papers for the sessions it has sponsored at the meetings of the AEA and the various regional associations.

It is not surprising, then, to find that in recent years there has been a perceptible increase in the representation of women actively participating in sessions at the AEA meetings. Between 1969 and 1971 only 7.3 percent of session chairs, 4.8 percent of authors of papers and 4.7 percent of discussants were women. Between 1972 and 1977 the comparable figures were 11.4 percent chairs, 13.7 percent authors and 11.6 percent discussants.[11]

Economic journals have been lagging behind those in the other social sciences in adopting double blind refereeing — where the referee does not know the identity of the author(s), as well as vice versa, but even so about half of them have by now adopted this practice. A 1978 survey[12] of acceptance rates of manuscripts written only by men, jointly

---

[8]Marina Von Neumann Whitman. Could it be a coincidence that it was one year later that the Council for the first time devoted a section of its annual Report to the President to economic issues concerning women?

[9]A study of the attitude of people toward women in typically male professions showed that those who had known women in such positions were far less likely to prefer men than those who had not. This was even more true when they judged these women to have been very competent. M. A. Ferber and J. A. Huber, 'Preference for Men as Bosses and Professionals', *Social Forces*, Vol. 58, No. 2, December 1979.

[10]See Footnote 4.

[11]It is not possible to make an equally meaningful comparison for journal articles published. New journals have been springing up at a rapid rate, so that comparing all journals now with all journals published, say, in 1970 is not useful. At the same time the existence of so many new, often more highly specialized outlets is likely to have influenced the choice of journals made by authors, so that a comparison of just the journals in existence during the earlier period is not useful either. The growing proliferation of double blind refereeing and the evidence that women are significantly more likely to have their manuscripts accepted by such journals, does however bode well for their progress in this respect as well.

[12]Sponsored by the Committee on the Status of Women in the Economics Profession of the American Economic Association.

by men and women, or women only, shows that women fare considerably better in journals where the referees do not know the sex of the author(s).[13]

III. Economics: The Broadening Perspective

As we have seen in the previous section, until recently practitioners of economics and *a fortiori* leaders of the profession have been predominantly men. It is therefore not altogether surprising that they showed little interest in those segments of the economy that have been largely the domain of women, namely household production and volunteer work. They also generally ignored the extent to which women were involved in the rest of the economy and the ways in which their behavior, their problems and their accomplishments differed from those of men. While no justification for this neglect was offered, it was presumably caused by the view that the importance of market work was secondary for women, destined to be wives and mothers, and that the importance of women's market work was secondary to the economy.

As women became both more visible and more audible outside the home with the rebirth of the women's movement in the sixties, the scope of economics began to change. The 'new home economics' emerged, focussing on allocation of time and other resources within the household. Volunteer work began to attract the attention of a few economists. An extensive literature sprang up dealing with the determinants of women's labor force participation and examining occupational segregation and continued earnings differentials between men and women. The effect of governmental policies and legislation on the economic status of women was examined. Special attention was also focussed on the role of women in economic development.

If we agree with Joan Robinson's definition that economics is the things economists are interested in, there has been a perceptible shift in the nature of this science by the end of the seventies. No longer is it true as Martha Griffith stated in hearings before the Joint Economic Committee of the U.S. Congress in 1973 that insofar as economic analysis has developed policy, 'it has not met the social concerns of the nation as defined by women, or as defined by men and women. It has met them as defined by men'. The traditional focus on economic man and his behavior in the market economy is being extended to encompass both men and women in virtually all spheres of activity.

1. *The New Home Economics.* While isolated scholars long studied the economic

---

[13]Since it was rather time-consuming to provide the requested information, it is not surprising that only 12 of the 36 journals contacted were willing to furnish it. The results (discussed at greater length in M. A. Ferber and M. L. Teiman, 'Are Women Economists at a Disadvantage in Publishing Journal Articles?' unpublished paper, 1979) are, nonetheless, instructive.

Among the journals which do have double blind reviewing the acceptance rate for manuscripts by only male authors was 15.2 percent, for those with at least one female author only 13.6 percent. Among journals with double blind reviewing, on the other hand, the rates were 19.0 and 26.4 percent respectively. Looking at individual journals, five of those with double blind reviewing had higher acceptance rates for manuscripts with at least one female author, and the rate for the sixth was virtually the same for both groups. Of journals without double blind reviewing, four had higher acceptance rates for manuscripts by men only.

These results clearly show that women, with or without male co-authors tend to do better than men when the referees do not know the sex of the authors, implying that they submit higher quality manuscripts. While it is less clear why this would be so (perhaps the relatively few women in a male field really tend to be better, or perhaps women have less self-confidence and are less likely to submit poor work) it indicates that a more or less equal acceptance rate by journals without double blind reviewing, so far from proving absence off discrimination rather tends to show its presence.

behavior of households[14] it was only in the nineteen sixties that economists in significant numbers began to analyze the division of labor between husband and wife in terms of each rationally specializing in order to maximize family welfare. Soon sophisticated techniques were used not only to examine allocation of tasks between spouses, but to study more generally the economics of marriage, fertility and divorce.[15] Ironically, however, the assumptions underlying the elegant models used by these authors abstract to a considerable extent from the complexities of the traditional family of the past, and take even less account of the realities of the present and the prospects for the future. As one feminist critic has commented, the economists' power to do intellectually clean, challenging and rigorously deductive, highly general work has been purchased at the price of obliterating most of the trees from the forest.[16]

There are at least four major problems with the approach which accepts the traditional family and the traditional division of labor between husband and wife as rational. It ignores the extent to which satisfaction (and dissatisfaction) is derived from work directly, not only from the consumption which work makes possible. The family is treated as though it did not change over time, and children did not grow up and leave home. No attention is paid to the status of the individual within the family. Last, but not least, there is the implied assumption that the family is a permanent, indivisible unit.

First, the division of labor where spouses specialize completely in market and homework respectively has the disadvantage that any type of activity is likely to become less pleasant and more tedious as one spends increasingly more time on it.[17] To the extent that variety is the spice of life, both husband and wife might find it more rewarding to share both types of work. Particularly, she is likely to appreciate the opportunity to get out of the house, and spend some of her time with other adults, while he may well enjoy the opportunity to get to know his children better.

Second, the wife who devotes much or all of her working time to the household finds the value of her contribution declining sharply as children grow up and require less care. At that time she may well consider reentering the labor market.[18] But during the years she was a full time homemaker her labor market skills became rusty. It may now be difficult for her to find work, let alone an interesting and well paid position. The seriousness of this problem will vary according to occupational category, and the length of absence from the labor market. In any case, however, the wife who stays home when

---

[14]Most notably M. G. Reid, *Economics of Household Production*, N.Y.: Wiley, 1934. A far less sophisticated work, written in the 19th century is C. P. Gilman, *Women and Economics.* Reissued in 1966, N.Y.: Harper and Row Publishers.

[15]Much of the seminal work was by G. S. Becker, such as 'A Theory of the Allocation of Time', *Economic Journal*, Vol. 75, No. 299, September 1965; 'A Theory of Marriage: Parts I and II', *Journal of Political Economy*, Vol. 81, No. 4, July/August 1973 and Vol. 82, No. 4, July/August 1974; and 'An Economic Analysis of Marital Instability', *Journal of Political Economy*, Vol. 85, No. 6, December 1977. A massive volume of related works is T. W. Schultz (Ed.) *Economics of the Family: Marriage, Children and Human Capital*, Chicago: University of Chicago Press, 1974.

[16]I. V. Sawhill, 'Economic Perspectives on the Family', *Daedalus*, Vol. 106, Spring 1977. The following critique of 'the new home economics' is based on that article, and one published almost simultaneously by M. A. Ferber and B. G. Birnbaum, 'The New Home Economics: Retrospect and Prospects', *Journal of Consumer Research*, Vol. 4, No. 1, June 1977.

[17]Although housework, and often market work as well, is itself heterogeneous, the differences between market and housework tend to be far greater than those within either category.

[18]The term reentry is used because the great majority of women today were in the labor market before their first child was born.

the children are young is far less likely to maximise family well-being in the long run, over the whole life cycle, even if she does so in the short run, during the early years of marriage.

A recent study of lifetime earnings of clerical workers with various patterns of labor force participation[19] indicates that a woman with two children and a high school education reduces her lifetime earnings by about 29 percent by dropping out of the labor market for 10 years. The comparable figure for a college graduate is 32 percent.

The losses in earnings are partially offset by the greater value of housework of the woman while she is out of the labor market. Using data from Robinson (1977) to determine the difference in time spent, and census data on earnings of housekeepers (with the same level of education as the woman concerned) to estimate the value of that time, we find that the total lifetime contribution of the high school graduate is nonetheless 18 percent lower, and of the college graduate 21 percent lower when she interrupts employment for 10 years.

The same study found that the total lifetime contribution of a high school graduate who leaves the labor market permanently after the birth of her first child is reduced by 57 percent compared to one who never leaves the labor market. The comparable figure for a college graduate is 50 percent.

The above estimates are based on a single occupational category, and would clearly vary for other occupations. Since the earnings profiles of clerical workers are relatively flat as compared, for instance, to most professionals, these estimates are rather conservative. The number of children would also influence the size of the gap, as would other individual variations in lifestyle. But there can be no doubt that the woman who continues to work outside the home makes a far larger contribution to the real income of the family, calculated as money income plus the market value of housework, than does the woman who spends any significant number of years as a full-time homemaker.

Third, in the family where the husband is the sole wage earner he is generally also the dominant decision maker. The wife with no money income of her own is less likely to have her own charge or bank accounts, has less say on when and how money is to be spent or where the family is to live.

From the wife's point of view it is also particularly unfortunate that the value of the homemaker to her family peaks at an early stage of the life cycle. A woman in her forties or fifties may well ask herself what she has done for her family, lately. Worse than that, she may begin to wonder whether the same question is on their minds. During these years the husband's earnings typically continue to increase, especially if he is in management or one of the professions. The relationship becomes more and more not one of two partners but that of the head of the household and a wife dependant on his economic contribution. It is easy to see what such a situation may do to her own perception of self-worth, and her status within the family.

This brings us to the fourth and most serious problem: the dependent homemaker who must suddenly fend for herself. The great majority of wives are sooner or later left without a husband, whether because of separation, divorce or death. Others find themselves in a position, temporarily or permanently, where they have to try to support

[19]Reported in M. A. Ferber and B. G. Birnbaum, 'Labor Force Participation Patterns and Earnings of Clerical Women', Forthcoming, *Journal of Human Resources*, and in M. A. Ferber and B. G. Birnbaum, 'One Job or Two Jobs: That is the Question', unpublished paper, 1979.

a husband who is unemployed or disabled. Such women, and their dependents, almost invariably find themselves faced by a severe reduction in their standard of living, and are frequently confronted by dire poverty. The most common case is that of the divorced woman, generally with children, who collects little if any alimony or child support and rarely manages to improve her economic status significantly except through remarriage.[20]

The husband, too, is disadvantaged when he has done virtually no housework previously and must suddenly manage on his own. Since courts frequently do award alimony to a wife who is unable to support herself, he may also feel a financial pinch if he is one of the conscientious minority, or at least be inconvenienced by the legal maneuvers that are necessary to avoid making the payments. Nonetheless, his earning power remains the same and his work goes on as before, so that he is far less vulnerable than the woman who becomes a displaced homemaker.

In addition to the disadvantages to the couple of such specialization, there are costs to the taxpayer as well. The loss of job experience and depreciation of skills which accompany the long term absence from the labor market make it difficult for a woman to support her family, should the need arise. Hence female headed families constitute a substantial proportion of families in need of public support (Ross and Sawhill, 1975).

The new tools developed for the economic analysis of the family have largely ignored these problems and have to a considerable extent been used to tacitly endorse the status quo. But the same tools have the potential for being used constructively to show the way forward from the traditional paternalistic union of man-as-head and wife-as-dependent, who all too often do not live happily forever, to a more egalitarian partnership of two individuals, each having a variety of options, sharing by choice rather than because they were trapped by behavior dictated by stereotypes.

2. *Nonmarket Production and the Gross National Product.* At about the time when economists turned their attention to household production, they also became concerned about the fact that goods and services produced in the home are not included in GNP.[21] Since then a number of researchers have attempted to estimate the value of time spent on housework, and also on volunteer work, in order to help remedy this deficiency. So far, however, there is no general agreement how this should be done.

One possibility is to value the time using opportunity cost. If a woman spends an hour cleaning house, minding the children, or serving a civic organization, the value of that hour is assumed to be equal to what she could earn if she were employed. There are a number of problems with this approach, of which only the two most serious ones are mentioned here. First, it is assumed that people make rational and informed decisions. If a woman accepts the traditional role of homemaker without even considering other possibilities, this is not a 'decision', which by definition involves weighing of alternatives, and certainly not 'rational' in the usual sense of the word. Nor is it easy to be 'informed', When a woman has not held a paying job for some time, it is difficult to

---

[20]According to the Census Bureau Report *Divorce, Child Custody, and Child Support,* Series P23, the amount of child support paid to most women is small: two-fifths received less than $1,000 during 1975 and three-fifths less than $1,500.

[21]The pioneering work in this field was W. D. Nordhaus and James Tobin, 'Is Growth Obsolete?' in *Economic Growth,* Fiftieth Anniversary Colloquium V, N.Y.: National Bureau of Econ. Res., 1972. Another interesting contribution pointing out the shortcomings of the traditional ways of calculating GNP was Tibor Scitovsky, *The Joyless Economy,* N.Y.: Oxford University Press, 1976.

estimate what she could earn. Second, the opportunity cost approach really says that when a person decides to spend time on nonmarket work it must be worth at least as much as she could earn. This does not preclude the possibility that it may be worth more, perhaps considerably more.

The second possibility is to value nonmarket work according to how much it would cost to hire someone to do it. There are difficulties with this approach as well. Perhaps the main one that troubles many people is that it is difficult to determine whether the quality of the product is the same when done by hired help. It is often argued that no one can do as well as the 'loving wife and mother'. Or, it might be that the hired specialist would do better than the non-expert homemaker.[22]

It may not be easy to resolve these problems and reach a resolution, but it is to be hoped that there will be agreement before too long to use even an imperfect estimate in preference to not including the value of non-market production in GNP at all.

3. *Labor Force Participation*. In the traditional theory of the supply of labor only two alternative uses of time are considered: market work and leisure. For a long time it was assumed that the amount of labor supplied would increase as wages go up, because workers would be more willing to give up leisure, and undertake potentially unpleasant tasks, as the rewards for doing so were greater. This was termed the substitution effect. As work was increasingly better paid, more of it would be substituted for leisure. Empirical studies did not, however, bear this out. It was, for instance, found that while real wages increased over time, the length of the work week declined, length of vacations increased and people retired increasingly earlier. In other words, higher pay resulted in less work. Eventually, economists found a perfectly plausible explanation for this. A worker with more income can afford a higher standard of living — more of all the good things in life, and one of those is leisure. This was termed the income effect. As earnings per hour increase, you can afford to work fewer hours.

Clearly the substitution and the income effect both exert an influence, and the extent of this varies as between different individuals. But it became increasingly obvious that beyond some level of wages[23] the income effect becomes dominant — for men. It was only in the 1960's as women's labor force participation continued to accelerate, while that of men was declining, that economists began to take notice of the fact that women's response to changing wage rates is different from that of men, and that there is an

---

[22]The following are among the interesting papers written on this topic. H. J. Adler and Oli Hawrylyshyn, 'Estimates of the Value of Household Work, Canada, 1961 and 1971', *The Review of Income and Wealth*, Series 24, No. 4, December 1978; Oli Hawrylyshyn, 'The Value of Household Services: A Survey of Empirical Estimates', *The Review of Income and Wealth*, Series 22, No. 2, June 1976. J. H. Hybels, 'The Value of Volunteer Work: Market Value vs. Opportunity Cost'. Paper presented at Chicago, 1978 meeting of the Association for the Study of the Grants Economy. Martin Murphy, 'The Value of Non-Market Household Production: Opportunity Cost versus Market Cost Estimates', *Review of Income and Wealth*, Series 24, No. 3, September 1978. Maurice Weinrobe, 'Household Production and National Production: An Improvement of the Record', *Review of Income and Wealth*, Series 20, No. 1, March 1974. See also M. A. Ferber and B. G. Birnbaum, 'Housework: Priceless or Valueless?' Paper presented at Chicago, 1980 meeting of the Midwest Economic Association. Forthcoming in *Review of Income and Wealth*.

[23]The level at which this happens varies considerably between different societies. European colonizers who found that 'natives' did not work as hard as they wanted them to generally used force, but on occasion used the carrot rather than the stick, and paid somewhat higher wages. They often found that the workers, whose desire for market goods was rather limited, responded by working less. In most modern countries, where the desire for market goods is very high, the negative response sets in only at a much higher wage level.

obvious explanation.[24] Their choice is not just between market work and leisure, but also between market work and housework. Therefore, the substitution effect dominates. As a woman can earn more in the labor market, this option becomes more attractive, and she will be inclined to spend more time working for money.

With this improved insight economists have made considerable progress in explaining one of the most significant, virtually world-wide, economic developments of the 20th century: the rapidly increasing labor force participation of women. Even so, there is room for further improvements. Projections by experts in the U.S. have consistently and significantly underestimated the actual rise in the number of women entering the labor market in recent decades. One possible explanation is their tendency to assume that women only react to changing economic conditions and ignore the impact of changing attitudes and ideologies brought about by the new feminist movement.

4. *Occupational Segregation and Women's Earnings.* At the same time economists have found it a challenge to explain the rapid influx of women into the labor market, they have also been confronted by the task of explaining why they have not been doing better in the labor market. In the U.S., for instance, occupational segregation[25] has not decreased over recent decades. Women tend to be clustered in a relatively few occupations and in the lower levels of all occupations, while men occupy the high-level positions even in those fields in which they constitute a small minority. And a woman who works full time, year round only earns somewhat less than 60 percent as much as a man.[26]

---

[24]The pioneering work was Jacob Mincer's 'Labor Force Participation of Married Women', in *Aspects of Labor Economics,* H. G. Lewis (Ed.) 1962 Universities National Bureau of Economic Research Conference Series No. 14, Princeton, N.J.: Princeton University Press, 63–97. Other important contributions were by W. G. Bowen and T. A. Finegan, *The Economics of Labor Force Participation*, Princeton, N.J.: Princeton University Press, 1969, and G. G. Cain, *Married Women in the Labor Force: An Economic Analysis*, Chicago: University of Chicago Press, 1966. An earlier descriptive study focusing attention on women's labor force participation was Gertrude Bancroft, *The American Labor Force: Its Growth and Changing Composition*, Washington, D.C.: Census Monograph Series, 1958.

[25]The extent to which women are in different occupations than men. The measure of segregation most often used is the percent of women in the labor force who would have to change jobs in order to duplicate the occupational distribution of men.

[26]Below is a representative list of works documenting these facts, mainly for the U.S., but also for some other countries. N. S. Barrett, 'Have Swedish Women Achieved Equality?' *Challenge*, November/December, 1973, F. D. Blau and W. E. Hendricks, 'Occupational Segregation by Sex: Trends and Prospects', *Journal of Human Resources*, Vol. 14, No. 2, Winter 1979. F. D. Blau, Pay Differentials and Differences in the Distribution of Employment of Male and Female Office Workers. Harvard Dissertation, 1975. M. A. Ferber and H. M. Lowry, 'The Sex Differential in Earnings: A Reappraisal', *Industrial and Labor Relations Review*, Vol. 29, No. 3, April 1976. M. A. Ferber and Ann Westmiller, 'Sex and Race Differences in Nonacademic Wages on a University Campus', *The Journal of Human Resources*, Vol. 11, No. 3, Summer 1976. B. G. Malkiel, and J. A. Malkiel, 'Male Female Pay Differentials in Professional Employment', *American Economic Review*, Vol. 63, No. 4, September 1973. William Moskoff, 'An Estimate of the Soviet Male-Female Income Gap', *ACES Bulletin*, Vol. XVI, No. 2, Fall 1974. M. Darling, *The Role of Women in the Economy*, Paris: OCED, 1975. Sanborn, Henry, 'Pay Differences Between Men and Women', *Industrial and Labor Relations Review*, Vol. 17, No. 4, July 1964. I. V. Sawhill, 'The Earnings Gap: Research and Issues', Paper presented at Workshop on Research Needed to Improve the Employment and Employability of Women. U.S. Department of Labor, D. C., June 1974. Scott, Hilda, *Does Socialism Liberate Women*? Boston: Beacon Press,1 1974. There is also a large amount of work which specifically focuses on women in academia. Among those are: A. E. Bayer and H. S. Astin, 'Sex Differentials in the Academic Reward System', *Science*, Vol. 88, 23 May, 1975. M. A. Ferber, J. W. Loeb and H. M. Lowry, 'The Economic Status of Women Faculty: A reappraisal', *Journal of Human Resources*, Vol. XIII, No. 3, Summer 1978. N. M. Gordon and T. E. Morton, 'Faculty Salaries: Is There Discrimination by Sex, Race, and Discipline?' *American Economic Review*, Vol. 64, No. 3, June 1974. E. P. Hoffman, 'Faculty Salaries: Is There Discrimination by Sex, Race, and Discipline? Additional Evidence', *American Economic Review*, Vol. 66, No. 1, March 1976.

Two very different, though not necessarily mutually exclusive approaches have been used to explain these three related phenomena. One essentially emphasizes the extent to which women's primary role as homemaker impacts on her performance in the labor market.[27] They prepare for and later enter those occupations where interruptions are not heavily penalized and the work does not unduly interfere with 'their family responsibilities', even if this deprives them of the opportunity for better careers and higher incomes. For the same reasons they have less upward mobility within each occupation. The crowding into female occupations and the clustering on the bottom rungs combine to keep women's earnings low. So does the fact that their lower labor force participation rate, their willingness to stay home in case of family emergencies, their readiness to follow a husband when he moves to advance his career reduce the amount of valuable experience — human capital, in the terminology of economists — they accumulate.

There is some truth to this interpetation — enough to make it superficially plausible. But it is not difficult to find flaws. None of the studies have succeeded in explaining all of the differential in earnings in these terms. Even when all these variables are taken into account, women are invariably paid less than would be expected, even though the differential becomes considerably smaller. Furthermore, upon more careful examination it becomes clear that there is considerable circular reasoning involved when traditional economists justify woman's specializing in homemaking by pointing to her lower earnings in the labor market, and explain her lower earnings in the labor market by pointing to her absorption in homemaking.

The alternative explanation differs from the former mainly by assigning some importance to discrimination in one form or another, whether by paying women less for doing essentially the same work, depriving them of equal opportunity to do the same work when they are fully qualified, or depriving them of equal opportunity to acquire the qualifications. This approach does not deny that women tend to give priority to homemaking while men concentrate on market work, but it raises the possibility that they do so because they are disadvantaged in the labor market, rather than vice versa.

There is an extensive literature exploring these various forms of discrimination, their possible causes and effects.[28] Attention was first focused on the possibility that employers may have a preference for hiring one type of person over another, hence are willing to pay the former more, will hire the latter only if they can pay them less. Proponents of this view recognized that people might sacrifice profit maximization in order to indulge their preferences, but they were also inclined to point out that they would be at a disadvantage compared to those who had no prejudices. Hence, it was argued, that in a competitive market this type of discrimination would be self-limiting.

---

[27]See, for instance, H. G. Birnbaum, Determinants of Earnings: The Economic Significance of Job Experience and the Effects of Cohorts on Age-Earnings Profiles. Harvard Dissertation, 1974. V. R. Fuchs, 'Recent Trends and Long Run Prospects for Female Earnings', *American Economic Review*, Vol. 64, No. 2, May 1974. Jacob Mincer and S. W. Polachek, 'Family Investments in Human Capital: Earnings of Women', *Journal of Political Economy*, Vol. 82, No. 31, March/April 1974. S. W. Polachek, 'Occupational Biases in Measuring Male-Female Discrimination', *Journal of Human Resources*, Vol. X, No. 2, Winter 1975. Several representative examples of this point of view applied specifically to women in academia are G. E. Johnson and F. P. Stafford, 'The Earnings and Promotion of Women Faculty', *American Economic Review*, Vol. 64, No. 6, December 1974. J. V. Koch and J. F. Chizmar, Jr., 'Sex Discrimination and Affirmative Action in Faculty Salaries', *Economic Inquiry*, Vol. 14, No. 2, March 1976. R. A. Lester, *Antibias Regulation of Universities: Faculty Problems and Their Solutions*, a report for the Carnegie Commission on Higher Education, 1974.

Soon, however, it was recognized that discrimination need not always be costly to those practicing it, and may even benefit them. For instance, if enough employers, or for that matter customers, prefer group A to B, they may be able to depress wages for B enough to compensate or more than compensate for the higher wages A will receive. Or if members of group A refuse to work alongside members of B, they might succeed in exacting a higher wage to compensate them for working with these 'undesirables', and depressing the wage of the B's correspondingly.

It was also recognized that pay differentials for the same work is by no means the only, or even the most common form of discrimination. For one, union rules and personnel practices, as well as equal pay legislation in recent years, make such practices difficult or impossible. Far more commonly, members of the unwanted group would be kept out of enterprises which pay relatively well, out of high income occupations, out of jobs which offer opportunity for upward mobility, and crowded into those few areas that are open for them. Thus we can explain the very substantial segregation of men and women in the labor market and the large earnings gap between them without resorting to the old game of blaming the victim.

5. *The Role of the Government.* Government today plays a large role in all economics, and its policies, whether inadvertently or by design, exert considerable influence both on the labor force participation of women and on their economic status in the labor market. Recent work is beginning to produce evidence that the rate at which earnings are taxed, and the tax treatment of single individuals as compared to one-earner and multiple-earner families particularly effects the incentive for married women to work for income.[29] This is understandable since they are still generally viewed as the marginal wage earners, so that the tax rate for the husband is calculated as though the family had

[28]K. J. Arrow, 'The Theory of Discrimination', in *Discrimination in Labor Markets*, Orley Ashenfelter and Albert Rees (Eds.) Princeton, N.J.: Princeton University Press, 1973. Gary Becker, *The Economics of Discrimination*, Chicago: University of Chicago Press, 2nd Ed., 1971. Barbara Bergmann, 'The Economics of Women's Liberation', *Challenge,* May/June, 1973. Andrea Beller, 'Occupational Segregation by Sex: Determinants and Changes', Bunting Institute of Radcliff College Working Paper, 1980. P. K. Brito and C. L. Jusenius, 'Career Aspirations of Young Women: Factors Underlying Choice of a Typically Male or Typically Female Occupation', paper presented at the ASA Meetings, San Diego, August, 1978. Harley Gunderson, 'The Influence of the Status and Sex Composition of Occupations on the Male-Female Earnings Gap', *Industrial and Labor Relations Review*, Vol. 31, No. 2, January 1978. J. F. Madden, *The Economics of Sex Discrimination,* Lexington, Mass.: Lexington Books, 1973. William Moskoff, 'The Effects of Occupational Segregation on the Male-Female Income Gap in the United States and the Soviet Union', paper presented at the San Francisco URPE-ASSA meetings, December 1974. I. V. Sawhill, 'The Economics of Discrimination Against Women: Some New Findings', *Journal of Human Resources*, Vol. 8, No. 3, Summer 1973. P. A. Wallace and M. A. LaMond, *Women, Minorities and Employment Discrimination*, Lexington, Mass.: Lexington Books, 1977. The case of academic women is examined by M. H. Strober and A. O. Quester, 'The Earnings and Promotion of Women Faculty: Comment', *American Economic Review*, Vol. 67, No. 2, March 1977, and M. H. Strober and B. B. Reagan, 'Sense and Nonsense in the Residual Method of Measuring Discrimination as Illustrated by the Analysis of Sex Differences in Economists' Income', unpublished paper, 1978. Some interesting work has also been done on the increasingly higher unemployment rate of women as compared to men. Barbara Bermann, 'Labor Turnover, Segmentation and Rates of Unemployment: A Simulation-Theoretic Approach', Working Paper, Project on the Economics of Discrimination, University of Maryland, 1974. Beth Niemi, 'The Female-Male Differential in Unemployment Rates', *Industrial and Labor Relations Review*, Vol. 27, No. 3, April 1974.
[29]J. H. Leuthold, 'The Effect of Taxation on the Hours Worked by Married Women', *Industrial and Labor Relations Review,* Vol. 31, No. 4, July 1978. J. H. Leuthold, 'The Effect of Taxation on the Probability of Labor Force Participation by Married Women', Public Finance, Vol. 33, No. 3, 1978. Rosen, H. S., 'Tax Illusion and the Labor Supply of Married Women', *Review of Economics and Statistics*, Vol. 58, No. 2, May 1976. F. P. Stafford, 'Would the ERAZ Lead to a Swedish-Style Tax System in the U.S.?' paper presented at the AEA Meetings, Atlanta, December 1979.

only his income, and the rest of the tax burden is allotted to the wife's income. This may well reduce the wife's net earnings to a level below the perceived value of her contribution as a full-time homemaker.

Similarly, it has been found that the impact of government payments to families is likely to have greatest impact on the labor force participation of women.[30] Again, this would be expected as long as the homemaker role is regarded as acceptable, or even preferable for a woman who does not need the income, while it is not a respectable alternative for a man.

Government can also affect women's labor force participation by providing, or subsidizing, services for the household. Of these most attention has been focused on day care centers, not only by social workers and child psychologists, but to some extent by economists.[31] They can make an important contribution by pointing out that the benefits of helping mothers to be in the labor market are not fully measured by current income, but must include the substantially greater earnings in the future associated with more experience. These benefits accrue not only to the family, but to some extent to the whole economy when the woman earns enough to pay taxes rather than so little as to be eligible to collect public assistance of one kind or another. It has also been found that children of working mothers achieve higher occupational status (Duncan and Duncan, 1969) providing one more long-run benefit of making it possible for mothers to take a job.

Government exerts its influence not only via taxes and expenditures, but also by passing and enforcing laws regulating economic behavior. Only a modest amount of work has been done by economists to investigate the economic impact of legislation.[32] Most of the findings so far are rather inconclusive, and more work is needed before it will be possible to shed much light on this subject.

6. *Economic Development*. Before 1960 in the vast and ever growing literature on economic development there were few reflections on the particular problems and contributions of women. Male economists simply tended to assume, without examining what was really happening, that modernization would break down sex inequality, because it replaces ascriptive bases of social organization by achieved ones. This

[30]G. G. Cain and H. W. Watts (Eds.) *Income Maintenance and Labor Supply: Econometric Studies*, Chicago: Rand McNally, 1973. J. F. Cagan, *Negative Income Taxation and Labor Supply: New Evidence for the New Jersey-Pennsylvania Experiment*. Report R-2155-HEW, Santa Monica, California, Rand Corporation, 1978. J. A. Pechman and P. M. Tipane, (Eds.) *Work Incentives and Income Guarantees: The New Jersey Negative Income Tax Experiment*, Washington, D.C.: Brookings Institution, 1975. H. W. Watts and Albert Rees (Eds.) *The New Jersey Income-Maintenance Experiment Vol. II, Labor-Supply Responses*, New York: Academic Press, 1977.

[31]R. D. Husby, 'Day Care for Families on Public Assistance: Workforce Versus Welfare', *Industrial and Labor Relations Review*, Vol. 27, No. 4, July 1974. R. R. Nelson and Michael Kraslunsky, 'Some Questions of Optimal Economic Organization: The Case of Day Care for Children', Urban Institute paper, 1971. A. M. Rivlin, 'Child Care', in C. L. Schultze, *et al.*, *Setting National Priorities: The 1973 Budget*, Washington, D.C., 1972. M. P. Rawe and R. D. Husby, 'Economics of Child Care: Costs, Needs and Issues', in Pamela Roby (Ed.) *Child Care – Who Cares? Foreign and Domestic Infant and Early Childhood Development Policies*, New York: Basic Books, Inc., 1973. M. H. Strober, 'Formal Extra-family Child Care — Some Economic Observations', in C. B. Lloyd (Ed.) *Sex, Discrimination, and the Division of Labor*, New York: Columbia University Press, 11975.

[32]Bellamy, Blanche, Goodman, Kelly and Stanley, Affirmative Action in Practice: A Preliminary Report to the Ford Foundation, 1975. Andrea Beller, 'The Impact of Equal Employment Opportunity Laws on the Male/Female Earnings Differential', paper presented at the Department of Labor and Barnard College Conference on Women in the Labor Market, N.Y.C., 1977. J. W. Loeb, M. A. Ferber and H. M. Lowry, 'The Effectiveness of Affirmative Action for Women', *Journal of Higher Education*, Vol. 49, No. 3, May/June 1978.

situation changed significantly with the publication of Ester Boserup's *Woman's Role in Economic Development* (1970). This pathbreaking work, encompassing information from all the regions of the world, points out the extent to which the transition from a traditional to a modern economy presents both threat and promise to the status of women. As the traditional division of labor disintegrates there is the danger that they will be deprived of their productive functions, reducing their role from that partner to helpmate, and simultaneously retarding the whole process of growth. On the other hand, with educational and training programs to increase their productivity, women in underdeveloped countries can make a far greater contribution to economic development than women in the now advanced countries did in earlier days.

Boserup's contributions not only influenced the work of scholars, but appears even to be having some impact on the policies of countries and international agencies providing aid and loans to developing economies.[33] Thus it is to be hoped that there will be less tendency to influence these poor countries to turn half of their population into mere facilitators of consumption, when they are in urgent need of more production.

IV. Economics: The Study of Man, and Woman

We have examined the volution of economics from a male dominated profession and a male oriented discipline into one perceptibly more open to women and women's concerns. Another way to gauge the extent of this development is to examine the changes that have taken place in textbooks. We focus specifically on the best-selling introductory text, published in ten editions since 1948: Paul Samuelson's *Economics*. Not only has this book dominated the market, but the author, a Nobel prize winner, is also one of the best known and most respected representatives of main stream economics in the post World War II period. A brief inspection of other widely used books proves our choice to be reasonably representative.

The first edition has no reference to 'Women' in the index, but does have references to 'Females, discrimination against' and 'Females, earnings of'. Upon examination it turns out that these are both contained in a two-page segment on 'The Position of Minorities'. The brief discussion deals with the reasons for lower earnings of 'Negroes, women, and old people'. It is suggested that women are at times paid less when doing equal work, on the grounds that they do not do it as well, and in any case do not need as much income, but that for the most part discrimination takes the form of not giving them the opportunity to do equal work. While this analysis is very perceptive for its time, it is

[33]Representative examples are: Boserup, Ester and Christina Liljenkrantz, *Integration of Women in Development: Why, When, How*, N.Y.: U.N. Development Programme, 1975. N. S. Chinchilla, 'Industrialization, Monopoly, Capitalism, and Women's Work in Guatemala', *Signs*, Vol. 3, No. 1, Autumn 1977. Steven Cohn, *et al.*, 'U.S. Aid and Third World Women: The Impact of Peace Corps Programme', unpublished paper, 1979. Achola Pala, 'Definition of Women and Development: An African Perspective', *Signs*, Vol. 3, No. 1, Autumn 1977. Hanna Papanek, 'Development Planning for Women', *Signs*, Vol. 3, No. 1, Autumn 1977. Niara Sudarhas, 'Women and Migration in Contemporary West Africa', *Signs*, Vol. 3, No. 1, Autumn 1977. Irene Tinker, 'The Adverse Impact of Development on Women', in Irene Tinber and M. B. Bramsen (Eds.) *Women and World Development*, Overseas World Development Council, 1976. Glaura Vasques de Miranda, 'Women's Labor Force Participation in a Developing Society: The Case of Brazil', *Signs*, Vol. 3, No. 1, Autumn 1977. World Bank, Integrating Women into Development, 1975. N. H. Youssef, *Women and Work in Developing Societies*, Population Monograph Series, No. 15, University of California, Berkeley, 1974. George Zeidenstein, *Including Women in Development Efforts*, N.Y.: The Population Council, 1977.

brief and superficial. Moreover, it is followed by the surprising statement that 'The position of women shows steady improvement. In fact there is evidence that they are burrowing [sic.] into those overhead white-collar jobs and service industries which are least sensitive to the ups and downs of the business cycle and which have more favorable long-run trends than the heavy capital goods sector of the economy in which men predominate'. Contrary to the implications of this statement we have seen that women's unemployment has been rising relative to that of men, and the earnings gap has not been decreasing.

In the same text entrepreneurs, workers and students, are always assumed to be men, as are the readers of the book. Females only make an appearance in the traditional roles of the widow who needs investment advice, the housewife, whose services are not included in National Income, and very occasionally as a consumer.

Small changes may be observed in later editions through the sixties. The references in the index are now to 'Women' rather than 'Females', though there are still only two. Women are occasionally acknowledged in non-traditional roles, as in a reference to '... men (and women) [being] needed to design, make, program, maintain, and correct machines'. The 1958 edition also takes note of the fact that women not only enter the labor market in recessions when their husbands are unemployed, but that there actually has been an increase in the number of women doing so during recent times of prosperity. But the author is sufficiently astonished to find that women would respond to better job opportunities to express his surprise by ending this sentence with an exclamation point.

The picture is significantly different by 1976. There are 15 references to 'Women' in the index, and two additional ones to 'Women's liberation'. While the male pronoun still dominates, the illustrations used have not improved much, there is a fairly extensive analysis of women's role in the economy, with references to most of the areas discussed in the previous section of this essay. Perhaps one may conclude that considerable progress is being made in raising the consciousness of economists, so that they are more likely to address themselves to women's issues. At the same time their subconscious continues to be rooted in tradition, so that old stereotypical attitudes still permeate much of their work.

The discussion in this chapter so far has dealt with 'mainstream' economics, which in the U.S. encompasses the vast majority of scholars in this field. Some comments are in order, however, on the relation between feminism and Marxism, if only because the issues involved are of considerably greater importance in the rest of the world.

To begin with, it should be noted that Marx himself focussed attention entirely on the market sector, just as 'bourgeois' economists did. In fact he goes so far as to consider workers engaged in the provision of services as unproductive, and defines only those goods produced for exchange, rather than for direct use, as commodities'. Marx did acknowledge that women (almost invariably speaking of 'women and children') were in the labor force, but appears to have considered this as a symptom of the unfortunate effects of capitalism. As he paints the picture (Capital, Vol. 1) it is with increasing mechanization, when 'The special skill of each individual insignificant factory operative vanishes as an infinitesimal quantity ...' and the worker becomes a mere 'living appendage' of the machine, that women and children begin to 'displace' men in factories. If further evidence is needed of Marx's traditional male point of view, let it be noted that he wrote that when Communism has been achieved, man will be able to hunt in the morning, fish in the afternoon, rear cattle in the evening, and criticize after dinner.

(The German Ideology). Can there be any doubt that man here means man, not man and woman?

In spite of this poor beginning by the founding father, many of his followers came to believe that Marxism stands for complete equality of women and men. Furthermore, his most famous disciple, Lenin, implemented legal equality in the U.S.S.R. He was also honest enough to write 'Notwithstanding all the laws emancipating woman, she continues to be a domestic slave, because petty housework crushes, strangles, stultifies and degrades her, chains her to the kitchen and nursery . . . ' (On the Heroism of Workers in the Rear). But when it came to making real changes, implementation sadly lagged behind intentions.

The really radical solution to what Marxists continue to call the 'woman question', that men should share household responsibilities, has never even been suggested. (The closest Lenin came was to suggest that men might 'lend a helping hand'.) The promise that is constantly held out is that housekeeping will be transformed into a large-scale socialist economy, but 60 years after Lenin acknowledged that in practice not enough was being done, remarkably little progress has been made in this direction in the U.S.S.R., let alone in the other countries professing to adhere to Marxism. Nor can one accuse recent leaders of breaking faith. Lenin, while extolling the contribution of women to the revaluation, castigates one of their most important leaders for discussing sex and marriage problems during their meetings.[34] His view is that 'all the thoughts of Communist women, of working women, should be centered on the proletarian revolution, which will lay the foundation, among other things, for the necessary revision of marital and sexual relations' (Dialogue with Clara Zetkin). His intellectual and political heirs to this day are urging women to support the revolution, and assuring them that true equality will thus be achieved — by and by.

It is not our intention to overstate the similarities between 'bourgeois' and 'Marxist' economists in their concern with, or solutions for 'the woman question'. Yet one cannot help but notice that both put higher priority on their primary, efficiency and revolution, respectively, than on achieving equality for women. Both continue to try to persuade women, and perhaps themselves, that women can be freed from household drudgery by gadgets (who is to use them?) or by socialized services (who is to perform them?). Both are making progress, though not necessarily at the same rate, in accepting women as more than helpers in the labor market, but are far from ready to accept a co-equal role for men in the household. There is more work for feminists to be done on both sides of the ideological dividing line.

References

BOSERUP, Ester (1970 *Woman's Role in Economic Development*, St. Martin's Press, New York.
DUNCAN, Beverly and O. D. DUNCAN (1969) 'Family stability and occupational success' in *Social Problems,* Vol. 16, No. 3, Winter.
ROBINSON, John P. (1977) *How Americans use time: A socio-psychological analysis of everyday behavior,* Praeger Publishers, New York.
ROSS, H. L. and I. V. SAWHILL (1975) *Time of Transition: The growth of families headed by women,* Urban Institute, Washington D.C.
SAMUELSON, Paul (1948) *Economics,* McGraw Hill, New York.

[34]Lenin, the man who swore at Philistines, was even more outraged at Inessa Armand who proposed to write a pamphlet favoring free love, and tried to organize prostitutes for the revolutionary struggle.

10

The Impact of Feminism on Media Studies — Just Another Commercial Break?

HELEN BAEHR

Anyone considering Media Studies will soon discover that its boundaries are faintly marked and always somewhere over the horizon.

Media Studies is hardly much older than the Women's Movement. Although its historical roots largely lie in postwar American theories of mass society and empirical communications research, Media Studies in Britain has yet to constitute itself properly as an academic 'discipline'. One is faced with the vexed problem: what is it exactly that feminism is having an impact on?

From its very beginnings the Women's Movement has responded critically, often angrily, to what it has rather loosely called 'sexism in the media'. Advertisements were an obvious first target and Betty Friedan devoted a large part of *The Feminine Mystique* to a content analysis of women's magazines and to a critique of advertising and market research techniques (Friedan, 1963). Since then the Women's Movement has continued to express concern over women's — and its own — representation in the mass media and feminist activity within media practice and Media Studies has steadily increased.

There are about 8,500 full-time degree students studying English Literature in Britain. There are very many fewer that 850 studying the media. At present there are just over 20 polytechnics and colleges of Higher Education offering courses on the media. Out of these only half offer a full-time media course. The rest simply include some kind of option usually in Education Studies or the Humanities.

The situation in schools and Further Education is hardly better. The subject is viewed with some hostility and not deemed worthy of serious academic consideration. Television, radio and newspapers do not come into the realm of 'high art' compared with a Dickens novel or a Wordsworth poem. It is estimated that only about 600 students at this level study the media.[1]

Putting such academic snobbery aside, there are serious practical constraints on teaching Media Studies. There is the lack of broadcast source materials since copyright legislation, as it stands in Britain, makes it almost impossible to resee material even for educational purposes. It is always helpful for students to have a practical component to introduce them to current practices in broadcasting and journalism, but the resources for this kind of work tend to be too expensive to be generally available.

[1]Figures taken from *The Media Reporter* (1978) Vol. II, No. 1, p.14–16.

There is also the fact that whereas Film Studies sought respectability at university level, Media Studies has developed over the last ten to fifteen years at polytechnics and colleges which were at one time less constrained by the heavy weight of an academic tradition. It grew out of an interdisciplinary approach and different courses have evolved different solutons to the problems of constructing and teaching across disciplines. Some hang on to, an albeit fragmented, notion of academic disciplines and employ a mix of sociology, social psychology, linguistic theory, semiology, aesthetics etc. Others make the brave attempt at abandoning conventional disciplinary bases by using a range of intellectual approaches to the major problems raised by a study of the media. But both suffer from the sexist assumptions and invisibility of women endemic in mainstream academe.

The quantitative and qualitative peculiarities of British Media Studies (and indeed the British education system) deserve some explanation. Media Studies in Britain has followed the traditionally British approach of 'education for education's sake'. It would rather die than dirty its hands with vocational enterprise. Whilst we do not actively discourage students from pursuing careers in the media industry, we take pains to assure them that a course does not offer a specific training for work in mass communications: 'We certainly don't dissuade those with an interest in journalism and broadcasting from applying, as long as they realise that getting a job may finally depend a good deal more on how well they convince an editor or selection board of their potential talent than on any academic qualifications which they may possess' (Corner, 1978: 14). Compare this 'apologia' with New York University's Department of Journalism and Mass Communications' prospectus which offers 'a professionally-oriented program, in which students are taught basic skills and theories necessary for careers in newspapers, broadcasting, magazines, public relations and survey research'. In Britain, graduates of Media Studies stand a good chance of gaining entry into the industry almost in spite of their academic qualifications. Many prospective employers are more likely to suspect, rather than welcome, their critical, at times even oppositional, views of existing professional practices and institutions.

Information about employment opportunities in the media industry tends to circulate by word of mouth and there are few clear career routes. There is a strong 'old-boy network' and even after formal training in journalism securing a position usually depends on pressing a personal case (Boyd-Barrett, 1970). Women can often be excluded from the normal recruitment and promotion channels. One reason given for the small number of women in top editorial positions on Fleet Street is that women are discouraged from subbing, working night shifts and from joining in the masculine pub culture of Fleet Street. The main reason why women journalists are concentrated in what may be termed 'women's fields' is not the one given by male journalists — that women are 'not tough enough' for hard news stories — but because they are not afforded the same opportunities to gain the relevant occupational knowledge (Smith, 1976).

In order to assess and outline the extent and direction of feminism's impact on Media Studies, it is necessary first to look at the development and dominant traditions of media sociology to see how a feminist perspective challenges the discipline's limited view of women's relationship to the mass media. Secondly, we need to examine the ways in which feminists involved in a study of the media have recognised the urgent need to specify a new area of enquiry — the representation of women. In some cases feminist attention to 'images of women in the media' has been less an assault on traditional bastions of academe and more another voice making a parallel demand for curriculum space. The ways in which some of the conventions and inbuilt assumptions of media sociology have been somewhat uncritically adopted by feminist media research will also be discussed.

*   *   *   *

Media sociology developed as a subject in search of academic respectability during and following World War II. In 1948 Harold Lasswell coined the dictum which was to characterise the discipline for several years. He suggested that the proper study of the media asked the question: 'Who says what, in which channel, to whom and with what effect?' (Lasswell, 1948). Lasswell's approach fragmented the study of the media into exclusive areas such as institutions, producers, content and audiences. It set the scene for a 'dominant paradigm' (Gitlin, 1978) in media sociology which looked at the short-term behavioural effects of the media, defining 'effects' so narrowly, microscopically and directly that at most only very slight effects could be indicated. The 'hypodermic needle' theory of early media psychologists and sociologists posited a stimulus-response mechanism between the medium and the individual — an injection of media content could produce a measurable behavioural or attitudinal outcome. This approach sought 'hard data' and followed the social-psychological mode of measuring content and effects experimentally and in surveys.

Research in the 1940's and 1950's proposed to dislodge this theory, arguing instead that the power of the media was 'limited' and located within existing structures of social relationships. (Katz and Lazarsfeld, 1955) 'Personal influence' and social variables such as age, social class, education — gender was not usually considered — were recognised as important intervening mechanisms operating between the message and the audience. Findings supported a 'two-step flow' of communication — from mass media, to opinion leaders, to people — and interpreted the media's role in affirming, rather than converting, people's existing attitudes and opinions as the media having 'no effect' (Klapper, 1960).

This research and its methodology has, in its turn, come under severe criticism. Its concentration on establishing that no direct causal connection exists between individual messages and their effects, deflects attention from questions of media structures, patterns of ownership and control, the media's relationship to the State and their role in constructing, mediating and distributing 'social knowledge' (i.e. their ideological role). As Gitlin affirms: 'Ideology and consciousness are concepts that fall through the sieves of both behaviourism and stimulus-response psychology. They have no ontological standing in the constraining conceptual world of mainstream media research' (Gitlin, 1978).

American media sociology developed as it did with the support and generosity of Madison Avenue and media conglomerates who were anxiously sharpening their tools of persuasion to ensure their millions of dollars spent on advertising would be millions well spent. The classic study of the 'two-step flow' was based on a survey of 800 women in Decatur, Illinois in 1945 and designed to assess the impact of the media and personal influence in four opinion areas — fashion, marketing, public issues and motion pictures

(Katz and Lazarsfeld, 1955). The selection of an all-female sample and the marketing orientation of this academic survey was probably determined by the fact that American women represented an enormously profitable pool of consumers whom it was vital to 'persuade' via advertising. In the flow of information to women on public issues, Katz and Lazarsfeld found that: 'Most marked in this sphere is the dominant role of husbands and male parents' (p. 332). They suggest that women are less influential and knowledgeable about public issues because their pre-occupation with domestic duties leads them 'to be less motivated to participate in the area' (p. 290). This emphasis on the lack of individual motivation obscures the real restrictions surrounding women's participation in 'public life'.

A comprehensive feminist critique of the sexist orientation and assumptions of this school of mainstream media sociology has yet to be written. The field is ripe for such examination but requires time and resources outside the scope of this paper. Media Studies has itself developed over the last years a critique and rejection of content analysis and 'effects' research, not on feminist grounds, but in favour of other approaches, most importantly 'uses and gratifications' research and studies of the ideological role of the mass media in society. The former aims to investigate not what the media do to people but what people do with the media, i.e. what uses and gratifications audiences derive. Such an approach assumes that individuals get what they 'need' from the media. Despite the fact that women form a major part of the media audience and come to the media with a particular set of needs resulting from their oppressed position, very few of these studies differentiate the audience according to sex.

Radio for example begins when the houseworking day starts and for many women is their only companion. At present radio's daily diet to 'housewives' often consists of programmes presented by male DJ's who chat to etherise the mind — a classic example of 'palliative radio' (Karpf, 1980). There are, however, to my knowledge very few studies of the particular needs and uses women bring to radio programmes. One early study of women listeners to daytime radio serials showed that women derived a number of gratifications which varied with their 'individual circumstances and problems' (Herzog, 1944). The serials, it was argued, allowed an identification with characters who enjoyed an exciting way of life and the women 'obtained emotional release and stimulus and some vicarious compensation for their own hardships by finding scapegoats in story characters'.

It is useful here to examine this study in the light of the problems 'uses and grats' raises for feminists engaged in media research. Firstly, individual needs tend to be emphasised without reference as to how they are universally related to social and economic conditions: what is it about women's lives that creates the need for emotional release and excitement? Secondly, there is an underlying assumption that part of the media's function is to provide 'vicarious compensation' thereby accepting the social conditions which create the need for such use of the media. In Herzog's study the sources of women's hardships and their need to identify with exciting characters are taken as given and unchangeable. Thirdly, this approach leads us into a circular argument: finding that women use the media to escape from the drudgery of their own lives infers that they 'need' escapist media content. What they really need is a different life! In a more recent study on children and television, Grant Noble observes that many women use TV as a childminder to occupy their children so that they can get on with housework (Noble, 1975). Once again the assumption seems to be that what women need

is more childminding television programmes and not increased childcare provisions.
Going back to the question of women and radio, what is missing from this approach is
an examination of what kind of needs are *not* gratified by media output.

Under different socio-economic conditions it might be possible for the mass media to
go beyond simply providing escapist 'entertainment' interspersed with the occasional
'balanced, objective and impartial' news bulletin or documentary. In Denmark
television programme-makers compiled a manifesto with tips on how to make children's
programmes. One prescribed that 'When you want to tell an exciting story — try to
relate the conflict in the story to the central conflict in society between labour and
capital'. (Bugler, 1976: 328). Even if this type of 'excitement' smacks a little of
propaganda we must not be led into the belief that entertainment can ever be neutral.
Without this realisation and some analysis of the material and ideological basis of the
production and consumption of media artefacts, 'uses and grats' media research can do
little more than beg and answer its own questions.

There has been in recent years a clear shift in Media Studies from the controlled
experiment, survey and interview situation to an examination of the social, economic
and political context of media organisations and professions and the role of the media as
ideological agencies playing a decisive and fundamental part in cultural production.
This critique of the media and its role in reproducing capitalist society stems from a neo-
Marxist position as expressed in Herbert Marcuse's notion of the media as a
'consciousness industry' propagating a 'one-dimensional' affirmative culture in which
the contradictions and barbarism of capitalism are falsely harmonised' (Marcuse, 1964).

Contemporary writers on the media have taken up and re-worked Marcuse's basic
premise: 'The fact remains that the mass media in advanced capitalist societies are
mainly intended to perform a highly 'functional' role: they too are both the expression
of a system of domination, and a means of reinforcing it' (Miliband, 1973). Stuart Hall
refers to the media as 'the site of an enormous ideological labour'. He goes on to
describe how the media offer 'preferred' meanings and interpretations which 'help us
not simply to know more about 'the world' but to make sense of it: ... The media serve,
in societies like ours, ceaselessly to perform the critical ideological work of 'classifying
out the world' within the discourses of the dominant ideologies' (Hall, 1977). A feminist
analysis requires us to extend the study of the way the media operate in relation to
the dominant bourgeois ideology to how they function within a patriarchal culture
where 'preferred' meanings reside in a male discourse: 'So the answer to the question
(can women speak?) is no, or only in a highly negotiated fashion, because the subject
position from which mastery of language is possible is a male construct — one which
women help to form but which we cannot operate' (Gledhill, 1978). The crucial question
then becomes: how are media images and representations of 'femininity' constructed
within patriarchal social and sexual relations of production and reproduction? Which
leads us to ask: how can representations of women (and men) change unless the
structures of patriarchal economic and social relations also change?

Pressure from the Women's Movement, and a growing recognition by feminists
involved in studying and teaching Media Studies of the inherent sexism of the subject,
has opened up the whole question of the special nature of women's relationship to the
media. The project on the representation of women has not been an even or unified one,
which makes it difficult to chart a direct route across its terrain.

Much of the feminist contribution to the debate on the ideological role of the media in society draws its theoretical framework from the massive input of new theories from France. It has looked to semiotics, described as the science of signs in society, especially to the work done by Roland Barthes in his *Mythologies* (1972) and to structural linguistics with its emphasis on language as a socially produced system actually providing the rules and constraints within which all signification has to work. It has been informed by the neo-Marxist philosophy of Louis Althusser which sees ideology as a level 'relatively autonomous' from the economic and political levels of capitalism and finally by Lacanian psychoanalysis, with its analyses of the human subject through language (Althusser, 1966; Lacan, 1968). Feminist film studies, like film studies itself, has developed independently — and in many ways more sophisticatedly — from feminist studies of broadcasting, newspapers and magazines. The intensity with which feminist film criticism has adopted psychoanalytic concepts — primarily those concerned with the processes of 'identification' and 'recognition' which draw women to films — has not been matched in feminist criticism of other mass media. This separation is due partly to film studies' historical roots which lie more in literary criticism than in sociology, and partly to the easier availability of film as an object of study. Independent feminist film-making has nourished the marriage between theory and practice which, given the monopolistic ownership structure of press and broadcasting, has not been possible in feminist media studies. Much of the research done on women and the media comes more from that strain of American social science empirical positivism outlined above, which organises mass communications research around concepts of 'effect' and 'function' and argues that behaviour resulting from exposure to the mass media obeys laws of conditioning, reinforcement, sublimation etc. Evidence cited is usually based on content analyses designed to measure certain aspects of a media message (e.g. how many male to female characters; what types of behaviour patterns do female characters exhibit as compared with male characters) and its results tend to remain at the descriptive level.

Studies which examine and document the images of females and males in the media reveal that:

> 'Regardless of the medium under examination or the scope of the particular study, the conclusions have been very similar: males dominate mass media content, both qualitatively and quantitavely. Roles of males in the mass media have been shown to be dominant, active, authoritative, while females have been shown to be submissive, passive and completely contented to subjugate their wills to the wills of media males. Males in all our mass media have varied roles emphasizing their importance in the spheres of employment, politics, science, history, and the family, while females have only two important spheres circumscribed by their sexuality and their domesticity' (Busby, 1975: 10).

Surveys of the ways in which media content has been dominated by males serve as a useful first step. But the limitations of content analysis are well documented (Burgelin, 1972). Studies which describe sexist content cannot help us to understand the relationship between the content described and the social structures which produce it and within which it operates.

Noreene Janus recognises that content analysis can provide a useful tool in researching sex roles in the media, but warns that its uses are 'limited' and its results should be interpreted with great care. She criticises many such studies of being consistent with a 'liberal feminist perspective':

'The studies of women and mass media ask questions that reflect a liberal feminist theoretical perspective since they set up Male vs. Female categories. All males are counted together as a general category and contrasted with an all-female category, with no reference made to the class, race or cultural divisions *within* each of these categories. Instead, the subjects are distinguished on the basis of visible personal traits (marital status, age etc.). The questions are ahistorical, apolitical, and in no way indicate how the images of women or men are related to the fundamental structures of society' (Janus, 1977).

A further consequence of setting up Male vs. Female categories is the implication that media content might be less sexist if women characters were shown to have the same occupational distribution as male characters or if more women were employed as newsreaders, TV presenters, DJ's etc. In an article on women and radio, Mileva Ross illustrates this position and her support of recent BBC moves to appoint women newsreaders: 'When the pressure was really on, the BBC discovered that, given the opportunities and the training, there were females who could be as 'acceptable' as male newscasters' (Ross, 1977: 19). The characteristics and roles associated with 'maleness' in media images here become the goals 'acceptable' for women in media images and the objective becomes one of integrating women into the system on an equal basis with men. men.

A major problem that arises out of many of the content analyses documenting images of women in the media stems from their failure to differentiate between different levels of meaning. For example, one woman newsreader reporting an item on 'militant bra-burning feminists' numerically equals one woman newsreader reporting on feminists' 'reasonable case for abortion on demand'. The method enumerates the visible form (i.e. both newsreaders are women) but leaves out the important question of the difference in the content presented. An increase in the number of female newsreaders here implies a change for the better. But as we already know that news coverage of women concentrates on their appearance, sexuality etc. (Epstein, 1978) more women reading the same old news simply reaffirms the very framework which reproduces sexism. That is not to say that more women should not be employed at all levels of media production, but it does suggest that content analysis as a methodology implicitly influences the kinds of questions asked and that the conclusions it draws may work against feminist interests.

A similar problem arises with the introduction into television and film of so-called independent, powerful 'liberated' women. Elizabeth Cagan writes: 'the assertive, ambitious woman is no longer an oddity but has become a new cultural type' (Cagan, 1978). Noreene Janus points out that the media have selectively presented issues that are 'marginal' to the Women's Movement. They define liberation in terms of women getting top white collar jobs, gaining equality in sports or having separate vacations from their husbands. She goes on: 'In advertising women are shown to have more control over consumption rather than production activities. The ways in which women's traditional roles reflect and conflict with the demands of the capitalist system are never dealt with' (Janus, 1977). The growing number of women playing policewomen, detectives or attorneys on television (*Policewoman, Charlie's Angels*) bear little ressemblance to feminist aspirations. Ironically, they are portrayed as enforcing rather than challenging the laws that oppress them (they usually end up needing to be rescued by their male partners/bosses) (Gerbner, 1978). Here we are seeing strong women reconstructed into redeemers of the patriarchy (Baehr, 1980).

The fact that heroic women have supplemented heroic men on the screen involves us in more than just media head-counting. It brings us back to questions concerning the media's crucial role in the construction of meaning and in the re-construction and representation of feminism and feminist issues within patriarchal discourse.

We need to consider seriously these problems and issues surrounding studies of women and media in order to map out more coherent future projects and approaches to feminist media research. The question of representation as it relates to the issue of realism seems to me to be a major problem in much of the existing research. Betty Friedan condemed the 'sexual sell' used to entice housewives to 'seek identity, purpose, creativity, the self-realization, even the sexual joy they lack — by the buying of things' (Friedan, 1963). She saw the media, through their relationship to the commercial market of commodities, as a major reason for the continued subordination of women. A more recent study of images of women in the media again suggests that media images determine what women are: 'We think we should look more closely at how our attitudes are conditioned, and even manipulated by the media through selection and suggestion. Are the images put out the real ones? In what ways are they 'unreal'? And is this due to omission or falsification?' (King and Stott, 1977). The very concept 'image' assumes that the media can somehow directly reflect 'reality' rather as if they were a mirror on the world. This view of the media inevitably leads to dismay and affront at the way the media 'falsify', 'omit' and 'distort' — i.e. create 'unrealistic' images of women (King and Stott, 1977; (Ed.) Tuchman, 1978; Friedan, 1963; Epstein, 1978; Weibel, 1977 and others).

Writing on the typical women's romance story in popular fiction, Tamar Karet illustrates this approach when she says: 'The female image these books present is largely a reflection of the real world, where it is men who govern nations, fly aeroplanes, make money and fight wars, so it isn't surprising that most of them show women as dependent beings. Nonetheless what they offer is a distorting mirror for this portrays a world that is even more sexist than reality' (in King and Stott, 1977: 103). To concentrate on a criticism of sexist (over sexist!) content or to question the verisimilitude of the women portrayed in popular fiction or in the mass media, is to accept such conventions as narrative, plot, hero/heroine characterisations without recognising that it is these forms, along with the media practices which produce them, which themselves construct very specific meanings and images of femininity. Christine Gledhill recognises the need for feminist analysis to understand the mechanisms which film employs to produce meanings: 'We cannot understand or change sexist images of women for progressive ones without considering how the operations of narrative, genre, lighting, *mise-en-scene* etc., work to construct such images and their meanings' (Gledhill, 1978, 460). For feminists these aesthetic structures and media practices occupy a central problematic operating as they do within a patriarchal discourse. Feminist film-makers have attempted an intervention into the male-dominated forms of cinema by trying to establish an alternative feminist language of film and allowing a more active and various construction of a film's meaning by encouraging audience discussion whenever possible. Independent film-makers are in a priviledged position compared to women working within established media institutions where the possibilities of introducing alternative modes of media production, distribution and consumption remain severely limited. (This is not to underestimate the considerable difficulties involved in funding and exhibition of independent film projects).

As I suggested previously in this chapter, feminist film criticism has addressed itself to questions of representational forms and audience identification in film, whereas a great deal of work on 'images of women in the media' has tended to use terms like 'conditioning' and 'falsification' which oversimplify women's complex relationship to the media and the processes involved in representation. They belong more to the dominant paradigm of media sociology in their suggestions that the media reflect/distort reality and that exposure to media messages has a direct — even measurable — effect on the audience.

The media are not transparent. They do not, and cannot, directly reflect the 'real' world any more than language can. To argue that they do along the lines of Friedan, King and Stott, Karet and others, is to deny the whole process of mediation which comprises a set of structures and practices which produce an ideological effect on the material they organise. By relying on a behaviourist type of 'direct-effects' model of the media these studies present a simplistic, unidirectional and reductive connection between media and behaviour, by arguing that the media determine and directly affect how we see ourselves and how we behave 'as women' in society: 'Watching lots of television leads children and adolescents to believe in traditional sex roles: Boys should work; girls should not. The same sex role stereotypes are found in the media designed especially for women. They teach that women should direct their hearts toward hearth and home' (Tuchman, 1978: 37). This approach mistakes the relationship between the media and their users as a causal one. It is not the media in themselves that determine what women are. Women are constructed outside the media as well, and it is their marginality in culture generally *and* in the media which contributes to their subordinated positions. 'The ideology of femininity as it is constructed through patriarchal capitalist determinations must always be seen both in relation to its overdetermination by 'masculinity' and as it is simultaneously included but set apart from the capitalist construction of the 'free' individual. Ideologically, women, as women, whatever their actual place in production, are negatively placed within the social relations of re/production' (Women's Studies Group, CCCS, Birmingham, 1978: 136.

It is a failure of many feminist studies that they neutralise and suppress the vital questions which explore the relationship between women's subordination in terms of their 'economic' place in patriarchal relations under capitalism and the representation of those relations in the ideological domain which women inhabit and construct. Janus proposes one alternative perspective from current 'liberal feminist' research on women and mass media: 'The problem must not be seen as a universal problem of males against females. Rather the problem must be viewed in its historical specific context. In researching the problem, our point of departure must be that we live in a capitalist-society which oppresses people in many diverse ways. Media images reflect not only sexism but also these other forms of oppression based on class, race, and nationality. A holistic and historical approach would recognise these relations when posing its problems for research and shaping its methodology' (Janus, 1977).

I have tried to indicate two major ways in which feminist scholarship has had an impact on Media Studies. Firstly, it has attempted to extend and redirect some of the central questions now being posed within the discipline and secondly, it has carved out for itself a specialised area of study concerning women's special relationship to the media. It is becoming increasingly clear that both of these strands are interconnected and can gain strength and nourishment from each other. A feminist perspective has shifted a crucial debate of Media Studies — the ideological role of the media in capitalist society — to a discussion on the construction of women's exploitation and subordination materially and ideologically within patriarchy.

A body of work, emerging from the Marxist-Feminist current in the Women's Movement has raised the problem of a radical feminist intervention into the forms of media aesthetics and practices already set by the dominant ideology. The growing interest in feminist film theory in the re-reading of Freud by Lacan has questioned the possibility of direct expression and insisted on the contradictory relationship between the language of the dominant class and that of oppressed groups: 'The real issue for feminism is the potential contradiction between woman as characterisation in terms of the independent woman stereotype and woman as sign in a patriarchal discourse' (Gledhill, 1978: 490).

This kind of approach provides an informed insight into some of the premises and limitations of content analysis and current reflection models of images of women. A theoretical examination of the media in terms of their signifying process means understanding that depictions of 'social reality' are mediated by a signifying mode with its own specific structures and determinations. We are now in a better position to move away from what has been a somewhat uncritical acceptance of content studies theoretically locked into the status quo, to asking some of the key questions already on the feminist film theory agenda. To accept that the media as a system of representation are a point of production of definitions is to address oneself to questions of cultural production and cultural reading and to the struggle towards the creation of alternative modes of media production and distribution and progressive images.

Feminist work into sexist content and female stereotyping has focussed attention onto the ways in which particular groups are portrayed and denied access to the media. The concept of 'stereotyping' has been taken up by Media Studies, although its application has been predictably restricted to images of gays, blacks, women, working-class youth etc., which leaves the representation of dominant groups as apparently unproblematic. In my own institution a course on women is included under 'Studies of Deviancy'.

With concern amongst feminists growing about the media industry's attempt to exploit the female (and male) market by selling 'new women' stereotypes, research is beginning to move away from mere description to an analysis of stereotypes as ideological concepts which can be mobilised to accommodate oppositional and alternative views and opinions. More work needs to be done on understanding the structural determinants of female stereotyping and how they function through the media to maintain women as an oppressed group: 'Stereotypes are selective descriptions — they select those features which have particular ideological significance ... In each case the oppressed group is characterised as innately less intelligent. It is particularly important for our ideology that attributes should be conceived of as being innate characteristics either of human nature in general (competitiveness) or of women/men/blacks in particular, since this supports the belief that they are not the effect of the socio-economic system' (Perkins, 1979: 157).

It is clear that there is still a considerable need for a thorough feminist 'working-over' of mainstream Media Studies. It remains a male-dominated discipline. As feminists working in the area, it is left to our small number to point out male bias and redirect student's interests and attention. It is up to us to point to women's absence and the sexist assumptions and conclusions behind much of the established literature and research. Thanks largely to the Women's Movement, there is now a whole range of books which look at the class, sexist and racist bias of the media. By using these we can make a start at dislodging and redirecting the overstudied and sterile debate about the effects of television on children into the more fruitful discussion of the media's role in sex-role socialisation. Up to now the heavy concentration on overt physical violence in programme content research has unquestioningly assumed non-violent content to be 'harmless'. We now have a firmer basis for a feminist perspective on women's employment and recruitment patterns in the media industry. Women have been gathering vital statistics which illustrate the patterns of discrimination which exist in the media professions (ACTT, 1975; Eddings, 1980; U.S. Commission on Civil Rights, 1977). As feminists we must rework the whole notion of the constituents of media 'professionalism' in terms of 'the clockwork of the male career' (Hochschild, 1971). It is left to us to draw students' attention to the fact that the latest fashion in Media Studies (the participant observation study of 'how television programmes are really made'), when conducted by male researchers regularly ignore the contribution made by production secretaries, production assistants, continuity and clerical back-up — the grades in television where women are concentrated (see Elliott, 1972; Schlesinger, 1978).

As an introductory text why not replace Harold Lasswell's revered dictum of 1948 with Virginia Woolf's infinitely more revealing one of 1928. In *A Room of One's Own* she recalls a lunchtime perusal of a daily newspaper after a morning spent reading academic testaments to female inferiority in the British Museum Reading Room: 'Some previous luncher had left the lunch edition of the evening paper on a chair, and, waiting to be served, I began idly reading the headlines. A ribbon of very large letters ran across the page. Somebody had made a big score in South Africa. Lesser ribbons announced that Sir Austen Chamberlain was at Geneva. A meat axe with human hair on it had been found in a cellar. Mr Justice .... commented in the Divorce Courts upon the Shamelessness of Women. Sprinkled about the paper were other pieces of news. A film actress has been lowered from a peak in California and hung suspended in mid air. The weather was going to be foggy. The most transient visitor to this planet, I thought, who picked up this paper could not fail to be aware, even from this scattered testimony, that England is under the rule of a patriarchy'. In these and other ways, feminist perspectives and feminist knowledge can greatly enrich, enliven and extend existing Media Studies. But the question remains: how much does a feminist intervention ultimately depend on the individual feminist who secures it? Are we the 'transient visitors'?

This paper has already indicated, critically at times, the very major contribution made be feminist research to the study of the mass media. It must be recognised, however, that studies of women's relation to the media has tended to occur as an 'option' and I have no reassurance that any of my feminist criticisms of media sociology are shared by, or even known to, my colleagues — all of whom are men. Like other 'women's subjects', Women and Media runs the risk of ghettoisation and the danger of confirming a subordinate status within the mainstream of the discipline. The institutionalisation of a separate strand which looks at women, carries with it the assumption that men's participation in the debate is marginal and that their representation in the media is unproblematic. The special study of women may be a necessary step in securing a firm feminist grounding in the attempt to understand and challenge existing media forms and structures. But the questions we raise are ones which will work best as critical ideas influencing and challenging the discipline as a whole. They are too important to be kept just to ourselves.

References

ALTHUSSER, Louis (1966) *For Marx,* Penguin, England.
ASSOCIATION OF CINEMATOGRAPH & TELEVISION TECHNICIANS (ACTT) (1975) *Patterns of Discrimination in Film and Television Industries.*
BAEHR, Helen (1980) The 'liberated' woman in television drama. In *Women's Studies International Quarterly,* Vol. 3, No. 1, pp. 29–39.
BARTHES, Roland (1972) *Mythologies,* Jonathan Cape, London.
BOYD-BARRETT, Oliver (1970) 'Journalism recruitment and training: problems in professionalization' In (Ed.) J. Tunstall, *Media Sociology,* Constable, London.
BUGLER, Jeremy (1976) 'What's in front of the children?' In *The Listener,* 16th September, p. 327–329.
BURGELIN, Oliver (1972) Structural Analysis and Mass Communication, In D. McQuail (Ed.) *Sociology of Mass Communications,* Penguin, England.
BUSBY, Linda (1975) 'Sex role research on the media', In *Journal of Communication,* 25 (4), Autumn.
CAGAN, Elizabeth (1978) 'The selling of the women's movement', In *Social Policy,* Vol. 8. p. 4–12.
CORNER, John (1978) 'Where students part company', In *Media Reporter,* Vol. 2, No. 1, p. 14–16.
EDDINGS, Barbara (1980) 'Women in Broadcasting', In *Women's Studies International Quarterly,* Vol. 3, No. 1, pp. 1–13.
ELLIOTT, Philip (1972) *The Making of a Tv Series,* Constable, London.
EPSTEIN, Laurily Keir (1978) (Ed.) *Women and the News,* Hastings House, New York.
FRIEDAN, Betty (1963) *The Feminine Mystique,* Victor Gollancz, London.
GITLIN, Todd (1978) 'Media sociology: The Dominant Paradigm', In *Theory and Society,* 6 (2) p. 205–253.
TUCHMAN, G, A. DANIELS and D. BENET (Eds.) *Hearth and Home,* Oxford University Press, Oxford.
GLEDHILL, Christine (1978) 'Recent developments in feminist criticism', In *Quarterly Revew Film Studies,* Vol. 3, No. 4, p. 457–493.
HALL, Stuart (1977) 'Culture, the Media and the 'Ideological Effect', In J. Curran, M. Gurevitch and J. Woollacott (Eds.) *Mass Communication and Society,* Edward Arnold, London.
HERZOG, H. (1944) 'What do we really know about day-time serial listeners?' In P. Lazarsfeld and F. Stanton (Eds.) *Radio Research* 1942–3; Duell, Sloan & Pearce, New York.
HOCHSCHILD, Arlie (1971) 'Inside the clockwork of the male career', In F. Howe, (Ed.) Women and the Power to Change, Carnegie Foundation, New York.
JANUS, Noreene (1977) 'Research on sex-roles in the mass media: toward a critical apprroach', In *Insurgent Sociologist,* Vol. VII (3), p. 19–32.
KARET, Tamar (1977) in J. King and M. Stott (Eds.) *Is This Your Life?* Virago, London.
KARPF, Anne (1980) 'Women and Radio', In *Women's Studies International Quarterly,* Vol. 3, No. 1, pp. 41–54.
KATZ, E. and P. LAZARSFELD (1955) *Personal Influence, the part played by people in the flow of mass communications,* Glencoe Free Press.
KING, J. and M. STOTT (1977) *Is This Your Life? Images of Women in the Media,* Virago, London.
KLAPPER, J. (1960) *The Effects of Mass Communication,* Free Press, New York.
LACAN, Jacques (1968) *The Language of the Self,* Delta, New York.
LASSWELL, H. D. (1948) 'The Structure and Function of Communication in Society', In L. Bryson, *The Communication of Ideas,* Harper, New York.
MARCUSE, Herbert (1964) *One Dimensional Man,* Routledge & Kegan Paul, London.
MILIBAND, Ralph (1973) *The State in Capitalist Society,* Quartet, London.
NOBLE, Grant (1975) *Children in front of the small screen,* Constable, London.
PERKINS, T. E. (1979) 'Rethinking Stereotypes', In M. Barrett, P. Corrigan, A. Kuhn and J. Wolff (Eds.) *Ideology and Cultural Production,* Croom Helm, London.
ROSS, Mileva (1977) In J. King and M. Stott (Eds.) *Is This Your Life?* Virago, London.
SCHLESINGER, Philip (1978) *Putting Reality Together: BBC News,* Constable, London.
SMITH, Roger (1976) 'Sex and Occupational Role on Fleet Street'. In D. Barker and S. Allen (Eds.) *Dependence and Exploitation in Work and Marriage,* Longman.
TUCHMAN, Gaye, A. DANIELS and D. BENET (1978) *Hearth and Home,* Images of Women in the Mass Media, Oxford University Press, Oxford.
U.S. Commission on Civil Rights, 1977. *Window Dressing on the Set. Women and Minorities in Television.*

WEIBEL, Kathryn (1977) *Mirror, Mirror,* Anchor, New York.
WOMEN'S STUDIES GROUP, Centre for Contemporary Cultural Studies, Birmingham University, 1978, *Women Take Issue,* Hutchinson, London.
WOOLF, Virginia (1945) *A Room of One's Own*, Penguin, London.

11

Education: The Patriarchal Paradigm and the Response to Feminism

DALE SPENDER

It can be established that feminism has made great gains within the field of education: the astounding growth of *Women's Studies* courses in many countries, the development of alternative and successful models of teaching and learning, the systematic and convincing critiques of the way in which knowledge is constructed and disseminated, and the establishment of diverse and far reaching research programmes are all testimony to the feminist achievement within the educational field. But from the point of view of education as a discipline, the generation of this new, challenging knowledge can be quite irrelevant: in Britain particularly, it is probable that there are many educationalists who are unaware of feminism and who remain oblivious to its educational insights and findings.

I think this is partly because of the way in which the parameters of education have been defined. Indicating his ignorance of the feminist stance (he uses *he* throughout to denote the researcher, the teacher, and the student) J. Eggleston (1979) in his article *The Characteristics of Educational Research* is critical of the tendency of educationalists to concern themselves solely with *schooling*, to confine their questions to problems which arise within the educational *system*, (in which they are of course influential), and to construe as successful research, only those results which can be applied to current educational practices. Although he does not state that by definition, feminism, which is outside these parameters is thereby excluded from consideration, Eggleston does make the general point that because education as a discipline has been constituted in this way, it leaves it open to the charge that its sole function is 'to increase the efficiency of the existing system in terms of accepted criteria' and to 'preclude the opportunity to explore potentially more effective alternatives' (Eggleston, 1979; 5). I would not quarrel with his assessment: by limiting its horizons to that which takes place within educational institutions, education has not only helped to promulgate the myth that the only genuine learning which occurs is that which is taught (and monitored and controlled) by educationalists, it has also — very conveniently — promulgated the accompanying myth that anything which educationalists do not provide is not worthy of attention: it is non-data. For many reasons education has ruled feminism as non-data and has therefore been able to protect itself in part from the feminist impact.

Eggleston argues that in his view it would be 'a salutory experience for educational researchers to look more often at instances in ... (the) ... wider context' than their own institutions (p. 7) and again, I would wholeheartedly concur, although I think it would be more than salutory. I suggest that educationalists begin to look at feminism. If they do then perhaps we will not have the absurd situation which confronts us at the moment, where on the one hand there is a dynamic and thriving feminist model of education and learning (which even has application to educational institutions) and on the other, a discipline which is ostensibly concerned with education and learning and yet which finds feminist educational theory and practice irrelevant.

Because of the limitations within the discipline itself I am obliged to divide this chapter into two parts. In the first part I will be concerned with legitimated or mainstream education, which is male controlled and which has remained almost impervious to feminism. In the second part I will document the achievements of feminist education and argue that it is more a case of what mainstream educationalists can learn from feminism than what feminism can learn from education.

It has been argued that it is difficult to talk about education in monolithic terms — even to call it a discipline[1] — and to assume that it has a paradigm which informs and circumscribes its parameters. As D. R. McNamara (1979) has pointed out in reference to Thomas Kuhn's conceptualisation, the existence of a paradigm would suggest that there is a single theory which provides educationalists with a means of explaining and understanding the world, and this is most certainly *not* the case. If education had a paradigm then we would expect to find a community of scholars who manifested a high degree of consensus working within a unified theoretical framework, whereas we find almost the reverse:

> There is hardly ever (never?) a sustained endeavour by a community of researchers investigating a specific issue within the context of a dominant theoretical perspective. There is no group of researchers working in similar fields and ready to replicate each other's research — even if a replication were possible. There is no series of classic experiments or exercises which students must practice in laboratory-like settings (McNamara, 1979; 169).

Because there is no consensus as to the substantive issues of education, the way in which problems are posed and the methods by which they are pursued, because there is no dominant theoretical perspective — in McNamara's terms — he thinks it more accurate to describe education (again, in reference to Kuhn) as in a pre-paradigmatic stage where 'there is variability in fact gathering and interpretation. There is a number of competing schools and subschools each with a comparatively free choice of observation and method' (McNamara, 1979; 170).

Admittedly this lack of cohesiveness in education causes problems when attempts are made to classify it as a discipline. Perhaps it is misleading to refer to the *paradigm of education* when one is talking more about an institutionalised practice than a theory. But within the theory and practice of education there are parameters and there are assumptions which can be identified. Eggleston suggested that education is sometimes circumscribed by its insistence on defining schooling as the context in which learning takes place and he has also quoted Patric Suppes (1973) to support his contention that educationalists start with a value system, with a belief structure which constrains and influences their research and their pronouncements, and which is in itself a legitimate — and necessary — field of enquiry: 'A central problem of ... (educational) ... research is to attack that belief structure when it is unsupported by data or systematic theory' (Suppes, 1973: quoted in Eggleston, 1979; 6).

[1]Mary Ann Elston has encountered similar difficulties in her chapter on Medicine where while there is a *practice* (both in education and medicine) it is difficult to establish the *theory* which informs it and which might constitute the *discipline*.

I am grateful to Eggleston for drawing attention to this facet of education as a discipline (although it is demonstrable that the words of Suppes and Eggleston often go unheeded) for while there is some debate as to whether there is a paradigm within education, I find it almost an incidental issue here. Although there may be some conceptual difficulties (what do I mean when I refer to *education*?) this does not pre-empt me from outlining some of the practices which are undertaken and justified in the name of education, nor from identifying some of the sexist and unacknowledged assumptions on which those practices are often based. Within education a sexist belief structure frequently operates and it is not supported by data or systematic theory. It seems to be accepted as the *natural order* and those who do challenge it, are regarded as unscholarly (see Elaine Reuben, 1978) and their challenge is dismissed as 'improper'.

While from Mr McNamara's point of view it may be difficult to detect a 'dominant theoretical perspective' or a unifying framework, I do not find it a difficult task at all, for as a feminist it is possible to see that the diverse theories and practices — and the assumptions on which they rest — share common features which bring them together within a coherent framework. Whether it be educational theory *or* practice which is analysed it can generally be claimed that it is a product of male experience and remains firmly within male control. Patriarchy is the educational paradigm.

Educational theories from student disaffection to curriculum innovation usually render women invisible; (as subject and as theorist); educational practices from the organisation of institutions, to classroom interaction usually help to exclude women. From the selection of 'good' and 'worthwhile' research topics to the methodologies which are employed in research, the sexism of education is blatant (Acker, 1980): it can readily be identified — if one chooses to engage in such a task. In Britain, education has not chosen to engage in such a task. 'Barriers' have been erected and while *outside* them there is an enormous amount of activity which is yielding challenging, stimulating, and useful data, *inside* the old order is preserved — at the moment.

From a feminist perspective one of the dominant theoretical frameworks of education is that of male dominance, but it is a framework which goes unquestioned and which has not been made the substance of educational enquiry. Unless and until education begins to examine male dominance as a fundamental issue in the entire educational process, the impact of feminism will be minimal. But while feminists continue to generate the 'alternative' findings of such great significance at such an extraordinary rate, education must be seen as under threat.

What I intend to do here is to (briefly) outline the nature and extent of male dominance in education and to comment on some of its implications. I want to show how that male dominance is used to perpetuate male dominance and to indicate the repercussions that would be the outcome of a successful feminist challenge to education. It is not an 'accident' that education has been so insistent on maintaining the boundary lines between education and feminism, between data and non data. I suspect that education as a theory and practice would be transformed if feminism were taken into account. And many of the current practitioners find the division to their liking and are prepared to put effort into maintaining it. Not only might their 'reputations' be at risk if women were to be included (a reason which Thomas Kuhn, 1972, gives for those who are in power suppressing novelty) but so too would some aspects of their way of life.

In terms of the organisation of education in Britain (and it seems that there are no marked differences in many other countries which are also male dominated) it is relatively easy to establish that education is male defined and controlled with the result that women — and their particular experience of the world — are excluded. To claim that education constitutes a male model invites a critical response only if the presence of women within education is used as evidence to the contrary. However, while it is indisputable that there are many women 'in' education the crucial issue is when they arrived and what influence they possess, for women are to be found concentrated in a particular, and not always prestigious activity,[2] that of teaching, and their entry even to this level is relatively recent.

Raymond Williams (1975) has claimed that the education model which we inherited in part and which we accept today (and which constitutes our notions of 'a good education' and how it can best be implemented) is in many respects one that 'was essentially created by the nineteenth century, following some eighteenth century models, and retaining elements of the medieval' (p. 172). Feminists do not need to be reminded that there were few — if any — women who were consulted or permitted to participate in the construction of that model in medieval times, in the eighteenth century or the nineteenth century. Indeed one of the features of that model was that it was most inappropriate for women; their brains would burst, their uteri atrophy, they would become unsuitable for motherhood if they were to receive what was considered 'a good education' for a man. Women were excluded then from conceptualising education and they are still excluded today.

For while in the twentieth century there are women in education, they are not the policy makers or decision makers. They still do not participate in the process of deciding what education could/should be. The model of education which passes as the society's model is the model generated by men, based on men's experience of the world, and women are required to be educated in a manner devised by men as befitting men.

Statistics can sometimes expose the fallacies of our own perceptions. It is sometimes thought that there are quite a few women in influential positions in education in Britain (and other countries) but if we believe this we are forgetting just how 'visible' one woman in an influential position can be. To those who think that women have some say in the policy making area of education Eileen Byrne's (1978) figures can come as a substantial shock for she states that 97% of the 'government of education' is male. She also notes that girls get an 'inferior' education and draws a link between the two. Because the policy making bodies are almost exclusively male, she says, women are given 'a different, often inferior education planned perhaps with no conscious ill-intent' (p. 15) but which nevertheless helps to maintain the asymmetry of the sexes.

While similar, Dorothy Smith's analysis is a more subtle one. She too notes that men are the predominant policymakers in education in Canada but rather than seeing this as a means by which women are given an 'inferior' education, she sees this as a means of keeping women, and women's experience, out of education and out of the culture in general. 'Women's participation in the educational process at all levels has increased this century' she says, and yet 'this participation remains within marked boundaries. Among the most important of these boundaries, I would argue, is that which reserves to

[2]Whether teaching enjoys low prestige because it is where women are primarily found, or whether women have been permitted entry to this level because of its low prestige — or whether both factors operate — is a debatable issue.

men control of the policy making and decision making apparatus in the educational system' (Smith, 1978; 287).

This is a substantial source of power for it allows men to legislate on the substantive nature of education. As Smith says, it is men who are the 'gatekeepers', it is they who are setting the standards, producing the social knowledge, decreeing what is significant, appropriate, relevant, and what will and will not be admitted to the systems of distribution, determining what will count as innovation in thought, or values, ruling what is legitimate in the light of their own *male* experience (p. 287). As a result, the male experience becomes the norm, the yardstick against which any female experience that is different is found to be 'deviant'.

While men continue to consult only men, to validate educational theory and practice in the light of male experience (as they must almost inevitably do in Britain if males comprise 97% of the government of education) then it is almost *structurally* impossible for women to 'have a voice'. They have no access to the circles in which models of education are conceptualised, with the result that any models which they generate — and which may be different from men's — remain outside the educational process. Smith says, 'Let us be clear that we are not talking about prejudice or sexism as a particular bias against women or as a negative stereotype of women'. This is not just the provision of an 'inferior' education in which girls are in receipt of less educational resources and are channelled into humanities and typing (although as Eileen Bryne rightly points out, this is part of the pattern of precluding them from being the *future* members of the government of education). 'We are talking about the consequences of women's exclusion from a full share in the making of what becomes treated as *our* culture' says Smith (p. 283), their exclusion from a full share in the making of what becomes *our* education.

This is why it is difficult for feminism to enter the educational arena: it is also why many established educationalists consciously or unconsciously resist feminist influence and even discount or ignore the feminist voice. The structure of education (and of our culture) would be altered if feminism were to be taken into account, for it would not be possible for male dominance to perpetuate male dominance in the manner which is currently employed.

If even 40% of the government of education were female considerable changes could take place and it is interesting to hypothesise what form those changes could take. If men's experience alone could no longer serve as the reference point, could that mean that males, and male experience could cease to the be norm, and if so, what implications would this have for our society? If women were in a position to vote they might not vote for many of the models which men have proposed. For example, if feminist educational models which have evolved in *Women's Studies* are any guide, women might vote for the *personal*, rather than the *impersonal* as a basis for education. They might not see the logic of confining education to that learning which takes place within institutions. They might not give consent to a model of education which is designed to *discriminate*, to 'sort out' the failures: they might prefer a more egalitarian and cooperative arrangement — if they were free to generate, and validate their own models from their own experience of the world.

But women are not 40% of the government of education and even those few women who are members are not necessarily free to propose models which are consistent with their experience as women. There are some women among the 'gatekeepers' and while it is theoretically possible that they could propose alternatives, practically, this possibility rarely, if ever, eventuates. This is because the women who occupy such positions frequently owe allegiance to men, who put them there.

In general, women depend upon men for promotion to influential positions. It is men who control who shall be admitted to their ranks (and in Britain, judging from the personal accounts I have access to, it seems, understandably, that they show little inclination to appoint feminists[3]). When it is men who can decree what shall be recognised as 'proper qualifications' then women who seek to join their ranks must indicate their familiarity with and adherence to those male values which legitimate 'proper qualifications'. According to Dorothy Smith, such women have minimum 'voting power', they can endorse, but not veto. The women who do obtain influential positions, says Smith 'are those who have passed through this very rigorous filter. They are those whose work and style of work and conduct have met with the approval of judges who are largely men'. She adds, 'And, in any case, they are very few' (Smith, 1978; 289).

In these circles even if the few women who were permitted access were to propose models which were 'different' then they could find they were treated individually, as women are collectively: their alternatives, by definition would be 'wrong' (de Beauvoir, 1972; Rowbotham, 1973). The chances of alternatives which have their origin in women's experience being treated as a 'refinement' an 'improvement' an 'extension' are remote, in a society where women are 'deviants' and in a context where women are tolerated (provided they are 'well behaved'). It is more likely that women who suggested that education should incorporate features of women's experience (cooperation rather than competition, for example) would themselves be viewed as inadequate, rather than that the male norm should be exposed as inadequate: it would be the women who were perceived as 'incompetent' or 'unbalanced' and not necessarily education.

Because education as we know it today has always been controlled by men, the educational model(s) which they have devised have always assumed the status of the norm, and this has circumscribed (and still does circumscribe) the model(s) which women may generate. When women began to claim education as a right in Britain in the nineteenth century, men had already agreed the general nature of education and how it could best be brought to fruition, and women found themselves either obliged to adopt the norm, or to develop a 'deviant' model, for there was little or no opportunity to generate an autonomous model of their own. Frances Buss, (the North London Collegiate School, Camden Girls' School) and Emily Davies, (Girton College), for example, adopted the male model, and sought to have girls excel in its terms, while Dorothea Beale (Cheltenham Ladies' College), and Anne Clough, (Newnham College, Cambridge) were concerned with protecting feminine accomplishments, with introducing academic work of a kind that was appropriate to girls, with special

[3]It is difficult to establish how many feminists there are within education but it is possible that some of those who are there have developed their interests (or made them known) *after* they received permanent appointments. Within feminist circles there is consensus that it is not always advantageous to have one's politics known before applying for a position but there is also an acknowledgement that in some institutions — particularly those which wish to project a 'progressive' image — token feminists are sometimes appointed. Unfortunately there is no research available on this topic but the absence of a feminist pressure group is noticeable: at the conference *Sex Differentiation and Schooling,* Cambridge, January 1980, when it was suggested that an association against sexism in education be formed, Eileen Byrne stated that it was important that it should *not* be a feminist association.

examinations for women, and they were among those who developed a subsidiary and subordinate form of education — for the subsidiary and subordinate sex (Jill Lavigueur, 1977; 66–69). In either case it was the male version of education that was taken as the reference point. That any values which women may have been able to contribute have been excluded is a point which is made by Rita McWilliams-Tullberg in her book on women at Cambridge for while women have been admitted (though not to full membership until 1948) they have been submerged, and Cambridge remains '*A men's university – though of a mixed type*'.

If women were to enter the arena, such arrangements would be at risk. Cambridge, for example, has only remained 'A men's university — though of a mixed type' because men have remained in power and have been able to decree arrangements. And this does not just apply to Cambridge: Jenny Shaw (1976) has claimed that although it was initially believed that the collapse of a single sex education would result in a 'mix' somewhere between an all male and an all female school, this has not happened. The identity of single sex girls' schools has been lost, has been submerged, with mixed sex schools actually more like boys' schools. Allowing females access but preserving the male ethos and definitions has been one way of 'accommodating' women without requiring modification from males. Feminism permits no such accommodation but demands modification: hence it is threatening.

Men have decreed the form and substance of education and they have designed it to serve their own interests. The have also developed numerous 'devices' for keeping it that way by structurally excluding females. I am not advocating a conspiracy theory — that is, that men have deliberately constructed a theory and practice designed to support and sustain male dominance — but that one outcome of taking *exclusively* for themselves the power to determine the parameters of education, has been to *exclude* women and thereby to perpetuate male dominance. Women's 'alternatives' are often dismissed and discounted within this system not because of what they might propose (although this in itself could give rise to alarm among some educationalists with a vested interest in current arrangements), but because it is *women* who are proposing them.

Within any discipline there are agencies which help to promote, assess, legitimate and generally monitor the knowledge which is generated within that discipline. Professional associations, conferences and periodicals all help to 'make' the individuals (who in turn, 'make' their successors) by selecting who is to speak, who is to publish, who validates courses, acts as a referee or examiner, and therefore, who will 'shape' the direction in which the discipline proceeds. But these individuals are more than 'gatekeepers'; they do not simply check what passes through their hands, passing that which is acceptable and eliminating that which is not. They can play a much more active role. By having a say in what does and does not get funded as research they are also able to influence what knowledge gets generated.

Lyn Lofland, (1975) has stated that '*he* who pays the piper calls the tune' (p. 156: my emphasis) in sociological research and this seems as true of education as of sociology. Lofland says:

> I do not mean to suggest that researchers are merely 'clerks,' answering specific and detailed questions supplied by funding agencies. I mean rather that funding agencies are important in setting the context in which research proceeds. What is generally 'problematic' to the funder, or what the funder is willing to 'buy' as problematic, draws the parameters . . . around what will be problematic to the researcher. But funding agency power is probably even more persuasive. For to the extent that the

products of funded research 'flood' the literature of a discipline or subdiscipline, they are undoubtedly influential in defining its central foci and thus in shaping the research of the nonfunded (Lofland, 1975; 156).

In a discipline which is male controlled there are two important issues here for feminists. The first is that what is perceived to be 'problematic', what requires explanation and research, is that which is problematic for men. The second is that because men fund their own research they are in a position to 'flood' the literature, to define the central foci as the problems of men and to perpetuate their own practices. At every level then, men are able to exclude women from the construction of knowledge: they can exclude them as subjects when they set up research which is problematic to men, they can exclude them as researchers and theorists by not allocating funding to projects which are perceived as problematic to women and by 'disallowing' women's unfunded research (the bulk of feminist research in education). By this means male dominance perpetuates male dominance; such male dominance is *very* problematic to feminists but as yet has not been funded for research.

While few of the agencies which monitor research acknowledge the extent, diversity and quality of (unfunded) feminist research in education (a point which I will return to later), the Women's Research and Resources Centre (in Britain) keeps a research index which indicates that much is happening *outside* the official parameters of the discipline. When women want to engage in research which is problematic to women they are usually obliged to leave the fold. And having completed that research there is no easy access back in, because their findings are not the central foci of the discipline; they are 'insignificant' in comparison to the findings of males, — while males are in control of the criteria!

Many of the women who are engaged in educational research outside educational institutions have stated that when they put forward their proposals *inside* the institutions, they were informed that they did not constitute a valid topic.[4] Others have said that although their proposals were initially accepted so many attempts were made to 'neutralise' them, to shift them towards the central foci, the more 'important' issues, that they could see little point in continuing. Some women have been told that they must remove the feminist element from their research because it constituted bias: in a context in which masculism runs rife through research (but which is endorsed as the norm and therefore perceived as neutral) it is clear that the 'bias' resides in the established practitioners rather than the feminist research. Women engaged in research outside the official parameters seem to readily agree that if they wished to work inside they were obliged to fit their research to male standards, thereby directly or indirectly facilitating the perpetuation of male ends. Given the vast number of feminist projects underway in education, the fact that the 1978 *Index to Theses* reveals that there were only three degrees awarded on what could be called, broadly speaking, issues that were 'problematic' to women, it seems that most women are working outside the system. This of course is perfectly understandable, even predictable.

The scale on which women have been omitted from educational consideration, is massive. Sandra Acker (1980) has surveyed the area of the sociology of education (in Britain) and from 184 articles published since 1960 she has been able to give some details

[4]When I proposed to undertake *Language and Sex* as a topic for my Ph.D. in Australia I was told by a number of university education departments that 'it was not a topic'.

of the absence of women. For example, the study of women has been minimal for while 58% of the articles purported to be studying both sexes, 37% had all male samples and only 5% all female samples (and as she points out, these all-female groups were often *mothers* who were being studied in relation to their influence on children).

More knowledge is generated about males, more attention and significance accorded to male experience, and if anthropologists were to use the literature of the sociology of education (and there is no reason to suspect that it is not representative of education as a whole) to 'crack the code' of our own culture in the way they do in other cultures, then, Acker says, they . . .

> . . . would conclude that numerous boys but few girls go to secondary modern schools; that there are no girls' public schools; that there are almost no adult women influentials of any sort; that most students in higher education study science and engineering; that women rarely make a ritual transition called 'from school to work' and never go into further education colleges. Although some women go to university, most probably enter directly into motherhood where they are of some interest as transmitters of language codes to their children. And except for a small number of teachers, social workers and nurses, there are almost no adult women workers in the labour market (Acker, 1980; 5).

This enormous bias, however, generally goes unacknowledged: as Acker notes, most researchers do not even think it necessary to give reasons for excluding women. The fact that virtually no one in the research community (feminists excluded) has ever drawn attention to this bias would seem to indicate that the assumption that women were not data, has been shared. It is understandable that within the relatively closed circle in which men have consulted with men, their theories and explanations should concentrate on men, and that this should not be seen as problematic — by men!

The feminist challenge, however, has made some impact. The male bias, once exposed, is indefensible, but the response of some researchers has been to provide 'explanations' for their exclusion of women — sometimes in the form of a footnote! A. H. Halsey, A. F. Heath and J. M. Ridge for example, recently produced their treatise *Origins and Destinations: family, class and education in modern Britain,* and although they provided what they thought to be a 'logical' explanation for the exclusion of women, Tessa Blackstone (1980) in her review of their book, suggests that their 'logic' leaves a lot to be desired. If we are to accept the explanation preferred by Halsey *et al.* then the future looks bleak for women, for they gave as their reason for the exclusion of women the fact that they had not been included in past studies. In such a way the structural exclusion of women is used to justify the continued structural exclusion of women.

Even where women have been included as subjects for study, however, their presence can still be discounted. Such is the bias in favour of men that it seems whether included or excluded, women can still be classified as non data. Having established their theories and formulated their hypothesis in terms of male experience, and having assumed that male experience constitutes human experience, many researchers have expressed surprise and bewilderment when they have 'encountered' women in their research and found the behaviour of women inconsistent with or contrary to male predictions.

In the articles which she surveyed, Acker found that . . .

[5]Sometimes researchers are 'surprisingly cavalier' about giving the sex of their sample, says Acker and refer to children or students. While she has given these researchers 'the benefit of the doubt' and classified their research as 'mixed sex' there is reason to believe that many such studies may have had all male samples but were using male to mean humanity.

Witkin is puzzled as 'the findings for girls in secondary modern schools were not anticipated'. For Synge, the high educational aspirations of rural girls were 'contrary to expectations'. Robinson and Rackstraw admit 'at present we have no supportable explanation to offer for these occasional sex differences in performance'. Liversidge is surprised that working class girls' occupational aspirations don't differ much between those in grammar schools and in modern schools, unlike those of boys. And Robertson and Kapur go so far as to say that their results for women students are bizarre (Acker, 1980: 9).

In her critique of the social sciences, Sheila Tobias (1978) indicated that women are often excluded on the grounds that they are unreliable subjects and provide confusing data, and that rather than modify their male oriented theories, male researchers have modified humanity. One wonders to what extent this practice has operated within education: it could be one of the reasons for the greater frequency with which males are studied. What is beyond speculation however is the reluctance of researchers to see beyond males as the representatives of humanity and to identify women as an autonomous group with perhaps different, but no less valid patterns of behaviour. The surprise and bewilderment expressed by some researchers at the 'abnormal' findings related to women has not always led them to question whether their theories apply to only half the human race. The 'deficiency' has been found in women and not the assumptions of male educationalists and by continuing to treat the different behaviour of women as 'deviancy' they have helped to reinforce the structural exclusion of women.

Research findings, however, are of little use if they go unreported. Part of the academic process is publication and here, again, we find that male control, and male interests, predominate. If it had been feasible Sandra Acker might have begun her survey of publications in the sociology of education, not with the material selected for publication, but with the material submitted for consideration. For if researchers are to be puzzled by the 'deviant' behaviour of females in their samples, is it not likely that articles which are concerned with women would surprise and bewilder editors who could well reject them?

Virginia Woolf (1929) has stated that the values of a woman are not the values of a man, but that the values of men predominate. When a women writes, says Woolf,

> ... she will find that she is perpetually wishing to alter the established values — to make serious what appears insignificant to a man, and trivial what is to him important. And for that, of course, she will be criticized; for the critic of the opposite sex will be genuinely puzzled and surprised by an attempt to alter the current scale of values, and will see in it not merely a difference of view but a view that is weak, or trivial, or sentimental because it differs from his own (Woolf, 1972; 146).

One suspects that the critics, the referees and editors of academic journals, find educational research on women, by women, of lesser significance. Few feminist articles are featured between their covers despite the volume of feminist research that is being undertaken.[6] But while the exclusion of women at the point of publication may be a matter of conjecture, their exclusion after publication (in 'straight' or feminist journals) is not.

[6] It could be that feminists don't submit articles for consideration because they are convinced that the odds are so heavily stacked against them, but I do not subscribe to this view (completely) because articles in 'straight' journals are usually viewed as more prestigious than articles within feminist journals by those who determine tenure/promotion etc., and feminists who are inside educational institutions and want to 'play the game' frequently do try to attain publication in educational academic journals.

In Britain, for example, there is a *British Research Index* which purports to 'list and analyse the subject content of all articles of permanent educational interest' and which through its operation provides a classic case of the structural exclusion of women. Criteria must be formulated and a selection must be made in determining which articles qualify for inclusion in the *Index* but from the outset there is little likelihood that feminist educational articles will ever get the stamp of approval for there are no feminist periodicals among the 195 used by the *British Research Index* to make their selection. Feminist material is by definition non-data despite the fact that in the two British based feminist journals, *Feminist Review* has had an article on education (Naish, 1979) and *Women's Studies International Quarterly* devoted an entire issue to education (Vol. I No. 4, 1978). While the feminist contribution is structurally excluded in this manner what can be stated with some certainty is that feminist models of education will never become of 'permanent educational interest,' through this channel.

But this is not the only consequence. By not including material from feminist periodicals the *Index* helps to construct the invisibility of women. In 1978, for example, out of the 3,384 listings in the *Index* there were only 14 under the heading of sex differences and this helps to suggest that sex differences is an issue of minimal significance and attracts a minimal amount of research — a most misleading suggestion. Sexism and feminism were not entries in the *Index* and anyone who attempted to use the *Index* as a guide to research and publications could be forgiven for concluding that sexism and feminism were absent from the educational agenda. The Women's Research and Resources Centre research index would of course suggest otherwise.

The exclusion of feminist material from the *British Research Index* cannot be simply explained however on the grounds that the editors do not consult feminist periodicals. Sometimes feminists do 'run the gauntlet' and attain publication in 'straight' journals but their articles — for some reason — do not get listed. It is extremely difficult to determine the criteria which operated for the selection of one article on the moral and legal rights to equality of educational opportunity in an issue of the *Oxford Review of Education* while an excellent feminist article by Carol Dyhouse (1977) in the same issue, did not. One is obliged to assume that Dyhouse's article alters 'the current scale of values' and is perceived not merely as a difference of view, but as an insignificant view.

Wherever one looks for the entry of women into the male controlled discipline, one finds that the way is barred. At every level, women are consistently consigned to the realm of non-data and are excluded. Male dominance is being used to perpetuate male dominance: nowhere is this more demonstrable than in the readers and texts used within education and which initiate new practitioners into the rules and values of the discipline.

Sandra Acker (1980) has also surveyed the major readers and textbooks in Britain in the sociology of education and has found that some of the textbooks are slightly more sensitive to women's issues which suggests that the feminist critiques, in this area at least, have had some impact. But with most of the readers, and with one particular introductory text, there have been few if any improvements.

The Sociology of Education: an introduction (Morrish, 1978) is supposed to be a revision of the 1972 version, but no revisions have been made in terms of women. Morrish does note that more women are undertaking paid work outside the home and he thinks this worthy of comment. He states that problems arise for children when mothers go out to work.

Basically, Morrish excludes women: where he does include them it is in terms of their 'deficiencies'. For example he notes that women tend to leave teaching and he sees this as a serious problem. The 'solution' he puts forward is to make entry to teaching more difficult and then only very committed women would join men in qualifying as teachers. He also thinks fewer women in teaching would have other benefits for 'much of the sense of a second-rate profession . . . has been the fact that it was predominantly female in membership' (Morrish, 1978; 234).

As Acker states, her study by no means exhausts the literature of the sociology of education and she says that it would be interesting to analyse the relevant Open University course units. 'All three sections of units I know of which deal with women' comments Acker, 'are entitled "case study"' (p. 13).

Such is the diet which new students are fed. If they wish to understand and operate the boundaries and the rules of education as a discipline they must begin to appreciate that women do not count.

Education is a classic case of *men's studies* but despite the apparent bleakness of the overall view, it does appear to be under threat and is, at least, in great danger of being modified. From being in a position where the patriarchal assumptions went unquestioned, the last ten years has seen those assumptions challenged, and some changes have been made.

There is an awareness that education is a male model, controlled by males, in their own interests. There is an awareness that males are the 'gatekeepers' and have used their position to keep women out. There is an awareness that males have defined females as 'other' as 'deviants' and there is every indication that they have been misguided and that their 'mistakes' will not be so readily tolerated in the future. There is a growing demand that women be included as equals in educational theory and practice, as theorists and as subjects.

That feminist critiques are finding their way into the educational arena (Sandra Acker's paper was given at the B.S.A. Annual Conference, 1980) suggests that educationalists are beginning to lose the battle to keep work by women about women, outside the parameters of education. All this is reassuring. While the circle of men who talk to men has been totally closed to women, there has been little chance of change, but allow feminists some access, and no matter how slight, they have the potential for transforming the patriarchal paradigm of education.

So far the impact of feminism on education has been to identify the way in which education has been constructed to exclude women, to recognise and expose the bias inherent in such an arrangement and to make education, as a discipline, problematic. It has been to identify the closed circle, to insist that men's view of the world is partial and if presented as the whole, is false. It has been to insist that women have the right to participate in the creation of *our* education. It has been to 'put the case': this may even prove to be the most significant part of the struggle. For given the body of knowledge which feminists bring with them, getting our foot in the door might have been the hardest act of all.

The Feminist Model of Education

There are difficulties associated with trying to conceptualise the feminist model of education in monolithic terms; this is partly because feminist education, unlike traditional education, has not been confined to narrow, institutionalised parameters, and partly because the feminist model is still evolving. Feminist education takes many forms, from consciousness raising sessions to post graduate courses in women's studies, and 'modifications' are constantly required in order to meet changing circumstances of time and place. But partly through necessity, all the many forms of feminist education share common assumptions and aims, common ways of organising and distributing knowledge. For the sake of clarity, however, rather than attempt to describe the current complexity of feminist education I am going to provide a chronological sketch of its development in order to outline its characteristics and the ways in which it departs from the conventional, patriarchal model. It is significant that despite the fact that this widespread and successful educational movement is ten years old, it is not documented in mainstream literature and therefore must be outlined here.

In the late 1960's when the modern women's liberation movement began to emerge[7] and women started to ask questions about the condition of women, there was, as Joan Roberts (1976) has pointed out (see Introduction) little or no readily available knowledge to help them in their quest. In terms of the criteria that women were using, there were no books, no courses, no 'experts' who could offer adequate explanations or data. It was in this context that the feminist model of education evolved, for women realised that if they wanted knowledge about women, authenticated by women, they would have to 'make it themselves'. If the knowledge produced by men was inadequate or false then there was no alternative but to set up a 'circle of women' to produce and validate knowledge about women.

Women believed (erroneously as we later discovered[8]) that there was no body of knowledge to transmit, no tradition, no heritage to impart; they believed that women had to become the authorities on women and that there was no better (or other) place to start than with themselves and their own lives. By placing this emphasis on personal experience and validation, they formed the basis of an educational model which constituted a radical departure from traditional education and which still distinguishes feminism from patriarchal education.

It was not that women consciously examined the transmission model of education, recognised its inadequacies, and dismissed it; in a sense they did not 'choose' a model based on personal experience, it was virtually that there was nothing else they could do.

'Beginning with the personal' laid the foundation for many subsequent significant developments. In the late 1960's, across the United States and the western world, women began to come together to describe the condition of being a woman in a patriarchal world. Connections were made, critiques developed, analyses undertaken, explanations offered and verified, as women checked with women about the collective nature of their experience. New knowledge was produced in a different way; it was 'collective' knowledge, 'made' rather than 'received' by all those who participated.

Again, this was not necessarily because women opted for the personal; in those first explosive years it is unlikely that such sophisticated rationales would have had sufficient time to evolve. (Even the definitions of consciousness raising have been provided in

[7]There is some difficulty in trying to pinpoint the starting date of the modern feminist movement, but Maren Lockwood Carden (1974) in her book *The New Feminist Movement,* outlines the early days in the USA.

[8]Much feminist scholarship has been archivist in nature and has 'recovered' the work produced by women in the past; this excision of women from history, from the history of many of the disciplines, is itself an example of the exclusion of women from cultural institutions.

retrospect.) While there is no agreement about why there was such an explosion[9] there is agreement about its occurrence. (Joan Cassell, 1977 says that it was estimated in 1972 that every block in Manhattan had at least one CR group, p. 34; it seems that this was the case in other cities and other countries as well.)

Women found themselves meeting with other women and talking about their personal experience (and validating it in the process); they were constructing a new reality without necessarily being able to state explicitly what it was they were doing. And because all those women who were involved, were to some extent, 'in the same boat', it was extremely difficult for any hierarchies to emerge. None of us (I recollect) had much more than our personal experience to go on. None of us was an expert who could rely on 'book learning'. We were all equal in the sense that we all felt that we had been 'misled' and we all wanted to come to understand how it had happened (and to make sure it didn't happen again). Under these circumstances it was not difficult for cooperative and collaborative activities to occur. The sharing of knowledge led to collective understandings which resulted in new knowledge; we 'recycled' the old and made the new together. And we called this 'learning process' consciousness raising.

There can be no doubt that we were engaged in a learning enterprise. Even some of the conventional aids associated with education were in use. Women left meetings to do their 'homework', to look up what men had said about women, and to return to the groups armed with notes, quotations, references, questions, hypotheses. Jointly women began to codify what they were doing; there were newsletters, mimeographed sheets, duplicated 'papers' appearing all over the place (almost spontaneously it has been suggested, see Carden 1974 and Freeman, 1975). There was 'cross fertilisation' of groups and for the women who were involved this was an exciting and dynamic — and *useful* process.

In attempting to describe feminist education there is a limit to the use which can be made of the customary terms in education. This was a learning experience, although qualitatively different from the learning which many of us had 'endured' in our own schooling.[10] It was part of living, not an activity which occurred in prescribed places and at prescribed times. That educationalists may not recognise this, says more about their restricted definition of learning than it does about feminism. The terms 'teacher' and 'learner' — as they have been defined by education — are also inadequate; while educationalists may wish to divide the world into these two polarised categories, they can become meaningless in a feminist context, where *all* are teaching and learning. Janet Robyns (1977) has described her experience of feminist education, which while it is much later and much more institutionalised than those first informal CR groups, shares some of those same features; she too finds the conventional terms inadequate and says of feminist teachers that they

> ... were not set up as knowers among a group of non knowers. They were more like part time assistants. They helped as much as they could by giving information about their experiences .... Another thing became apparent. The 'teacher' did not remain the same person. In sharing our knowledge, our thoughts and experiences, the 'teacher' rotated among us. Each functioned as teacher at times because each had something to offer. There was no knower/non knower, judge/judged hierarchy (Robyns, 1977: 53).

[9]There still seems to be no acceptable explanation for the rise of the modern women's movement although Carden and Cassell have tried to formulate explanations.

[10]Perhaps the closest model is that of Freire; some work has been done indicating the parallels between Freire's version of education and that of feminism.

This form of education, of course, stands in sharp contrast to traditional forms and suggests one of the reasons behind the 'dismissal' of feminist education. To conventional educationalists the failure to establish definite 'authority figures' no doubt resembles something approaching anarchy and the lack of a 'prescribed' curriculum (in conventional terms) would seem to pose a threat to standards. In one sense, educationalists are not mistaken, for feminists do seek an end to hierarchies and standards, as they have been constructed, on the grounds that they are *not* an inherent part of learning, but of a stratified society!

The success of feminism in developing an egalitarian and cooperative model of education (which appears to be more beneficial for students) would be difficult to dispute. Although currently this non-hierarchical structure is an explicit feminist goal, I do not think that the *aim* alone, accounts for the achievement. It seems to me that equality and cooperation were almost the inevitable outcome of the circumstances in which feminists found themselves. However, in the current context where a body of knowledge is rapidly becoming available, and where the possibility of 'transmission' exists — with all its concomitant attributes of hierarchies and competition — it may be very important for feminism to focus on past achievements and to keep the cooperative model in mind, for it could begin to get 'lost' as feminism enters institutions. While this is a risk it is by no means inevitable, for even in institutionalised courses the feminist model of education still makes its presence felt (which is one of the reasons that it has met resistance).

In commenting on the reception that Women's Studies courses sometimes get in institutions, Janet Wolff (1977) says of such courses that they are 'less a question of teaching and learning, or of imparting a body of information, and more a process of cooperative discovery' (156) and Janet Robyns has also outlined the way in which the non-competitive nature of feminist education (inside or outside institutions) makes learning a markedly different activity. She states that things are very different when there is no need to get to the top. 'We found that if competition was out, we could relax, no one was trying to win' and this had many repercussions. 'We didn't hoard what we had learned' she says, 'Learning was no longer isolated' it was exciting, with these sessions being 'the high point in our lives .... Incentive and enthusiasm were bred here'. We didn't dread our sessions, she adds, contrasting feminist learning with traditional education (p. 52–53).

Within the framework that Wolff and Robyns (and others) outline, many of the traditional theories of teaching and learning, motivation and memorisation, appear most inappropriate. For women who have participated in feminist education it is not necessary to make a conscious effort to commit to memory the facts of oppression; it is not as if they are likely to forget — or even to be 'tested' on what they know! While learning is so closely linked with living, as it is within feminism, the premise that it is necessary to introduce external factors to induce human beings to learn, and to help them retain what they could learn, seems inapplicable.

By emphasising the role that the personal plays in learning, feminists have developed an educational paradigm which is at times diametrically opposed to the patriarchal one (where the personal is seen as a source of contamination and the subjective, something to be avoided). If all were going well within the patriarchal framework, if schooling could be seen as effective and successful, with students emerging from the process as literate, numerate, socially skilled, politically aware and responsible for themselves then perhaps any comparison between the two models would be little more than an interesting exercise. But given that women are coming from the feminist experience testifying to (and exhibiting) its advantages, and students are coming from schooling and testifying to (and exhibiting) its disadvantages, then this ceases to be just an interesting exercise and becomes a significant issue. One woman I interviewed helped to sum it up when she said

> After institutionalised education you feel worse. After feminist education, you feel better. I left university convinced I was dim, I was always sure everyone around me was brighter than I was, and I was always frightened of being found out. I was frightened of the world. I felt incompetent. I had the mentality of a victim. All that changed after my women's studies course. I felt much more in charge of my own life, though I was more aware of the things that were against me. But I felt capable. I thought it was possible to do something about them.

Becoming a victim in educational institutions is not an uncommon experience; 'victims' are the predictable outcome given the way educational theory and practice are organised. Fundamental to the patriarchal model of education are the concepts of 'compete and eliminate'. Students are isolated from one another, required to compete, frequently have their personal lives and experiences discounted (see Douglas Barnes, 1976) and are generally deprived of any autonomy or responsibility. Because the educational ladder has fewer places on each ascending rung, an arbitrary number of students must be designated as 'failers' at each stage, with the result that their educational experience is terminated. Only within a patriarchal and hierarchical framework could it be seen as logical that those who are classified as less able — determined by objective tests of course — should be given the least educational experience. It is no wonder that women leave feminist education feeling good (Freeman, 1975) and students leave patriarchal education, feeling devalued.

The difference between the feminist model and the patriarchal model is in essence political and it has been a political manouvre on the part of educationalists to keep the feminist forces out of education. But I suspect that the traditional forces are being undermined — and not only from the outside, but from within.

Feminism is a social and political movement, a revolutionary movement, aimed at the redistribution of power. It has developed its own form of organisation and dissemination of knowledge which reflects its political nature and aspirations. If feminism had remained outside educational institutions its model could still constitute a threat, but the fact that it has moved inside as well, (while still retaining many of its outside and informal bases) makes it an even greater threat. Given the conservative nature of curriculum construction and the usual methods by which knowledge becomes incorporated in the curriculum (Williams, 1975), the establishment of so many women's studies courses in so many institutions, at so many levels, and in so many countries in such a short space of time, is little short of astonishing.

There has been method in what some might see as the madness of taking feminism into educational institutions. There has been a deliberate policy of bringing politics into education, and this in part explains the resistance which feminists have encountered. The main aims of the women's studies course — at Cambridge — states Joanna Mack (1977) are to challenge 'the male monopoly of intellectual thought' and to 'change the content and viewpoint of such work' and to 'establish the political and personal connections of what is studied'. Mack goes on to say that 'it is important to study what political use has been made of academic disciplines to justify discrimination and oppression' and to 'raise the consciousness of many of the students' (Mack, 1974: 162). With such avowed political intentions, it is not surprising that educationalists have not welcomed feminists with open arms; there is a lot at stake and they have a lot to lose.

Ann Fitzgerald, (1978) has said that 'women's studies confronts head-on the two shibboleths of the traditional curriculum; disciplinary specialization and apolitical objective knowledge' (p. 3). There are many ramifications which arise from the feminist premise that the personal is political, and the challenge which the multi/interdisciplinary, explicitly subjective nature of feminism, makes to the educational community should not be underestimated;

> Women's studies . . . is necessarily interdisciplinary and frankly political. It is problem centered and challenges the ways in which social structures (the curriculum very much included) create and foster ideas about ourselves and the world. In acknowledging the male centeredness of the traditional curriculum, it points out the biases inherent in all disciplines and thus the political nature of education itself . . . . Questioning the underlying assumptions about the truth and supposedly objective knowledge of academic fields is to recognize that the very chopping up and categorizing of knowledge in the academy is itself a political act (Fitzgerald, 1978: 3).

From the feminist model where women have posed questions about women, discipline boundary lines have blurred and even collapsed. The traditional compartmentalisation of knowledge has even been put forward as a possible 'divide and rule' strategy which has permitted the production and perpetuation of false meanings about women; feminists have come to appreciate that many divisions are arbitrary, often unnecessary, frequently misleading, and the product of a male view of the world. The existence of multi/inter/predisciplinary feminist knowledge is in itself a testimony to the dispensability of many discipline divisions and this constitutes another threat to the patriarchal model of education.

It is becoming increasingly difficult to keep feminism out of education, particularly as it infiltrates educational institutions.[11] What we have at the moment is a complex situation in which there is a patriarchal paradigm of education where men have not only decreed the boundaries, the rules, the definitions and methodologies, but where they have done it in such a way that females are excluded. Along side this, often in the same institutions, and sometimes in the same departments, is a feminist model of education which not only challenges those boundaries, rules, definitions and methodologies, but which also posits female experience as a viable alternative for organising the theory and practice of education. The impact of feminism on education must be viewed in terms of the challenge it makes to *both* male versions of educational theory and practice *and* to male supremacy.

Thomas Kuhn (1972) has suggested that the history of scientific knowledge is the history of the shift from one paradigm which no longer adequately explains, which contains too many inaccuracies and contradictions to be tolerated, to a new paradigm which takes account of more evidence and which offers a more comprehensive

---

[11]In the *Women's Studies Newsletter,* Fall 1979, Florence Howe states that there are now over 300 Women's Studies programmes in the United States and 21 research institutes. The *Women's Research and Resources Centre Newsletter* in Britain indicates that there is constant expansion in Women's Studies in schools, adult education, and higher education with the first M.A. in Feminist theory beginning at Kent University in 1980. Other westernised countries report similar growth.

explanation. It will be interesting to see whether this applies to education, for currently the feminist paradigm seems to take much more into account, provides a much more comprehensive explanation of human learning and a much more successful educational model.

Conclusion

Feminists have brought politics into education; they have issued a challenge. Educationalists, until now, have chosen to ignore it. It is not possible to say what the final outcome will be but it is possible to suggest that the odds are not on the side of patriarchy; the feminist achievement is too substantial for it to remain 'non-data'.

Feminists have developed their own structures for producing their own meanings about women; they have exposed the discrepancies between their meanings and those that have been enshrined as legitimated (objective) knowledge, and in the process they have exposed the political nature of education and the means by which male supremacy has been used to perpetuate male supremacy. One of the substantive issues that women's studies addresses is that of the construction, organisation and distribution of knowledge. While traditional education has been only marginally concerned with this issue, for reasons of necessity women's studies has been centrally concerned with the politics of knowledge, and can now provide data and explanations which raise questions about the role played by education as a discipline.

Men may have set up their own circle and kept women out, and one way of assessing the impact of feminism upon education would be to document the extent to which women have been able to penetrate that circle. But it would be a distortion of the role that feminism has played if this was the *only* form of assessment; for women have set up their own circle, have produced their own knowledge and are now challenging the very existence and authenticity of the male model. Men may even keep their own circle but the impact of feminism could be to shift the locus of power.

References

ACKER, Sandra (1980) 'Feminist perspectives and the British Sociology of Education', *Paper presented at British Sociological Association,* Annual Conference, Lancaster, April 8.

BARNES, Douglas (1976) *From Communication to Curriculum,* Penguin, Middlesex.

BLACKSTONE, Tessa (1980) 'Falling short of meritocracy' in *The Times Higher Education Supplement,* January 18th, p. 14.

BYRNE, Eileen (1978) *Women and Education,* Tavistock, London.

CARDEN, Maren Lockwood (1974) *The New Feminist Movement,* Russel Sage Foundation, New York.

CASSELL, Joan (1977) *A group called women; sisterhood and symbolism in the feminist movement,* David McKay, New York.

DYHOUSE, Carol (1977) 'Good wives and little mothers; social anxieties in the schoolgirls' curriculum, 1890–1920' in *Oxford Review of Education,* Vol. II, No. 1, pp. 21–35.

EGGLESTON, J. (1979) 'The characteristics of educational research; mapping the domain' in *British Educational Research Journal,* Vol. V, No. 1, pp. 1–12.

FITZGERALD, Ann (1978) 'Teaching interdisciplinary women's studies' in Great Lakes College Association *Faculty Newsletter,* March 27.

FREEMAN, Jo (1975) *The politics of women's liberation,* David McKay, New York.

FREIRE, Paulo (1972) *CulturalnAction for Freedom,* Penguin Education, Middlesex (1973) *Pedagogy of the Oppressed,* Penguin Education, Middlesex.

HALSEY, A. H., A. F. HEATH and J. M. RIDGE (1980) *Origins and destinations: family, class and education in modern Britain,* Oxford University Press, Oxford.

HOWE, Florence and Paul LAUTER (1980) *The impact of women's studies on the campus and the disciplines,* National Institute of Education, U.S. Dept H.E.W., Washington D.C.

KUHN, Thomas (1972) *The Structure of Scientific revolutions* (2nd Ed.) University of Chicago Press, Chicago.

LAVIGUEUR, Jill (1977) 'Equality of educational opportunity for girls; and its relation to coeducation', Unpublished M.A. Dissertation, University of Sheffield.

LIVERSIDGE, W. (1962) 'Life Chances', in *Sociological Review,* 10, pp. 17–34, Quoted in ACKER, S., 1980.

LOFLAND, Lyn H. (1975) 'The 'thereness' of women; a selective view of urban sociology' in Marcia Millman and Rosabeth Kanter (Eds.) *Another Voice; feminist perspectives on social life and social science,* Anchor Press, Doubleday, New York, pp. 144–170.

MACK, Joanna (1974) 'Women's studies in Cambridge' in *The New Era,* Vol. 55, No. 6, July/Aug., pp. 162–164.

McNAMARA, D. R. (1979) 'Paradigm lost; Thomas Kuhn and educational research' in *British Educational Research Journal,* Vol. V, No. 2, pp. 167–174.

McWILLIAMS-TULLBERG, Rita (1975) *Women at Cambridge; a men's university — though of a mixed type,* Victor Gollancz, London.

MORRISH, I. (1978) *The sociology of education; an introduction,* Methuen, London, Quoted in ACKER, S. 1980.

NAISH, Julia (1979) 'The chance to say what they think: Teaching English as a second language' in *Feminist Review,* No. 3, pp. 1–11.

PORTER, Nancy M. and Margaret EILEENCHILD (1980) *The Effectiveness of Women's Studies Teaching,* National Institute of Education, U.S. Dept H.E.W., Washington, D.C.

REUBEN, Elaine (1978) 'In defiance of the evidence; notes on feminist scholarship' in *Women's Studies International Quarterly,* Vol. I, No. 3, pp. 215–218.

ROBERTS, Joan I. (Ed.) (1976) *Beyond Intellectual Sexism; a new woman, a new reality,* David McKay, New York.

ROBERTSON, A. and R. L. KAPUR (1972) 'Social change, emotional distress, and the world view of students: an empirical study of the existential ethic and the spirit of suffering' in *British Journal of Sociology,* 23, pp. 462–477, Quoted in ACKER, S., 1980.

ROBINSON, W. O. and S. J. RACKSTRAW (1978) 'Social class differences in posing questions for answers' in *Sociology,* 12, pp. 265–280, Quoted in ACKER, S., 1980.

ROBYNS, Janet (1977) 'Reproductive versus Regenerative education; the extension of English education through reference to feminism', Unpublished Associateship Report, University of London Institute of Education.

SHAW, Jenny (1976) 'Finishing schools; some implications of sex-segregated education' in Diana Barker and Sheila Allen (Eds.) *Sexual Divisions and Society; Process and Change,* Tavistock, London, pp. 150–173.

SMITH, Dorothy (1978) 'A peculiar eclipsing; women's exclusion from man's culture' in *Women's Studies International Quarterly,* Vol. I, No. 4, pp. 281–296.

SUPPES, Patric (1973) 'Facts and fantasies of education' in M.C. Wittrock (Ed.) *Alternatives from educational research,* Prentice Hall, London, Quoted in EGGLESTON, J., 1979.

SYNGE, J. (1973) 'Scottish regional and sex differences in school achievement and entry to further education' in *Sociology,* 7, pp. 107–116, Quoted in ACKER, S., 1980.

TOBIAS, Sheila (1978) 'Women's Studies; its origins, organization and prospects' in *Women's Studies International Quarterly,* Vol. I, No. 1, pp. 85–98.

WILLIAMS, Raymond (1975) *The Long Revolution,* Penguin, Middlesex.

WITKIN, R. (1971) 'Social class influence on the amount and type of positive evaluation of school lessons' in *Sociology,* 5, pp. 169–189, Quoted in ACKER, S., 1980.

WOLFF, Janet (1977) 'Women's Studies and Sociology' in *Sociology,* Vol. II, No. 1, Jan., pp. 155–161.

WOOLF, Virginia (1929) 'Women and Fiction' in *The Forum,* March 29, Reprinted in Leonard Woolf (Ed.) 1972, *Collected Essays; Virginia Woolf,* Vol. II, Chatto and Windus, London, pp. 141–148.

YOUNG, Michael (1975) *Knowledge and Control; new directions for the sociology of education,* Collier MacMillan, London.

12

Before and After: The Impact of Feminism on the Academic Discipline of Law

KATHERINE O'DONOVAN

Legal academics usually write in complacent terms of the progress made by the law over the past hundred years towards the equality of women with men. 'As we shall see, during the past century the wife's position has steadily changed from something in many respects inferior to that of a servant (who could at least quit her master's service by giving notice) to that of the joint, co-equal head of the family' (Bromley, 1976: 108). Explanations for this change are couched in general terms of 'the movement for the equality of the sexes' (Bromley: 110); and the changes in the law since 1857, when civil divorce was introduced (although not on equal terms for women petitioners), and which particularly occurred with the Married Women's Property Acts 1870–82 are seen as evidence of legal enlightenment. Whilst it is true that the law has changed gradually during the past hundred years and now recognises that women may be independent legal subjects, there has been little attempt in legal literature to analyse and explain the previous subordination of women in law, the processes of alteration, or the remaining injustices.

Legal writers generally consider that it is outside the purview of the lawyer to discuss reasons for legal provisions, other than purely technical explanations. Their job is to deal with the how rather than with the why. This is partly because such explanations are inevitably complex, raising as they do socio-economic questions, and because law-making and the interpretation of law are seen as different tasks, but it is also the case that issues relating to women have remained unperceived, and therefore undiscussed. The law is an instrument of social control in the rational world of men; one of its major functions is the resolution of conflict. It is not seen to enter the lives of women, indeed it does not do so directly. In its regulation of the family the law is concerned not to interfere overtly, but to create a space in which the male head of the household can exercise power and authority. Here the lack of legal provision is as significant as its presence.

The invisibility of women in academic work has evoked a good deal of comment in recent years, but not from lawyers. Since legal academics view their role as that of reporting and analysing actual legal provisions, they do not comment on areas which the law ignores. Until the advent of the Equal Pay Act, 1970 and the Sex Discrimination Act, 1975 the desirability of legislation to enforce equality of women with men was not discussed in British law journals. However, even these two legislative acts only affect the lives of women in the public domain. They leave untouched certain issues of discrimination by the state itself,[1] and they do not impinge on the private domain at all. Again, the lack of legal commentary on this has been disappointing, but it is symptomatic of the lawyer's outlook. Even women lawyers welcoming and explaining the new legislation have not remarked on its failure to deal with discrimination by the state (Richards, 1976; Rendel, 1978).

The reasons for this invisibility of legal woman stretch further, though, than simple omission. There is abundant evidence of the subordination of women to men and differentiation between them even in the twentieth century (Graveson and Crane, 1957); although as late as 1974 these are referred to as 'slight' by the author of a new textbook on family law (Cretney, 1974: 148). Women traditionally appeared in textbooks only as incapable persons aligned with the insolvent and the inebriate and confined with lunatics and children to a chapter entitled 'legal disabilities'. Textbook writers accepted this without question. The judges, whose handiwork and creation the common law was, offered a number of rationalisations for their perpetuation of male dominance. The traditional judicial attitude to women was that they were not legal subjects but creatures whose 'natural and proper timidity and delicacy unfits (them) ... for many of the occupations of civil life'.[2] Behind this opinion lay the assumption that (alleged) biological inferiority and social inferiority were to be equated. Rationalisations for this view were couched in terms of male protectiveness or of each sex belonging to a separate sphere, but it is hard to resist the conclusion of Albie Sachs that 'English common law, which has so often been extolled as being the embodiment of human freedom, had in fact provided the main intellectual justification for the avowed and formal subjection of women' (Sachs and Wilson, 1978: 40).

I think it is fair to say that lawyers no longer overtly hold the opinion that women are inferior to men. Accepted however, is an account of the legal position of women in which they are located in the private domain 'in which the King's writ does not seek to run, and to which his officers do not seek to be admitted'.[3] Confined to the domestic sphere where 'the house of everyone is to him as his castle and fortress'[4] women have remained remote from legal discussion. And any challenge to this can safely be dismissed with the comforting cliché of 'separate spheres' or 'separate but equal'. In this analysis a separate social role leads to different legal rights. The assumptions which underlie the allocation of women and men to separate legal spheres are that men are in the public domain of politics, commerce, property, and work. Law regulates only the public domain and confers legal rights on those who work, that is, who are economically productive. Women, being in the private domain which is unregulated by law, are not full legal subjects and are therefore not entitled to the same legal rights as men.

Feminists have attacked the premises which lead to the denial of equal legal rights to all human beings. Their challenge has been made in four main areas, each of which I propose to consider in turn: equality and women's rights; sex-based legal classification; economic implications at current arrangements in family life; and the relationship of women to the state.

---

[1] The Sex Discrimination Act, 1975 gives its purpose as 'promoting equality of opportunity between men and women generally'. Yet it covers only discrimination in employment, education, and the provision of goods and services. It does not affect discrimination by the state through laws on social security, pensions, taxation, and the family.

[2] *Bradwell* v. *Illinois,* (1873) 130, 21 L.Ed. 442.   83 U.S. (16 Wall)

[3] *Lord Justice Atkin, Balfour* v. *Balfour* (1919) 2 K.B. 571 at p. 579.

[4] *Semayne's Case,* 77 E.R. 194 at p. 195.   5 Co. Rep. 91a

Equality and Women's Rights

For the non-lawyer equality and justice may be synonymous with law. A reading of jurisprudential classics will quickly show that in legal theory this is not so. Legal positivism, the ruling theory, is concerned not with substantive justice but with the concept of law — what it is, how it is defined. A major debate has centred on whether law requires moral content, but since the basic tenet of positivism holds that law is the expression of the will of the sovereign, that is, of those in power, the answer has been negative. The content of legal rules thus depends on the desires of the dominant group in society. Bentham, the revered founder of this school of thought, justified the allocation of power and superior legal rights to men on the pragmatic ground that they already had physical power; but he showed his belief in the more general inferiority of women in describing them as 'delicate, inferior in strength and hardiness of body, in point of knowledge, intellectual powers and firmness of mind' (Bentham, 1948: 58). Bentham's other major contribution to liberal theory of law was utilitarianism, which holds that law and its institutions should serve the general welfare, and nothing else. He called the idea of individual human rights 'nonsense on stilts'.

Hart, the current leading exponent of legal positivism, has acknowledged that Bentham's 'insistence that the foundations of a legal system are properly described in the morally neutral terms of a general habit of obedience opened the long positivist tradition in English jurisprudence' but that this epoch may now be closing. 'Utilitarianism is now on the defensive, if not on the run, in the face of theories of justice which in many ways resemble the doctrine of the unalienable rights of man' (Hart, 1976: 547).

The traditional requirement of justice is that of the generalisation principle. In essence this means that the principle of what is right (or wrong) for one person must be right (or wrong) for all other similarly placed (Singer, 1963). This is incorporated into the law through the operation of precedent. In the past the common law was created by judges looking to what has been decided in previous cases when faced with a legal conflict and choosing which preceding cases to follow. A body of cases known as precedents, was built up. The problem with the classical theory of justice and with precedent is that when faced with a moral or legal problem a decision must be made as to whether the circumstances are essentially similar or essentially different. The determination of whether persons are essentially similar or different is made with reference to the concepts of status and class.

The legal term status has long been used to identify the privileges and obligations of a given individual or class in the currently prevailing social order, with naturally occurring characteristics serving as the means of identifying a certain status. 'Women, lunatics, blacks, Indians, and others have been limited from time to time in their legal rights and capacities by reason of their sex, colour, ethnic background or mental abilities — characteristics over which the individual has little control' (Hunter, 1976: 1043). The concept of status serves to justify the separate classification of women from men and their consequential differentiation by the law.

Demands for women's rights have usually involved a demand for equal status with men. Feminists regard law as a touchstone of the advancement of women's progress towards equality, perhaps without realising that the nature of legal reasoning is to differentiate amongst human beings and to classify them according to this differentiation. But the feminist starts from a different major premise than does the lawyer. The feminist assumes that all persons are equal and anticipates that they will have the same legal rights, whereas the lawyer starts out with a process of classification. The impact of feminism has been to raise questions about this legal approach.

Questions about equality have caused political controversy in recent years because of demands made by racial minorities and by women. Ronald Dworkin has given considerable attention to the concept of equality. He makes a distinction between the right to equal treatment, 'which is the right to an equal distribution of some opportunity or resource or burden' and the right to treatment as an equal, 'which is the right, not to receive the same distribution of some burden or benefit, to be treated with the same respect and concern as anyone else' (Dworkin, 1977: 227). He gives the example of two children, one dying from a disease that is making the other uncomfortable and says, 'I do not show equal concern if I flip a coin to decide which should have the remaining dose of a drug' (p. 227). This shows, he claims, that the right to treatment as an equal is fundamental, and the right to equal treatment is derivative. He concludes 'we may therefore say that justice as fairness rests on the assumption of a natural right of all men and women to equality of concern and respect, a right they possess not by virtue of birth or characteristic or merit or excellence but simply as human beings with the capacity to make plans and give justice' (p. 182).

The inclusion of rights of women in debates about human rights has been an important step, obvious though it may now seem. 'In a global community aspiring towards human dignity, a basic policy should ... be to make the social roles of the sexes, with the notable exception of childbearing, as nearly interchangeable or equivalent as possible'. To achieve genuine equality between the sexes, it is vital that 'nobody be forced into a pre-determined role on account of sex, but each person be given better possibilities to develop his or her personal talents' (McDougal, Lasswell, Chen, 1975: 509).

Sex-based Legal Classification

The pervasiveness of classification in legal processes and its centrality in legal reasoning has already been indicated. Formal logic and taxonomies depend on classification and in ancient and medieval thought it was believed that from classification truths would be learned about the world (Woody, 1973). This is no longer believed today and classification is said to be a matter of tradition and administrative convenience. Separate classification of women from men has been challenged by feminists and the repercussions of this challenge have been both academic and practical, for a new way of viewing the world is demanded.

Academic recognition of the chance nature of sex as a basis for legal rights has concentrated on the inequity of using ascribed characteristics to determine a persons's legal status. Susan Woody has argued that a distinction should be drawn between classifications based on characteristics which are ascribed and those which are chosen. The ascribed characteristics such as race or sex where used as a basis for classification should be viewed with suspicion, especially where a reduction in personal freedom is involved. Otherwise that dimension over which a person has no control is an occasion for penalty (Woody, 1973). There is however a difficulty with this argument and that of Smith (1976: 122) that a chosen status such as marriage or parenthood is not included amongst ascribed characteristics as voluntary human action is involved. Smith argues that special rights or duties based on assumed (i.e. chosen) status are not repugnant to equality. But what he overlooks is that these choices are not necessarily made by one sex only and that legal requirements resulting from marriage and parenthood are capable of expression in non-gender specific words such as parent or spouse. As we shall see, gender roles enshrined in the law, and especially those related to marriage and the family, are a major source of inequality between women and men.

In the United States challenges to sex-based classification in legislation have been upheld in a number of cases.[5] Although the Supreme Court does not apply to this classification as strict a scrutiny as that applied to race or ethnic origins, nevertheless, it requires that important governmental objectives be satisfied by a classification based on sex. American feminists continue to press for an amendment to the Constitution which would outlaw sex as a factor in determining legal rights as follows: 'Equality of rights under the law shall not be denied or abridged by the Unite States or by any state on account of sex' (Peratis and Cary, 1978: 44).

Courts in Britain do not have power to review legislative classification for constitutionality, and classification based on sex is not forbidden by law. The Sex Discrimination Act 1975 does not affect areas such as family law, welfare law, tax law and parts of employment law. Here legislative schemes continue to be based on gender roles as husband or wife, and the state itself takes an active part in promoting this division. The idea that all separate classification of women and men should be eliminated has received scant official attention and even amongst feminists there seems to be a division of opinion on this issue. A number of complex questions are raised concerning assimilation of women and men, special provision for women, and affirmative action or positive discrimination (Wasserstrom, 1977: 581). Certain feminists believe in total assimilation of the sexes with no public recognition of biological or physiological differences. The logic of this position leads Shulamith Firestone to advocate the cessation of the current method of child-bearing and the substitution of extra-uterine reproduction (Firestone, 1971: 233). With this view-point can be associated the belief that language must be reformed to eliminate its current gender associations (Jagger, 1974; Lakoff, 1975). Legal discourse is undeniably masculine in character, with its reference to the 'reasonable man', its misogynistic jokes that the reason that legislation refers to the masculine gender only is that 'the male embraces the female', but there has been little discussion on this. Many feminists thus fear that assimilation means women disappearing into a male model of the world, and becoming 'honorary men' or 'social males' (Stacy and Price, 1979: 28).

The argument that the law must continue to classify men and women separately in order to make special provision for women is usually associated with either the biological functions of maternity or a social role within the family. Insofar as biological functions are concerned it may be necessary for the law to protect individuals' reproductive and procreative organs by safeguards at work, maternity leave etc. But social roles and sex are not necessarily synonymous (O'Donovan, 1979: 147), and there

[5]*Reed* v. *Reed*	404 U.S. 71(1971)
Frontiero v. *Richardson*	411 U.S. 677(1973)
Weinberger v. *Wiesenfeld*	420 U.S. 636(1975)
Stanton v. *Stanton*	421 U.S. 7(1975)

is no reason why, in all other cases, the law should not be couched in neutral terms of 'parent', 'spouse' etc. The protection of social roles by the law is a matter for public policy. The point here is that these roles do not have to be sex based.

Positive or reverse discrimination has been justified intellectually by American legal philosophers. 'The case for programmes of preferential treatment can plausibly rest on the view that the programmes are not unfair ... and on the view that is it unfair to continue the present set of unjust — often racist and sexist — institutions that comprise social reality' (Wasserstrom, 1977: 622). And although the official British view is that positive discrimination involves the very evil of inequality that it purports to cure, a leading academic lawyer has written that 'the law may have to create inequalities to make up for natural or social inequalities which are not of its own creation ... and to treat as equal that which is unequal may ... be a very odious form of discrimination' (Kahn-Freund, 1971: 510).

The general acceptance that separate classification may involve discrimination against women is the major change in this area so far. The law Commission of Canada has stated: 'It is apparent that substantial progress towards the elimination of such discrimination is seriously impeded by sexually-based classifications in the law governing the primary social and economic relationship between the sexes' (1976: para. 3.3).

Economic Implications of Current Arrangements in Family Life

'At no time has the English lawyer regarded marriage as a mere contract. It must be admitted then that the word marriage, apart from describing a social institution or ceremony, creates a relationship recognised by the law conferring rights and duties' (James, 1957: 21). This statement sums up the legal view of marriage, a view which has been strongly criticised by feminists. In her analysis of the marriage contract, Lenore Weitzman has shown that the marriage contract is unlike any other. Its provisions are unwritten, its penalties are unspecified, its terms are unclear and the parties cannot either write their own terms or vary the existing terms. She has analysed the ways in which present laws assign certain roles and obligations to each spouse and in so doing place an unfair burden on married women. She argues that it is no longer possible to assume, as does conventional marriage law, that marriage is 'the voluntary union for life of one man and one woman to the exclusion of all others',[6] or as stated in Matthew Bacon's Abridgement, 'a compact between a man and a woman for the procreation and education of children' (1832), or that it is the first marriage, or that there will be a strict division of labour between the couple (Weitzman, 1974: 1169). Weitzman's solution is to suggest a freely negotiated contract between the couple prior to marriage, but John Eekelaar has pointed out that economic circumstances may change over the years as may expectations and that in any case the courts have flexibility and discretion to deal with the circumstances of the marriage (Eekelaar, 1978: 53).

'In most families the husband's duties will be largely conditioned by the fact that he is the breadwinner; the wife will usually be primarily responsible for the running of the home, a duty which may take the form of supervising a large domestic staff or of doing the household 'chores' herself, such as cooking, cleaning, and mending and looking

---

[6]Lord Penzance, *Hyde* v. *Hyde & Woodmansee,* (1866) L.R. I P.D. 130 at p. 133.

after the children' (Bromley, 1976: 112). This view is that of the author of the leading textbook on family law. The statement not only ignores the views of feminist writers, but also shows a failure to appreciate that the law reinforces the allocations of these social roles within the family and assigns rights and duties on the basis of sex.

'Marriage however, is not just a 'natural' or social necessity — though these are the terms in which marriage is frequently seen by the participants, by sociologists and by the judiciary. The interrelationship of unwaged domestic labour and the wage-labour market make marriage an *economic* necessity for nearly all women, and a wife is an economic asset for a man' (Leonard Barker, 1977: 241). Nevertheless, there is little economic security in marriage for a non-wage earner. According to English law agreements between spouses are unenforceable in the courts because they are private, and property belongs to the person who has acquired it, or in whose name it has been registered, usually the husband. The financial plight of the dependent wife and the unfairness of laws which push women into the role of wife and then punish her for not having acquired her own assets has been recognised for some time (see Kahn-Freund, 1971). Feminists have added a new dimension however, by insisting on the economic value of the work done by the housewife (Glazer-Malbin, 1976), and by pointing out how legal and other institutional arrangements coerce women into housewives (O'Donovan, 1979).

Housework as an area of academic study has been taken seriously by sociologists for some time (Oakley, 1974). Recently there is evidence that lawyers also recognise its importance in ascertaining the contribution of spouses to family life, since that is the method of quantification adopted by legislation relating to termination of marriage (Gray, 1977: Ch. II). And the approach of the courts in valuing a wife on her accidental death has also been studied (Clarke and Ogus, 1978: O'Donovan, 1978a). This has led to debates about matrimonial property which remain inconclusive. Even the most enlightened of lawyers seem to regard child-bearing and child-rearing as synonymous: 'The inequality of the sexes dictated by nature imposes a necessary inequality of access to gainful occupation — from the birth of the first child at least until the youngest child begins to go to school the wife's contribution to the family cash income will either cease or be greatly reduced. At other times too, her natural functions as a mother and housewife restrict her earning capacity, (Kahn-Freund, 1971: 504). The English Law Commission is still struggling with this problem, but essentially the solution proposed is that of equal rights in family property for both spouses, with some exceptions. Commenting on this Olive Stone recently stated: 'there are many in the legal profession and perhaps within the Law Commission itself who still hold out against giving the English wife equal rights in the home . . . . The Law Commission has finally emerged with recommendations which would greatly improve the position of the non-owner spouse in the matrimonial home but subject to some exceptions that speak both loudly and disturbingly for the power still exercised by those who could still deny legal personality to women, particularly if married' (Stone, 1979: 193).

Certain feminists have put forward a solution to the problem of marital property which harks back to the nineteenth century; it is that of separate property. 'Current English and American law reform efforts in the area of marital property are concentrating on the problem of mitigating the harsh effects of our traditional system of

---

[7]See The Law Commission: Third Report on Family Property (Law Com. No. 86) (1978).

separate property on the situation of the propertyless housewife, through legal devices designed to recognise her contribution by giving her a share in the property acquired by the spouses during the marriage regardless of its source or of how title is held' (Glendon, 1974: 315). Glendon argues that women are no longer housewives but participants in the workforce; 'that marriage exists primarily for the personal fulfillment of the individual spouses and that it should last only so long as it performs this function to the satisfaction of each' (Glendon 1974: 324); and that the modern independent woman would prefer to manage her own property. This approach has been criticised on the grounds that there has been insufficient attention to the relevance of behaviour within marriage and marriage-like relationships and that 'there are aspects of personal relationships which militate strongly toward sharing principles regardless of whether equality is in fact realised' (Westerberg Prager, 1977: 22).

A similar debate has taken place in Britain over the question of maintenance or alimony. Academic lawyers have argued that the equality of the sexes now enshrined in the law requires that maintenance be abolished or strictly limited. This view is exemplified in the work of Gray (1977) and Deech (1977). Gray argues that it is only consistent with no-fault divorce and cultural acceptance of serial marriage that maintenance should be abolished. 'There is, after all, no logical reason why a man should bear financial responsibility in the aftermath of an event which the law no longer declares to be attributable to his fault: a law which imposes such responsibility is in reality an unconstitutional form of taxation' (Gray, 1977: 348). He advocates a limited form of rehabilitative maintenance during the transitional period following divorce, acknowledging that such an approach 'contains a quite remarkable hortatory element, in that it provides an incentive for women to retain a degree of financial independence during marriage and thereby minimise the risk of severe, if not insuperable, disadvantage in labour market terms in the event of marriage breakdown' (p. 299).

Deech argues that the concept of marriage as a partnership of equals is 'incompatible with a maintenance law which rests on a foundation of female dependency' (Deech, 1977: 230); that marriage is thus regarded as 'a career alternative to an economically productive one' and this may reinforce 'the tendency on the part of some to search for a spouse who can provide a life-long meal ticket' (p. 231). She points to anti-discrimination legislation saying that a precondition for its success may be the abolition of dependency in all laws including maintenance. Her conclusion is that the aim of maintenance should be rehabilitative and that it should be permanent only for the elderly and the incapacitated not already cared for by the state.

Criticism of Gray's and Deech's views has been expressed on the grounds that their proposals will not ensure equality, but merely perpetuate an unfair situation for divorced women, who already suffer long-term economic prejudice because of the current arrangements of family life. Neither reformer sees the distinction between continuing existing privatised family life, housework and childcare arrangements which exploit women, whether it is the state or the husband providing financial support, and the transference of these tasks to the public economy. Without such a revolution in family life women will remain dependent in fact if not in law (O'Donovan, 1978b).

This debate has been discussed in the leading British law journal by John Eekelaar who comments that there must be a middle ground between these two positions. However, he goes on to say 'It is possible that, in the justified concern felt for children and wives on the breakdown of marriage, the position of the spouse (usually the husband) who enters a second marriage after the divorce has received insufficient attention' (Eekelaar, 1979: 268).

The question of economic dependence within marriage is crucial to recent academic writing on the family. A vigorous assault on state social policies which ensure the primacy of the husband as breadwinner has been made by Hilary Land. She has shown how the social security system is based on the premiss that men are breadwinners and women housewives, regardless of the realities, and 'that the British social security system, by perpetuating inegalitarian family relationships, is a means of reinforcing, rather than compensating for, economic inequalities' (Land, 1976: 108). In her work on the taxation system Land has shown that there also the official assumptions contained in the law are that the marriage relationship is unequal. And although the state claims to be supporting the family, it is in fact supporting marriage through the married man's tax allowance, which is allowed regardless of whether there are children (Land, 1978). The difficulty with Land's approach is that she attacks the concept of dependency on the grounds that it does not correspond to the reality of female participation in the workforce, but she overlooks the clear statistics which show the low levels of women's earnings. And elsewhere she admits that the task of caring for the young, the sick and the aged has been allocated by society to women who are usually unpaid, or paid only at subsistence (Parker and Land, 1978).

The Relationship of Women to the State

Conventional legal analysis admits that the state is the source of law either through legislation or through the agents of the state — those officials who administer the law — the judiciary, government servants, the police. However, the state retains a mask of neutrality and impartiality in its administration and creation of the law. Recent research has shown that the content of legal rules is not neutral as far as women are concerned (O'Donovan, 1979), and that the agents of the state are not impartial in their administration of the law. As Albie Sachs has pointed out: 'The notion of impartiality itself is not neutral. It is a value-laden concept that presupposes that it is both feasible and desirable for the machinery of state to operate in a neutral manner 'without fear or favour'. In this context the very idea of neutrality pre-supposes social inequality. To say that judges should be unbiased between rich and poor, white and black, male and female is to accept that these are enduring social categories' (Sachs and Wilson, 1978: 52). Sachs has shown the judicial bias against women in the nineteenth century; and there is evidence to indicate its continuation today, even in the administration of anti-discrimination legislation (Byrne and Lovenduski, 1978).

Family lawyers believe that the role of the state is to strengthen and cherish the family through legal support; and that the woman, as the economically and physically weaker party in marriage, is in need of the protection of the law (Cretney, 1976: 258). Feminists have challenged this assumption on a number of grounds. First, it is argued that the state does not support the whole family. Instead state policies are directed towards the support of marriage (as evidenced by the married man's tax allowance), and towards the support of 'a specific form of household: the family household dependent largely upon a male wage and upon female domestic servicing' (McIntosh, 1978: 255). The kind of marriage that the state reinforces is the breadwinner/housewife marriage in which the husband engages in paid labour and the wife is dependent. Evidence for this can be drawn from the infamous cohabitation rule in supplementary benefits which denies a woman living with man, whether married to him or not, the access to state benefit in her own right (Land, 1976).

Secondly, it is argued that since the impact of state policy is to continue the dependence of women, even when they engage in waged labour, this provides an excuse for low wages for women. The notion that married women work for 'pin-money' dies hard, and there is clear evidence of average earnings of women being considerably lower than those for men (Stacey and Price, 1979). This view can be supported from social security provisions which deny married women the increases for children received by married men drawing sickness or employment benefit, even though both are paying the same contribution (O'Donovan, 1979). Women are also unable to provide widower's benefits on the same basis as widow's benefits. This goes to indicate that waged work by married women is not treated by the state as being directed towards the support of a family, since it is considered that it is the husband's duty to maintain the family.

Thirdly, feminists argue that breadwinner/housewife marriage supported by the state provides a work incentive for men. 'There are enormous advantages to the economically powerful groups in our society in sustaining the belief that men are breadwinners and women, at most, are supplementary earners, whose primary duties lie in the home. In this way work incentives for men are preserved even among low-wage earners whose wives also have to work to support the family. At the same time it justifies paying women lower wages than men. Women when they enter the labour market do so in the belief that they do not need as high a wage as a man' (Land, 1978: 142).

Fourthly, Veronica Beechey has argued that women's, and above all married women's, place in wage labour is that of a reserve army. They are available to be used in times of economic expansion but at times of unemployment they can 'disappear almost without trace back into the family' (Beechey, 1978). The unemployed married woman is classified as her husband's dependent, with the occupation of housewife, 'not entering the statistics of the 'economically active' until there are job openings' (McIntosh, 1978: 278).

Finally, what is the primary role of the married woman in the eyes of the state? According to contemporary feminist analysis it is that of reproduction of the labour force and of labour power, including the socialisation of future workers. Mary McIntosh has linked the family household system, in which a number of people are expected to be dependent primarily on the wages of the male breadwinner and in which the domestic and caring work is performed unpaid by the wife and mother, to the reproduction of the conditions of capitalism (McIntosh, 1979). She argues that this particular form of household, supported by the state, serves to meet the needs of unwaged individuals — children and sick, elderly or incapable relatives through the unwaged work of the wife and the earnings of the husband. Parker and Land point out that although the state has taken over certain functions which used to be attributed to the family, such as education and housing, it has not taken over the functions attributed to the wife. 'The state less readily shares, let alone takes over, the caring and nurturing work usually ascribed to the dependent wife. Support for the family would seem to be regarded as best achieved via the husband, with least risk to his dominant position. This may be because the subordinate position of women in marriage, and hence the family, is implicitly seen as indispensable yet brittle keystone to the maintenance of long-established inequalities within wider social and economic institutions' (Land and

Parker, 1978: 362). The leading textbook in family law states however: 'In most families the husband's duties will be largely conditioned by the fact that he is the breadwinner; the wife will usually be primarily responsible for the running of the home, a duty which may take the form of supervising a large domestic staff or of doing the household 'chores' herself, such as cooking, cleaning, mending and looking after the children' (Bromley, 1976: 112).

Recent developments in legislation suggest that law-makers recognise that unpaid care in the home should be remunerated by the state (see O'Donovan, 1978a). As female participation in the workforce has increased (see Mayhew, 1976), woman may be less willing to drop out of paid employment to provide care for children, the sick and the elderly. Thus child benefit is now paid to the mother (and not to the parent undertaking childcare) and invalid care allowances have been introduced for those caring for the infirm at home. But here contradictions abound, as with the housewife's non-contributory invalidity pension, for married women are ineligible for the former and can only receive the latter if they can show that they are unable to perform housework. Again, the assumption that a married woman is dependent on her husband is underlined.

From the feminist critique of state oppression of women we can conclude that the state has not and cannot confront its own sexism and stereotyping of women. Social policies are sex-based. Social roles are allocated to women and reinforced by law. Any major change in state policy would involve nothing less than social revolution and the probable removal of the family from the base of society. Such an outcome has already been anticipated by a former Master of the Rolls, Lord Evershed who stated in 1957: 'To what end are we moving? I have read that in Russia the social circle of a man's wife will depend upon her own status rather than that of her husband. . . . Carried to their logical conclusions, such tendencies would appear to lead to the result that husband and wife in law and in form would become . . . partners in the firm of marriage. . . . For my part I greatly hope that the English race will in this, as it has done in many other aspects of life, resist the logical conclusion' (Foreword to Graveson and Crane, 1957: xvi).

Conclusion

It is difficult to analyse change whilst in its midst. Legal philosophy is in a state of flux and academic legal scholarship is undergoing a period of re-thinking which may prove to be fundamental. Feminism has contributed to this change, not least because feminists have adopted inter-disciplinary approaches to academic work and have ignored the traditional boundaries between disciplines. New light has been brought to bear on old problems, as in the discussion of the nature of justice and equality. Areas of study have emerged, such as the legal recognition of housework, where none existed hitherto. Generations of legal scholars have been shown to have been unaware of real social and legal inequalities which now appear obvious. New ways of seeing, new insights into the nature of law and society — these are the feminist contributions.

It would be foolish to argue that all areas of law have been equally affected. Jurisprudence, family law, criminology, employment law, and welfare law are the places of impact so far as the academic subjects within law are concerned. But more important may prove to be the new questions being asked and the new methodology. An illustration of this can be given from legal history. Traditional legal history involved the collection of reported cases, the analysis and parsing of the opinions of the judges with definite statements about legal doctrine. Non-lawyer historians, on the whole, took little interest in legal history. All this has changed. County archives are being researched to find out how the law treated the common people, hitherto unrepresented in history (see e.g. Carroll, 1976; MacFarlane, 1978; Middleton, 1979). A recent example is an article on witchcraft trials where the author concludes that ' ... witchcraft charges were a useful method for men to keep women inferior and in fear' (Geis, 1978: 39). Geis accuses Chief Justice Hale who sentenced women to death for witchcraft of 'systematic biases against women' (p. 43). We can contrast this view with that of Holdsworth, a leading legal historian, who said of the death sentences of two 'witches': 'We should remember that the sentence was in accordance with the law, and that the existence of witches was vouched for in the Bible. ... It is probable, too, that his sincere religious beliefs led hm to see no harm in the act ... ' (Holdsworth, 1966: 578). The deference with which legal scholars regard the past seems to be waning at last.

References

BEECHEY, Veronica (1978) 'Some Notes on Female Wage Labour in Capitalist Production' in A. Kuhn and A. M. Wolpe (Eds.) *Feminism and Materialism,* Routledge and Kegan Paul, London.

BENTHAM, Jeremy (1948) *The Principles of Morals and Legislation,* Hafner, New York.

BROMLEY, P. (1976) *Family Law,* 5th Edition, Butterworths, London.

BYRNE, P. and J. LOVENDUSKI (1978) 'Sex Equality and the Law' in *British Journal of Law & Society,* Vol. 5, pp. 148–165.

CARROLL, B. A. (1976) *Liberating Women's History,* University of Illinois Press, Illinois.

CLARKE, K. A. and OGUS, A. I. (1978) 'What is a Wife Worth?' in *British Journal of Law & Society,* Vol. 5, pp. 1–25.

CRETNEY, S. M. (1974) *Principles of Family Law,* Sweet and Maxwell, London.

DEECH, Ruth (1977) 'The Principles of Maintenance' in *Family Law,* Vol. 7, No. 8, pp. 229–233.

DWORKIN, Ronald (1977) *Taking Rights Seriously,* Harvard U.P., Cambridge, Mass.

EEKELAAR, John (1978) *Family Law and Social Policy,* Weidenfield and Nicolson, London.

FIRESTONE, Shulamith (1971) *The Dialectic of Sex,* Jonathan Cape, London.

GEIS, G. (1978) 'Lord Hale, Witches, and Rape' in *British Journal of Law Society,* Vol. 5, pp. 26–44.

GLAZER-MALBIN, Nona (1976) 'Housework: Review Essay' in *Signs,* Vol. 1, pp. 905–922.

GLENDON, Mary Ann (1974) 'Is There a Future for Separate Property?' in *Family Law Quarterly,* Vol. 8, pp. 315–328.

GRAVESON, R. H. and F. R. CRANE (Eds.) (1957) *A Century of Family Law,* Sweet and Maxwell, London.

GRAY, Kevin (1977) *Reallocation of Property on Divorce,* Professional Books, Abingdon, Oxon.

HART, H. L. A. (1976) 'Bentham and the U.S.A.' in *Journal of Law & Economics,* Vol. 19, pp. 547–567.

HOLDSWORTH, W. (1966) *A History of English Law,* Vol. VI, Menthuen, London.

HUNTER, Howard O. (1978) 'An Essay on Contract and Status' in *Virginia Law Review,* Vol. 64, pp. 1039–1097.

JAGGER, Alison (1974) 'On Sexual Equality' in *Ethics,* Vol. 84, pp. 285–291.

JAMES, T. E. (1957) 'The English Law of Marriage' in R. H. Graveson and F. R. Crane (Eds.) *A Century of Family Law,* pp. 20–38. Sweet and Maxwell, London.

KAHN-FREUND, Otto (1971) 'Matrimonial Property & Equality Before the Law: Some Sceptical Reflections' in *Human Rights Journal,* Vol. 4, pp. 493–510.

LAKOFF, Robin (1975) *Language and Woman's Place,* Harper and Row, New York.

LAND, Hilary (1976) 'Women: Supporters or Supported?' in S. Allen and D. Leonard Barker (Eds.) *Sexual Divisions and Society: Process and Change,* pp. 108–132, Tavistock, London.

LAND, Hilary (1978) 'Sex-Role Stereotyping in the Social Security and Income Tax Systems' in J. Chetwynd and O. Hartnett (Eds.) *The Sex Role System,* pp. 127–142, Routledge and Kegan Paul, London.

LAND, Hilary and Roy PARKER (1978) 'Family Policy in the United Kingdom' in S. B. Kamerman and A. J. Kahn (Eds.) *Family Policy,* pp. 331–366, Columbia U.P., New York.

LAW COMMISSION (1978) *Third Report on Family Property:* The Matrimonial Home (Co-ownership and Occucaption Rights) and Household Goods, Law Com. No. 86, H.M.S.O., London.

LAW REFORM COMMISSION OF CANADA (1976) *Report on Family Law,* Government Publications, Ottawa.

LEONARD BARKER, Diana (1977) 'The Regulation of Marriage: Repressive Benevolance' in G. Littlejohn, B. Smart, J. Wakeford and N. Yuval-Davis (Eds.) *Power and the State,* pp. 239–266, Croom Helm, London.

McDOUGAL, M. S., H. D. LASSWELL AND L. C. CHEN (1975) 'Human Rights for Women and World Public Order: The Outlawing of Sex-Based Discrimination' in *American Journal of International Law,* Vol. 69, pp. 497–533.

MacFARLANE, Alan (1978) *The Origins of English Individualism: The Family, Property and Social Transition,* Blackwell, Oxford.

McINTOSH, Mary (1978) 'The State and The Oppression of Women' in A. Kuhn and A. M. Wolpe (Eds.) *Feminism and Materialism,* pp. 254–289, Routledge and Kegan Paul, London.

McINTOSH, Mary (1979) 'The Welfare State and the Needs of the Dependent Family' in S. B. Burman (Ed.) *Fit Work for Women,* Croom Helm, London.

MAYHEW, Judith (1976) 'Women at Work: A lawyer discusses the legislation relating to women employees' in P. Carlen (Ed.) *The Sociology of Law,* pp. 134–142. University of Keele, Staffordshire.

MIDDLETON, Christopher (1979) 'The Sexual Division of Labour in Feudal England' in *New Left Review,* Jan-Apr 1979, pp. 147–168.

OAKLEY, Ann (1974) *Housewife,* Allan Lane, Harmondsworth, Middlesex.

O'DONOVAN, Katherine (1978(a)) 'Legal Recognition of the Value of Housework' in *Family Law,* Vol. 8, No. 7, pp. 215–221.

O'DONOVAN, Katherine (1978(b)) 'The Principles of Maintenance: An Alternative View' in *Family Law,* Vol. 8, No. 6, pp. 180–184.

O'DONOVAN, Katherine (1979) 'The Male Appendage — Legal Definitions of Women' in S. B. Burman (Ed.) *Fit Work for Women,* pp. 134–152, Croom Helm, London.

PERATIS, Kathleen Willert and Eve CARY (1978) *Women and the Law,* National Textbook Company, Skokie, Illinois.

RENDEL, Margherita (1978) 'Legislating for Equal Pay and Opportunity for Women in Britain' in *Signs,* Vol. 3, No. 4, pp. 897–908.

RICHARDS, Margaret A. (1976) 'The Sex Discrimination Act — Equality for Women?' in *Industrial Law Journal,* Vol. 5, pp. 35–41.

SACHS, Albie and Joan Hoff WILSON (1978) *Sexism and the Law,* Martin Robertson, London.

SINGER, M. G. (1963) *Generalization in Ethnics,* Eyre and Spottiswoode, London.

SMITH, J. C. (1976) *Legal Obligation,* Athlone Press, London.

STACEY, Margaret and Marion PRICE (1979) 'The Law is Not Enough: The Continued Oppression of Women', Paper presented at the *B.S.A. Conference,* April 1979, University of Warwick.

WASSERSTROM, Richard, A. (1977) 'Racism, Sexism and Preferential Treatment: An Approach to the Topics' in *University of California Los Angeles Law Review,* Vol. 24, pp. 581–622.

WEITZMAN, Lenore J. (1974) 'Legal Regulation of Marriage: Tradition and Change' in California Law Review, Vol. 62, pp. 1169–1288.

WESTERBERG PRAGER, Susan (1977) 'Sharing Principles and the Future of Marital Property Law' in *University of California Los Angeles Law Review,* Vol. 25, pp. 1–22.

WOODY, Susan Minot (1973) 'The Legal Classification of Persons: A Search for Standards' in *American Journal of Jurisprudence,* Vol. 18, pp. 18–30.

13

Medicine as 'Old Husbands' Tales': The Impact of Feminism

MARY ANN ELSTON

Introduction

When I first discussed the topic of this paper, namely, the impact of feminism on medicine, almost without exception I received the same response. 'Has there been any?' My short answer is 'probably not much', at least in Britain. A casual glance through most medical journals still suggests a male dominated professional world. Women, when they appear, are regarded as abnormal, deficient or troublesome members of the human race, despite, or even because of, their special feminine characteristics. If, however, the topic had been the impact of feminism on women's health the comments I would have received and the answer I would have given would have been quite different. For the changes brought about by the women's health movement have been mainly outside rather than within that body of knowledge and practice normally defined as medicine. That this has been so is only in part due to the opposition of the medical profession to feminist ideas.

The feminist critique questions both the content of medical knowledge and the form in which it is reproduced, to both patients and health workers. The changes that feminists have sought are not ones that can be achieved solely by increasing the numbers of women doctors. For the hundreds (maybe more) of British women who have been active in women's health groups; for the thousands who have read feminist health handbooks or attended women's health or women's studies courses; and for the hundreds of thousands who have taken part in the campaign to preserve and extend women's rights to abortion, to cite just three of the many aspects of the women's health movement; for all of us, health has become a political issue, too important to be left to doctors.

Not all doctors approve this change. Many are unaware, or oblivious to it, or at least pretend to be. Others deny its existence or significance but perhaps their denial is indicative of their awareness of the feminist pressure. Thus, one response to feminist attacks on gynaecology textbooks (e.g. Diane Scully and Pauline Bart, 1973), which were concerned to show that many of the legitimated medical texts put forward erroneous and sexist ideas about women's sexuality, has been the clarification of the author's position in subsequent editions. One of the books which has received particularly critical attention is Norman Jeffcoate's *Principles of Gynaecology*, first published in 1957. In the preface to the first edition Jeffcoate stated that he had not hesitated to 'enunciate views which in many respects are conjectural if not fanciful' (p. vii). (All page references are to the 1975 edition.) In the latest (1975) edition he assures us that in revising his book he has endeavoured to preserve this 'original personal flavour'. He continues,

> In so doing I restated some of my firmly — and allowing for up-dating from time to time — consistently held views tested by *clinical observation and experience*. This was against a background of recent developments in knowledge and techniques ... and in the light of *supposed and much advertised, yet probably non-existent*, major modifications in the basic outlook and behaviour of the women and girls of Western societies (Jeffcoate, 1975: v; emphasis added).

I shall consider medical textbooks including this one in more detail below but these prefaces illustrate some of the themes of the feminist critique. For example, they show that doctors (or some of them) do not hesitate to speak for all women, and to discredit feminists as deviant; their clinical observation and experience is *more* valid than women's experience even when it is women's experience that is being referred to. This clinical experience is paramount even when unsupported by more systematic evidence such as controlled trials.

In this paper I will outline some of the reasons that medicine is so important for women and the ways in which medicine can be seen as 'men's studies'. I have tried to give an account of some of the ways feminists have begun to construct an alternative paradigm for analysing health and health care and of some of the changes in medicine that have occurred. I am painfully aware that in the space available I have done scant justice to the range of issues raised by feminists. In accordance with the themes of this book I have concentrated on changes in the professionally defined discipline rather than try and give an exhaustive history of the women's health movement. I have focussed almost exclusively on medicine and the medical profession as it is primarily these which have been the object of feminist criticism, rather than, for example, nursing. To ignore nursing may run the risk of perpetuating medical dominance but to consider the impact of feminism on a profession whose professional identity has been rooted in the subservience of women to men would need, and needs, another paper. I have concentrated on the women's health movement in Britain, as that with which I am most familiar, and I have tried to consider some of the reasons which make the experience of women in Britain different from that of women in the United States. But it is important to bear in mind that we are considering an *international* movement which addresses itself to a common fundamental problem.

Assessing Change

In systematically assessing the impact feminism has had on medicine there are two major problems. The first is that it is not easy to compare the situation 'before' feminism with the present. This is not just because women's invisibility in research into medicine and medical education in the past means there is very little 'before' data (see Judith Lorber, 1975). It is also because the development of a feminist perspective gives us new ways of seeing beliefs and practices which previously were accepted as part of the 'natural' order between men and women, or were felt by women to be the result of their personal failure. In the past, for example, if an internal examination hurt, despite the doctor's reassurance that it would not, it was your fault because you were not relaxed enough. That the doctor might be rough and inadequately trained seldom came to mind as an explanation. Today it is not enough for the doctor to warn that the speculum may be cold, failure to warm it is grounds for complaint.

In the absence of systematically comparable data I shall on occasions use 'anecdotes', accounts of events that are significant because they happened at all, whether or not they are 'representative' of some statistical universe. For a professor to be challenged for referring to menopausal women as 'prunes' as happened recently in a London teaching hospital is an indication of change, as is prefacing a statement in a lecture with 'You girls aren't going to like this'.

'Atrocity stories' are common in health. Gerry Stimson and Barbara Webb (1975) suggest that these may be a way of patients redressing the balance of power against professionals from a safe distance. They noted that most of their stories were told by women, though their methodology did not include comparison between the sexes. Among feminist women the nature and significance of 'atrocity stories' has changed and this may be either because the atrocious behaviour of the professionals has changed, (for better or worse) or that we perceive it differently. For example, how would you have reacted to the following ten years ago?

> A middle class woman being treated for salpingitis (infection of the Fallopian tubes) at a central London teaching hospital was in such pain that she went to the outpatients' clinic a week before her next appointment. While waiting, the intensity of the pain made her burst into tears. The consultant, walking past and seeing this said, 'What are you crying for? I haven't touched you yet.'

The second problem, is the classic problem of the human sciences; attributing cause. Where changes have occurred that are in line with feminist demands it does not of course follow that they are necessarily due to feminism, or to women's demands (and the two are not always synonymous). Negative changes (often a backlash against feminism) may reveal more about cause and effect. In the small number of cases where change has occurred in medicine that might be attributed to feminism this appears to have been a necessary but not a sufficient cause. There are instances where women's complaints have led to 'scientific' investigations of procedures where it has been found that all is not well. Examples would include the reconsidering of methods of inducing labour that occurred in the mid-seventies in Britain (see below) and further investigation of side effects of the oral contraceptive pill following research by feminists (e.g. Barbara Seaman, 1969). However, the criteria used and causes for concern in this medical research may not correspond to those of feminists. For example, further research into counselling and information giving when intra-uterine contraceptive devices (IUDs) are inserted, may be called for as a way of reducing the economic waste of a high incidence of 'discontinuers' in population control programmes, (Anthony Reading, 1979) rather than as relevant to women's health. There is no recognition that explaining the procedures and possible side effects should be an unquestioned part of good practice. Reading's article suggests that it is 'the significance attached to the side effects rather than their objective severity' Reading, 1979: 631) which determines the response to IUD insertion (The implication is that women are reacting subjectively and therefore irrationally). There is however no discussion of what could be meant by 'objective severity'; is it some absolute level of blood loss or perhaps some objective way of measuring pain?

Other cases of change within medicine seem to have come about through a *combination* of different pressures, not all of them sharing the same assumptions. For example, the liberalisation of some regimes that has occurred in a number of maternity hospitals may be due to the natural childbirth movement which is by no means entirely feminist in outlook. (For example, few hospitals today would totally exclude a woman's husband from a normal delivery but many would exclude a more 'irregular' companion.)

It is not just within feminism of course that the problem of determining cause and effect arises (although feminism is probably more open to the difficulties and more ready to acknowledge them): trying to assess the impact of any social movement is a complex exercise. What is not difficult to establish, however, is why feminists seek change and where their demands meet resistance from the medical profession.

Why is Medicine an Important Issue for Women?

That health and health care have been central pre-occupations of the contemporary women's movement is clear if one looks at, for example, the content of feminist journals, directories of women's groups or the content of women's studies courses and women's conferences. Sheryl Burt Ruzek (1978) lists twenty-eight American feminist periodicals covering women's health issues (including the irresistibly titled *The Monthly Extract, An Irregular Periodical*) and her list of women's health groups around the world takes up twenty pages. In Britain the position is similar for journals: *Women's Report*, published bi-monthly from 1973 to 1979, had a regular Mind/Body feature. *Wires,* the movement's newsletter has many features and news items on health. When *Spare Rib* (1980: 18) recently listed articles from previous issues which might be useful for women planning a women's health course 53 out of 94 issues were cited and the list was not exhaustive (*Spare Rib,* No. 94, 1980, 18). *Women's Studies International Quarterly* (1979, Vol I No 1) has had a special issue on Mind and Body, and both *M/F* and *Feminist Review* have carried articles relevant to women's health, especially on abortion. Women's health handbooks, both feminist and non-feminist, have been best sellers (see below and Elston 1979 for further discussion).

Why has this explosion of interest occurred? One succinct formulation is to be found in Barbara Ehrenreich and Deirdre English's pamphlet, *Complaints and Disorders, the sexual politics of sickness* (now a feminist classic). They write,

> The medical system is strategic for women's liberation. It is the guardian of reproductive technology-birth control, abortion, and the means of safe childbirth. . . . When we demand control over our own bodies, we are making that demand above all to the medical system. It is the keeper of the keys. But the medical system is also strategic to women's oppression. Medical science has been one of the most powerful sources of sexist ideology in our culture. Justifications for sexual discrimination . . . must ultimately rest on the one thing that differentiates women from men; their bodies. Theories of male superiority ultimately rest on biology. Medicine stands between biology and social policy . . . biology traces the origins of disease; doctors pass judgement on who is sick and who is well. *Medicine's prime contribution to sexist ideology has been to describe women as sick, and as potentially sickening to men* (Ehrenreich and English, 1973: 5 emphasis original).

Central therefore to contemporary (and previous) feminist movement has been the demand for women's right to control their own bodies, to seize the means of reproduction back from expropriators, in this case doctors. But seizing the means of control is insufficient if the means themselves are formulated in male terms. Medicine has claimed the right to define what 'woman' is or should be since the nineteenth century, according to many feminist historians.

Rewriting History

Feminists' concern with control over reproduction and male dominated medicine is then not new, as Ehrenreich and English (1973) have pointed out. One of the most important contributions to our understanding of medicine has been the recent work of historians, many of them feminists, who have shown the inaccuracy of a history of medicine that depicts it as the unidirectional progress of great men's scientific ideas. Instead, what has emerged is a picture which suggests that the rise of the male medical profession is linked, at least in part, to the ousting of women healers from autonomous healing work and to the capturing of a lucrative and high status group of patients — middle class women — in the nineteenth century (see Ben Barker-Benfield, 1976; Jean Donnison, 1977; Lorna Duffin, 1977 and Martha Vicinus, 1973).

Theories about women being slaves to their reproductive organs, to be replaced by the end of the nineteenth century by Freudian accounts of women's psychology, were weapons in the battle over women's entry into higher education, and particularly the medical profession in the 1850s. The argument put forward by male doctors was ostensibly one about preserving the purity and modesty of genteel women, a danger not apparently threatening entrants to Nightingale reformed nursing. But such arguments could be, and were, turned against men, by women pointing out that women patients had purity and modesty to be preserved too. An underlying issue was the financial threat that women doctors would pose, particularly to the emerging speciality of obstetrics and gynaecology. The opposition to women's entry into obstetrics and gynaecology that still prevails has historical roots (see Duffin 1977 and Mary Roth Walsh, 1977).

This rewriting of history is not just important because it sets the academic record straight. Jane Lewis has discussed some of the issues raised by feminist historians on health: my concern is with its effect on women's understandings of health and medicine. Knowledge of 'the horrors of the half-known life' (Barker-Benfield 1976) has not only informed, it has politicised women. For if medicine in the nineteenth century functioned to legitimate sex discrimination by specious science, may not this still be true today? Feminist analyses of the history of birth control campaigns (e.g. Linda Gordon, 1974 and Jane Lewis, 1979) have shown how in the past feminist campaigns were at times opposed by, at times in concert with and at times co-opted by other movements, notably eugenicist ones. There are lessons to be learnt from these histories for today's struggle to differentiate women's rights from population control issues.

Medicine as Feminists have Seen it

We have seen that medicine is charged by feminists with being particularly involved in our oppression through its control over legal access to abortion, most forms of contraception and the management of childbirth. In this feminists are united. Different groups within the broadly defined women's health movement would disagree as to the origins of this medical control, and the appropriate strategy for overcoming it, including the importance of achieving change within medicine. (Elizabeth Fee has described three broad tendencies within the American women's health movement: liberal, radical and Marxist (Fee, 1975); these differences however are not discussed here both for reasons of limited space and because it seems more appropriate to focus on the common ground.)

Whatever the origins of the power of the medical profession they have been accused of using their control over reproduction to maintain women individually and collectively in subordinate positions. This may be literally, through the degradations involved in gynaecological examinations, or by controlling women's access to information and resources. Like most of the other disciplines considered in this book medicine is seen by feminists as both a body of knowledge and a practice based on the 'tacit belief that men are 'normal' whereas women are 'abnormal' 'and' that the 'natural' role of women is to reproduce, and that is the central determining characteristic of a woman's being' (Lesley Doyal, 1979: 219).

However, women as the object of research and practice are not invisible as they are in some subjects. As Lorber (1975) has pointed out in relation to medical sociology, which derives many of its assumptions from medicine, women appear as 'ubiquitous patients but invisible professionals'. As in such areas as the sociology of the family (see Ann Oakley, 1974) there is the contradiction that women are 'invisible' even when they are most 'visible'. It is partly because of their invisibility as *human beings* but their visibility as *patients* that the medical model of women has arisen in which many aspects of women's lives are defined as areas of increasing medicalisation. While medicine has been predominantly controlled by men — who could perhaps reach consensus about the difference, deviance, and 'disease' of women, the exclusion of women from medical circles has meant that there has been little or no challenge from within medicine to this concept of women.

But there are further contradictions: for as some aspects of women's lives have come under increasing medical control, other aspects — which women themselves may define as an area for medicalisation — have been ignored. So, many of women's specific health complaints, such as cystitis, dysmennorhea, vaginal infections, have been largely ignored in medical education and research. Typically dismissed as 'trivial' or attributed to a woman's inadequate personality or 'over-emotionality' one is required to ask whether these complaints have not been conceptualised as problems precisely because they are not problems for men (i.e. for 'normal' human beings). And certainly, the medical profession has also constructed an extensive body of knowledge (under the rubric of psychiatry) which lends substance to this dismissal of women, by portraying them as more emotional, more subjective, more passive and less rational than men (Broverman *et al.*, 1970; Phyllis Chesler, 1972; Dorothy Smith and Sara David, 1975). This has other implications as well: women's ostensible subjectivity and emotionality makes their testimony suspect when research is done on health issues that effect women. Jill Rakusen (1975) has pointed out that the major studies in Britain on the safety of oral contraceptives regarded women's evidence on headaches, loss of libido etc. as too subjective to be assessed. It seems the male controlled medical profession has it all 'sewn up' when it comes to women, without hearing our testimony.

The other aspect in the medicalisation of stages of women's lives is the medical model of women as primarily a reproducer. By appropriating 'reproduction' as a medical area, women are brought increasingly under medical control — when well! Menarche, the menopause, and most of all motherhood or the desire to avoid it have become occasions for medical intervention. And it is in these areas that the clash between a medical frame of reference and a woman's frame of reference is likely to be greatest.

Hilary Graham and Ann Oakley (in press) have documented the contrasting and conflicting paradigms of pregnancy they encountered in their research on childbirth.

Ann Oakley's study indicates that you do not have to look for 'explanations' in terms of psychological theories about the feminine role when it comes to adjustment to pregnancy. Apart from the fact that it requires genuine adjustment there is also the suggestion that high levels of technological intervention in the birth can have negative effects on mothers after birth. That these possibilities (skillfully dissected by Oakley, 1980) have not occurred to medical practitioners would be surprising if it were not for the fact that medicine has been controlled by those who cannot experience the procedures.

Most doctors claim that such interventions are justified by scientific 'knowledge' of their efficacy, but as in other aspects of medicine, such 'knowledge' can frequently be demonstrated to be a myth (Archibald Cochrane, 1972). Feminists have exposed the emperor's nakedness on many occasions, and shown how *moral* decisions are frequently disguised as *scientific* ones, based for example on a belief in women's 'natural' instincts (Sally MacIntyre, 1976). New techniques and treatments are introduced with little investigation of physical effects, let alone psychological consequences. Wendy Farrant's research on the introduction of pre-natal screening for foetal abnormalities for example has shown how the risks of the procedure are often underestimated, and the impact of the introduction of screening programmes on women not considered (Farrant, 1980).

Whether or not less testing is carried out on drugs and other treatments intended for women than on those intended for men or for use on members of both sexes (or if women are used more as guinea pigs in general) is not established. What does seem clear is that there are many instances of women's lives being endangered when safer alternatives are available, often when the women are not ill. This is particularly the case with contraceptives where possibly harmful methods are often preferred to statistically safer early abortion (see for example Christopher Tietze and Sarah Lewitt, 1977). The lives of women from ethnic minorities and in the Third World are particularly at risk. Jill Rakusen has analysed the medical evidence and the circumstances of the use of Depo-Provera (Rakusen, in press). This is an injectable hormonal contraceptive which is not approved as safe for use in the United States. In Britain it has approval for short-term use in particular circumstances but was recently (1980) refused full approval by the Committee on Safety of Medicines. This refusal may have been influenced by the feminist 'Ban the Jab' campaign which was taken up by national newspapers like the *Guardian*. Feminists have criticised the use of Depo-Provera not only for its possible carcinogenicity and the side effects that many women suffer with it. There is well documented evidence that it has been given, especially to Asian and West Indian women in Britain without their knowledge let alone information as to its dangers (e.g. Wendy Savage, 1978). Its use has been greater in the Third World where it is just one of the many suspect or banned health products that are 'dumped' by Western firms often under aid programmes (Barbara Ehrenreich *et al.*, 1979).

As Lorber (1975) has indicated, one way in which women are invisible in the medical frame of reference is in the process of defining what is important, or even what *exists*, in health care work. Women are some seventy-five per cent of the paid National Health Service labour force (Joyce Leeson and Judith Gray, 1978) and a similar proportion among paid health workers in the USA (Carol Brown, 1975), and the vast majority of unpaid health workers in the home (Janet Finch and Dulcie Groves, 1980 and Jane Taylor, 1979). But as in most fields the form that the work takes and the terms of the division of labour are predominantly set by men and set in a hierarchical way. Within medicine itself, the profession has for the most part continued the pattern set over one hundred and fifty years ago, of presenting barriers to the entry of women to the profession and to the achievement of equality by those who surmount the entry hurdle. It is to this that we now turn.

Women in Medicine

The male dominance of the medical profession is sometimes represented as changing, or being about to change. Increases in the number and proportion of women entering medical school have been widely publicised. In 1978 women were thirty-eight per cent of entrants to medical schools in Great Britain and it has been predicted, without any good evidence, that they will soon be over half the intake. The upturn in women's entry to medical school is usually attributed to the 1973 decision of the Committee of Vice-Chancellors and Principals and the 1975 Sex Discrimination Act which outlawed quotas on women's entry. While it is clear that the enforced formal abolition of quotas did have a marked effect on some schools they did not bring about massive overnight change. There had been a steady increase in both numbers and percentage of women entrants since 1968. The expansion must in part be credited to the changing methods in selection, and expansion in the number of places available. In more recent years there has been a fall in the number of male applicants from the United Kingdom (which raises some interesting questions).

Whatever the reasons for the increased intake of women it is clear that 'positive discrimination policies' have not been among them. Most medical schools in Britain are reluctant to admit mature students and one London school is currently facing a suit under the Sex Discrimination Act for the exercise of an age barrier that indirectly discriminates against women. Elsewhere I have discussed in more detail the recent history of medical school selection (Elston, 1977, 1980). Here the important point is not the recent expansion but the fact that ever since 1948 the proportion of women entering medical school *has never fallen below 22%* overall. In the United States the invisibility of women in post-war medical schools, can perhaps be understood for there were very few of them until recently, but in Britain, there is no such excuse for the continued assumption that medical practitioners are males — though, of course, representation is very different from control.

Entry into medical school is only the first stage in a medical career. Despite increasing numbers, and increasing visibility, medical education and professional career structures still assume male patterns as the norm and women must follow or become 'problems'. In recent years the so called 'wastage' of and the 'problem of married women doctors' have occupied much space in the medical press. The remedies to these problems have been sought on an individualistic basis, by providing special training schemes on a part-time basis which are difficult to obtain, tend to push women into specialities where male doctors are reluctant to work, and have no guarantee of permanent work at the end (see Elston 1977, 1980 for more detailed discussion).

As in other occupations, women in medicine are disproportionately concentrated in low-paid, low status specialities and grades (Leeson and Gray 1979, Elston 1977, 1980). Most crucially they are virtually absent from professional bodies concerned with determining either terms and conditions of service (such as British Medical Association (BMA), with overall professional standards and codes of conduct, (the General Medical

Council (GMC)) or establishing the content and form of specialist knowledge (e.g. the Royal Colleges and their faculties whose professional examinations are the passport to specialist status).

In 1975 Beulah and Thomas Bewley documented women's exclusion from positions of influence and power (Bewley and Bewley, 1975). Since then, there have been a few changes. 1979 saw a woman president of the BMA, and there has been an increase in female membership of the GMC but for the most part the situation described by the Bewleys is substantially unchanged. Women are also rarely found in senior positions in teaching hospitals and so are absent as sponsors and role models for younger women doctors in a profession where informal patronage is important for professional success (see Lorber, 1975, Elston, 1980). Women in senior positions are not necesarily feminists. Indeed some senior women doctors are well known for their hostility to suggestions of special consideration for women, on the grounds that they themselves succeeded without such assistance, often either by 'choosing' not to have families or delegating childcare in ways that may not be possible even if acceptable to younger generations. (It should be pointed out that opposition to change on the grounds that 'we managed it' is not uncommon among senior members of the profession as a whole e.g. when junior doctors of both sexes have pressed for reduction in on call commitments.)

The policies pursued by the Medical Women's Federation (MWF), the main pressure group for women doctors, have been mainly constructed along traditional lines e.g. an emphasis on part-time work. Much of their energy in the past has been spent in getting recognition that women doctors exist at all. There are however signs of increasing politicisation among women doctors as exemplified by the content of some of the papers given at an MWF conference last year (MWF, 1979) and the formation of other groups such as the Women Doctors' Action Group. Many women doctors (and many men) have been active in the campaigns against restrictive legislation on abortion, particularly in Doctors for a Woman's Choice on Abortion (DWCA). This group was started in 1976 and had 300 members after its first announcement. By 1979 there were over five hundred members and it has been active and influential in demonstrating that there are substantial numbers of doctors who do believe in 'a woman's right to choose'.

But to 'come out' as a feminist at work for a doctor may still be to commit professional suicide. Success as a woman doctor is still primarily achieved through accepting and achieving male standards. There are fields where it is sometimes suggested that women's 'special qualities' are particularly appropriate. But one field where this is not the case is obstetrics and gynaecology. Actual or potential experience with the subject matter, whether dysmennorhea or childbirth is apparently a disqualification. It remains one of the few specialities in Britain where part-time training is not acceptable for professional accreditation (Membership of the Royal College of Obstetricians and Gynaecologists). In 1979 twelve per cent of consultants in obstetrics and gynaecology were women, compared with the average for all specialities of ten per cent. So, while slightly above average, this level does not suggest recognition of its being a suitable speciality for women, and it is well below the level of preference for it as a career shown by graduating women doctors (Elston, 1980). Yet personal experience is not thought wholly inappropriate in obstetrics and gynaecology by some. Jeffcoates writes in *Principles of Gynaecology,*

> If every husband were a gynaecologist in the widest sense, we would see fewer clinical problems, and if *every gynaecologist were a husband and a father of girls* he might be better fitted for his work (1975: 2).

The Reproduction of Medical Knowledge and Practice

Like education, considered in another chapter in this book, Medicine cannot be regarded as consisting of a highly integrated set of theoretical constructs that can be codified in textbooks. There are, as we have seen, shared beliefs and assumptions such as those about women that can be inferred from sources such as textbooks, and these are considered in detail below. Medicine is, above all, institutionalised *practice* and there production of medical knowledge takes place primarily in a practical setting, in Britain at least (i.e. through clinical teaching). Paul Atkinson has concluded from his study of clinical teaching in a Scottish medical school, that

> Clinical and bedside teaching provide the milieu in which components of medical training are fused. They provide the combination of 'theory' and 'practice', of 'science' and 'practical experience' which are together taken to be necessary for the production of the competent practitioner (Atkinson, 1977: 87).

Atkinson goes on to suggest this direct clinical experience, as managed by clinical teachers, can be seen as an invisible pedagogy in which what constitutes 'real' medicine and good medical practice are produced for students. Competent practice involves not just knowledge but appropriate behaviour.

Earlier analysts of medical education have tended to stress the training for uncertainty that is involved. Atkinson suggests that 'the reverse side of the coin — the certainty and dogmatism of personal experience' (*ibid.* p. 103) has received less attention. One way of dealing with uncertainty is to base knowledge on personal experience, and this gives rise to dogmatism. A recent television programme, *The Boys from Horseferry Road* (*sic*) (ITV, 24th June, 1980) showed very clearly the processes by which medical students are taught to 'stick to their guns' even when they may be uncertain or wrong. This emphasis on the 'privileged knowledge' granted by the clinical gaze (Atkinson, 1977: 86) and consequent assertiveness is relevant to feminist critiques of medical practice in two ways.

Firstly, clinical experience may clash with the personal experience of women, the starting point for many feminists' critiques. But doctors' knowledge is legitimated by a higher place in the credibility hierarchy and by appeals to science. Patients are socialised to expect certainty and knowledge from their doctors and the distinction between knowledge based on experience and on observation is not always recognised. Ann Oakley quotes an example from her observations of ante-natal clinics where the male doctor is seen as the possessor of privileged information.

> Male Doctor: 'Will you keep a note in your diary of when you first feel the baby move?'
> Patient: 'Do you know — well, of course you would know — what it feels like?'
> Male Doctor: 'It feels like wind pains — something moving in your tummy' (Oakley, 1980: 15).

Feminists have argued that a less patronising way of treating women, or indeed any patients, would be for doctors to admit more often to their uncertainty, either as individuals, or because of the state of medical knowledge.

The second aspect of clinical dogmatism that is relevant relates to the model of competent behaviour. The qualities that are seen as desirable — such as assertiveness — are qualities that are characteristically seen as male qualities, and probably more likely to be exhibited by males in our culture. Thus the medical model of 'woman' as patient has its counterpart in a medical model of doctor as 'man'. Gail Young (in press) has argued that women doctors in our society are still seen as honorary men ' by virtue of society's concept of what a doctor is and what a woman is'. Curing is man's work, caring is what women do.

Where Feminism and Medicine Meet; The Conflicts of being a Feminist Doctor

We have seen that numbers alone are insufficient to change the nature of medicine. Women doctors may have to choose between compromising their feminist principles and working in alienating environments in order to achieve positions whence they believe they may be able to make changes, or working outside the system. For most of those who work in the National Health Service a daily conflict is likely to be faced between the kind of treatment that they would like to give and what it is possible to give (given shortage of resources, time and skills). Mary Howell, a former senior administrator in an American medical school who gave up that position in order to work as a paediatrician in an inner city clinic, has written a powerful plea for support, rather than criticism of, professional women from within the women's movement (Howell, 1979). For, the possibility, or even the desirability, of being a feminist doctor is not something all feminists would accept. The commitment to non-hierarchical ways of working and non-expert controlled forms of care may leave little scope for a doctor. Some feminist health centres in the USA only employ doctors in a minimal capacity to comply with legal regulations (e.g. to sign prescription forms). Medical practitioner contact with women seeking health care may be very restricted, and even controlled by the lay workers.

The appropriate role of feminist doctors is one of the areas of disagreement between different strands of the women's movement. But such disagreement should not be allowed to obscure the enormous contribution made to women's health by the many feminist doctors who, as individuals often working in isolation, have changed their practices and supported the movement, particularly by sharing their knowledge with us.

Have Medical Schools Changed what they Teach about Women?

Medical textbooks and studies of medical education have been one source of evidence for the existence of the medical model of woman outlined above. There is no British equivalent of Mary Howell's book, *Why Would a Girl Go Into Medicine?*, published under the pseudonym, Margaret Campbell, (1974). In this she documents both the sexist behaviour towards female medical students exhibited by male students and faculty and the belittling manner in which material dealing with women's health was taught. My own experience doing participant observation research among pre-clinical medical students in 1973–4 was a politicising one. My field notebooks for a study not concerned with sexual divisions are full of examples of sexism; e.g. jokes shared by lecturers and students about the answers to an examination question on the effects of removal of the ovaries: such diverse effects as the development of beards and blackheads, and the improvement of driving skills were recorded.

It may well be that such incidents would not occur today. I have already cited some examples of protest at teachers' behaviour. A lecturer was removed from a course after protests from women students at one medical school. Some medical schools and teaching hospitals have women's groups where support is available for individuals and where some of the barriers between different groups of health workers can be broken down. At one London school when, in 1976, women students requested a session on women and health as part of their sociology course the lecturer agreed eventually to invite a (woman) guest lecturer as he declared he did not know anything about the subject matter and anyway there was no proper evidence on the topic. By 1979 he was giving the lecture himself.

Change for the better (as far as women are concerned) may be balanced by backlash on the part of men. Mary Howell (Campbell, 1974) has expressed concern that in her experience in America the response to protests by women against attacks on women as a self-explanatory biological category may be to replace them with attacks on feminist women as unreasonable, unrepresentative and unhealthy. A recent edition of *General Practitioner,* a journal distributed free to all general practitioners and heavily subsidised by drug advertisements, carried a feature on women and their health (*General Practitioner,* April 25, 1980). It may be significant progress that such a journal should carry one article on the social origins of depression in women and one on doctors' stereotypes of women. But this gain is neutralised by the sandwiching of the article between another which purports to show that there are new ills brought about *by* sexual equality and one on the psychology of pregnancy, which is fine example of the kind of article feminists have been criticising for a decade.

Medical assumptions about women may be more explicit in this popular literature produced for doctors as a medium for drug advertisements than in medical textbooks and more academic journals, but the assumptions are still there in the more prestigious literature, and have not remained immune from feminist criticism.

Medical Textbooks

Because of the practical emphasis in medical education, clinical textbooks for undergraduate medical students consist mainly of 'lecture note' type precis of 'facts' and a major function of lectures is to update these outlines. However analysis of the 'facts' presented and the content of the more discursive books used more for post-graduate examinations, suggest that they are 'facts' defined by the medical paradigm already outlined. Thus Scully and Bart's (1973) analysis of 27 gynaecology textbooks used in the USA showed that two-thirds of them failed to incorporate the findings of Kinsey and Masters and Johnson about female sexuality into their texts. The sexual satisfaction of the patient's husband (and husbands were the only partners considered) was treated as more important than that of the woman herself. Mary Howell's informal analysis of paediatrics textbooks suggests paediatricians see themselves as rescuing children from those who damage them. Those who do damage are primarily parents, normally referred to by the pronoun 'she'. Contempt for mothers was manifested firstly by blaming mothers for the child's illness e.g. malnutrition, which was discussed in terms of maternal irresponsibility, and not poverty. Secondly, these books disparaged where they did not ignore 'the central and essential contributions made by mothers to promote, maintain, restore and protect the health of their children' (Howell, 1978).

There are some indications of change during the Seventies either in direct response to feminist criticisms or because of 'the changing position of women' or, indeed, changes in medical knowledge. Ruzek notes that several authors and publishers did respond to Scully and Bart's criticisms, (1978: 274–26). My own 'informal' content analysis comparing recent editions of obstetrics and gynaecology and psychiatry texts does indicate there have been some changes for the better and there are some texts which are relatively acceptable.

For example, homosexuality now seems to receive less attention as a medical problem; (male homosexuality though is still seen as more of a social problem than women's.). Discussions of sterilisation, though still almost always assuming that the only reason for sterilisation is when a married woman has too many children, have changed in some cases. For example, Josephine Barnes' book, *Lecture Notes in Gynaecology* states that 'it is wise to obtain the consent of the spouse' in the latest (1978) edition compared with the previous assertion that both partners must consent. In several books more concern still is expressed about the physical and psychological consequences of sterilisation for the male than for the female, a concern not warranted by available evidence.

Reference is more frequently made in recent textbooks to the importance of considering women's feelings and wishes in labour in discussions of childbirth but these may quickly be counterbalanced by such statements as the following: 'In my view ... the doctor now has a duty to recommend to his patient that labour be pain-free in order to facilitate better control of monitoring techniques' (Dewhurst, 1976, p. 205–6). On episiotomy, the making of an incision in the perineum to assist delivery which has been condemned as an unnecessary routine practice leading to extra discomfort by radical midwives and others, we find in the same book: 'The modern accoucheur simply looks for reasons why an episiotomy should not be performed. There are few' (Dewhurst, 1976: 484).

So, while there have been some changes they are not on the whole fundamental or feminist. One book which has some changes which appear to be specifically in response to the women's movement is the afore-mentioned *Principles of Gynaecology* by Norman Jeffcoate. As indicated by the preface to the latest edition quoted near the beginning of this chapter, Jeffcoate rejects the validity of feminist ideas. On female sexuality and orgasm he writes:

> In the woman sexual feelings are dormant compared with those of the man and only develop gradually with experience .... Some women never achieve vaginal orgasms and always depend on stimulation of the clitoris, vulva and extra-genital erogenous zones for satisfaction. Indeed one current view denies the existence of the phenomenon of the vaginal orgasm ... but most women with satisfactory sex lives have no doubt that vaginal orgasm is real and much more powerful than that induced by *superficial stimulation* .... The above views [his] long established and confirmed by nearly all normal women are an *anathema to small pressure groups, agitating for the liberation of women* and equality of the sexes in all matters. They protest that the concepts of masculine initiation of sexual activity ... reflect the prejudice of males in general and of male gynaecologists in particular. And such protagonists maintain that sex drive and desire are spontaneously just as strong in girls and women as they are in boys and men, being motivated by *personal pleasure rather than by a procreational instinct or anxiety to satisfy their lover.* If this is what they really believe to be true in general, rather than in isolated cases, *they deceive themselves*, but not others, not even the majority of women.
>
> Sex equality in many respects is desirable; but equality in sex desire is unattainable being contrary to an all *powerful inherent law of nature* (Jeffcoate 1975: 568, emphasis added).

The book continually presents a double standard with respect to female sexuality. Frigidity in women is caused primarily by constitutional and psychological factors, but it is not necessarily a problem because some women are 'so constitutionally devoid of capacity for orgasm they will not feel frustrated' (1975: 575). Male impotence, seen by Fish (1978) as primarily caused by women's behaviour, is for Jeffcoate mostly due to psychological problems but sometimes caused and often exacerbated by women's scorn. 'Her man needs his confidence raised and if ever his manliness is questioned, or she makes him feel he is failing her the cure is inevitably postponed' (1975: 578).

So while it might appear that some gains have been made there is still a long way to go. We will see later that this is also the case in health handbooks written for women by doctors. To understand the significance of these it is necessary to outline some aspects of the feminist paradigm for health care, and some strategies for reconstructing health knowledge.

An Alternative Model of Women and their Health

That feminist strategies for reconstructing health knowledge should have begun outside the established medical framework will probably come as no surprise. If, for example, the object is to provide non-hierarchical ways of giving health care then to attempt change in a service as dominated by hierarchy as the National Health Service (NHS) may be futile. Yet not to attempt change within the service that most women use may be to limit the benefits of feminist approaches to health care to a privileged few. This is one of the issues that has most exercised feminists in Britain.

The early stages of the women's health movement had four main strands, redefining ourselves as healthy, overcoming our ignorance, attacking sexist beliefs and seizing the means of reproduction for ourselves. The channels women have used to achieve these include setting up women's health groups, producing articles, books and pamphlets, setting up alternative services and establishing single issue campaigns and pressure groups. (For reasons of space I will only consider selected aspects of the first three here. For more detailed discussion see Ruzek, 1978 and Leeson and Gray, 1978). The traditions of consciousness raising groups, collective ways of sharing experience and learning to see personal experience as politically structured, have been carried on into women's health groups. Small groups of women meet in their own houses or women's centres to learn about their bodies. A core activity for many groups has been self-examination, where, using plastic speculums, lamps and mirrors women are able to examine their own vaginas. To do this, to be privy to a view previously confined to doctors, and to learn that they are healthy and normal 'down there' is for many women a deeply emotional and political act. From here groups may go on to develop their skills in many different ways. Some get involved in 'health education', writing articles, setting up health courses and other self-examination groups; spreading the knowledge they have about how to monitor your menstrual cycle to detect abnormalities and pregnancy, to treat vaginal infections, and about some of the misconceptions women have learnt from doctors about retroverted uteruses and cervical erosions etc.

Other groups have concentrated on developing practical skills, learning to fit diaphragms and IUDs and to do menstrual extractions. For women, having learnt that many doctors perform procedures they have no specific training for, see no reason why they should not learn how to do them for themselves, slowly and carefully and with other women who are aware of and share the risks. Learning that the illegal abortionist they referred women to was not a doctor was one reason why women in Chicago set up

Jane, an illegal abortion collective that carried out over 11,000 abortions in the four years between 1969 and 1973 (Pauline Bart, in press). Another area where feminists have defied the law to seize back control of reproduction in the United States has been in childbirth where midwives (who are illegal in many states) have 'caught' babies and risked prosecution (Suzanne Arms, 1975).

Women's Clinics

Being illegal or operating only within small groups are not the ideal conditions for reaching large numbers of women. The obvious extension of health groups in some countries, notably the United States, has been the establishment of feminist clinics, staffed by women for women. Some of these clinics are organised on what Ruzek (1978) calls traditional feminist lines. Though female lay workers and para-professionals have a greater role than in conventional gynaecological settings, and the emphasis is on information giving and support, it is still assumed that doctors should provide the routine services. In radical feminist clinics, by contrast, doctors are merely technicians. Routine care is provided by lay women and women are encouraged to learn basic health care procedures for themselves and to discuss their health problems in groups. Both sorts of clinics have faced opposition and attempts at co-option from the established profession but have also led to some modifications of practice by gynaecologists threatened by an alternative service.

In Britain there is as yet no equivalent network. There do exist a number of well-woman clinics run by the local Area Health Authorities (AHAs), and sessions are set aside in some general practices, within the NHS. There are also clinics providing services for women (such as cervical cytology), run by charities or by profit-making concerns. But these are not necessarily feminist as Katy Gardner, a feminist general practitioner, has pointed out (Gardner, in press). She argues that it is important for women to press for such clinics to be established within the NHS. Some groups have done this, often through Community Health Councils, set up in 1974 to look after the patients' interests in the NHS (Leeson and Gray, 1978).

General practitioners in the National Health Service are legally self-employed, undertaking to work for the NHS by contract and preserving a substantial degree of autonomy in organising their work. This self-employed status has been criticised by the political left long before the inception of the NHS but it does allow general practitioners some freedom to innovate (as well as to resist innovation). A few practices have been established where work is organised at least in part according to feminist principles. Several groups have begun campaigns to establish feminist clinics with a substantial involvement of lay health workers but they have all foundered so far. At a time of reduction in public expenditure on health in Britain where trained health workers may be losing their jobs such alternatives have been unlikely to gain political support. Conventional well-women clinics may be seen by doctors as opportunities to delegate routine work to lower paid workers freeing doctors' valuable time (Edwards, 1974; Marsh, 1976).

To press for clinics outside the NHS is to court the danger of promoting the private, profit-making sector of medicine and is politically unacceptable to most British feminists. In some areas where abortions are difficult to obtain within the NHS because of the attitudes of local gynaecologists, women's pressure has led to the establishment of links between the NHS and the charities who provide a non-profit making service. Such compromises have presented local feminists with a dilemma; on the one hand more abortions are likely to be available, on the other, the underlying problem is left untouched and a national law is still being differentially implemented. The charitable sector however should not be confused with the private sector. As women's health has become profitable so clinics funded by the pharmaceutical companies and organisations such as British United Provident Association (BUPA), the main provider of private health care insurance, have been established.

Feminist Health Education

Learning to feel good about ourselves and our bodies has definite health implications and feminists have tried to pass their knowledge on through health courses and through writing. Books like Susie Orbach's *Fat is a Feminist Issue* (1978) have changed many women's attitudes to the way they look and helped them lose weight. Formerly taboo subjects like menstruation have become topics for best sellers (Paula Weidegger, 1978). The feminist health classic, *Our Bodies, Ourselves* (Boston Women's Health Collective, 1971, British edition edited by Angela Phillips and Jill Rakusen, 1978) encapsulates this process of self-redefinition in its title. Elsewhere I have compared it with other health handbooks for women, both feminist and non-feminist (Elston, 1979). For the feminist books have also brought a commercial response. These are predominantly written by doctors and often contain little precise information about treatments (whether from doctors or self-help); self-examination is rarely mentioned and the attitude is 'ask your doctor as he knows best'.

One example where the impact of the women's health movement can be detected is the differences between the first (1971) and second (1977) editions of Derek Llewellyn Jones' *Everywoman*. A second edition was considered appropriate because of,

> changes in attitudes to women's role in society, her sexuality, and because medical science has made considerable advances. . . . None of this alters my belief that modern woman is interested in her *femininity* and wants information, which all too often she is not given when she consults a doctor. Too many doctors still behave in an authoritarian way (1977: 13).

This passage suggests a partial recognition of change, assuming it is not just a publisher's shrewd recognition that women will no longer buy certain kinds of books. Throughout the new edition there are small changes and subtle re-emphases. The right analgesia is no longer described as allowing the mother to co-operate, even to help, in the process of childbirth (1971: 185). By 1977,

> whichever method (of analgesia) she chooses it is the duty of those *helping her* during childbirth to inform her of the progress of her labour, to obtain her co-operation and to treat her as a participant (1977: 13 emphasis added).

These non-feminist health handbooks lack any political perspective as to why doctors behave in the way they do, except that 'they are busy men' (1977: p. 318). It is even possible that by raising women's expectations of reasonable treatment without an account of why they might not get it may provoke more dissatisfaction with medical men. But their existence and their changing nature, whether a product of commercial acumen or changing attitudes, must be in part due to feminism.

Making Women Visible

One area where feminists have generated new knowledge and raised new questions is in relation to the hazards women face at work, and not just with respect to reproduction. Health and safety issues and occupational medicine are neglected in most systems of medicine. Health and safety of women workers, except in a few instances (e.g. where known damage to foetuses from lead and radiation has led to restrictions on women's employment) has been virtually ignored officially and in medicine until recently. This reflects both the assumption that women do not work and that if they do, they do not work in hazardous environments. Yet recent research has shown there are many toxic chemicals and hazardous procedures used constantly in clerical work (Women and Hazards Group, in press). In reality many women's working environments, laundries, kitchens, hospitals and homes, are dangerous environments.

During the Seventies there has been a regeneration of concern in Britain and the USA with health and safety issues, partly stimulated by new legislation (Health and Safety at Work Act in 1974 in Britain, the establishment of the Occupational Safety and Health Administration (OSHA) in 1977 in the USA). Local health and safety groups have challenged many of the assumptions about the ways health and safety standards are measured (see Patrick Kinnersley, 1974). Women's hazards groups have shown in particular how standards are set for 'average males' and have investigated the health risks particular to women's work. Where possible damage to foetuses has been recognised in the past the recommendation has usually been that women should leave the work when pregnant. Feminist researchers and activists like Jean Stellman (1977) and Vilma Hunt (1975) have pointed out that by the time most women know they are pregnant the most likely stage for foetal damage is past. Moreover, the traditional view assumes that damage is primarily via toxins crossing the placenta, and this ignores the possiblity of mutagens which may be transmitted by the father or the mother. So here is an example where feminist knowledge has pointed to the need for better protection for everyone. Naomi Fett, in an article in a special issue of the journal *Preventive Medicine* has shown that women's involvement in health and safety at work struggles is not confined to recent years but has a long but often obscured history (Fett, 1978).

Challenging Medical Practices and Beliefs

As already suggested one area where the conflict between medical paradigms and women's paradigms is greatest is in that of childbirth. Over the past ten to fifteen years obstetrics has, in the eyes of many, been transformed from an art into a science. New techniques for the active management of labour have been introduced, one of the latest being foetal heart monitors. Inspection of the literature suggests that this trend has been accompanied by a marked increase in the dissatisfaction expressed by women with obstetric care, an increase in the number of deliveries involving forceps and Caesarian sections (and I recognise that it is claimed this is what a 'no risks' policy necessitates) and no clear evidence that this policy has led to an improvement in reproductive success (e.g. as measured by the perinatal mortality rate) (Ian Chalmers *et al.*, 1980).

It would be impossible to summarise either the feminist analyses of medically controlled childbirth or the debate over the value of interventionist obstetrics. Many aspects of the former are discussed in Arms (1975), Oakley (1980), Graham and Oakley (in press) and in the newsletters and literature of the various groups pressing for changes in obstetric policies; in Britain these include the Association of Radical Midwives (ARM), the Association for Improvements in Maternity Services (AIMS) and the Society to Support Confinements. Discussions of the latter are to be found in Martin Richards (1975), Tim Chard and Martin Richards (1977). Sheila Kitzinger and John Davis (1978) and in Christine Beels' feminist guide to birth *The Childbirth Book* (1978).

In the limited space available I want to focus on one aspect of the conflict over childbirth, induction of birth. This issue illustrates a partial success for women, and how such success is achieved. Induction of labour, starting by means of rupturing the membranes or the use of hormones such as oxytocin, showed a marked increase in use in NHS hospitals since the early fifties, when its use for women who had reached the 41st week of their pregnancy became widespread. Chalmers and Richards (1977) present figures suggesting that in 1967, 16.8 per cent of all births were induced, by 1971 the rate was 26.3 per cent and by 1974, 39.9 per cent.

Such a rapid increase did not go unnoticed by those women who felt their labours were more painful and less controllable. A public campaign began in 1974 which was not initially specifically feminist though it became increasingly so. Television programmes, articles in Sunday newspapers and questions in Parliament focussed on the 'childbirth revolution'. A leading article in the *Lancet* (1974), entitled 'A Time to be Born' noted women's concern was no longer muffled and recognised that the public might be right to express concern over the use of unproven procedures for convenience (Nov 16, 1974, ii, pp. 1183–4). For, as the public were pointing out, there was little or no evidence as to the benefits or dangers of the widespread use of induction. Controversy over the issue filled many pages in the medical press.

In 1975, Jean Robinson, then chairwoman of the Patients' Association (a pressure group that exists to safeguard the interests of patients in health care) wrote to the *Lancet*, criticising a recently published article's research design and use of other information about induction (*Lancet*, 1975 p. 1088). In a subsequent issue a letter from a male obstetrician was published (*Lancet*, 1975 p. 1242). Jean Robinson's letter was commended for its marshalling of the evidence on the consequences of induction. The doctor concluded that the Patients' Association had an anonymous obstetrician 'ghosting' its letters on clinical matters and asked for this individual to come forward. The inference was that letters from anonymous doctors could not be taken seriously as their clinical standing could not be assessed and that the Patients' Association had no right to be interested in clinical questions. (It is probably superfluous for me to point out that the issue raised in the original letter was primarily one of interpreting published statistical data, not a question of clinical acumen and that Jean Robinson has no need of doctors to write her letters.)

The Department of Health commissioned a survey on mothers' experience of induction. But in 1976 the terms of the debate changed. Ian Chalmers and his colleagues published the results of a long term study of births in Cardiff that found that there had not been a significant decline in still births and perinatal deaths associated with the increased use of induction and other interventionist procedures. Chalmers and his colleagues called for caution and for further research that could establish casual links between obstetric procedures and birth outcomes (see Chalmers *et al.*, 1976, Chalmers and Richards, 1977). These findings and others in the context of widespread public concern did lead to some reduction in induction rates in many hospitals and a more cautious attitude on the part of many to intervention. But how much of a reduction this was is difficult to assess because of problems with the definition of 'induction' in hospital statistics and changing techniques. As a professor of obstetrics recently remarked to a woman researching maternity care policies, 'We have ways of doing it now so women don't know it's happening'. This may or may not be an advance.

This example illustrates:

> Firstly, that even if it was not feminist criticisms that generated the debate and led to the medical research, feminist criticisms of the indiscriminate use of procedures that have not been adequately tested have been validated.
>
> Secondly, women's complaints of their experience of induction were not sufficient reason for changes in medical practice. They are too 'subjective'. The emphasis in much of the medical debate over the value of induction was over the possible benefits and hazards for the baby, rarely over the benefits and hazards for the mother (see Oakley, 1980, for discussion of the limitations of indices of reproductive success).
>
> Thirdly, women, and the public in general, have had to enter such debates on the medical profession's terms to receive much medical attention. Even then, their ability and right to do this may be challenged. In this way the argument may remain at the level of the adequacy of medical claims for the scientific basis for their knowledge rather than possibly questioning the definition of what is counted as 'scientific knowledge'.

The Women's Health Movement in Britain; Some Conclusions

The women's health movement in Britain has sometimes been accused of lagging behind our sisters abroad. We have not the range of feminist clinics, the record of hospital and clinic occupation and government sponsored conferences on women's health that some countries have seen. Whether or not this means we are backward is not possible to judge. Our experience has certainly been different from that of women in America, just as their experience has been different from that of women in Italy and Australia. To understand the origins of these differences would involve an analysis of the historical differences in women's economic, political and social position and, indeed, of political conditions and traditions and economic and social forces in the different societies: a task yet to be undertaken.

However, there are some differences in the structure of medical care in, for example Britain and the United States, which may give us a partial understanding of some of the differences. Since 1948, most women in Britain have received their medical care from the National Health Service. Entry to medical care is usually from the general practitioner, with whom one is registered and sees when well or ill. The difficulties of changing doctors and the potential dependence on her/his care in case of need may make confrontation even more difficult than for a middle-class American woman seeing a gynaecologist for well-woman care only. The chances of seeing a woman doctor (14 per cent of GPs) may be higher in Britain, and this is particularly true in area health authority family planning clinics where many women go for contraceptive services. This may make offensive encounters less likely. There are different traditions of practice, for our problem may not be degrading examinations but getting them at all. But more importantly, the lack of a direct cash relationship between doctor and patient may both save us from the worst excesses of defensive and heroic medicine and limit the possibilities of direct economic sanctions on doctors (either by individuals changing doctors or by the setting up of alternative services). The centralised bureaucratic nature of the NHS compared with the fragmented system of health care in the USA may give us more equitably distributed health care but it may also hinder innovation. Because the women's health movement was initially primarily a middle class white movement there has been less attention paid to the situation of the thousands of women in the USA whose problem is getting access to any kind of health care and who use public clinics so it is difficult to compare their experience with that of women in Britain.

It may be that the experience of (some) American women of health care is more oppressive than in Britain. My impression is that it is more overtly so. But a high level of oppression does not automatically lead to more radical feminist consciousness any more than levels of material suffering directly determine the level of class consciousness (John Foster, 1974; Edward Thompson, 1963).

Feminists in Britain have had to continually engage with the apparent paradoxes the existence of the NHS poses. We simultaneously make demands of the state while recognising that state ideologies and institutions play a major part in our oppression. We find ourselves defending the principle and the continued existence of the NHS in the face of public expenditure cuts while arguing that these services may degrade and damage women. I am not suggesting that this paradox does not exist in the USA, only that there, the greater extent and visibility of capital's direct involvement in health care makes different strategies appropriate.

In the early years of the women's health movement particularly in the USA the emphasis was primarily on the 'cultural critique' of the quality of medicine. This critique was markedly different from the more traditional 'political economic' tradition of socialist analyses of health care which saw the problems of American (and, to some extent, British) medicine as being ones of lack and maldistribution of resources (see John Ehrenreich, 1978). In the past decade it has become commonplace to refer to Western medicine as being in a state of crisis. Apparently inexorably rising costs are not matched by improvements in health, and there has been the growth of public, especially women's, concern about the quality of services. As Doyal (1979) and Ehrenreich (1978) have argued, it is not possible to explain the origins of this 'crisis' within a paradigm that assumes medicine is unquestionably scientific and beneficial.

Feminist theories have played a major part in the development of a more critical understanding of health care but in so doing we have learnt that some of our early accounts and arguments are insufficient on their own (and, of course, on occasions unfounded). Self-help and overcoming ignorance and lack of confidence are essential preliminary steps but they cannot in themselves bring about radical changes in the distribution of power (see for example Charlotte Ryan, 1975). The power of the medical profession is not solely a product of their predominantly male membership. It cannot be understood without reference to questions of class and the relationship between the professions and the state in a class dominated society. As Doyal (1979) has argued the social production of health and health care is structured by class and race domination as well as sex domination.

So, in this chapter I have argued that feminism has had some impact on medicine, a major impact on women's understanding of health, and, I believe, some impact on the quality of women's health. We have learnt that some of our original claims were inaccurate, but many were not and that our original demands for more information and more testing etc. are both insufficient for change and more problematic than we first realised (see Rakusen, in press). We have learnt that some of our concerns are not specific to women and that we need to analyse both the control of reproduction when we are well and what happens when we are ill, including what makes us ill in the first place.

In short, we have learnt that understanding health and medicine is much more complex a project than we first thought and that we must look outside medicine to understand why it is involved in our oppression. We are learning the confidence to tackle these complexities. Through our learning it has become clear that health and health care are a lot more complicated than most doctors have told us, more complicated, indeed, than many of them realise.

The current situation then is one in which feminism is challenging not just medical myths about women, but the right of a male dominated profession to make myths at all about women and to proceed to pass them off as scientific facts which are not open to challenge or investigation. Ultimately, it may be the impact we have on the right to legitimate knowledge, rather than the particular forms of knowledge produced, which may prove to be the most significant contribution. When male medical practitioners excluded women and denied their right to generate knowledge about women's health on the grounds that such knowledge was 'old wives' tales' they helped to structure the split which we witness today whereby male dominated medical practice is likely to define women as ill and female dominated women's health care is likely to define women as well. That women have had to develop their understandings *outside* the control of the medical profession is a commentary on the principles and practices of that profession. But from that *outside* position we can look at many of the medical facts as they pertain to women, and challenge their legitimacy with our label 'old husbands' tales': as yet it may not carry the same force as its predecessor (although it could even in the forseeable future) but that it can be conceptualised — and validated among women — is testimony to the impact of feminism on medicine.

Acknowledgements

In the writing of this paper I have been helped by the suggestions and ideas of many friends. I would particularly like to thank Sue Barlow, Lesley Doyal, Maggie Eisner, Claire Lawton, Jill Rakusen and Gill Yudkin for their help. Dale Spender made many helpful suggestions and was a patient editor of a chapter that suffered more than most from the contingencies of everyday life in its production. Responsibility for the final version is of course my own.

References

ARMS, Suzanne (1975) *Immaculate Deception*, Houghton Miflin, Boston.
ATKINSON, Paul (1977) 'The reproduction of medical knowledge' in Robert Dingwall, Christian Heath, Margaret Reid and Margaret Stacey (Eds.) *Health Care and Health Knowledge*, Croom Helm, London, pp. 85–106.
BARKER-BENFIELD, Ben (1976) *The Horrors of the Half-Known Life*, Harper, New York.
BARNES, Josephine (1978) *Lecture Notes in Gynaecology*, Pitman Medical, London, 4th edn.

BART, Pauline (in press) 'Seizing the means of reproduction' in Helen Roberts (Ed.) *Women, Health and Reproduction*, Routledge & Kegan Paul, London.

BEELS, Christine (1978) *The Childbirth Book*, Turnstone, London.

BEWLEY, Beulah and Thomas BEWLEY (1975) 'Hospital doctors' career structure and misuse of medical womanpower', *Lancet*, ii, pp. 270–72.

BOSTON WOMEN'S HEALTH COLLECTIVE (1971) *Our Bodies, Ourselves*, Simon Schuster, New York. Boston Women's Health Collective; and Angela PHILLIPS and Jill RAKUSEN (1978) *Our Bodies, Ourselves*, Penguin, London. British edn.

BROVERMAN, I. K., D. M. BROVERMAN, F. E. CLARKSON, P. S. ROSENCRANTZ and S. R. VOGEL (1970) 'Sex Role stereotyping and clinical judgements of mental health' *Journal of Consulting Psychology*, Vol. 34, No. 1 pp. 1–7.

BROWN, Carol (1975) 'Women workers in the health service industry', *International Journal of Health Services*, Vol. 5, No. 2, pp. 173–184.

CAMPBELL, Margaret (1974) *Why Would a Girl go into Medicine?*, Feminist Press, Westbury, New York.

CHALMERS, Ian, J. G. LAWTON and A. C. TURNBULL (1976) 'Evaluation of different approaches to obstetric care', *British Journal of Obstetrics & Gynaecology*, Vol. 83, pp. 921–929 and 930–933.

CHALMERS, Ian and Martin RICHARDS (1977) 'Intervention and causal inference in obstetric practice' in Tim Chard and Martin Richards (Eds.) *Benefits and hazards of the New Obstetrics*, Heinemann, London, pp. 34–61.

CHALMERS, Ian, Ann OAKLEY and Aidan MACFARLANE (1980) 'Perinatal health services; an immodest proposal', *British Medical Journal*, i., pp. 842–45.

CHARD, Tim and Martin RICHARDS (Eds.) (1977) *Benefits and Hazards of the New Obstetrics*, Heinemann, London.

CHESLER, Phyllis (1972) *Women and Madness*, Avon Books, New York.

COCHRANE, Archibald (1972) *Effectiveness and Efficiency*, Nuffield Provincial Hospitals Trust, London.

DEWHURST, C. J. (Ed.) (1976) *Integrated Obstetrics and Gynaecology*, Blackwell, Oxford, 2nd edn.

DONNISON, Jean (1977) *Midwives and Medical Men*, Heinemann, London.

DOYAL, Lesley, with Imogen PENNELL (1979) *The Political Economy of Health*, Pluto Press, London.

DUFFIN, Lorna (1977) 'The conspicious consumptive; woman as invalid' in Sara Delamont and Lorna Duffin (Eds.) *The Nineteenth Century Woman: Her Cultural and Physical World*, Croom Helm, London, pp. 26–56.

EDWARDS, D. (1974) 'Gynaecological abnormalities found at a cytology clinic', *British Medical Journal*, iv, p. 218.

EHRENREICH, Barbara, Mark DOWIE and Steve MINKIN (1979) 'The Charge: Gynocide; The Accused: The U.S. Government' *Mother Jones*, 4, Nov., pp. 26–37.

EHRENREICH, Barbara and Deidre ENGLISH (1973) *Complaints and Disorders; the Sexual Politics of Sickness*, Feminist Press, Westbury, New York.

EHRENREICH, John (1978) 'Introduction' to John Ehrenreich (Ed.) *The Cultural Crisis of Modern Medicine*, Monthly Review Press, New York, pp. 1–35.

ELSTON, Mary Ann (1977) 'Women doctors: whose problem?' in Margaret Stacey, Margaret Reid, Christian Heath and Robert Dingwall (Eds.) *Health Care and Health Knowledge*, Croom Helm, London, pp. 115–138.

ELSTON, Mary Ann (1979) 'Reclaiming our bodies: health handbooks by and for women', *Women's Studies International Quarterly*, Vol. 2, No. 1, pp. 117–125.

ELSTON, Mary Ann (1980) 'Half our future doctors?' in Rosalie Silverstone and Audrey M. Ward (Eds.) *The Careers of Professional Women*, Croom Helm, London, pp. 99–139.

FARRANT, Wendy (1980) 'North-East Thames Regional Screening Programme for the detection of fetal abnormality: some priorities for CHC action', Background paper for South Camden Community Health Council.

FEE, Elizabeth (1975) 'Women and health care: A comparison of theories', *International Journal of Health Services*, Vol. 5, No. 3, pp. 397–425.

FETT, Naomi (1978) 'Women's occupational health and the Women's Health Movement', *Preventive Medicine*, 7, pp. 366–371

FINCH, Janet and Dulcie GROVES (1980) 'Community care and the family: A case for equal opportunity', forthcoming in *Journal of Social Policy*, Vol. 9, No. 4.

FISH, T. (1978) *Outline of Psychiatry*, Wright, Bristol, 3rd edn., Edited by M. Hamilton.

FOSTER, John (1974) *Class Struggle and the Industrial Revolution*, Methuen, London.

GARDNER, Katy (in press) 'Well woman clinics' in Helen Roberts (Ed.) *Women, Health and Reproduction*, Routledge & Kegan Paul, London.

GORDON, Linda (1974) *Woman's Body, Woman's Right*, Grossman, New York.

GRAHAM, Hilary and Ann Oakley (in press) 'Competing ideologies of reproduction: medical and maternal perspectives on pregnancy and childbirth' in Helen Roberts (Ed.) *Women, Health and Reproduction.*

HOWELL, Mary (1978) 'Paediatricians and mothers' in John Ehrenreich (Ed.) *The Cultural Crisis of Modern Medicine*, pp. 201–211.

HOWELL, Mary (1979) 'Can we be both feminists and professionals?' *Women's Studies International Quarterly*, Vol. 2, No. 1, pp. 1–7.

HUNT, Vilma R. (1975) *Occupational Health Problems of Pregnant Women* SA-53-4-75. U.S. D.H.E.W., Washington, D.C.

JEFFCOATE, Norman (1975) *Principles of Gynaecology*, Butterworths, London, 4th edn.

KINNERSLEY, Patrick (1974) *The Hazards of Work*, Pluto Press, London.

KITZINGER, Sheila and John DAVIS (Eds.) (1978) *The Place of Birth*, Oxford University Press, Oxford.

LEESON, Joyce and Judith GRAY (1978) *Women and Medicine*, Tavistock, London.

LLEWELLYN-JONES, Derek (1971) *Everywoman*, Faber & Faber, London, 2nd edn., 1977.

LEWIS, Jane (1979) 'The ideology and politics of birth control in inter-war England', *Women's Studies International Quarterly*, Vol. 2, No. 1, pp. 33–48.

LORBER, Judith (1975) 'Women and medical sociology; invisible professionals and ubiquitous patients' in Marcia Millman and Rosabeth Kanter (Eds.) *Another Voice*, Doubleday, New York, pp. 75–105.

MACINTYRE, Sally (1976) 'Who wants babies? The social construction of instincts' in Diana Leonard Barker and Sheila Allen (Eds.) *Sexual Divisions and Society: Process and Change*, Tavistock, London, pp. 150–173.

MARSH, G. N. (1976) 'Further nursing care in general practice', *British Medical Journal*, iii, p. 626.

MEDICAL WOMEN'S FEDERATION (1979) 'Careers symposium'.

OAKLEY, Ann (1974) *The Sociology of Housework*, Martin Robertson, London.

OAKLEY, Ann (1980) *Women Confined*, Martin Robertson, London.

ORBACH, Susie (1978) *Fat is a Feminist Issue*, Paddington Press, London.

RAKUSEN, Jill (1975) 'The Pill Report: Information or propaganda?' *Spare Rib*, 32, pp. 6–8.

RAKUSEN, Jill (in press) 'Depo-provera: the extent of the problem — a case study in the politics of birth control' in Helen Roberts (Ed.) *Women, Health and Reproduction*.

READING, Anthony (1979) 'The role of psycho-social factors in IUD continuation', *Social Science and Medicine*, Vol. 13, No. 6, pp. 631–640.

RICHARDS, Martin (1975) 'Innovation in medical practice: Obstetricians and the induction of labour in Britain', *Social Science and Medicine*, Vol. 9, pp. 595–602.

RYAN, Charlotte (1975) 'Our Bodies, Ourselves: The fallacy of seeking individual solutions for societal contradictions', *International Journal of Health Services*, Vol. 5, No. 2, pp. 335–38.

RUZEK, Sheryl Burt (1978) *The Woman's Health Movement*, Praeger, New York.

SAVAGE, Wendy (1978) 'The use of depo-provera in East London', *Fertility and Contraception*, Vol. 2, No. 3, pp. 24–30.

SCULLY, Diane and Pauline BART (1973) 'A funny thing happened on my way to the orifice; woman in gynaecology textbooks', *Americal Journal of Sociology*, 78, pp. 1045–1050.

SEAMAN, Barbara (1969) *The Doctors' Case Against the Pill*, Avon Books, New York.

SMITH, Dorothy E. and Sara J. DAVID (Eds.) (1975) *Women Look at Psychiatry*, Press Gang Publishers, Vancouver.

STELLMAN, Jeanne M. (1977) *Women's Work, Women's Health*, Pantheon, New York.

STIMSON, Gerry and Barbara WEBB (1975) *Going to See the Doctor*, Routledge & Kegan Paul, London.

TAYLOR, Jane (1979) 'Hidden Labour and the National Health Service' in Paul Atkinson, Robert Dingwall and Anne Murcott (Eds.) *Prospects for the National Health Service*, Croom Helm, London, pp. 130–44.

THOMPSON, Edward P. (1963) *The Making of the English Working Class*, Gollancz, London.

TIETZE, Christopher and Sarah LEWITT (1977) 'Mortality and fertility control', *Women and Health*, Vol. 2, No. 1, pp. 3–7.

VICINUS, Martha (Ed.) (1973) *Suffer and be still; Women in Victorian Life*, Indiana University Press, Bloomington.

WALSH, Mary Roth (1977) *Doctors Wanted: No Women Need Apply: sexual barriers in the medical profession, 1835–1975*, Yale University Press, New Haven, Connecticut.

WEIDEGGER, Paula (1978) *Female Cycles*, The Women's Press, London.

WOMEN AND HAZARDS GROUP (in press) *Office Work is Dangerous to Your Health*, British Society for Social Responsibility in Science, London

YOUNG, Gail (in press) 'A woman in medicine; Reflections from the inside' In Helen Roberts (Ed.) *Women, Health and Reproduction,* Routledge and Kegan Paul, London.

14

The Emperor doesn't Wear any Clothes: The Impact of Feminism on Biology*

RUTH HUBBARD

While many people have long acknowledged that social context inevitably affects and often structures perceptions of reality, most continue to believe that the scientific methodology guarantees objectivity to scientists and science. But science is the result of a process in which scientists — who, like everyone else, live in a particular time, place and stratum of society — observe what goes on in nature. And they do so by taking note of things that for some reason command their attention. Science, therefore, is made by a process in which nature is filtered through a coarse-meshed sieve; only items that scientists notice and structure into a cohesive system are retained. Since scientists are rather a small group of people — predominantly male — and mostly economically and socially privileged, university educated males at that, there is every reason to assume that like all other human productions, science — and biology — reflect the outlook and interest of the producers.

Scientists (and biologists among them) do not ask all possible questions that are amenable to their methodology, only those that arouse their curiosity and interest, or the curiosity and interest of supporting organisations. They do not accept all possible answers; only those congruent with the implicit assumptions that form the basis of their understanding of the world (an understanding shared with most of their 'educated' contemporaries). Furthermore, the very methodology of science limits its applicability to repeatable and measureable phenomena. This discounts vast areas of human experience, indeed, most facets of our relationships with ourselves, fellow humans, other living beings, and the inanimate world, and hence imposes grievous limitations on biology, the science of living (and hence constantly changing) organisms.

When scientific knowlege is held superior to other ways of knowing it serves to devalue or invalidate much of people's daily experience. Thus science, and hence biology, as it has developed, stands often in sharp contrast to feminist principles. While there has been a growing number of feminist accounts of the ways in which social science disciplines often serve the narrow interests of disciples and social peer groups, the myth of scientific objectivity has minimized similar critical appraisals in the natural sciences. But the time has come to evaluate the 'interesting' questions in biology, and to ask why androcentric scientists find them interesting.

*This is a revised version of the Introductions and of the article 'Have only men evolved?' which appeared in *Women Look at Biology Looking at Women,* edited by Ruth Hubbard, Mary Sue Henefin and Barbara Fried, and thanks are due to Barbara Fried who coauthored the Introductions, and to Schenkman Publishing Co., for their kind permission to reprint.

For instance, among billions of animal species, why have certain ones been studied repeatedly and in great detail, while others have been ignored? Until very recently, greater attention has been focused on the social structure among Savannah baboons than on chimpanzees or gibbons. Could this be because it has been easy to stereotype baboon social behaviour as hierarchical, with relatively rigid sex roles? Could it be because chimpanzees have very fluid relationships with one another that are difficult to stereotype by sex except for the fact that females nourish the unweaned young?

Is it an accident that among billions of insect species, those whose social behaviour easily conforms to rigid roles are the ones that have caught the imaginations of naturalists from the nineteenth century onward? The 'scientific' language of the last century is still in use — ant and bee societies still contain slaves and queens, as well as workers and soldiers. Yet we hear almost nothing about the behaviour of insects whose social arrangements do not lend themselves to analogies reinforcing human social arrangements that many people think of as 'natural'.

Turning to studies of our own species, is it an accident that scientists have been primarily interested in exploring contraceptive techniques that tamper with the *female* reproductive system, following the curious logic that because 'fertility in women depends upon so many finely balanced factors . . . it should be easy to interfere with the process at many different stages . . . ?' Would it not be more sensible to conclude that it is more difficult and riskier to tamper with a woman's reproductive system than a man's *because* the woman's system is made up of 'so many finely balanced factors?' (Wood, 1969: 36–37).

These examples suggest a few of the ways in which the objects selected for scientific study and the manner of study are used to reinforce the interests or preconceptions of the studiers. There is clearly not enough time or money for scientists to ask all possible questions. So one asks only those that promise to lead somewhere. The question is *who gets to decide where?*

For those who make the decisions are powerful figures in the construction of scientific knowledge, and scientific knowledge is a powerful influence in our lives.

It is not just the choice of questions which is significant, but also the way in which answers are presented. Other contributors to this volume have commented on the role which language plays in the construction of our sexist reality, and scientific language is no exception.

The limits of our language present the limits of 'reality' as we know it. Scientists control our thought not only by their choice of subjects but in their manner of description. Much scientific writing for example employs the passive voice, a ponderous, authority-laden style that carries an automatic sanctification of the subject under discussion. As linguist Julia Stanley (1972) points out, when B. F. Skinner writes that 'The punishment of sexual behavior changes sexual behavior', he makes passive the statement '*someone* is choosing to punish and thereby change the sexual behavior of certain people'. Sexual behavior is punishable. Women are reinforceable. The ecosphere is manipulable. The missing questions that this linguistic structure conceals are: *by whom? for what purpose? in whose interest? under what conditions?*

Looking at scientific language, we must provide answers to these questions and delegitimatize language that masks authority and authorship. Behind every statement that something is doable are a doer and a motive.

The development of a highly technical language has always been defended by scientists as necessary for 'precision'. Whether this is true or not, it is important to look at the *social* function of technical language. Learning what scientists are talking about requires a long period of apprenticeship, a molding of one's consciousness to fit the information into a precise, *publicly inaccessible* mode.

Scientific knowledge should be made maximally accessible and minimally obfuscated through language. Language is power in the scientific mode as elsewhere; if we want the power that comes with information to be more widely shared, we must dispense with the elite protection of unnecessary complexities (including nomenclature) and challenge them wherever we find them.

There is another pitfall that has been largely ignored, or at least underrated. It is called by all sorts of jargon such as 'experimenter expectancy', but what it boils down to is that more often than not, we find what we look for. Indeed, one can prove almost any hypothesis if one gets to set the terms of the experiment: to choose appropriate conditions, ask appropriate questions, select appropriate controls. And if one does a thorough job, the conclusion will have that quality of obviousness that scientists so enjoy at the end of meticulous research. And it really *is* obvious, for it fits what we believe about the world; but the reason it fits so well is that it is founded on those very beliefs. Thus were discovered the four humors of the body, leeching to cure disease, the inheritance of acquired characteristics, and countless cast-off theories with which we engender feelings of superiority in present-day biology students. But so also were discovered the accepted theories which today are part of biology, and which are androcentric — male biased.

Most self-fulfilling theories are devised without intent to defraud, and when they are debunked, they — at worst — damage the reputations of their authors. When such theories become effective tools for oppression, however, they are social dangers. So for example, if some scientists who believe (wish?) that women's mental lives are controlled by the physical demands of their reproductive systems (or that blacks are intellectually inferior) proceed to 'prove' these hypotheses by devising the necessary tests, asking the right questions, finding appropriate subjects, and then come to the obvious conclusions, sexism (or racism) becomes part of the scientific dogma.

For two centuries men have avoided the ethics of the 'woman question', as they have avoided issues of racial oppression, by claiming to base the relevant political decisions on laws of nature. 'It would no doubt be a great boon to the human race', men might say 'if women *could* do the marvelous things men have done, like vote, own property, and get a proper education. But such was clearly not nature's design when she gave females a 'head almost too small for intellect but just big enough for love" (Meigs, 1847; see also Walsh, 1979). If women had been meant to vote, we would not have been born with a uterus.

That the division by sex of power and privilege in society is politically motivated and not based on biology is sufficiently obvious to have been said often by many different people. But in practically every generation, there arise new prophets of 'biology as destiny', and each is fêted as a new Galileo who must be protected against political persecution — this time from enraged women rather than from the church.

The new science of sociobiology would have us believe that women stay home with the children because their eggs are large (hence metabolically more expensive) than their husbands' sperm and that women's 'nurturing instinct' has evolved to guard these biological 'investments'. Though the message to women has been somewhat altered in the century since Darwin, it remains intact: we reproduce, therefore we are. And if our reproductive functions are no longer our sole destiny, they certainly remain our most sanctioned calling. Almost fifty years ago, Virginia Woolf noted Mr. John Langdon Davies' warning that 'when children cease to be altogether desirable, women cease to be altogether necessary' (Woolf, 1957: 116). From all appearances, androcentric scientists still remain comfortable in that conviction.

What can we do to restructure and name the scientific world? We can document the impact that science and biology have on our lives; we can challenge. We must fight with science's own tools, refuting illogical and self serving explanations, exposing unsubstantial claims, disclaiming poorly conceived and inadequately controlled experiments. In the process we change the assumptions from which science proceeds, we change the paradigm of biology. We can become, and are becoming, a force to be contended with.

We can start at the beginning with the question that has so fascinated scientists of the past century: What *is* a woman? After years of speculation, there is very little that can be added to what our ancestors observed millenia ago, without the aids of rats, baboons, electrodes and personal interviews. Most women can menstruate, become pregnant, and breast feed their babies. Most men, for their part, can inseminate women, thereby contributing half the genetic material of the next generation.

To these bare bones, each society has fitted its own notions about behaviors appropriate to each sex. Anthropologists have shown that these notions can be diametrically opposed in different societies; what may be considered fit only for the goose in one, will be the sole province of the gander in another.[1] This fact, however, has hindered few from proclaiming their particular assignment of roles as natural, innate, and commendable. From the moment of birth, each of us is admitted to a social club whose membership, at least until the recent advent of trans-sexual surgery, has been considered fixed for life. The rules of this membership are often the most stringent that will ever be invoked to govern our conduct.

What name we will be called, what will be the color of the first article of clothing hung on our still unselfconscious bodies, what toys we will play with, what we will be taught in school (indeed whether we go to school), what books we will read, what our life's work will be, how much (if at all) we will be paid for it — no aspect of our lives has seemed too large or too small to be subject to sexual differentiation.

No wonder, then, that we need rarely resort to physical examination to determine the sex of an individual. Society provides us with clues more readily detected.

The fact is, we can never see each other with our 'societal clothes' off. Rather, scientists have offered us a reverse 'emperor's new clothes' by proclaiming that they can undress the emperor. *Homo sapiens,* they tell us, stands splendidly naked before us if only we carefully observe the behavior of rats, monkeys, apes, and peahens, as though these animals were humans stripped of enculturation. Scientists have compared humans across history and continents, thinking to discard all our varying, societal 'clothes' as acquired characteristics, while establishing the remainder as innate. They have tried to isolate 'pure' behavior — that not subject to environmental influence — by measuring

[1]See for example Margaret Mead, *Male and Female: A Study of the Sexes in a Changing World* (New York: Dell, 1949); Ernestine Friedl, *Women and Men: An Anthropolgist's View* (New York: Holt, Rinehart, Winston, 1975); and C. J. Matthiasson (Ed.). *Many Sisters: Women in Cross-cultural Perspective* (New York: Free Press, 1974).

brain waves, or observing pre-language infants. And they have tried to cancel out interference from 'impure' behaviour by drawing their subjects from what they perceive to be identical environments.

So far each approach has proved inadequate to the herculean task — rather like poking around the ruins of a great fire to find the match that started it all. We cannot regulate human environments as we do the life of a laboratory rat; we can match up quantifiable statistics, but we can't measure the quality of a person's world. Often correspondences we think we see between ourselves and other species are invented by us. When we study our history, other cultures, infants, or possibly even our brain waves, we are looking at phenomena which are themselves products of sexually dimorphic societies. We are looking at these phenomena with eyes accustomed to find, perhaps even hoping to find, sexual dimorphism in everything we see.

'The story of our lives becomes our lives', writes Adrienne Rich (1976: No. 18) a truth perhaps nowhere more apt than in the story of our lives as women or men. We live in a world which for so long has reported our differences as essential, that our lives have come to assume the shape of this profound conviction. How, then, are we to disentangle the two, how do we isolate nature from nurture? How can we expect to discover what is responsible for each of the differences we observe between the sexes? And why do we care?

It is difficult to understand the investment so many people have in believing sex differences to be profound, and biologically based, unless one realizes that the ideology of sex differences serves a social function. Like other forms of biological determinism, it can be used to reinforce the *status quo* by implying that what is, must be. In a scientifically oriented, politically liberal society like ours, existing inequalities between the sexes can no longer be derived from Laws of God or Man. Hence there is every motivation to shore them up with appropriate Laws of Nature.

But we cannot accept this version of reality. It has been made by men and used against women. We need to construct a more inclusive and, in that sense truer reality by pulling forth facts that have previously been ignored, while pushing back others which have received more notoriety than their substance merits. In our critique of biology, one thing becomes clear: not only must we not believe that biology is our destiny: we must reexamine whether it is even our biology.

Although there are numerous examples of the way in which the discipline of biology has developed to exclude or distort the experiences of women, I have chosen to use Charles Darwin (1809–82) and his theories of evolution and human descent to illustrate this point. For Darwin, rather than being a lone hero swimming against the social stream — as he is often portrayed — is of course, a product of his time and place, and Darwinism has wide areas of congruence with the social and political ideology of nineteenth century Britian and with Victorian precepts of morality, particularly as regards the relationships between the sexes. And the same Victorian notions still dominate contemporary biological thinking about sex differences and sex roles.

But first I must reiterate my concern with language and reality, for all acts of naming (and Darwin's evolutionary theory is an act of naming) happen against a backdrop of what is socially accepted as real. The question is *who* has social sanction to define the larger reality into which one's everyday experiences must fit in order that one be reckoned sane and responsible. In the past, the Church had this right, but it is less looked to today as a generator of new definitions of reality, though it is allowed to stick by its old ones even when they conflict with currently accepted realities (as in the case of miracles). The State also defines some aspects of reality and can generate what George Orwell called Newspeak in order to interpret the world for its own political purposes. But, for the most part, at present science is the most respectable legitimator of new realities.

Every theory is a self-fulfilling prophecy that orders experience into the framework it provides. Therefore, it should be no surprise that almost any theory, however absurd it may seem to some, has its supporters. The mythology of science holds that scientific theories lead to the truth because they operate by consensus: they can be tested by different scientists, making their own hypotheses and designing independent experiments to test them. Thus, it is said that even if one or another scientists 'misinterprets' his or her observations, the need for consensus will weed out fantasies and lead to reality. But things do not work that way. Scientists do not think and work independently. Their 'own' hypotheses ordinarily are formulated within a context of theory, so that their interpretations by and large are sub-sets within the prevailing orthodoxy. Agreement therefore is built into the process and need tell us little or nothing about 'truth' or 'reality'. Of course, scientists often disagree, but their quarrels usually are about details that do not contradict fundamental beliefs, whichever way they are resolved (see Kuhn, 1970). To overturn orthodoxy is no easier in science than in philosophy, religion, economics, or any of the other disciplines through which we try to comprehend the world and the society in which we live.

The very language that translates sense perceptions into scientific reality generates that reality by lumping certain perceptions together and sorting or highlighting others. But what we notice and how we describe it depends to a great extent on our histories, roles, and expectations as individuals and as members of our society. Therefore, as we move from the relatively impersonal observations in astronomy, physics and chemistry into biology and the social sciences, our science is increasingly affected by the ways in which our personal and social experience determine what we are able or willing to perceive as real about ourselves and the oganisms around us. This is not to accuse scientists of being deluded or dishonest, bur merely to point out that, like other people, they find it difficult to see the social biases that are built into the very fabric of what they deem real. That is why, by and large, only children notice that the emperor is naked. But only the rare child hangs on to that insight; most of them soon learn to see the beauty and elegance of his clothes. One task of feminism within biology has been to point out when the emperor is naked, and there is evidence that the emperor is embarrassed by the charge.

In trying to construct a coherent, self-consistent picture of the world, scientists come up with questions and answers that depend on their perceptions of what has been, is, will be, and can be. There is no such thing as objective, value-free science. An era's science is part of its politics, economics and sociology: it is generated by them and in turn helps to generate them. Our personal and social histories mold what we perceive to be our biology and history as organisms, just as our biology plays its part in our social behavior and perceptions. As scientists, we learn to examine the ways in which our experimental methods can bias our answers, but we are not taught to be equally wary of the biases introduced by our implicit, unstated and often unconscious beliefs about the nature of reality. To become conscious of these is more difficult than anything else we do. But difficult as it may seem, we must try to do it if our picture of the world is to be more than a reflection of various aspects of ourselves and of our social arrangements.[2]

Darwin's Evolutionary Theory

It is interesting that the idea that Darwin was swimming against the stream of accepted social dogma has prevailed, in spite of the fact that many historians have shown his thinking fitted squarely into the historical and social perspective of his time. Darwin so clearly and admittedly was drawing together strands that had been developing over long periods of time that the questions why he was the one to produce the synthesis and why it happened just then have clamored for answers. Therefore, the social origins of the Darwinian synthesis have been probed by numerous scientists and historians.

A belief that all living forms are related and that there also are deep connections between the living and non-living has existed through much of recorded human history. Through the animism of tribal cultures that endows everyone and everything with a common spirit; through more elaborate expressions of the unity of living forms in some Far Eastern and Native American belief systems; and through Aristotelian notions of connectedness runs the theme of one web of life that includes humans among its many strands. The Judaeo-Christian world view has been exceptional — and I would say flawed — in setting man (and I mean the male of the species) apart from the rest of nature by making him the namer and ruler of all life. The biblical myth of the creation gave rise to the separate and unchanging species which that second Adam, Linnaeus (1707–78), later named and classified. But even Linnaeus — though he began by accepting the belief that all existing species had been created by Jehovah during that one week long ago ('Nulla species nova') — had his doubts about their immutability by the time he had identified more than four thousand of them: some species appeared to be closely related, others seemed clearly transitional. Yet as Eisley has pointed out, it is important to realize that:

> Until the scientific idea of 'species' acquired form and distinctness there could be no dogma of 'special' creation in the modern sense. This form and distinctness it did not possess until the naturalists of the seventeenth century began to substitute exactness of definition for the previous vague characterizations of the objects of nature.

And he continues:

> ... it was Linnaeus with his proclamation that species were absolutely fixed since the beginning who intensified the theological trend. ... Science, in its desire for classification and order, ... found itself satisfactorily allied with a Christian dogma whose refinements it had contributed to produce (Eiseley, 1961: 24).

Did species exist before they were invented by scientists with their predilection for classification and naming? And did the new science, by concentrating on differences which could be used to tell things apart, devalue the similarities that tie them together? Certainly the Linnaean system succeeded in congealing into a relatively static form what

---

[2]Berger and Luckmann have characterized this process as 'trying to push a bus in which one is riding' [Peter Berger and Thomas Luckmann. *The Social Construction of Reality* (Garden City: Doubleday & Co., 1966) p. 12]. I would say that, worse yet, it is like trying to look out of the rear window to *watch* oneself push the bus in which one rides.

had been a more fluid and graded world that allowed for change and hence for a measure of historicity.

The hundred years that separate Linnaeus from Darwin saw the development of historical geology by Lyell (1797–1875) and an incipient effort to fit the increasing number of fossils that were being uncovered into the earth's newly discovered history. By the time Darwin came along, it was clear to many people that the earth and its creatures had histories. There were fossil series of snails; some fossils were known to be very old, yet looked for all the world like present-day forms; others had no like descendants and had become extinct. Lamarck (1744–1829), who like Linnaeus began by believing in the fixity of species, by 1800 had formulated a theory of evolution that involved a slow historical process, which he assumed to have taken a very, very long time.

Possibly one reason the theory of evolution arose in Western, rather than Eastern, science was that the descriptions of fossil and living forms showing so many close relationships made the orthodox biblical view of the special creation of each and every species untenable; and the question, how living forms merged into one another, pressed for an answer. The Eastern philosophies that accepted connectedness and relatedness as givens did not need to confront this question with the same urgency. In other words, where evidences of evolutionary change did not raise fundamental contradictions and questions, evolutionary theory did not need to be invented to reconcile and answer them. However one, and perhaps the most, important difference between Western evolutionary thinking and Eastern ideas of organismic unity lies in the materialistic and historical elements, which are the earmark of Western evolutionism as formulated by Darwin.

Though most of the elements of Darwinian evolutionary theory existed for at least a hundred years before Darwin, he knit them into a consistent theory that was in line with the mainstream thinking of his time. Irvine writes:

> The similar fortunes of liberalism and natural selection are significant. Darwin's matter was as English as his method. Terrestrial history turned out to be strangely like Victorian history writ large. Bertrand Russell and others have remarked that Darwin's theory was mainly 'an extension to the animal and vegetable world of laissez faire economics'. As a matter of fact, the economic conceptions of utility, pressure of population, marginal fertility, barriers in restraint of trade, the division of labor, progress and adjustment by competition, and the spread of technological improvements can all be paralleled in *The Origin of Species*. But so, alas, can some of the doctrines of English political conservatism. In revealing the importance of time and the hereditary past, in emphasizing the persistence of vestigial structures, the minuteness of variations and the slowness of evolution, Darwin was adding Hooker and Burke to Bentham and Adam Smith. The constitution of the universe exhibited many of the virtues of the English constitution (Irvine, 1972: 98).

One of the first to comment on this congruence was Karl Marx (1818–83) who wrote to Friedrich Engels (1820–95) in 1862, three years after the publication of *The Origin of Species:*

> It is remarkable how Darwin recognizes among beasts and plants his English society with its division of labour, competition, opening up of new markets, 'inventions', and the Malthusian 'struggle for existence'. It is Hobbes's 'bellum omnium contra omnes', [war of all against all] and one is reminded of Hegel's *Phenomenology,* where civil society is described as a 'spriritual animal kingdom', while in Darwin the animal kingdom figures as civil society (quoted in Sahlins, 1976: 101–102).

A similar passage appears in a letter by Engels:

> The whole Darwinist teaching of the struggle for existence is simply a transference from society to living nature of Hobbes's doctrine of 'bellum omnium contra omnes' and of the bourgeois-economic doctrine of competition together with Malthus's theory of population. When this conjurer's trick has been performed ... the same theories are transferred back again from organic nature into history and now it is claimed that their validity as eternal laws of human society has been proved (*ibid.*).

The very fact that essentially the same mechanism of evolution through natural selection was postulated independently and at about the same time by two English naturalists, Darwin and Alfred Russel Wallace (1823–1913), shows that the basic ideas were in the air — which is not to deny that it took genius to give them logical and convincing from.

Darwin's theory of *The Origin of Species by Means of Natural Selection,* published in 1859, accepted the fact of evolution and undertook to explain how it could have come about. He had amassed large quantities of data to show that historical change had taken place, both from the fossil records and from his observations as a naturalist on the Beagle. He pondered why some forms had become extinct and others had survived to generate new and different forms. The watchword of evolution seemed to be: be fruitful and modify, one that bore a striking resemblance to the ways of animal and plant breeders. Darwin corresponded with many breeders and himself began to breed pigeons. He was impressed by the way in which breeders, through careful selection, could use even minor variations to elicit major differences, and was searching for the analog in nature to the breeders' techniques of selecting favorable variants. A prepared mind therefore encountered Malthus's *Essay on the Principles of Population* (1798). In his *Autobiography,* Darwin writes:

> In October 1838, that is, fifteen months after I had begun my systematic enquiry, I happened to read for amusement Malthus on *Population,* and being well prepared to appreciate the struggle for existence which everywhere goes on from long-continued observation of the habits of animals and plants, it at once struck me that under these circumstances favourable variations would tend to be preserved and unfavourable ones to be destroyed. The result of this would be the formation of new species. Here, then, I had at last got a theory by which to work (Darwin, Francis, 1958: 42–43).

Incidentally, Wallace also acknowledged being led to his theory by reading Malthus. Wrote Wallace:

> The most interesting coincidence in the matter, I think, is, that I, *as well as Darwin,* was led to the theory itself through Malthus ... It suddenly flashed upon me that all animals are necessarily thus kept down — 'the struggle for existence' — while *variations,* on which I was always thinking, must necessarily often be *beneficial,* and would then cause those varieties to increase while the injurious variations diminished' (ibid.; original emphasis).

Both, therefore, saw in Malthus's struggle for existence the working of a natural law which effected what Herbert Spencer had called the 'survival of the fittest'.

The three principal ingredients of Darwin's theory of evolution are: endless variation, natural selection from among the variants, and the resulting survival of the fittest. Given the looseness of many of his arguments — he credited himself with being an expert wriggler — it is surprising that his explanation has found such wide acceptance. One reason probably lies in the fact that Darwin's theory was historical and materialistic, characteristics that are esteemed as virtues; another, perhaps in its intrinsic optimism — its notion of progressive development of species, one from another — which fit well into the meritocratic ideology encouraged by the early successes of British mercantilism, industrial capitalism and imperialism.

But not only did Darwin's interpretation of the history of life on earth fit in well with the social doctrines of nineteenth-century liberalism and individualism. It was used in turn to support them by rendering them aspects of natural law. Herbert Spencer is usually credited with having brought Darwinism into social theory. The body of ideas came to be known as social Darwinism and gained wide acceptance in Britain and the United States in the latter part of the nineteenth and on into the twentieth century. For example, John D. Rockefeller proclaimed in a Sunday school address:

> The growth of a large business is merely the survival of the fittest . . . The American Beauty rose can be produced in the splendor and fragrance which bring cheer to its beholder only by sacrificing the early buds which grow up around it. This is not an evil tendency in business. It is merely the working-out of a law of nature and a law of God (Hofstadter, 1955: 45).

The circle was therefore complete: Darwin consciously borrowed from social theorists such as Malthus and Spencer some of the basic concepts of evolutionary theory. Spencer and others promptly used Darwinism to reinforce these very social theories and in the process bestowed upon them the force of natural law.[3]

Sexual Selection

It is essential to expand the foregoing analysis of the mutual influences of Darwinism and nineteenth-century social doctrine by looking critically at the Victorian picture Darwin painted of the relations between the sexes, and of the roles that males and females play in the evolution of animals and humans. For although the ethnocentric bias of Darwinism is widely acknowledged, its blatant sexism — or more correctly, androcentrism (male-centeredness) — is rarely mentioned, presumably because it has not been noticed by Darwin scholars, who have mostly been men. Already in the nineteenth century, indeed within Darwin's life time, feminists such as Antoinette Brown Blackwell (1975),[4] and Eliza Burt Gamble (1894) called attention to the obvious male bias pervading his arguments. But these women did not have Darwin's or Spencer's professional status or scientific experience; nor indeed could they, given their limited opportunities for education, travel and participation in the affairs of the world. Their books were hardly acknowledged or discussed by professionals, and they have been, till now, merely ignored and excluded from the record. However, it is important to expose Darwin's androcentrism, and not only for historical reasons, but because it remains an integral and unquestioned part of contemporary biological theories.

---

[3]Though not himself a publicist for social Darwinism like Spencer, there can be no doubt that Darwin accepted its ideology. For example, near the end of *The Descent of Man* he writes: 'There should be open competition for all men; and the most able should not be prevented by laws or customs from succeeding best and rearing the largest number of offspring'. Marvin Harris has argued that Darwinism, in fact, should be known as biological Spencerism, rather than Spencerism as social Darwinism. For a discussion of the issue, *pro* and *con, see* Marvin Harris, *The Rise of Anthropological Theory; A History of Theories of Culture* Thomas Y. Crowell, New York, 1968), Ch. 5: Spencerism; and responses by Derek Freeman and others in *Current Anthropology* 15 (1974), 211–237.

[4]Antoinette Brown Blackwell, *The Sexes Throughout Nature* (G. P. Putnam's Sons, New York, 1975); reprinted Westport, Conn.: Hyperion Press, 1978). Excerpts in which Blackwell argues against Darwin and Spencer have been reprinted in Alice S. Rossi (Ed.) *The Feminist Papers* (New York: Bantam Books, 1974), pp. 356–377.

Early in *The Origin of Species,* Darwin defines sexual selection as one mechanism by which evolution operates. The Victorian and androcentric biases are obvious:

> This form of selection depends, not on a struggle for existence in relation to other organic beings or to external conditions, but on a struggle of individuals of one sex, generally males, for the possession of the other sex (Darwin, Charles: 69).

And,

> Generally, the most vigorous males, those which are best fitted for their places in nature, will leave most progeny. But in many cases, victory depends not so much on general vigor, as on having special weapons confined to the male sex (*ibid.*).

The Victorian picture of the active male and the passive female becomes even more explicit later in the same paragraph:

> the males of certain hymenopterous insects [bees, wasps, ants] have been frequently seen by that inimitable observer, M. Fabre, fighting for a particular female who sits by, an apparently unconcerned beholder of the struggle, and then retires with the conqueror (*ibid.*).

Darwin's anthropomorphizing continues, as it develops that many male birds 'perform strange antics before the females, which, standing by as spectators, at last choose the most attractive partner'. However, he worries that whereas this might be a reasonable way to explain the behavior of peahens and female birds of paradise whose consorts anyone can admire, 'it is doubtful whether [the tuft of hair on the breast of the wild turkey-cock] can be ornamental in the eyes of the female bird'. Hence Darwin ends this brief discussion by saying that he 'would not wish to attribute all sexual differences to this agency'.

Some might argue in defense of Darwin that bees (or birds, or what have you) do act that way. But the very language Darwin uses to describe these behaviors disqualifies him as an 'objective' observer. His animals are cast into roles from a Victorian script. And whereas no one else can claim to have solved the important methodological question of how to disembarrass oneself of one's anthropocentric and cultural biases when observing animal behavior, surely one must begin by trying.

After the publication of *The Origin of Species,* Darwin continued to think about sexual selection and in 1871, he published *The Descent of Man and Selection in Relation to Sex,* a book in which he describes in much more detail how sexual selection operates in the evolution of animals and humans.

In the aftermath of the outcry *The Descent* raised among fundamentalists, much has been made of the fact that Darwin threatened the special place Man was assigned by the Bible and treated him as though he was just another kind of animal. But he did nothing of the sort. The Darwinian synthesis did not end anthropocentrism or androcentrism in biology. On the contrary, Darwin made them part of biology by presenting as 'facts of nature' interpretations of animal behavior that reflect the social and moral outlook of his time.

In a sense, anthropocentrism is implicit in the fact that we humans have named, catalogued, and categorized the world around us, including ourselves. Whether we stress our upright stance, our opposable thumbs, our brain, or our language, to ourselves we are creatures apart and very different from all others. But the scientific view of ourselves is also profoundly androcentric. *The Descent of Man* is quite literally *his* journey. Elaine Morgan rightly says:

> It's just as hard for man to break the habit of thinking of himself as central to the species as it was to break the habit of thinking of himself as central to the universe. He sees himself quite unconsciously as the main line of evolution, with a female satellite revolving around him as the moon revolves around the earth. This not only causes him to overlook valuable clues to our ancestry, but sometimes leads him into making statements that are arrant and demonstrable nonsense ... Most of the books forget about [females] for most of the time. They drag her on stage rather suddenly for the obligatory chapter on Sex and Reproduction, and then say: 'All right, love, you can go now', while they get on with the real meaty stuff about the Mighty Hunter with his lovely new weapons and his lovely new straight legs racing across the Pleistocene plains. Any modifications of her morphology are taken to be imitations of the Hunter's evolution, or else designed solely for his delectation (Morgan, 1973: 3–4).

To expose the Victorian roots of post-Darwinian thinking about human evolution, we must start by looking at Darwin's ideas about sexual selection in *The Desecent,* where he begins the chapter entitled 'Principles of Sexual Selection' by setting the stage for the active, pursuing male:

> With animals which have their sexes separated, the males necessarily differ from the females in their organs of reproduction; and these are the primary sexual characters. But the sexes differ in what Hunter has called secondary sexual characters, which are not directly connected with the act of reproduction; for instance, the male possesses certain organs of sense or locomotion, of which the female is quite destitute, or has them more highly-developed, in order that he may readily find or reach her; or again the male has special organs or prehension for holding her securely (Darwin, Charles, p. 567).

Moreover, we soon learn:

> in order that the males should seek efficiently, it would be necessary that they should be endowed with strong passions; and the acquirement of such passions would naturally follow from the more eager leaving a larger number of offspring than the less eager (*ibid.*: 580).

But Darwin is worried because among some animals, males and females do not appear to be all that different:

> a double process of selection has been carried on; that the males have selected the more attractive females, and the latter the more attractive males ... But from what we know of the habits of animals, this view is hardly probable, for the male is generally eager to pair with any female (*ibid.*: 582).

Make no mistake, wherever you look among animals, eagerly promiscuous males are pursuing females, who peer from behind languidly drooping eyelids to discern the strongest and handsomest. Does it not sound like the wishfulfillment dream of a proper Victorian gentleman?

This is not the place to discuss Darwin's long treatise in detail. Therefore, let this brief look at animals suffice as background for his section on Sexual Selection in Relation to Man. Again we can start on the first page: 'Man is more courageous, pugnacious and energetic than woman, and has more inventive genius'.(*ibid.*: 867), Among 'savages', fierce, bold men are constantly battling each other for the possession of women and this has affected the secondary sexual characteristics of both. Darwin grants that there is some disagreement whether there are 'inherent differences' between men and women, but suggests that by analogy with lower animals it is 'at least probable'. In fact, 'Woman seems to differ from man in mental disposition, chiefly in her greater tenderness and less selfishness' (*ibid.*: 873), for:

> Man is the rival of other men; he delights in competition, and this leads to ambition which passes too easily into selfishness. These latter qualities seem to be his natural and unfortunate birthright.

This might make it seem as though women are better than men after all, but not so:

> The chief distinction in the intellectual powers of the two sexes is shown by man's attaining to a higher eminence, in whatever he takes up, than can women — whether requiring deep thought, reason, or imagination, or merely the use of the senses and hands. If two lists were made of the most eminent men and women in poetry, painting, sculpture, music (inclusive both of composition and performance), history, science, and philosophy, with half-a-dozen names under each subject, the two lists would not bear comparison. We may also infer ... that if men are capable of a decided pre-eminence over women in many subjects, the average of mental power in man must be above that of woman ... [Men have had] to defend their females, as well as their young, from enemies of all kinds, and to hunt for their joint subsistence. But to avoid enemies or to attack them with success, to capture wild animals, and to fashion weapons, requires the aid of the higher mental faculties, namely, observation, reason, invention, or imagination. These various faculties will thus have been continually put to the test and selected during manhood (*ibid.*: 873–874).

'Thus', the discussion ends, 'man has ultimately become superior to woman' and it is a good thing that men pass on their characteristics to their daughters as well as to their sons, 'otherwise it is probable that man would have become as superior in mental endowment to woman, as the peacock is in ornamental plumage to the peahen'.

So here it is in a nutshell: men's mental and physical qualities were constantly improved through competition for women and hunting, while women's minds would have become vestigial if it were not for the fortunate circumstance that in each generation daughters inherit brains from their fathers.

Another example of Darwin's acceptance of the conventional mores of his time is his interpretation of the evolution of marriage and monogamy:

> ... it seems probable that the habit of marriage, in any strict sense of the word, has been gradually developed; and that almost promiscuous or very loose intercourse was once very common throughout the world. Nevertheless, from the strength of the feeling of jealousy all through the animal kingdom, as well as from the analogy of lower animals ... I cannot believe that absolutely promiscuous intercourse prevailed in times past ... (*ibid.*: 895).

Note the moralistic tone; and how does Darwin know that strong feelings of jealousy exist 'all though the animal kingdom?' For comparison, it is interesting to look at Engels, who, working largely from the same early anthropological sources as Darwin, had this to say:

> As our whole presentation has shown, the progress which manifests itself in these successive forms [from group marriage to pairing marriage to what he refers to as 'monogamy supplemented by adultery and prostitution'] is connected with the peculiarity that women, but not men, are increasingly deprived of the sexual freedom of group marriage. In fact, for men group marriage actually still exists even to this day. What for the woman is a crime entailing grave legal and social consequences is considered honorable in a man or, at the worse, a slight moral blemish which he cheerfully bears ... Monogamy arose from the concentration of considerable wealth in the hands of a single individual — a man — and from the need to bequeath this wealth to the children of that man and of no other. For this purpose, the monogamy of the woman was required, not that of the man, so this monogamy of the woman did not in any way interfere with open or concealed polygamy on the part of the man (Engels, 1972: 138).

Clearly, Engels did not accept the Victorian code of behavior as our natural biological heritage.

Sociobiology: A New Scientific Sexism

The theory of sexual selection went into a decline during the first half of this century, as efforts to verify some of Darwin's examples showed that many of the features he had thought were related to success in mating could not be legitimately regarded in that way. But it has lately regained its respectability, and contemporary discussions of reproductive fitness often cite examples of sexual selection.[5] Therefore, before we go on to discuss human evolution, it is helpful to look at contemporary views of sexual selection and sex roles among animals (and even plants).

Let us start with a lowly alga that one might think impossible to stereotype by sex. Wolfgang Wickler, an ethologist at the University of Munich, writes in his book on sexual behavior patterns (a topic which Konrad Lorenz tells us in the Introduction is crucial in deciding which sexual behaviors to consider healthy and which diseased):

> Even among very simple organisms such as algae, which have threadlike rows of cells one behind the other, one can observe that during copulation the cells of one thread act as males with regard to the cells of a second thread, but as females with regard to the cells of a third thread. The mark of male behavior is that the cell actively crawls or swims over to the other; the female cell remains passive (Wickler, 1973: 23).

The circle is simple to construct: one starts with the Victorian stereotype of the active male and the passive female, then looks at animals, algae, bacteria, people, and calls all passive behavior feminine, active or goal-oriented behavior masculine. And it works! The Victorian stereotype is biologically determined: even algae behave that way.

But let us see what Wickler has to say about Rocky Mountain Bighorn sheep, in which the sexes cannot be distinguished on sight. He finds it 'curious':

> that between the extremes of rams over eight years old and lambs less than a year old one finds every possible transition in age, but no other differences whatever; the bodily form, the structure of the horns, and the color of the coat are the same for both sexes.

Now note: ' . . . the typical female behavior is absent from this pattern.' Typical of what? Obviously not of Bighorn sheep. In fact we are told that 'even the males often cannot recognize a female', indeed, 'the females are only of interest to the males during rutting season'. How does he know that the males do *not* recognize the females? Maybe these sheep are so weird that most of the time they relate to a female as though she were just another sheep, and whistle at her (my free translation of 'taking an interest') only when it is a question of mating. But let us get at last to how the *females* behave. That is astonishing, for it turns out:

> that *both* sexes play two roles, either that of the male or that of the young male. Outside the rutting season the females behave like young males, during the rutting season like aggressive older males (*ibid.*: original emphasis).

[5]One of the most explicit contemporary examples of this literature is E. O. Wilson's *Sociobiology: The New Synthesis* Harvard University Press, Belknap Press, (Cambridge: 1975); *see* especially chapters 1, 14–16 and 27.

In fact:

> There is a line of development leading from the lamb to the high ranking ram, and the female animals (♀) behave exactly as though they were in fact males (♂) whose development was retarded ... We can say that the only fully developed mountain sheep are the powerful rams. ...

At last the androcentric paradigm is out in the open: females are always measured against the standard of the male. Sometimes they are like young males, sometimes like older ones; but never do they reach what Wickler calls 'the final stage of fully mature physical structure and behavior possible to this species'. That, in his view, is reserved for the rams.

Wickler bases this discussion on observations by Valerius Geist, whose book, *Mountain Sheep,* contains many examples of how androcentric biases can color observations as well as interpretations and restrict the imagination to stereotypes. One of the most interesting is the following:

> Matched rams, usually strangers, begin to treat each other like females and clash until one acts like a female. This is the loser in the fight. The rams confront each other with displays, kick each other, threat jump, and clash till one turns and accepts the kicks, displays, and occasional mounts of the larger without aggressive displays. The loser is not chased away. The point of the fight is not to kill, maim, or even drive the rival off, but to treat him like a female (Geist, 1971: 190).

This description would be quite different if the interaction were interpreted as something other than a fight, say as a homosexual encounter, a game, or a ritual dance. The fact is that it contains none of the elements that we commonly associate with fighting. Yet because Geist casts it into the imagery of heterosexuality and aggression, it becomes perplexing.

There would be no reason to discuss these examples if their treatments of sex differences or of male/female behavior were exceptional. But they are in the mainstream of contemporary sociobiology, ethology, and evolutionary biology.

A book that has become a standard reference is George Williams's (1975) *Sex and Evolution.* It abounds in blatantly biased statements that describe as 'careful' and 'enlightened' research reports that support the androcentric paradigm, and as questionable or erroneous those that contradict it. Masculinity and femininity are discussed with reference to the behavior of pipefish and seahorses; and cichlids and catfish are judged downright abnormal because both sexes guard the young. For present purposes it is sufficient to discuss a few points that are raised in the chapter entitled 'Why Are Males Masculine and Females Feminine and, Occasionally, Vice-Versa?'

The very title gives one pause, for if the words masculine and feminine do not mean of, or pertaining, respectively, to males and females, what *do* they mean — particularly in a scientific context? So let us read.

On the first page we find:

> Males of the more familiar higher animals take less of an interest in the young. In courtship they take a more active role, are less discriminating in choice of mates, more inclined toward promiscuity and polygamy, and more contentious among themselves.

We are back with Darwin. The data are flimsy as ever, but doesn't it sound like a description of the families on your block?

The important question is who are these 'more familiar higher animals?' Is their behavior typical, or are we familiar with them because, for over a century, androcentric biologists have paid disproportionate attention to animals whose behavior resembles those human social traits that they would like to interpret as biologically determined and hence out of our control?

Williams' generalization quoted above gives rise to the paradox that becomes his chief theoretical problem:

> Why, if each individual is maximizing its own genetic survival should the female be less anxious to have her eggs fertilized than a male is to fertilize them, and why should the young be of greater interest to one than to the other?

Let me translate this sentence for the benefit of those unfamiliar with current evolutionary theory. The first point is that an individual's *fitness* is measured by the number of her or his offspring that survive to reproductive age. The phrase, 'the survival of the fittest', therefore signifies the fact that evolutionary history is the sum of the stories of those who leave the greatest numbers of descendants. What is meant by each individual 'maximizing its own genetic survival' is that every one tries to leave as many viable offspring as possible. (Note the implication of conscious intent. Such intent is not exhibited by the increasing number of humans who intentionally *limit* the numbers of their offspring. Nor is one, of course, justified in ascribing it to other animals.)

One might therefore think that in animals in which each parent contributes half of each offspring's genes, females and males would exert themselves equally to maximize the number of offspring. However, we know that according to the patriarchal paradigm, males are active in courtship, whereas females wait passively. This is what Williams means by females being 'less anxious' to procreate than males. And of course we also know that 'normally' females have a disproportionate share in the care of their young.

So why these asymmetries? The explanation: 'The *essential* difference between the sexes is that females produce large immobile gametes and males produce small mobile ones' (my italics). This is what determines their 'different optimal strategies'. So if you have wondered why men are promiscuous and women faithfully stay at home and care for the babies, the reason is that males 'can quickly replace wasted gametes and be ready for another mate', whereas females 'can not so readily replace a mass of yolky eggs or find a substitute father for an expected litter'. Therefore females must 'show a much great degree of caution' in the choice of a mate than males.

E. O. Wilson says the same thing somewhat differently:

> One gamete, the egg, is relatively very large and sessile; the other, the sperm, is small and motile . . . . The egg possesses the yolk required to launch the embryo into an advanced state of development. Because it represents a considerable energetic investment on the part of the mother the embryo is often sequestered and protected, and sometimes its care is extended into the postnatal period. *This is the reason why* parental care is *normally* provided by the female . . . . [6] (my italics)

[6]Edward O. Wilson, *Sociobiology: The New Synthesis. (Harvard University Press,* Belknap Press, Cambridge, 1975), pp. 316–317. Wilson and others claim that the growth of a mammalian fetus inside its mother's womb represents an energetic 'investment' on her part, but it is not clear to me why they believe that. Presumably the mother eats and metabolizes, and some of the food she eats goes into building the growing embryo. Why does that represent an investment of *her* energies? I can see that the embryo of an undernourished woman perhaps requires such an investment — in which case what one would have to do is see that the mother gets enough to eat. But what 'energy' does a properly nourished woman 'invest' in her embryo (or, indeed, in her egg)? It would seem that the notion of pregnancy as 'investment' derives from the interpretation of pregnancy as a debilitating disease (see Datha Brack, 1979).

Though these descriptions fit only some of the animal species that reproduce sexually, and are rapidly ceasing to fit human domestic arrangements in many portions of the globe,[7] they do fit the patriarchal model of the household. Clearly, androcentric biology is busy as ever trying to provide biological 'reasons' for a particular set of human social arrangements.

The ethnocentrism of this individualistic, capitalistic model of evolutionary biology and sociobiology with its emphasis on competition and 'investments', is discussed by Sahlins (1976) in his monograph. *The Use and Abuse of Biology.* He gives many examples from other cultures to show how these theories reflect a narrow bias that disqualifies them from masquerading as descriptions of universals in biology. But, like other male critics, Sahlins fails to notice the obvious androcentrism.

About thirty years ago, Ruth Herschberger (1948) wrote a delightfully funny book called *Adam's Rib,* in which she spoofed the then current androcentric myths regarding sex differences. When it was reissued in 1970, the book was not out of date. In the chapter entitled 'Society Writes Biology', she juxtaposes the then (and now) current patriarchal scenario of the dauntless voyage of the active, agile sperm toward the passively receptive, sessile egg to an improvised 'matriarchal' account. In it the large, competent egg plays the central role and we can feel only pity for the many millions of miniscule, fragile sperm most of which are too feeble to make it a fertilization.

This brings me to a question that always puzzles me when I read about the female's larger energetic investment in her egg than the male's in his sperm: there is an enormous disproportion in the *numbers* of eggs and sperms that participate in the act of fertilization. Does it really take more 'energy' to generate the one or relatively few eggs than the large excess of sperms required to achieve fertilization? In humans the disproportion is enormous. In her life time, an average woman produces about four hundred eggs, of which in present-day Western countries, she will 'invest' only in about 2.2.[8] Meanwhile the average man generates several billions of sperms to secure those same 2.2 investments!

Needless to say, I have no idea how much 'energy' is involved in producing, equipping and ejaculating a sperm cell along with the other necessary components of the ejaculum that enable it to fertilize an egg, nor how much is involved in releasing an egg from the ovary, reabsorbing it in the oviduct if unfertilized (a partial dividend on the investment), or incubating 2.2 of them to birth. But neither do those who propound the existence and importance of women's disproportionate energetic investments. Furthermore, I attach no significance to these questions, since I do not believe that the details of our economic and social arrangements reflect our evolutionary history. I am only trying to show how feeble is the 'evidence' that is being put forward to argue the evolutionary basis (hence *naturalness*) of woman's role as homemaker.

The recent resurrection of the theory of sexual selection and the ascription of asymmetry to the 'parental investments' of males and females are probably not unrelated to the rebirth of the women's movement. We should remember that Darwin's

---

[7] For example, at present in the United States, 24 per cent of households are headed by women and 46 per cent of women work outside the home. The fraction of women who work away from home while raising children is considerably larger in several European countries and in China.

[8] Furthermore, a woman's eggs are laid down while she is an embryo, hence at the expense of her mother's 'metabolic investment'. This raises the question whether grandmothers devote more time to grandchildren they have by their daughters than to those they have by their sons. I hope sociobiologists will look into this.

theory of sexual selection was put forward in the midst of the first wave of feminism.[9] It seems that when women threaten to enter as equals into the world of affairs, androcentric scientists rally to point out that our *natural* place is in the home.

The Evolution of Man

Darwin's sexual stereotypes are doing well also in the contemporary literature on human evolution. This is a field in which facts are few and specimens are separated often by hundreds of thousands of years, so that maximum leeway exists for investigator bias. Almost all the investigators have been men; it should therefore come as no surprise that what has emerged is the familiar picture of Man the Toolmaker. This extends so far that when skull fragments estimated to be 250,000 years old turned up among the stone tools in the gravel beds of the Thames at Swanscombe and paleontologists decided that they are probably those of a female, we read that 'The Swanscombe woman, or her husband, was a maker of hand axes . . . ' (Howells, 1973: 88). (Imagine the reverse: The Swanscombe man, or his wife, was a maker of axes. . . .) The implication is that if there were tools, the Swanscombe *woman* could not have made them. But we now know that even apes make tools. Why not women?

Actually, the idea that the making and use of tools were the main driving forces in evolution has been modified since paleontological finds and field observations have shown that apes both use and fashion tools. Now the emphasis is on the human use of tools as weapons for hunting. This brings us to the myth of Man the Hunter, who had to invent not only tools, but also the social organizations that allowed him to hunt big animals. He also had to roam great distances and learn to cope with many and varied circumstances. We are told that this entire constellation of factors stimulated the astonishing and relatively rapid development of his brain that came to distinguish Man from his ape cousins. For example, Kenneth Oakley writes:

> Men who made tools of the standard type . . . must have been capable of forming in their minds images of the ends to which they laboured. Human culture in all its diversity is the outcome of this capacity for conceptual thinking, but the leading factors in its development are tradition coupled with invention. The primitive hunter made an implement in a particular fashion largely because as a child he watched his father at work or because he copied the work of a hunter in a neighbouring tribe. The standard hand-axe was not conceived by any one individual *ab initio,* but was the result of exceptional individuals in successive generations not only copying but occasionally improving on the work of their predecessors. As a result of the co-operative hunting, migrations and rudimentary forms of barter, the traditions of different groups of primitive hunters sometimes became blended (Oakley, K., 1972: 81).

It seems a remarkable feat of clairvoyance to see in such detail what happened some 250,000 years in pre-history, complete with the little boy, and his little stone chipping set just like daddy's big one.

[9]Nineteenth-century feminism is often dated from the publication in 1792 of Mary Wollstonecraft's (1759-1797) *A Vindication of the Rights of Woman;* it continued right through Darwin's century. Darwin was well into his work at the time of the Seneca Falls Declaration (1848), which begins with the interesting words:

> When, in the course of human events, it becomes necessary for one portion of the family of man to assume among the people of the earth a position different from that which they have hitherto occupied, but one to which the *laws of nature and of nature's God* entitle them . . . (my italics).

And John Stuart Mill (1806-1873) published his essay on *The Subjection of Women* in 1869, ten years after *Darwin's Origin of Species* and two years before the *Descent of Man and Selection in Relation to Sex.*

It is hard to know what reality lurks behind the reconstructions of Man Evolving. Since the time when we and the apes diverged some fifteen million years ago, the main features of human evolution that one can read from the paleontological finds are the upright stance, reduction in the size of the teeth, and increase in brain size. But finds are few and far between both in space and in time until we reach the Neanderthals some 70,000 to 40,000 years ago — a jaw or skull, teeth, pelvic bones, and often only fragments of them.[10] From such bits of evidence as these come the pictures and statues we have all seen of that line of increasingly straight and upright, and decreasingly hairy and ape-like men marching in single file behind *Homo sapiens,* carrying their clubs, stones, or axes; or that other one of a group of beetle-browed and bearded hunters bending over the large slain animal they have brought into camp, while over on the side long-haired, broad-bottomed females nurse infants at their pendulous breasts.

Impelled, I suppose, by recent feminist critiques of the evolution of Man the Hunter, a few male anthropologists have begun to take note of Woman the Gatherer, and the stereotyping goes on as before. For example Howells, who acknowledges these criticisms as just, nontheless assumes 'the classic division of labor between the sexes' and states as fact that stone age men roamed great distances 'on behalf of the whole economic group, while the women were restricted to within the radius of a fraction of a day's walk from camp'. Needless to say, he does not *know* any of this.

One can equally well assume that the responsibilities for providing food and nurturing young were widely dispersed through the group that needed to cooperate and devise many and varied strategies for survival. Nor is it obvious why tasks needed to have been differentiated by sex. It makes sense that the gatherers would have known how to hunt the animals they came across; that the hunters gathered when there was nothing to catch, and that men and women did some of each, though both of them probably did a great deal more gathering than hunting. After all, the important thing was to get the day's food, not to define sex roles. Bearing and tending the young have not necessitated a sedentary way of life among nomadic peoples right to the present, and both gathering and hunting probably required movement over large areas in order to find sufficient food. Hewing close to home probably accompanied the transition to cultivation, which introduced the necessity to stay put for planting, though of course not longer than required to harvest. Without fertilizers and crop rotation, frequent moves were probably essential parts of early farming.

Being sedentary ourselves, we tend to assume that our foreparents heaved a great sigh of relief when they invented argriculture and could at last stop roaming. But there is no reason to believe this. Hunter/gatherers and other people who move with their food still exist. And what has been called the agricultural 'revolution' probably took considerably longer than all of recorded history. During this time, presumably some people settled down while others remained nomadic, and some did some of each, depending on place and season.

We have developed a fantastically limited and stereotypic picture of ways of life that evolved over many tens of thousands of years, and no doubt varied in lots of ways that we do not even imagine. It is true that by historic times, which are virtually now in the scale of our evolutionary history, there were agricultural settlements, including a few

[10]There are also occasional more perfect skeletons, such as that of *Homo errectus* at Choukoutien, commonly known as Peking Man, who was in fact a woman.

towns that numbered hundreds and even thousands of inhabitants. By that time labor was to some extent divided by sex, though anthropologists have shown that right to the present, the division can be different in different places. There are economic and social reasons for the various delineations of sex roles. We presume too much when we try to read them in the scant record of our distant prehistoric past.

Nor are we going to learn them by observing our nearest living relatives amongst the apes and monkeys, as some biologists and anthropologists are trying to do. For one thing, different species of primates vary widely in the extent to which the sexes differ in both their anatomy and their social behavior, so that one can find examples of almost any kind of behavior one is looking for by picking the appropriate animal. For another, most scientists find it convenient to forget that present-day apes and monkeys have had as long an evolutionary history as we have had, since the time we and they went our separate ways many millions of years ago. There is no theoretical reason why their behavior should tell us more about our ancestry than our behavior tells us about theirs. It is only anthropocentrism that can lead someone to imagine that 'A possible preadaptation to human ranging for food is the behavior of the large apes, whose groups move more freely and widely compared to gibbons and monkeys, and whose social units are looser' (Howells, 1973: 133). But just as in the androcentric paradigm men evolved while women cheered from the bleachers, so in the anthropocentric one, humans evolved while the apes watched from the trees. This view leaves out not only the fact that the apes have been evolving away from us for as long a time as we from them, but that certain aspects of their evolution may have been a response to our own. So, for example, the evolution of human hunting habits may have put a serious crimp into the evolution of the great apes and forced them to stay in the trees or to hurry back into them.

The current literature on human evolution says very little about the role of language, and sometimes even associates the evolution of language with tool use and hunting — two purportedly 'masculine' characteristics. But this is very unlikely because the evolution of language probably went with biological changes, such as occurred in the structure of the face, larynx, and brain, all slow processes. Tool use and hunting, on the other hand, are cultural characteristics that can evolve much more quickly. It is likely that the more elaborate use of tools, and the social arrangements that go with hunting and gathering, developed in part as a consequence of the expanded human repertory of capacities and needs that derive from our ability to communicate through language.

It is likely that the evolution of speech has been one of the most powerful forces directing our biological, cultural, and social evolution, and it is surprising that its significance has largely been ignored by biologists. But, of course, it does not fit into the androcentric pardigm. No one has ever claimed that women can not talk; so if men are the vanguard of evolution, humans must have evolved through the stereotypically male behaviors of competition, tool use, and hunting.

How to Learn Our History? Some Feminist Strategies

How *did* we evolve? Most people now believe that we became who we are by a historical process, but, clearly, we do not know its course and must use more imagination than facts to reconstruct it. The mythology of science asserts that with many different scientists all asking their own questions and evaluating the answers independently, whatever personal bias creeps into their individual answers is cancelled out when the large picture is put together. This might conceivably be so if scientists were women and men from all sorts of different cultural and social backgrounds who came to science with very different ideologies and interests. But since, in fact, they have been predominantly university-trained white males from privileged social backgrounds, the bias has been narrow and the product often reveals more about the investigator than about the subject being researched.

Since women have not figured in the paradigm of evolution, we need to rethink our evolutionary history. There are various ways to do this:

(1) We can construct one or several estrocentric (female-centred) theories. This is Elaine Morgan's approach in her account of *The Descent of Woman* and Evelyn Reed's in *Woman's Evolution* (1975). Except as a way of parodying the male myths, I find it unsatisfactory because it locks the authors into many of the same unwarranted suppositions that underlie those very myths. For example, both accept the view that our behavior is biologically determined, that what we do is a result of what we were or did millions of years ago. This assumption is unwarranted given the enormous range of human adaptability and the rapid rate of human social and cultural evolution. Of course, there is a place for myth-making and I dream of a long poem that sings women's origins and tells how we felt and what we did; but I do not think that carefully constructed 'scientific' mirror images do much to counter the male myths. Present-day women do not know what prehistoric hunter/gatherer women were up to any more than a male paleontologist like Kenneth Oakley knows what the little toolmaker learned from his dad.

(2) Women can sift carefully the few available facts by paring away the mythology and getting as close to the raw data as possible. And we can try to see what, if any, picture emerges that could lead us to questions that perhaps have *not* been asked and that should, and could, be answered. One problem with this approach is that many of the data no longer exist. Every excavation removes the objects from their locale and all we have left is the researchers' descriptions of what they saw. Since we are concerned about unconscious biases, that is worrisome.

(3) Rather than invent our own myths, we can concentrate, as a beginning, on exposing and analyzing the male myths that hide our overwhelming ignorance, 'for when a subject is highly controversial — and any question about sex is that — one cannot hope to tell the truth' (Woolf, 1945: reprinted 1970: 6)- Women anthropologists have begun to do this. New books are being written, such as *The Female of the Species* (Martin and Voorhis, 1975) and *Toward an Anthropology of Women* (Reiter, 1975), books that expose the Victorian stereotype that runs through the literature of human evolution, and pull together relevant anthropological studies. More important, women who recognize an androcentric myth when they see one and who are able to think beyond it, must do the necessary work in the field, in the laboratories, and in the libraries, and come up with ways of seeing the facts and of interpreting them.

None of this is easy, because women scientists tend to hail from the same socially privileged families and be educated in the same elite universities as our male colleagues. But since we are marginal to the mainstream, we may find it easier than they to watch ourselves push the bus in which we are riding.

As we rethink our history, our social roles, and our options, it is important that we be ever wary of the wide areas of congruence beteen what are obviously ethno- and androcentric assumptions and what we have been taught are the scientifically proven facts of our biology. Darwin was right when he wrote that 'False facts are highly injurious to the progress of science, for they often endure long . . . ' (Darwin, C., p. 909). Androcentric science is full of 'false facts' that have endured all too long and that serve the interests of those who interpret as women's biological heritage the sexual and social stereotypes we reject. To see our alternatives is essential if we are to acquire the space in which to explore who we are, where we have come from, and where we want to go.

We are still in the early stages of a journey. The impact of feminism on biology has been to show the way androcentrism has gone, to expose its limitations and misuses, and to demonstrate that there are other ways to go. This has been no mean achievement.

Feminism has made a crucial contribution by introducing a change in the construction of reality. We have helped to make the shift from a reality in which there was often unquestioned acceptance of the scientific 'facts' about the sexes to a reality in which not only the 'facts' about the sexes are problematic but where the authority of male scientists to construct those facts — frequently in their own interest — is also problematic. The distance travelled already should not be underestimated.

We are helping to change the climate in which biology is produced. We are helping to change the assumptions and the expectations and thereby to promote the emergence of *different* biological knowledge. We have declared that the Emperor isn't wearing any clothes, and he can either insist that he is — and become increasingly absurd — or he can acknowledge his nakedness. Either way he must not pass unchallenged.

References

BLACKWELL, Antoinette Brown (1975) *The sexes throughout nature,* G. W. Putnam's Sons, N.Y., reprinted 1978, Hyperion Press, Westport, Conn.

BRACK, Datha Clapper (1979) 'Displaced — The Midwife by the Male Physician' in Ruth Hubbard *et al.* (Eds.) *Women Look at Biology Looking at Women,* Schenkman Publishing Co., Cambridge, Mass., pp. 83–102.

DARWIN, Charles, *The Origin of the Species and the Descent of Man* New York (Modern Library Edition, New York).

DARWIN, Francis (Ed.) (1958) *The Autobiography of Charles Darwin,* Dover Publications, New York.

EISELEY, Loren (1961) *Darwin's Century,* Doubleday, Anchor Books, Garden City.

ENGELS, Frederick (1972) *The Origin of the Family, Private Property and the State,* E. B. Leacock (Ed.) International Publishers, New York.

GAMBLE, Eliza Burt (1894) *The Evolution of Woman: an inquiry into the dogma of her inferiority to man,* G. P. Putnam's Sons, New York.

GEIS, Valerius (1971) *Mountain Sheep,* University of Chicago Press, Chicago.

HANSBERRY, Lorraine (1969) 'To be Young, Gifted and Black' adapted by Robert Nemiroff from *In Her Own Words,* Prentice Hall, Englewood Cliffs, N.J.

HERSCHBERGER, Ruth (1948) *Adam's Rib,* reprinted edition, Harper and Row, New York, 1970.

HOFSTADTER, Richard (1955) *Social Darwinism in American Thought,* Beacon Press, Boston.

HOWELLS, William (1973) *Evolution of the Genus HOMO,* Addison Wesley Publishing Co. Reading.

IRVINE, William (1972) *Apes, Angels and Victorians,* McGraw Hill, New York.

KUHN, Thomas (1970) *The Structure of Scientific Revolutions* (2nd Ed.) University of Chicago Press, Chicago.

LEWIS, Edwin C. (1968) *Developing Women's Potential,* Iowa State Uni. Press, Ames IA.

MARTIN, M Kay and Barbara VOORHIS (1975) *Female of the Species,* Columbia University Press, New York.

MEIGS, C. D. (1847) 'Lecture on some of the distinctive characteristics of the female' (Paper delivered at the Jefferson Medical College, Philadelphia, Pa.) See Mary Roth Walsh's essay, 'The Quirls of a Woman's Brain' in Ruth Hubbard *et al., Women Look at Biology Looking at Women,* 1979, Schenkman Publishing Co, Cambridge, Mass., pp. 103–125.

MORGAN, Elaine (1973) *The Descent of Woman,* Bantam Books, New York.

OAKLEY, Kenneth P. (1972) *Man the Toolmaker,* British Museum, London.

REED, Evelyn (1975) *Woman's Evolution,* Pathfinder Press, New York.
REITER, Rayna R. (Ed.) (1975) *Toward an Anthropology of Women,* Monthly Review Press, New York.
RICH, Adrienne (1976) *Twenty One Love Poems,* Effie's Press, Emery, Ca.
SAHLINS, Marshall (1976) *The Use and Abuse of Biology,* University of Michigan Press, Ann Arbor.
STANLEY, Julia P. (1972) 'Nominalized Passives' (Paper delivered at the *L inguistic Society of America,* Chapel Hill, N.C., July).
WALSH, Mary Roth (1979) 'The Quirls of a Woman's Brain', in Ruth Hubbard *et al.* (Ed.) *Women Look at Biology Looking at Women,* Schenkman Publishing Co., Cambridge, Mass., pp. 103–125.
WICKLER, Wolfgang (1973) *The Sexual Code: the social behavior of animals and men,* Doubleday, Anchor Books, Garden City.
WOOD, Clive (1969) *Birth Control; Now and Tomorrow,* Peter Davies, London.
WOOLF, Virginia (1957) (first published 1928) *A Room of One's Own,* Harcourt, Brace, Jovanovich, N.Y.

15

Dirty Fingers, Grime and Slag Heaps: Purity and the Scientific Ethic[1]

KATHY OVERFIELD

Science — An Editorial Note

That there is a general chapter to cover all the physical and natural sciences (with the exception of biology) is significant; that this is neither an area of well developed critiques of individual disciplines, nor an area of successful feminist impact, is also significant. The assumptions of 'science' however, are the assumptions of our daily lives with the control of science concentrated in male hands, and in terms of the general framework of this book, it could be expected that a case would be made for 'getting more women into science' so that the direction of scientific research could change, so that different values and assumptions could be included in that circle in which scientific knowledge is produced and distributed. Because there are so few women involved in the scientific enterprise* it would constitute a major task to have them equally represented among the 'powerful' but such a proposal is probably most common among those who address themselves to the problem of women and science.

This however, is not the 'solution' put forward here by Kathy Overfield. She argues that science *is* men's studies and cannot be modified and that a 'woman-centred-science' would be so radically different that it would no longer be invested with the meaning of 'science' as we understand it. It would not be 'science' and therefore, in a society where science is the frame of reference, would be without validity.

Despite the fact that it is possible to perceive science as a dogma and no less open to challenge and enquiry as, for example, the religious dogma which preceded it, science itself permits few heretics. Its system of beliefs must be accepted and rather than taking up the challenge of non-believers, science denigrates them with labels such as spiritualist, mystic of telepath. While much of substance may come from sources outside science, such is the hold of the scientific dogma or ethic over our minds, we are capable of dismissing it, as superstition or mythology, of trivialising it, of spurning its non-rational nature.

Women as well as men have been impressed by the scientific ethic and have acquiesced to its values. Yet, argues Overfield, the scientific ethic *is* the male ethic; it is the ethic of dominance and control, it is the ethic which encodes a dichotomous and unequal division of the objects and events of the world into man/woman, norm/deviant, dominant/subordinate, rational/emotional. To enter science is to accept this scientific ethic, to accept these unequal dichotomies, and for this reason Overfield urges women to eliminate, not modify, the basic constructs of science.

Because all the other 'sciences' which have been analysed in this volume are also party to the 'scientific ethic' and have been directly, and indirectly exposed, it is fitting that this is the most severe and yet perhaps the most significant critique of science, should be the concluding chapter.

Nowhere is the exclusion and absence of women more obvious than in the sciences.[2] The feminist movement too, largely ignores science and technology — except in specific

*That there are so few feminist scientists, in Britain, is a fact that has been appreciated; the organising collective for the Women's Research and Resources Centre Summer School in 1979 had to abandon sessions on women and science/technology for there were no feminist scientists or technologists to be found. Since then the question as to why feminists come from the arts or social sciences has acquired new significance.

[1] My thanks are due to Diana Marquand, who has given me support and helpful criticism in the writing of this chapter.

[2] I use the term 'science' and 'sciences' rather loosely here, in regard to both the 'pure' and 'applied' sciences, reasoning that the same scientific ethic is common to all. The same process and validation is equally necessary to the social sciences.

instances or campaigns. Scientific practice and theory have been going long enough to enable us to draw some conclusions from the present situation. One inescapable conclusion — quite quickly drawn by a woman and certainly a feminist — is that there are remarkably few women involved in science at any level. I would qualify this: there are fewer and fewer women the higher you look in the sciences (particularly among those who control and select the research programmes and carve up the money in consultation with governments and multi-national corporations). There are more women in biology (since biology, it seems, in the popular and scientific view is to do with soft, furry things, and therefore suitable for women — Brighton Women and Science Group [BWSG], 1980) and hardly a sprinkling in nuclear physics or engineering. (In socialist countries, the situation is slightly altered, but the logic is plain to see: there are more women in the lower branches and in those sciences regarded as inferior, such as medicine.)

There is a strict and rigid hierarchy of scientific importance — that is, physics stands much higher in esteem than engineering and chemistry. The social sciences (the debate still rages) have blatantly *not* fitted into a scientific framework pure and simple though nor, in general, have they been any more woman-orientated. Since in subjects such as sociology and anthropology, direct reference must be made to people and societies it has been difficult to limit these to pure dichotomies, to pure 'objectivity'. (What happens then, however, is that 'subjectivity' is introduced as another factor, and turned into an approach in itself — as exemplified in phenomenology, for instance.)

Women, in fact, are excluded both in practice from scientific activity and — more importantly for us to realise — from and by the scientific ethic, ideology, and image-making process. (So are sensitive people generally, but women suffer the double handicap of being rigidly confined by virtue of their sex.) Logically, the exclusion — the substantiation of women's absence — starts very early on and is present, working its way through, at all levels. It's rather late, at university professorship stage, to wonder incredulously why so very few women are in these posts; and it becomes all too easy to fall back on deterministic or biologistic[3] explanations for this (strange!) situation.

The British statistics hold remarkably steady insofar as women's entry to both scientific training and employment is concerned (this though Sex Discrimination Acts and Government reports on education) and show a consistent trend:

In Great Britain in 1975, there were, for every one woman at any particular stage of education, the following ratio of men:

Ratio of men to every one woman:	In all subjects	In science	In engineering and technology
	men/women	men/women	men/women
A level (college)	1.3/1	2.8/1	—
Undergrad.	1.8/1	2.4/1	*24.0/1*
Postgrad.	2.8/1	*5.0/1*	*19.5/1*

(HMSO, 1975, my italics)

[3]Biologism or biological determinism is expressed in arguments, supposedly drawn from biological research and observation, and then maintained to be rigid patterns applicable to human beings. For example, women are said to be 'naturally' nurturant, or 'naturally' intellectually inferior — on the basis of some obscure species' behaviour. 'Sociobiology' is the most recent of this kind of purportedly rational prejudice.

On the teaching side, a comparison between different subjects shows the following ratio:

Ratio of men to every one woman:	In all subjects men/women	In science men/women	In engineering and technology men/women
Professor	48.0/1	*113.4/1*	*No women*
Reader/senior lecturer	15.0/1	25.8/1	*108.6/1*
Lecturer or Assistant	6.5/1	12.0/1	28.7/1

(HMSO, 1975, my italics)

Is it any wonder women feel outnumbered?

Now, there are several explanations put forward for this state of affairs (and if it remains the same, feminist explanations have hardly even started). Some educational experts, Government reports, and most scientists, would have it that this is due to the innate inferiority of women (which must eventually show itself) or, more liberally, that women, for reasons best known to themselves, do not *choose* to enter or pursue the sciences in a persistent, conscientious way (thus reducing the problem to an individualistic/psychological level). For believers of these schools of thought what is needed is more promotion of science, and scientific research, in the schools, in order to attract more women of suitable calibre; or more incentives for women scientists to remain in the jobs.

This approach has never worked and can never work, for it is based on a complete untruth. Science now is the embodiment of values currently esteemed as male and masculine. It is not feminine or female; nor are women or female values wanted. Secondly, we are looking at the wrong end and the wrong reasons (most researchers have not actually asked women scientists why they 'dropped out') if we look at university entrants and teaching posts. Careful analysis of the scientific ethic, as it is now put forward (since its proponents have now managed to eliminate or suppress dissenters) shows just what it means and what feminists are really up against. (And, by the by, what it does, particularly to women but also to sensitive people in general if they do manage to survive and remain in science — Watson and Crick, 1968.)

It is patently not a question of getting more girls to do scientific courses, or of 'sexism' on the part of individuals or institutions. While the scientific ethic and its selection process continue to operate in their present, patriarchal form (and they are firmly embedded in all education and research), one of the weedier entrants to be thinned out will continue to be women.

It is always helpful to look at any system of thought with some reference to who is putting it forward — in other words, in whose interests it is. The story of science is particularly checkered for in its early days it was something not so very different from the alchemist procedure which preceded it. In form and ideology, however, it was miles from both alchemy and orthodox religion. Its roots are very tangled among the rise of capitalism and the influence and growth of the protestant ethic (Weber, 1974) but now

the title 'science' has been exclusively reserved for that knowledge and those skills which can be
systematised and incorporated into the academic culture of the ruling capitalist class. All other
knowledge and skills ... have been denigrated and labelled 'unscientific' (Alam, 1978).

The greater part of the ruling capitalist class has always consisted of men. Patriarchy
requires some sort of legitimation for the fact that women are necessarily kept powerless
and unequal to men, and science has conveniently provided such deterministic
explanations. This has been accomplished largely through the media of biology and
medicine — while female-centred skills (such as midwifery and herbalism) were
eliminated and scorned (Donnison, 1977; Ehrenreich and English, 1976). Our function
has been, and is (supposed) to be, only defined in terms of male hopes and fears. The
widely-accepted view until very recently was neatly summed up in the early 20th century
by a respected scientist:

If the feminine abilities were developed to the same degree as those of the male [woman's] maternal
organs would suffer and we should have before us a repulsive and useless hybrid (Morgan, 1970: 37).

This quotation clearly illustrates two points: firstly, woman has always been seen in
terms of her reproductive functions, and this has led to a concentration on our
reproduction and biology as an explanation for all sorts of differences between women
and men. Secondly, the male is always taken as the starting point for any definition.
Men never see fit to study themselves in the way they study women, for they create the
definitions and the standards from which we can only deviate. A very good example of
the way in which woman is thus objectified by science/scientists is found in the (so-
called) study of female sexuality — which has always been the object of fear, loathing
and male manipulation. Neither the original ideas for research, nor the eventual results,
are 'objective' or 'neutral'. 'Many of the ideas ... reflect particular social values
concerning women .... The concept of female sexuality ... is essentially a passive
one ... ' (Birke, unpublished, 1979).
    Science has appropriated the glories of 'progress' to itself, by attributing these to the
scientific method, and the objectivity of a logically-followed procedure, which has no
reference to its practitioners or the society in which they live. 'Objectivity', in fact, is the
cornerstone of all science. Unfortunately, however, merely to temper it with a little
'subjectivity' is no solution at all: the basic ethos that there is a dichotomy represented
by objectivity and subjectivity remains unchanged. So, too, does woman's position as
the, inevitable, Object. (I have developed these ideas further in Overfield, 1980.)
    The sciences rest on the premise that 'scientific' explanations are a particular way of
interpreting the world and what happens in it, by a process of rational, logical thought
(as against meditation, say). It is almost impossible to disentangle how this philosophy
has remained unchanged and unchallenged, for in its early days and still largely today
(Wallsgrove in BWSG, 1980) science is carried out by particular individuals who hold
certain ideas and assumptions, and who proceed in their work by hunches, illuminated
guesswork, and fits and starts. The ethic, nevertheless, is that science, *per se*, is objective,
rational, logical, untarnished by emotion or prejudice and that it is individual *scientists*
or other people who use or abuse the resulting products or theories either for good or
for bad.
    These basic assumptions (the 'use/abuse' dichotomy; the 'objectivity/subjectivity'
dichotomy) result in several things: science is seen as a collection of pure and objective

facts, almost to the extent of being a reified thing in itself. What individuals choose to do with these simple facts, then, is their affair. The pursuit of scientific 'truth' is an end in itself and bears no relation to the society in which we live, or the circumstances or prejudices under which this pursuit is carried out. Political questions are regarded as anathema; science is not a political form of knowledge according to this argument — and political involvement on the part of individual scientists is regarded as good enough reason to get them out. Thus, scientists are given a *carte blanche* to persist in their role of maintaining the *status quo* under the guise of (and with all the glory of) objectivity (Janson-Smith in BWSG, 1980). As a result, individual scientists are both absolved from blame should their scientific discoveries be 'perverted' or misused, and are prevented from seeing science as a political force, and its practitioners as having some responsibility in how it is used.

Some of these questions about political responsibility have already been asked, however (Rose and Rose, 1976; Kuhn, 1970): my concern is, more specifically, if or where women can 'fit' the scientific model and, further, if we really want to (bearing in mind that alternatives have hardly even been thought up as yet).

The second point is, in a representation of things as dichotomies as in the above examples, what is it which is conjured up in your mind in thinking of the opposite of the scientific ethic as I have described it — irrational, moody, emotional, flighty, intellectually incapable? Could it be — woman?

The form of scientific development had a great deal to do with its origins and rise, when capitalism and imperialism were also intensifying. More than this, however, all these developments were characterised by a certain way of seeing the world (*weltanschaung*: world view), and a certain way of naming what was seen. All these phenomena grew enormously in Western Europe and gave the Europeans the wherewithal to reach other nations and other people. They did not stop at that, however: the scientific ethic, as much as the capitalist and imperialist ethics, was based on exploitation, elimination of rivals, domination and oppression.

This ideology embodied the essential dividing/dichotomising ethos. Now 'rationalist thought' as reflected in the sciences has become the dominant mode, eliminating or denigrating any ideas or cultures in any way at variance. It is based essentially on an aggressive, go-getting, domineering and exploitative view of all things. Since most of its practitioners were (and are) men, some feminists have traced this kind of thought pattern to something inherent in male thought which, by naming itself Subject, must create in opposition, Object (de Beauvoir, 1976; Daly, 1973). Bacon, for instance, pointed out that, in knowing how something works, you can then *control* it. He advocated trying to understand nature precisely for this reason — to find out in order to manipulate and dominate nature (Easlea, 1974).

Feminists have tried to find the source of such a conceptualisation of the world by tracing how female power was different from male power. There is little we can be sure of, but it does seem that societies where women held power were probably not based on this kind of exploitative rationale (Firestone, 1972). It seems more that they were based on harmony than domination; on cooperation than destruction. Mary Daly extends this to imply that societies where men ultimately hold power, will always be based on such an ethic, for ''on top' thinking, imagining and acting is essentially patriarchal' (1973: 94). Daly links this to patriarchal religion ('to be human is to be male is to be the son of God') — which has the effect of totally excluding women from a positive identity in our humanity and womanfulness; while de Beauvoir refers to the distinction between Self and Other as the fundamental presumption. In any case, woman in patriarchal societies — as she is always defined by and in reference to men — is inevitably Other, and more, Object.

More than this however, is the conception of things in the world as being dichotomies, divisions — in distinction to, for example, the Eastern philosophers' understanding of things. Dichotomy runs through the whole of the scientific approach to the world: things are either rational or irrational; thesis or antithesis; objective or subjective; us or them; pure or impure; and perhaps more importantly — I would say, most fundamentally — male or female. Since men were — as far as we know — much more interested in pursuing this kind of understanding and using it for their own ends, they have also been in the envied position of being able to produce all the definitions. The whole point of having categories is to classify and reduce whatever is the *object* of study to a collection of common factors. Science appropriates for itself what are seen as the 'good' bits: logic, rationality, objectivity, experimental proof — and, whether as origin or result — *maleness*. If the male, or masculine, is the baseline from which everything is compared, anything else tends automatically to be defined as deviant, prohibited, or an expression of 'otherness' (Mathieu, 1978; de Beauvoir, 1976). As anthropologists and others have noticed, in a patriarchal society it does not matter *what* is defined as the ethic/esteemed — indeed this varies quite considerably — so long as it also becomes the birthright of men as against women (Miller, 1978). Conversely, it is seen as an achievement to *reach* male standards, to become *equal* on male terms, to attain accredited status. (This is what the liberal approach to women's entry into science represents.)

Protestantism was supposedly more amenable to rationalist understanding and application than was Catholicism. Presumably since the threat to this new knowledge was so great, Protestantism drew its strength from a reversion to Judaism, and science reflected these beliefs in its takeover by an élite of respected 'founding fathers' and its shoring up against opposition by secret (select) Academies and Brotherhoods. (I do not suggest that Catholicism is in any way 'better' or less oppressive of women than Protestantism; it would be more true to say that the oppression takes a different form in different religions. The fact is, however, that Catholic countries tend to be more backward scientifically and less sure about their scientific ethic. This is perhaps partly because Catholic thinking is more closely interwoven with mythology and its Christian roots are more deeply embedded in earlier — sometimes matriarchal — religions. Catholicism is strongest in peasant societies where herbal remedies and ritual observances take account of the changing seasons, etc. Such practices cannot be dismissed as mere "magic" or "superstition": they are in fact a form of science and have actually provided a viable knowledge of medicine for many centuries. This type of "science" or "magico-science" is in fact more global in its approach, relating spiritual, emotional , physical and environmental disorders and seeking to remedy them in a way which restores balance and respects the living organism. It is perhaps no accident that ancient and primitive medicine people were often women and that many of them were burned as witches by an increasingly patriarchal society eager to promote its own aggressive and divisive world-view. Nor is it surprising that patriarchal science should be so involved in splitting the atom and promoting germ warfare: the underlying principle being that natural energy be harnessed, controlled and divided against itself, rather than observing a respect for life in all its contradictions. In fact science has now become the modern religion, and reflects the existing divisions in society. I would argue, however, that science is much more than this, precisely because it is so firmly on the 'good' side of the rational ethic: science can only be disproved by yet more science; and all the esteemed qualities represented by the 'goodies' are in total opposition to what woman is ever (supposed) to be. To be female, according to this ethic (and it has been well sustained and 'proved' — BWSG,1980) is to be irrational, incapable of persistence or conscientiousness (but very good at boring, repetitive tasks), emotional, and subject to all sorts of weird lunar and psychic influences. (I am not saying women are not ever any of these things, but trying to point out the result of using rigid dichotomies.) To be female in a male world is not Self — it must be Other; it is not Subject, but Object — and women have certainly been, and continue to be, prime *objects* of scientific enquiry.

Woman is therefore not simply excluded on a practical level by selection procedures and employment policies; she is only able to enter and pursue a scientific career by virtue of denying everything the scientific ethic says is woman's nature, or by becoming a surrogate man. This choice — to be schizophrenic or a surrogate man — does not appear very attractive to me, nor to most self-respecting women. It is reflected in either a conscious or subconscious withdrawal or removal from patriarchal science. The image, moreover, of 'femininity' propagated by a misogynist form of knowledge is only 'proved' over and over again by the number of female dropouts. Instead of questioning the assumptions of the scientific ethic, explanation is usually sought in biologistic explanations of female character — which of course gets more and more difficult to fathom. If this seems like a vicious circle, it is.

The realisation of what woman's 'nature' is supposed to be, and how women do not fit into science, becomes more and more obvious to girls and women the higher in the scientific process they get (Curran in BWSG, 1980). It is not simply a question of implied imbecility and irrationality (as if that were not enough); it is a constant, subtle and insidious devaluation of everything seen as 'female' — and, obviously therefore, women. To assert oneself powerfully *as a woman*, is impossible. It is only to be expected, therefore, that girls at undergraduate level opt out in larger and larger numbers; or that they divert into the 'softer', lower-ranking sciences such as biology or the social sciences. (Rather than a constant reiteration of woman's inferiority, in these disciplines denigration of woman is accomplished more by ignorance and denial of woman's contribution to knowledge.)

It isn't just a question either of what something is, but also of what it is not: science is not, as it stands, a sensitive, aware, open, challenging field of knowledge. Recognising its inherent powerfulness — and the reflected power of those involved — individuals and corporations have more and more directed science to the ends of exploitation and rape (taking all, giving back nothing). Thus, larger and larger chunks of all countries' scientific budgets are allocated to 'defence' (us/them); and individual scientists have no say whatsoever in what their discoveries will be put to (use/abuse). Scientific research is also a thoroughly cut-throat business, and sensitive people in general are phased out or drop out (Watson and Crick, 1968). It is based on patronage, and the only way to get anywhere is by conforming, not by revolting.

So, the next question is, do women really want to be part of *this* science? For there is no way that we can be on our terms: it is only by accepting woman's inferiority, the stereotypical view of woman's nature, and the consequent, emotionless exploitation of the world, that we will even be allowed in.

In fact there has been an alternative critique of science for as long as the discipline has been in existence, at least in its 'modern, objective' form. Romanticism has criticised science precisely because of its propensity to divide the world, and its refusal to recognise feeling and emotion. The poetic movement which flourished in the 19th century along with science, and which derived much of its energy and ideas from Goethe (poet, scientist, philosopher and politician) stressed, by contrast, wholeness, sensitivity, emotional awareness. In England, Byron, Shelley, Wordsworth, Keats, to name a few, rejected the rationalist, objective approach: they emphasised the importance of feeling and intuition rather than logic in human relationships, and advocated a harmonious living with nature rather than the domination and exploitation of the natural world. They are perhaps the archetypal sensitive 'feminine' men that imperialist England grudgingly spewed forth. Perhaps it was Mary Shelley's particularly feminine intuition which prompted her to foresee some of the possible horrors of the scientific world-view in the story of the monster 'Frankenstein' (much retold and elaborated in our own society).

Poets, since then, have tended to be dismissed as 'effeminate'. S/he is not a figure to be taken seriously in the same way as a football star, pop singer, or white-coated scientist. Indeed it is not commonly known that the Romantic poets wrote about science, politics, ethics and philosophy.

Feminists, too, have dismissed the Romantic tradition. Since it was in fact the only alternative to 19th century rationalism and science, it has been deliberately ridiculed and kept down by the increasingly powerful and encapsulating male capitalist superculture of the 20th century. Many of the important texts of the French and German Romantic movements remain untranslated so that their significance is lost to the mass of the American and English speaking feminist movement. Feminists therefore tend to see Romanticism as male supremacist ideology would like them to see it: a spineless and emasculated preoccupation with love and heartache ; a silly trick used by advertisers to con young women into lipsticks and deodorants. Yet it is in fact an important part of our heritage as women. Jung clearly recognised the relationship between femininity and feeling, emotion, creativity: that 'inner self' which perceives things in a non-rational way. He also warned against the emphasis on the 'outer', masculine, rational self. Where too much importance is placed on this, there is danger of psychic repression which is bound to result in sickness. A dire warning against the over-use or abuse of the scientific method.

I have tried to indicate that the introduction of more 'subjectivity' with regard to science is a total red herring (though I would be the last person to prevent some *feeling*). More subjectivity might enable a few male scientists here and there to burst into tears when their discovery was turned into an 'anti-personnel' killer; it would not alter anything in the funding of such research, the choice of scientists to carry it out; and the appropriation by outside interests for exploitation (Rose and Rose, 1976). Thus, once embarked on a programme of 'science for social control' (which all the 'advanced' nations already are), there is no stopping it. (This is not to reify science, but to recognise the hugely powerful interests involved in science now.) The introduction of 'subjectivity' is also reflected in approaches such as phenomenology and ethnomethodology — totally dominated by men, inevitably. If the fundamental élitist ethic persists, certain individuals or groups will have the right to categorise others, and to pursue their policies willy-nilly on the basis of such categories. Such disasters as Thalidomide, Hiroshima and di-ethyl stilboestrol[4] will recur, again and again — and the scientific concern will be to excuse, to preserve reputations, to mutter about inadequate testing and 'human error'.

Perhaps because there are so few women involved in science generally, the role of most women is — common to any group kept out, in ignorance — to gasp at the horrific results and effects of certain scientific practice. In general we do not have the power to change anything from within — and the scientific enterprise has proven itself fairly immune to gentle change. On the other hand, women will continue to be prime objects of the sciences both because of our powerlessness and because of the way the scientific ethic works itself through. This is particularly the case as regards biology, medicine and the social sciences — for it is to involve women in an impossible contradiction, employing us in greater numbers, only at the price of losing any self-identify — or, rather, to identify *against* ourselves, with the oppressor, per *his* definitions. (I am not saying that any women doctors, biologists, etc. are bound to be nervous wrecks: what I am saying is that we are allowed in only as tokens, on male terms which — so far as the scientific ethic is concerned — completely devalues anything which is regarded as 'female/feminine'.)

The language of science is as important in this alienating process as the practice of sexism: not only the heavy emphasis placed on 'objectivity', but the use of female/male as descriptive, qualitative and fixed categories (based on the social stereotypes of the scientists' world-view). In engineering, *male* parts are those which are active and which penetrate; *female* parts are passively penetrated. *Dominance* and *subordination/slavery* are also used in biology and engineering. This kind of 'naming' process, in such terms, is totally unnecessary — but reflects the real divisions in society, and the basis of oppression.

And of course there is the very word 'objectivity'. Scientific activity is supposed to be objective, value-free, and responsible (see Hubbard, this volume). The underlying ethic, however, is far from any of these. For one thing, the decision-making process, whether it involves the amount of money allocated to scientific research or the way in which the results of that research are used, is totally subjective. The values are those of exploitation and dominance: the abuse of nature and destruction of the environment if not directly of populations. The secrecy of the whole nuclear energy programme and experimental germ warfare are but two results of this so-called 'objectivity' — having defined, the powerholders must keep others out by mystification and secrecy (or academic jargon). But women still see this male activity as objective and responsible. Men being, therefore, more objective and responsible, we tend too readily to allow them authority, to leave them unchallenged in their important work while we get on with cleaning the house and giving the children their tea. Yet what could in fact be more utterly irresponsible than this man-made threat which hangs over our lives, our children's lives, and the lives of our children's children? Man, it seems, reverts to the

---

[4]DES was a drug given, particularly in the US, as a 'morning-after' pill. Thousands of women were not told that the drug they were being prescribed was still on trial, and had certain possible hazards. In fact, well after the time it was realised that DES caused vaginal cancer in the *daughters* of the women to whom it was given, the FDA was reluctant to ban its prescription because of the private corporate interests involved. Depoprovera is an even more recent example. It is indicative that both these products are directed against women as reproducers: a good example of woman as Object.

behaviour of the archetypal patriarch, the great god Saturn who ate his children rather than concede his power to them . . . .

In the face of this totally ingrained dichotomy, producing textbooks showing more girls doing experiments and working in science hardly scratches the surface of oppression. There can be no doubt either, that if women are encouraged to take part in an unchanged science, all we will have will be more women divorced from themselves who have been forced, in order to survive, to see 'female' as equivalent to passive, weak, irrational, emotional and hopeless. Is this what a self-respecting womanhood is asking?

The traditional solution has been that 'more women must get in and kick up a fuss' — however, the stock response to that has been that anyone who kicks up a fuss is unlikely to be promoted, or to stay, within the scientific enterprise for long. The alternative has been suggested that women should still go into science, take all this into themselves day after day, and then, once they have achieved positions of power, set about changing things. Unfortunately, this ignores both the effect of being in any system of thought for any time and yet being able to shake if off easily; and what happens to people once in power in any hierarchical, oppressive society. Tyrants — as much as slaves — tend to absorb and subscribe to the ethic which legitimates their position in the hierarchy.

At the moment, however, we are not even at first base. We have neither the power within the old ethic, nor have we rejected it for what it is. The point about the subjectivity/objectivity argument is that it is always a dichotomy — and the question then becomes, just who has the power to decide what the alternatives are to be? In a patriarchal society, even if objectivity were thrown out of the window tomorrow and subjectivity became the 'in' quality, women could never be the holders of *that* esteemed quality. Until patriarchy is uprooted and the male/female ceases to be a symbol of power/powerlessness it won't much matter to most women, if, instead of being accused and put down for subjectivity and emotion (as now), we were accused of being, say, blue rather than green.

What *do* we want, if not this science? — and it is no solution at all to turn our backs on something which holds so much power over all our lives.

There are, I think, two main effects on women of participating in patriarchal science, which must be recognised and changed. Firstly, we absorb all the hatred and denial (in both women and men) of any qualities which are not valued within the dichotomised ethic. Thus emotion, concern, sensitivity, awareness — are all despised and eliminated (or ghettoised) from day-to-day scientific and social activity. Secondly, this is a very good basis for women to deny our strength to act together *as women*. The first problem is for women to realise that we must act together, if we are to change anything. (I am not saying some men, too, do not want to see a change — but the oppressed must first of all realise their own oppression and act.) This isn't easy, because science is only one reflection of the dichotomies which exist in our society, and is an accurate image of the divisions therein. While a patriarchal, hierarchical, oppressive society exists, so too will a science of that form. (I do not know if patriarchy necessarily implies the rest, but on the basis of evidence so far accrued, it seems fair to say it does.) And so will the objectivity/subjectivity division: male/female being opposing sides, representing opposing qualities. In fact, dichotomy is a complete invention: most things are not, in truth, polar opposites, but are at points on a continuum. There is no such thing, for example, as light or dark: colours merge into each other and are only perceived by us as different colours according to the amount of light let through. Hot is not the opposite of cold; woman is not the opposite of man. (Nevertheless, this is the way we are all taught to read, to think and to conceptualise the world. Children, at school, acquire language and vocabulary by using the concept of opposites. Thus, tall is taught to be the *opposite* of short; fat the opposite of thin; and girls and boys are allocated different colours and different activities according to this dividing ethos. Most languages, in themselves, are also genderised, so the idea of dichotomy is totally ingrained in speech and writing.)

Male science furthers the capitalist, imperialist tradition in which it was begotten: it exploits, rapes, destroys. It mutilates the earth and pollutes the air in its insatiable consumption of carbon-based fuels: it poisons the sea and leaves radioactive waste to destroy our children's children. Meanwhile, mothers in the Thirld World watch their babies die of malnutrition, incapable of absorbing reconstituted, skim milk promoted by multinational corporations. While the male commandos of the world prepare for the biggest punch-up ever (a perverted desire to produce one final all-consuming orgasm from Mother Earth before final re-entry into the womb of nothingness), relatively nothing is spent, for example, on the project to drain the Sud (Sudan) which could provide food for all our children. Are these the priorities of a life-loving society?

It is time women understood what the real dichotomy is: life versus death. As the colonised victims of white male oppression have challenged the dichotomy with their slogan 'black is beautiful' so must we: 'women are strong'. Our strenght must lie, not in semantic arguments about rationality, subjectivity, emotionalism and so on, but in the realisation that the male scientific ethic as it now stands, call it what you will, is utter insanity — but permeates our lives at every level.

It is essential to realise that, as women, we have not only the right, but the responsibility to understand and organise every area of scientific activity; not just as campaigns for free abortion, better ante-natal care, or a faster, drug-aided birth. If women do not get it right, we will carry on being scientific 'objects' and acceding in our own — and humanity's — elimination. Until now, women have not seen the need for a woman-orientated science, or a woman-orientated society: we cannot expect it to be handed us on a gilded plate (except an engraved name-plate for our coffins).

References

ALAM, A. (1978) Science and imperialism, *Race and Class 19.*

De BEAUVOIR, Simone (1976) *The Second Sex*, Penguin, London.

BIRKE, Lynda (1979) 'Sex and the Single Rat: an exploration of ideas concerning animal sex', unpublished.

Brighton Women and Science Group (BWSG) (Eds.) (1980) *Alice Through the Microscope: The Power of Science Over Women's Lives*, Virago, London.

CURRAN, Libby (1980) 'Science education: did she drop out or was she pushed?' in BWSG.

DALY, Mary (1973) *Beyond God the Father*, Beacon Press, Boston.

DONNISON, Jean (1977) *Midwives and Medical Men*, Heinemann, London.

EASLEA, Brian (1974) *Liberation and the Aims of Science*, Chatto and Windus, London.

EHRENREICH, Barbara and Deirdre ENGLISH (1976) *Complaints and Disorders – the sexual politics of sickness*, Writers' and Readers' Publishing Cooperative, London.

FIRESTONE, Shulamith (1972) *The Dialectic of Sex*, Bantam, New York (1975) London. HMSO Statistics of Education.

JANSON-SMITH, Deirdre (1980) 'Sociobiology: so what?' in BWSG.

KUHN, T. (1970) *The Structure of Scientific Revolutions*, Chicago University Press.

MATHIEU, Nicole Claude (1978) *Ignored by Some, Denied by Others*, WRRC Explorations in Feminism No. 2, London.

MILLER, Jean Baker (1978) (Ed.) *Psychoanalysis and Women*, Pelican, London.
MORGAN, Robin (Ed.) (1970) *Sisterhood is Powerful*, Vintage, New York.
OVERFIELD, Kathy (1980) 'The packaging of women: science and our sexuality' in WRRC Summer School collection — Heterosexuality, Coupledom and Parenthood, London.
ROSE, Hilary and Steven (Eds.) (1976) *The Radicalisation of Science*; and *The Political Economy of Science*, Macmillan, London.
WALLSGROVE, Ruth (1980) 'Towards a Radical Feminist philosophy of science' in BWSG.
WATSON, D. and CRICK, F. (1968) *The Double Helix*, Penguin, London.